NUMBERS

Brazos Theological Commentary on the Bible

NUMBERS

D A V I D L. S T U B B S

BrazosPress
a division of Baker Publishing Group
Grand Rapids, Michigan

© 2009 by David L. Stubbs

Published by Brazos Press
a division of Baker Publishing Group
P.O. Box 6287, Grand Rapids, MI 49516-6287
www.brazospress.com

Printed in the United States of America

Library of Congress Cataloging-in-Publication Data
Stubbs, David L. (David Leon), 1964–
    Numbers / David Stubbs.
        p.   cm. — (Brazos theological commentary on the Bible)
    Includes bibliographical references (p.   ) and indexes.
    ISBN 978-1-58743-140-1 (cloth)
    1. Bible. O. T. Numbers—Commentaries. 2. Bible. O. T. Numbers—Theology. I. Title. II. Series.
BS1265.53.S78 2009
222′.1407—dc22   2009013059

To Lynn, Connor, and Anna,
treasured fellow travelers

The LORD bless you and keep you;
the LORD make his face to shine upon you, and be gracious to you;
the LORD lift up his countenance upon you, and give you peace.

—Numbers 6:24–26

CONTENTS

SERIES PREFACE

Near the beginning of his treatise against Gnostic interpretations of the Bible, *Against the Heresies*, Irenaeus observes that scripture is like a great mosaic depicting a handsome king. It is as if we were owners of a villa in Gaul who had ordered a mosaic from Rome. It arrives, and the beautifully colored tiles need to be taken out of their packaging and put into proper order according to the plan of the artist. The difficulty, of course, is that scripture provides us with the individual pieces, but the order and sequence of various elements are not obvious. The Bible does not come with instructions that would allow interpreters to simply place verses, episodes, images, and parables in order as a worker might follow a schematic drawing in assembling the pieces to depict the handsome king. The mosaic must be puzzled out. This is precisely the work of scriptural interpretation.

Origen has his own image to express the difficulty of working out the proper approach to reading the Bible. When preparing to offer a commentary on the Psalms he tells of a tradition handed down to him by his Hebrew teacher:

> The Hebrew said that the whole divinely inspired Scripture may be likened, because of its obscurity, to many locked rooms in our house. By each room is placed a key, but not the one that corresponds to it, so that the keys are scattered about beside the rooms, none of them matching the room by which it is placed. It is a difficult task to find the keys and match them to the rooms that they can open. We therefore know the Scriptures that are obscure only by taking the points of departure for understanding them from another place because they have their interpretive principle scattered among them.[1]

---

1. Fragment from the preface to *Commentary on Psalms 1–25*, preserved in the *Philokalia* (trans. Joseph W. Trigg; London: Routledge, 1998), 70–71.

As is the case for Irenaeus, scriptural interpretation is not purely local. The key in Genesis may best fit the door of Isaiah, which in turn opens up the meaning of Matthew. The mosaic must be put together with an eye toward the overall plan.

Irenaeus, Origen, and the great cloud of premodern biblical interpreters assumed that puzzling out the mosaic of scripture must be a communal project. The Bible is vast, heterogeneous, full of confusing passages and obscure words, and difficult to understand. Only a fool would imagine that he or she could work out solutions alone. The way forward must rely upon a tradition of reading that Irenaeus reports has been passed on as the rule or canon of truth that functions as a confession of faith. "Anyone," he says, "who keeps unchangeable in himself the rule of truth received through baptism will recognize the names and sayings and parables of the scriptures."[2] Modern scholars debate the content of the rule on which Irenaeus relies and commends, not the least because the terms and formulations Irenaeus himself uses shift and slide. Nonetheless, Irenaeus assumes that there is a body of apostolic doctrine sustained by a tradition of teaching in the church. This doctrine provides the clarifying principles that guide exegetical judgment toward a coherent overall reading of scripture as a unified witness. Doctrine, then, is the schematic drawing that will allow the reader to organize the vast heterogeneity of the words, images, and stories of the Bible into a readable, coherent whole. It is the rule that guides us toward the proper matching of keys to doors.

If self-consciousness about the role of history in shaping human consciousness makes modern historical-critical study critical, then what makes modern study of the Bible modern is the consensus that classical Christian doctrine distorts interpretive understanding. Benjamin Jowett, the influential nineteenth-century English classical scholar, is representative. In his programmatic essay "On the Interpretation of Scripture," he exhorts the biblical reader to disengage from doctrine and break its hold over the interpretive imagination. "The simple words of that book," writes Jowett of the modern reader, "he tries to preserve absolutely pure from the refinements or distinctions of later times." The modern interpreter wishes to "clear away the remains of dogmas, systems, controversies, which are encrusted upon" the words of scripture. The disciplines of close philological analysis "would enable us to separate the elements of doctrine and tradition with which the meaning of Scripture is encumbered in our own day."[3] The lens of understanding must be wiped clear of the hazy and distorting film of doctrine.

Postmodernity, in turn, has encouraged us to criticize the critics. Jowett imagined that when he wiped away doctrine he would encounter the biblical text in its purity and uncover what he called "the original spirit and intention of the authors."[4] We are not now so sanguine, and the postmodern mind thinks

---

2. *Against Heresies* 9.4.

3. Benjamin Jowett, "On the Interpretation of Scripture," in *Essays and Reviews* (London: Parker, 1860), 338–39.

4. Ibid., 340.

interpretive frameworks inevitable. Nonetheless, we tend to remain modern in at least one sense. We read Athanasius and think him stage-managing the diversity of scripture to support his positions against the Arians. We read Bernard of Clairvaux and assume that his monastic ideals structure his reading of the Song of Songs. In the wake of the Reformation, we can see how the doctrinal divisions of the time shaped biblical interpretation. Luther famously described the Epistle of James as a "strawy letter," for, as he said, "it has nothing of the nature of the Gospel about it."[5] In these and many other instances, often written in the heat of ecclesiastical controversy or out of the passion of ascetic commitment, we tend to think Jowett correct: doctrine is a distorting film on the lens of understanding.

However, is what we commonly think actually the case? Are readers naturally perceptive? Do we have an unblemished, reliable aptitude for the divine? Have we no need for disciplines of vision? Do our attention and judgment need to be trained, especially as we seek to read scripture as the living word of God? According to Augustine, we all struggle to journey toward God, who is our rest and peace. Yet our vision is darkened and the fetters of worldly habit corrupt our judgment. We need training and instruction in order to cleanse our minds so that we might find our way toward God.[6] To this end, "the whole temporal dispensation was made by divine Providence for our salvation."[7] The covenant with Israel, the coming of Christ, the gathering of the nations into the church—all these things are gathered up into the rule of faith, and they guide the vision and form of the soul toward the end of fellowship with God. In Augustine's view, the reading of scripture both contributes to and benefits from this divine pedagogy. With countless variations in both exegetical conclusions and theological frameworks, the same pedagogy of a doctrinally ruled reading of scripture characterizes the broad sweep of the Christian tradition from Gregory the Great through Bernard and Bonaventure, continuing across Reformation differences in both John Calvin and Cornelius Lapide, Patrick Henry and Bishop Bossuet, and on to more recent figures such as Karl Barth and Hans Urs von Balthasar.

Is doctrine, then, not a moldering scrim of antique prejudice obscuring the Bible, but instead a clarifying agent, an enduring tradition of theological judgments that amplifies the living voice of scripture? And what of the scholarly dispassion advocated by Jowett? Is a noncommitted reading, an interpretation unprejudiced, the way toward objectivity, or does it simply invite the languid intellectual apathy that stands aside to make room for the false truism and easy answers of the age?

This series of biblical commentaries was born out of the conviction that dogma clarifies rather than obscures. The Brazos Theological Commentary on the Bible advances upon the assumption that the Nicene tradition, in all its diversity and

5. *Luther's Works*, vol. 35, ed. E. Theodore Bachmann (Philadelphia: Fortress, 1959), 362.
6. *On Christian Doctrine* 1.10.
7. *On Christian Doctrine* 1.35.

controversy, provides the proper basis for the interpretation of the Bible as Christian scripture. God the Father Almighty, who sends his only begotten Son to die for us and for our salvation and who raises the crucified Son in the power of the Holy Spirit so that the baptized may be joined in one body—faith in *this* God with *this* vocation of love for the world is the lens through which to view the heterogeneity and particularity of the biblical texts. Doctrine, then, is not a moldering scrim of antique prejudice obscuring the meaning of the Bible. It is a crucial aspect of the divine pedagogy, a clarifying agent for our minds fogged by self-deceptions, a challenge to our languid intellectual apathy that will too often rest in false truisms and the easy spiritual nostrums of the present age rather than search more deeply and widely for the dispersed keys to the many doors of scripture.

For this reason, the commentators in this series have not been chosen because of their historical or philological expertise. In the main, they are not biblical scholars in the conventional, modern sense of the term. Instead, the commentators were chosen because of their knowledge of and expertise in using the Christian doctrinal tradition. They are qualified by virtue of the doctrinal formation of their mental habits, for it is the conceit of this series of biblical commentaries that theological training in the Nicene tradition prepares one for biblical interpretation, and thus it is to theologians and not biblical scholars that we have turned. "War is too important," it has been said, "to leave to the generals."

We do hope, however, that readers do not draw the wrong impression. The Nicene tradition does not provide a set formula for the solution of exegetical problems. The great tradition of Christian doctrine was not transcribed, bound in folio, and issued in an official, critical edition. We have the Niceno-Constantinopolitan Creed, used for centuries in many traditions of Christian worship. We have ancient baptismal affirmations of faith. The Chalcedonian definition and the creeds and canons of other church councils have their places in official church documents. Yet the rule of faith cannot be limited to a specific set of words, sentences, and creeds. It is instead a pervasive habit of thought, the animating culture of the church in its intellectual aspect. As Augustine observed, commenting on Jeremiah 31:33, "The creed is learned by listening; it is written, not on stone tablets nor on any material, but on the heart."[8] This is why Irenaeus is able to appeal to the rule of faith more than a century before the first ecumenical council, and this is why we need not itemize the contents of the Nicene tradition in order to appeal to its potency and role in the work of interpretation.

Because doctrine is intrinsically fluid on the margins and most powerful as a habit of mind rather than a list of propositions, this commentary series cannot settle difficult questions of method and content at the outset. The editors of the series impose no particular method of doctrinal interpretation. We cannot say in advance how doctrine helps the Christian reader assemble the mosaic of scripture. We have no clear answer to the question of whether exegesis guided by

8. *Sermon* 212.2.

doctrine is antithetical to or compatible with the now-old modern methods of historical-critical inquiry. Truth—historical, mathematical, or doctrinal—knows no contradiction. But method is a discipline of vision and judgment, and we cannot know in advance what aspects of historical-critical inquiry are functions of modernism that shape the soul to be at odds with Christian discipline. Still further, the editors do not hold the commentators to any particular hermeneutical theory that specifies how to define the plain sense of scripture—or the role this plain sense should play in interpretation. Here the commentary series is tentative and exploratory.

Can we proceed in any other way? European and North American intellectual culture has been de-Christianized. The effect has not been a cessation of Christian activity. Theological work continues. Sermons are preached. Biblical scholars turn out monographs. Church leaders have meetings. But each dimension of a formerly unified Christian practice now tends to function independently. It is as if a weakened army had been fragmented, and various corps had retreated to isolated fortresses in order to survive. Theology has lost its competence in exegesis. Scripture scholars function with minimal theological training. Each decade finds new theories of preaching to cover the nakedness of seminary training that provides theology without exegesis and exegesis without theology.

Not the least of the causes of the fragmentation of Christian intellectual practice has been the divisions of the church. Since the Reformation, the role of the rule of faith in interpretation has been obscured by polemics and counterpolemics about *sola scriptura* and the necessity of a magisterial teaching authority. The Brazos Theological Commentary on the Bible series is deliberately ecumenical in scope, because the editors are convinced that early church fathers were correct: church doctrine does not compete with scripture in a limited economy of epistemic authority. We wish to encourage unashamedly dogmatic interpretation of scripture, confident that the concrete consequences of such a reading will cast far more light on the great divisive questions of the Reformation than either reengaging in old theological polemics or chasing the fantasy of a pure exegesis that will somehow adjudicate between competing theological positions. You shall know the truth of doctrine by its interpretive fruits, and therefore in hopes of contributing to the unity of the church, we have deliberately chosen a wide range of theologians whose commitment to doctrine will allow readers to see real interpretive consequences rather than the shadowboxing of theological concepts.

Brazos Theological Commentary on the Bible has no dog in the current translation fights, and we endorse a textual ecumenism that parallels our diversity of ecclesial backgrounds. We do not impose the thankfully modest inclusive-language agenda of the New Revised Standard Version, nor do we insist upon the glories of the Authorized Version, nor do we require our commentators to create a new translation. In our communal worship, in our private devotions, in our theological scholarship, we use a range of scriptural translations. Precisely as scripture—a living, functioning text in the present life of faith—the Bible is not semantically fixed. Only a modernist, literalist hermeneutic could imagine that this modest fluidity is a liability. Philological precision and stability is a consequence of, not a basis for, exegesis. Judgments about the meaning of a text fix its literal sense, not the other way around. As a result, readers should expect an eclectic use of biblical translations, both across the different volumes of the series and within individual commentaries.

We cannot speak for contemporary biblical scholars, but as theologians we know that we have long been trained to defend our fortresses of theological concepts and formulations. And we have forgotten the skills of interpretation. Like stroke victims, we must rehabilitate our exegetical imaginations, and there are likely to be different strategies of recovery. Readers should expect this reconstructive—not reactionary—series to provide them with experiments in postcritical doctrinal interpretation, not commentaries written according to the settled principles of a well-functioning tradition. Some commentators will follow classical typological and allegorical readings from the premodern tradition; others will draw on contemporary historical study. Some will comment verse by verse; others will highlight passages, even single words that trigger theological analysis of scripture. No reading strategies are proscribed, no interpretive methods foresworn. The central premise in this commentary series is that doctrine provides structure and cogency to scriptural interpretation. We trust in this premise with the hope that the Nicene tradition can guide us, however imperfectly, diversely, and haltingly, toward a reading of scripture in which the right keys open the right doors.

R. R. Reno

AUTHOR'S PREFACE

Israel's forty-year sojourn in the wilderness, much of which is recorded in Numbers, was a time of revelation and care by God, a time of testing, and a time of judgment and blessing. Just as Jacob-Israel wrestled with God (Gen. 32:24) after crossing the ford of the Jabbok River, so too Israel wrestled with God during those forty years after crossing the Red Sea. They too came away limping but blessed. One of the lessons of Numbers is that encountering God and the things of God is no light thing. God desires to bring blessing to his chosen people, to all nations, and to all creation, and central to this blessing is the gift of God's presence. For us sinful mortals, however, the warmth of God's life-giving presence is also a burning fire that tests us and ultimately cleanses us to make us holy. All this, in fact, is blessing.

When I accepted the invitation to participate in this commentary series, I knew that I was in for a challenging yet rewarding journey as I encountered more fully this particular "thing of God," the book of Numbers. Certainly part of the challenge and reward of this project is its cross-disciplinary nature. For a theologian to tread in the territory of the great Old Testament scholars, past and contemporary, who have commented on Numbers and the issues contained in it is no light thing. My appreciation for the work of those who have gone before me has only increased. And yet I also see the need for Christian theologians and ethicists to be more deeply immersed in the biblical witness. The particular vision and expertise that we bring to the exegetical task will make a helpful contribution, for there is a great need for Christian interpreters of the Bible to speak forthrightly from and to the full doctrinal and lived tradition of the church. As a result of this project, my own vocation as a Christian scholar was further refined, and I came away with deeper questions about the way the theological disciplines have been divided.

Working on Numbers has also challenged me on another level. The high vision this part of Christian scripture paints of who the people of God are to be, especially in the first ten chapters, is deeply challenging. It has increased my dedication to the church as a visible and holy body of people and made me glad for the ways that God has been faithful to shape the church over time. Yet it also showed me more clearly ways that the church bodies I am part of, and I as an individual, fall short of God's intentions. Numbers does contain words of grace, but it also reminds us that God's work in our lives is often painful. "Count the cost" is one of its implicit messages, while the images of the Nazirite, Joshua, Caleb, and Phineas call us to accept that challenge. Listening to that message over and over changes one.

I would like to express my gratitude to all the people and institutions that have supported me and walked beside me during this long encounter with Numbers. Western Theological Seminary, my professional home, is a wonderful community in which to work. My thanks go to all the faculty, staff, and students who have provided resources, time, conversation, questions, and encouragement to me throughout my research and writing. I especially appreciate the time and trouble that Tom Boogaart and Brent Strawn, colleagues at Western and Candler, took to read and make helpful suggestions on draft portions of the manuscript. I am also grateful to Western for the sabbatical leave that allowed me to devote a year to this project while living in St. Andrews, Scotland. Many thanks to all the people of St. Mary's College and the congregation at All Saints Church in St. Andrews for creating a welcoming and warm space for my family and me during our year there. Jonathan Mason, the people at All Saints, and our neighbors Alec and Marlene went above and beyond good Scottish hospitality and opened their lives and hearts to us; their gift of friendship and community was priceless and will not be forgotten. Nathan MacDonald not only gave me access to his astute intellect and expertise in Numbers, but also to his office and library—both were great gifts to me. My immediate family, ever patient with fascinating details about Balaam and the laws of Numbers, deserves special thanks for all their love, support, and understanding during what I know seems to them like a very long journey. The great joy that they give me is like water in the desert. And finally, thanks to the good and visionary people at Brazos Press. I am grateful for their trust and encouragement at all points during the project. Robert Wilken's early comments and Rusty Reno's careful reading, comments, suggestions, and encouragement were invaluable. I am also appreciative of David Aiken's careful editorial work.

May God bless all these wonderful people. I hope this work will be a blessing to others, helping them to hear God speaking through Numbers to guide, comfort, and challenge us all to live as saints.

All Saints Day 2008

ABBREVIATIONS

General

→	indicates a cross-reference to commentary on a Numbers passage
BDB	Francis Brown, S. R. Driver, and C. A. Briggs, *A Hebrew and English Lexicon of the Old Testament*. Reprinted Oxford: Oxford University Press, 1966.
NIDOTTE	Willem A. VanGemeren, ed., *New International Dictionary of Old Testament Theology and Exegesis*. 5 vols. Grand Rapids: Zondervan, 1997.
NRSV	New Revised Standard Version

Biblical

Acts	Acts	Gal.	Galatians
Amos	Amos	Gen.	Genesis
1 Chr.	1 Chronicles	Hab.	Habakkuk
2 Chr.	2 Chronicles	Hag.	Haggai
Col.	Colossians	Heb.	Hebrews
1 Cor.	1 Corinthians	Hos.	Hosea
2 Cor.	2 Corinthians	Isa.	Isaiah
Dan.	Daniel	Jas.	James
Deut.	Deuteronomy	Jer.	Jeremiah
Eccl.	Ecclesiastes	Job	Job
Eph.	Ephesians	Joel	Joel
Esth.	Esther	John	John
Exod.	Exodus	1 John	1 John
Ezek.	Ezekiel	2 John	2 John
Ezra	Ezra	3 John	3 John

Jonah	Jonah	2 Pet.	2 Peter
Josh.	Joshua	Phil.	Philippians
Jude	Jude	Phlm.	Philemon
Judg.	Judges	Prov.	Proverbs
1 Kgs.	1 Kings	Ps.	Psalms
2 Kgs.	2 Kings	Rev.	Revelation
Lam.	Lamentations	Rom.	Romans
Lev.	Leviticus	Ruth	Ruth
Luke	Luke	1 Sam.	1 Samuel
Mal.	Malachi	2 Sam.	2 Samuel
Mark	Mark	Song	Song of Songs
Matt.	Matthew	1 Thess.	1 Thessalonians
Mic.	Micah	2 Thess.	2 Thessalonians
Nah.	Nahum	1 Tim.	1 Timothy
Neh.	Nehemiah	2 Tim.	2 Timothy
Num.	Numbers	Titus	Titus
Obad.	Obadiah	Zech.	Zechariah
1 Pet.	1 Peter	Zeph.	Zephaniah

INTRODUCTION

My child, when you come to serve the Lord,
   prepare yourself for testing.

—Sirach 2:1

Numbers begins with the words "the LORD spoke to Moses in the wilderness of Sinai," a phrase that alerts readers they are with Moses and Israel in the middle of a story, the story of the chosen yet sinful people of God on their way from the slavery of Egypt through the wilderness toward life in the promised land.

Many readers of Numbers, coming across the words "in the wilderness" know that this phrase is more than simply a geographical designation. It is a phrase linked with the many foundational experiences of Israel during its forty years on the way from Egypt to the promised land, experiences that form the heart of the Pentateuch. The basic plot of this time is this: God frees the people of Israel from their slavery in Egypt and brings them to Sinai. There God reveals himself to them and gives them a vision and covenant that tells them they are to be "a priestly kingdom and a holy nation" (Exod. 19:6), living out God's designs for a renewed humanity amid the nations. Numbers begins at Mount Sinai, where Israel gladly and obediently accepts this vision and begins its journey to the promised land, where it will put this vision into practice. But very quickly the people of Israel start grumbling about their food, about their social status, and amid fears and lies they end up rejecting God's plans for them. The situations and hardships they encounter in the wilderness are occasions of testing for them, and through them their sin and unfaithfulness to God and his plans are revealed. God punishes them and disciplines them, delaying their entrance into the promised land until they spend forty years in the wilderness. Toward the end of these forty years God leads them to confession and a newfound obedience. God is determined to bless them in spite of their sin. He gives Israel a renewed start and finally leads it to the edge of the promised land of Canaan.[1]

While those foundational experiences of Israel with God are in one sense unrepeatable, later Israelite and Christian traditions have often understood aspects of Israel's forty years in the wilderness as patterns or figures for their own experiences. Israelite prophets before and during Israel's Babylonian exile prophesy about a new wilderness journey from exile to the promised land. Even after their return from exile, the people of God come to expect they will be led by God into yet another new beginning in the wilderness. The gospel writers portray Jesus's life as a final wilderness experience of God's chosen people—"final" here in the sense of goal or *telos*—in which Christ overcomes the temptations that Israel succumbed to, fulfilling in his own life the calling of the whole people. The life of the church before the expected return of Christ as well as the life of believers between their baptism and their own resurrection are also likened to the experience of Israel in the desert. As such, Numbers not only informs us of Israel's historical, physical journey, but as scripture, it authoritatively shapes and finds itself in mutual conversation with Christian understandings of the calling, purposes, and commandments given to the people of God in other times and places; tells us much about God's reactions to sin and plans for blessing his people; and also alerts us to the temptations common to God's people.

This, at least, is how Christians have often read this scriptural text in the past.

Given the advent of modern historical-critical scholarship, such readings that focus on the narrative continuity of Numbers with the rest of scripture and its figural resonances with Christ and the church have been called into question on a number of fronts. But a central conviction of the Brazos Theological Commentary on the Bible is that reading scripture with an eye to the "rule or canon of truth" passed on through the Nicene tradition of the church will help clarify rather than obscure the meaning of Numbers. Accordingly, I will approach the text as Christian scripture, as an authoritative part of a larger canon of writings. This mosaic of writings refers to a unified work of God that encompasses both the economy of creation and the economy of redemption and that has a christological shape and center.

One implication of these commitments is that priority will be given to the final form of the text. I will seek to uncover the distinctive voice of the final form of Numbers while, on the one hand, noting how this form grew out of earlier traditions and, on the other hand, attending to the place of Numbers within the Pentateuch and the larger witness of Christian scripture. I will also highlight how this voice interacts with other theologians and traditions within Christian

---

1. Israel's wilderness time stretches from crossing the Red Sea out of Egypt to crossing the Jordan River into the promised land. More precisely, the forty years in the wilderness is officially marked from the time they departed Egypt (33:38; cf. Exod. 12) to the death of Aaron (Num. 20:22–29).

history. Numbers has a distinctive voice that both harmonizes with and at times adds a contrapuntal and tension-filled melody to the larger chorus of scripture and later tradition. It is this voice that I hope to make come alive through this commentary, trusting that this voice is a usual means in, under, and through which God's voice can be heard.

Besides these foundational assumptions, a few other assumptions about the structure and themes of Numbers and the relationship between its laws and narratives should be made clear.

Numbers is not easy reading. Just as the books of the Old and New Testaments, depending on how one views them, can appear to be either a jumble of ill-matched pieces from perhaps different puzzles or a complex yet beautiful mosaic whose bold and subtle patterns continue to surprise us, so too the different parts of Numbers. It presents us with a variety of genres, primarily narrative and lawlike material, that seem to interrupt each other and whose connections to each other are neither explicitly stated nor easily seen. Furthermore, its integrity as a book—that it has an overall sense on its own—is often called into question. Yet there is a way to understand its coherence—and this perspective guides my commentary—which clarifies its subtle yet quite beautiful patterns and shows Numbers to be an artfully constructed text in which seemingly disparate parts work together to emphasize central themes.

The structure of Numbers has been a matter of debate within recent scholarship. Dennis Olson's landmark study *The Death of the Old and the Birth of the New* discerned the structure of the book and its place within the larger structure of the Pentateuch, this in light of little sustained attention having been given to the question and even less agreement about it in modern (specifically after 1861) biblical studies.[2] Part of the problem Olson found is that modern scholars mainly focused on the sources that went into the composition of Numbers, rather than on the final composition itself.[3] For example, the theology and themes of the theoretical Yahwist (J) source were thoroughly examined, while the final form of Numbers was neglected. As a result, the forest was lost for the trees.

A related but opposite problem emerged as scholars began attending to the shape of the Pentateuch (or Hexateuch). Some proposed ways of understanding

2. Olson 1996: 31 writes: "The central problem in the interpretation of the book of Numbers . . . is the failure to detect a convincing and meaningful structure for the book. Little systematic discussion of the structure of Numbers can be found in the scholarly literature. Commentaries often simply propose an outline with little or no comment or defense. Numerous interpreters lament the difficulty of determining any coherent plan or outline. Martin Noth's observations are typical: 'From the point of view of its contents, the book lacks unity, and it is difficult to see any pattern in its construction.'" Stephen Sherwood, whose commentary focuses on literary issues, writes: "Apart from an outline of the book, I have not found any proposed structure convincing" (*Leviticus, Numbers, Deuteronomy*, Berit Olam [Collegeville, MN: Liturgical Press, 2002], 110).

3. Olson's analysis (1996: 9–31) of the scholarship on Numbers suggests this, and Won Lee, *Punishment and Forgiveness in Israel's Migratory Campaign* (Grand Rapids: Eerdmans, 2003), xi, writes: "Until the mid-twentieth century, pentateuchal scholarship predominantly focused on the formation of parts of the Pentateuch rather than the entire work."

the larger literary structure of the first five (or six) books of the Bible have a tendency to undermine the integrity of the individual books. This is especially true for Numbers. The first part of the book (1:1–10:10) tends to get lopped off and attached to the "Sinai cycle" that extends from the arrival of Israel at Mount Sinai (Exod. 19), through Leviticus, up to their departure from "the wilderness of Sinai" (Num. 10:11–12).[4] Now our "tree," Numbers, gets lost in the forest of the Pentateuch. The question of structure thus becomes one of making sense of the integrity and structure of the whole book while also seeing the part it plays in the larger shape of the Pentateuch.

There are two main keys to this structural puzzle, each of which has important implications for the interpretation of Numbers: the tripartite structure of the book and the seven rebellions in its middle section. The book has three major parts that form an ABA' pattern:

A   1:1–10:10
B   10:11–25:18
A' 26:1–36:13

The first part of the book has many parallels to the last part (cf. Olson 1996: 5–6):

- censuses taken (1–4 and 26)
- lists of leaders (1 and 34)
- laws concerning gō'ēl (5 and 35)
- laws concerning a woman (5) or women (27, 30, 36)
- laws concerning a vow (6) or vows (30)
- attention to holy places (7–8) and holy land (34)
- setting aside of Levites (8) and Levitical towns (35)
- Passover celebrated (9) and its offerings detailed (28)
- details of the silver trumpets (10) and Trumpets Festival offerings (29)

4. Rolf Rendtorff's proposed cycles in Genesis (*Das Überlieferungsgeschichtliche Problem des Pentateuch* [Berlin: Gruyter, 1977]) is extended to the whole Pentateuch by Wenham 1981: 14–18, who understands Numbers to have three main blocks of material grouped around locations: the Sinai cycle, the Kadesh cycle, and the Plains of Moab cycle. This broad tripartite division is right, but on grounds that go beyond location. Gray 1903: xxiii writes: "The first section of Numbers (1:1–10:10) may be regarded as an appendix to the Books of Exodus and Leviticus." Noth 1968: 2 writes: "From this indication of the contents it is already clear that the book is not a self-contained unit" and must be seen only as a part of the larger Pentateuch, having no clear structure of its own. Seeing a clear structure in 10:11–36:13, Lee, *Punishment and Forgiveness*, 288–90, divides 1:1–10:10 from the rest of the book and groups it with either the priestly materials in Exod. 25:1–Num. 10:10 or a larger block of preparatory events of the failed campaign for the conquest of the promised land (Exod. 1:1–Num. 10:10).

Olson helpfully highlights the importance of the censuses of the people and the Levites as key indicators of the "obedient beginnings" of the exodus generation in Num. 1–10 and the "rise of a new generation of hope" in Num. 26.[5] While the theme of God's faithfulness to Israel in assuring the passing on of his blessings and promises from one generation to the next is important, on its own it does not illuminate clearly enough the way the book pivots around the central rebellion section and, more specifically, the events of Num. 13–14. Instead, the book is better understood as beginning with a summary vision of who Israel is to be (A) and then moving to an extended narrative (B) of the failure of Israel to live up to this vision. While Israel's failure is centered on the rebellion of Num. 13–14, the narratives in the central third of the book also highlight the persistence of God in his work to ultimately bless his people in spite of their sin. The final third of the book is devoted to the renewed start and reorganization of the people for life in the promised land (A').

This tripartite understanding of the overall structure of Numbers can account for many features of the text. On a literary level, it coheres with the text's physical markers (i.e., topographical and geographical references), chronological markers, and the shifts in tone (from positive to negative to positive)—all of which point to a three-part division of the book. It accounts for the central place of the rebellion (Num. 13–14) in the book. It also has place for the chiastic structure of the seven rebellions, which in turn helps to illuminate the relationship between the book's laws and narrative material. Most important, it provides the book with a coherent overall thematic structure that in large and small ways helps make good sense of the individual pieces of the book. While I will briefly overview how this thematic movement clarifies the role of the different pieces of Numbers in the larger whole, the full fruit of this will be seen in the commentary proper.

The three-part thematic movement of the book concerns the shifts in Israel's relationship to God, three different legs of its spiritual journey as a community or nation.[6] This movement may be summed up in three phrases: (1) the identity and organization of God's holy people, (2) the struggles of Israel and God with Israel's unfaithfulness, and (3) the reorganization of Israel for life in the promised land.[7] Every section of the book can be seen to cohere with and add to these summative themes.

Numbers 1–10 focuses on the structure of the people, their politics, so to speak. God is organizing Israel to be a holy people, as he has done already since the people arrived at Sinai. This opening third of the book functions like an

---

5. While he primarily divides the book in two (Num. 1–25 and Num. 26–36), Olson 1996: 133 also observes that "a positive tone is struck" in the "major break" in Num. 21.

6. "Spiritual" here simply points to Israel's relationship to God. It is not spiritual in any sort of a reductive sense—their relationship to God embraces every aspect of their lives.

7. Ashley 1993: 8 applies Brueggemann's terms—"orientation, disorientation, reorientation"— to Numbers; see Walter Brueggemann, "Psalms and the Life of Faith," *Journal for the Study of the Old Testament* 17 (1980): 3–32.

overall summary of who Israel is to be, touching on all the major aspects of its life. Its tribal and leadership structures (Num. 1–4), the role of law in the formation of its ethical vision (Num. 5–6), and the worship life of the people (Num. 7–10) all play central parts in the identity and life of Israel. For example, the ordering of the five representative laws in Num. 5–6 shows that the goal of God's law and work with Israel is to move it toward blessing and a life of shalom (→6:22–27).

In the central part of the book, the people's lack of faithfulness to this vision and covenant and God's effort to move Israel from faithlessness to faithfulness and holiness are clearly the main themes. As the people move away from the mountain of revelation toward life in the promised land (10:11), they begin obediently. But as they enter into the journey, their obedience and faithfulness go only so far. In the wilderness the hearts of the people are laid bare—their hardships test them and their sins are revealed. Their unfaithfulness also tests the patience of the Lord, revealing God's holiness and mercy. Israel eventually rejects the promised land and the kind of relationship with God it represents at the very heart of the book (Num. 14). However, this rejection is not the end of the story. The end of the book offers signs of hope that one day God's purposes for Israel will be fulfilled, and Israel does take steps toward this goal. A change occurs in both the vow that Israel takes (21:1–3) and the direction of God's action toward Israel in the episode of the bronze serpent (21:4–9). Both episodes point to an inner change in Israel that occurs as the older generation dies out and the new comes of age. Their vow indicates that Israel is coming to accept God's leadership. In the bronze serpent episode, Israel is directed to see its sin, and it symbolically triumphs over it by turning to and accepting God's goodness. The physical healing of the poison in Israel indicates the possibility of an inner spiritual healing of the people. As a result of this partial "sanctification," battles and movements in the wilderness take on a more positive tone as Israel moves toward the blessing of God through Balaam.

The final four chapters of this central section bring the wrestling of God and Israel in the wilderness to an unexpected, but fitting, climax. In the chapters concerning Balaam (Num. 22–24), the original vision of who Israel is called to be is spoken again, and God is faithful to bring his intentions to pass. Israel will be blessed by God, in spite of the machinations of the nations and powers that surround it. But in a stunning turn of events, sin within rather than evil without threatens Israel's fulfillment of its vocation. Israel's apostasy in the episode of the Baal of Peor (Num. 25), juxtaposed as it is with the Balaam chapters, shows that even in spite of Israel's sin, God will not abandon it, but will continue to move Israel toward blessing. And in this episode, the best of the new generation is represented in Phineas. In his zeal for the holiness of God, he is a seed of hope and role model for what Israel should be. Altogether, the central part of the book speaks clearly of the temptations that the people of God face, of God's faithfulness and longsuffering patience with his people, and of the way that God uses the trials and temptations of his people to form them (or at least key representatives of the new generation) into people of holiness.

In the final third of the book, which recapitulates the first part, the people are again organized as a holy people. Their forty-year punishment and testing, which eventually leads them to the renewed blessing by Balaam, is over. Even though they do not live completely according to the ideal set for them in the first part of the book, they overcome the temptations and obstacles that would keep them from crossing the Jordan. More specific directions are given for what their life as the people of God should look like when they reach the promised land, instructions that fill out what it means to be a holy and priestly people living among the nations.

The holiness and faithfulness required of the people of God in order to live into their covenantal vocation is the central theme throughout the book. The first and third parts show what Israel's vocation entails in visible polity and worship life. The crucial middle part of the book shows the struggle needed to create a holy zeal and faithfulness in this sinful yet chosen people who are called to be blessed, to be holy, and to bear the name of God among the nations.

Just as the ABA' structure sheds light on the book's overall thematic movement and the role the individual sections play in the book, a second key element of the book's structure does something similar. Within the central part, Israel rebels against God and his will seven times. The number seven plays a role in the opening chapters of the book, as the phrase "at the command of the LORD" appears seven times in Num. 3–4 and seven times in Num. 9, underscoring Israel's obedience. Perhaps these groupings are meant to contrast with the seven rebellions (Milgrom 1990: xxxi), which are arranged in a chiasm. Attending to this chiastic structure helps with both the interpretation of these rebellions and another interpretational challenge of the book: the relationship between its lawlike and narrative pieces.

Comprised of a series of elements presented and then paired in inverted order, chiastic structures are common in the Pentateuch. Milgrom notes that "the main structural device, to judge by its attestation in nearly every chapter in Numbers, is chiasm and introversion" (1990: xxii).[8] I am convinced that the seven rebellions follow the pattern ABCDC'B'A'.[9] The patterning of these episodes shows a deci-

8. Milgrom distinguishes between chiasm, which has two paired elements (ABB'A'), and introversion, which has at least three (ABxB'A'). While chiasms can be purely esthetic devices, introversions are meant to teach something: "The central member frequently contains the main point of the author, climaxing what precedes and anticipating what follows" (1990: xxii). Milgrom points out a major chiasm in the structure of the Pentateuch (i.e., elements of Numbers have similarities to elements recorded in Exodus, and these pairings center on the revelation of God at Mount Sinai) and also points out introversions in many chapters of Numbers; he does not, however, notice the chiastic structure of the rebellions. Admittedly, there is danger in finding chiasms everywhere; I will let the reader decide whether the chiasm of the rebellions is persuasive and illuminates the interpretation.

9. The only modern writer who notices this structure is Thomas Römer, "De la périphérie au centre: Les livres du Lévitique et des Nombres dans le débat actuel sur la Pentateuque," *Colloquium biblium lovaniense* 55 (2006): 1–21, but perhaps Matthew noticed it (Matt. 4:1–11): the three

sive, yet subtle, editorial hand by the writer or redactor, which draws attention to the central element: the important story of the spying out of the promised land and Israel's rejection of it and desire to go back to Egypt.[10]

This chiastic structure divides the lawlike material and minor narrative material in the central part of the book into four sections (15:1–41; 17:12–20:1; 20:14–29; 21:10–35), which follow the last four rebellions. The major themes of these four sections correspond to the themes of the rebellions that precede them. In general, these laws and narratives suggest positive characteristics and practices of the people of God that are opposite to or help correct the negative characteristics and sins that beset Israel in the previous rebellions.

This relationship suggests three things about how to interpret the lawlike material in Numbers: (1) the larger narrative is primary; (2) the laws are not simply deposited in Numbers in a haphazard fashion, but were carefully placed in order to comment on the narrative; and (3) these laws should be read with an eye for how the law, if properly obeyed, would shape the character of Israel over time. Understanding the significance of the laws in Numbers in this way naturally opens up figural readings of them, for the virtuous characteristics implied in obedience to the laws are of continuing interest to the people of God, even if the precise form of the law cannot be obeyed given changed cultural contexts.

Read in these ways, Numbers is a book that focuses on the vocation of the people of God and the sins that constantly work to keep Israel from fulfilling it. Because of this, Numbers is a wonderful book for the Christian church to reflect on in the midst of the important contemporary discussions about the nature and mission of the church. Numbers pushes the Christian church toward an incredibly high view of its calling, while at the same time being utterly realistic about the ways the people of God fail to fully live into it. It pushes us to be a people of zeal and hope and of humility and honesty. My hope is that this commentary will help Christians attune their ears to the divine speech that will correct, form, and guide us into truth and action concerning the matters touched on in this rich part of Christian scripture.

---

temptations of Christ seem to roughly correspond to B (food), C (temple or priestly leadership), and D (kingdom or promised land). The A elements can be seen as introductions and summaries.

10. The centrality of the spy episode is well argued by Lee, *Punishment and Forgiveness*, 213–82, who divides Num. 10:31–36:13 at 15:1, right after this episode. However, given the chiastic structure, there is no need to *divide* the book at this episode; rather Num. 13–14 is at the *center* of the *central* section, and the spy episode may well be the key text for understanding the redaction of the Pentateuch.

PART 1

IDENTITY AND ORGANIZATION
OF GOD'S HOLY PEOPLE (1:1–10:10)

God Prepares Israel for the Journey
to the Promised Land

As Numbers begins, Israel is in its final days at Sinai. The yearlong experience of Israel at Mount Sinai forms the foundation of its life as the covenant people of God. After Israel was freed from bondage to Egypt and cared for by God on the way to Mount Sinai, God revealed himself to Moses and Israel at the mountain. God also established the covenant there, revealing to them the basic patterns of worship and holy living that would structure their lives. The narratives of that experience in Exod. 19–Num. 10 form the heart of the Torah and "present the Sinaitic experience as disclosing the essential, normative relationship of YHWH to his people Israel. Sinai was a kind of archetype."[1] The laws and patterns of worship disclosed at Sinai form "a model of cosmic harmony," and the relationship of law and love between YHWH and Israel disclosed in them reveals "the prototype of redeemed life."[2]

1. Jon D. Levenson, *Sinai and Zion: An Entry into the Jewish Bible* (Minneapolis: Winston, 1985), 18.
2. Ibid., 79.

But God did not intend for Israel to stay on the mountain. God gave it a vocation to be "a priestly kingdom and a holy nation" (Exod. 19:6). That vocation required it to move from the Sabbath-like experience of Sinai to its life in the promised land of Canaan. There Israel was to live out the patterns of Sinai among the nations. The promised land is thus not a cipher for an escape out of earth into heaven, but rather the place where God's heavenly and holy designs for humanity are to be lived out on earth by his priestly people. In these opening chapters of Numbers, God through Moses organizes and orients the people of God for this transition, and Israel begins to put into practice aspects of the vision of Sinai in preparation for its departure.

This organization and orientation of the people contains three main parts. First, through the census and directions given in Num. 1–4, the vision of the basic structure of Israel as a priestly kingdom is put into practice. The people are physically structured in a way that is symbolic of who they are; they become a living icon that reveals their *identity* and calling to be a holy and priestly people. In Num. 5–6 laws are given that touch upon different aspects of what it means to be holy and give insight into the process of sanctification required for Israel to live into that calling. These chapters give a brief overview of the *ethics* of the people of God and hint at the difficulties it will face in the journey toward Canaan. Finally, in Num. 7–10:10 Israel is given directions for worship and tabernacle practices. As in Num. 1–4, God's presence and the worship practices associated with the tabernacle form the center of the people of God. Thus it is fitting that the final activities and directions that orient Israel in its journey to Canaan are related to its life of *worship*.

The patterns of Israel's organization, ethics, and worship are not only of historical interest. Reading these chapters as Christian scripture, these patterns also inform our understanding of what the church is, the central aspects of our ethical life as a people, and the main impulses of our worship.

1

A PICTURE OF THE PRIESTLY
KINGDOM (1:1–4:49)

At the beginning of the Sinai narratives, the Lord reveals to Moses the core of Israel's identity as a people: they are God's "treasured possession out of all the peoples," and they are to be "a priestly kingdom and a holy nation" (Exod. 19:5–6). In Num. 1–4, in preparation for Israel's departure from Sinai, this vision is put into practice: they are counted like a treasure, in this way establishing the boundaries of the people. They are then organized in a way that highlights their vocation as a priestly and holy people. The way the people are organized can be represented graphically: the twelve tribes of Israel form a square, three tribes to each side, and the whole is centered on the tabernacle. The priests and Levites form an inner square around the tabernacle, between it and the twelve tribes. As Israel marches, this square unwinds into a line, with the priests and the tabernacle still at the center. Exegesis of these chapters thus can take the form of a contemplation of this living icon of the people of God.[1] What are its striking features? What view of God and Israel underlies this form? How might this picture inform our understanding of the Christian church?

The Census as a Political Act: Election of a Holy Nation (1:1–54)

The first activity during the movement away from the experience of Sinai is the counting of the people, the census commanded by God (1:1–2). This census, the

1. See Balentine 1999: 74–76 for the need to reassess how to read ritual texts.

census of the Levites in 3:14–16, and the census in Num. 26 provide the Greek and English titles given to this fourth book of the Pentateuch: "Numbers." This taking of a census tells us several things about God and Israel.

Taking a census is a political act in which a ruler demarcates and makes a claim upon the people being numbered. Such knowledge was used for various military, religious, economic, and political purposes. In Israel these purposes included military service ("able to go to war"; 1:3), the tabernacle-related service of the Levites (Num. 4), and the allocation of the promised land (Num. 26).[2] That God commands such an action tells us that God is king of Israel and that these are his elect, delimited, and quite visible people, who are to be organized for various activities as a political entity. God acted as king in the defeat of Pharaoh's army (Exod. 15:3, 18) and in establishing the covenant with Israel (24:3–8), and here again God acts as a king, counting the people and further establishing their political organization.

Censuses of the people of God do not occur frequently in scripture, but when they do, a dark cloud often hangs over the process, except when God explicitly commands them. Exodus 30:11–15 stipulates how to take censuses: those registered are to give "half a shekel as an offering to the LORD," an offering that functions as "a ransom for their lives to the LORD, so that no plague may come upon them for being registered." It seems that "counting is tantamount to usurping divine knowledge and authority" just as eating the fruit in the garden was a "primordial act of hubris."[3] Such an act is permitted, but seemingly only if the claim of the Lord over his people is also acknowledged through this act of ransom—a term that suggests that some kind of ownership or debt is at stake.[4] The census that David takes of Israel (2 Sam. 24; 1 Chr. 21) is seen as blameworthy, in fact instigated by "satan" (21:1).[5] The way David's commander Joab tries to dissuade him from doing this suggests that part of David's census-taking was a further claim upon the people that usurps or ignores God's claim over them: "Are they not, my lord

---

2. Some commentators understand the census primarily as a means to raise and organize an army (e.g., Levine 1993). But since censuses are commanded in Numbers for at least three reasons, a broader understanding of the censuses is called for.

3. William Henry Propp, *Exodus 19–40*, Anchor Bible 2a (New York: Doubleday, 2006), 535.

4. In cultures surrounding Israel, census-taking was also a religiously charged activity. In Mari and Rome sacrifices to the gods accompanied the taking of a census (Propp, *Exodus 19–40*, 534; Robert P. Gordon, *First and Second Samuel* [Exeter, England: Paternoster, 1986], 316). While the reasons for these sacrifices are not explicitly stated, perhaps there is a sense that writing down someone's name (as at Mari) signified that part of the person was being held by those taking the census. This reticence may be similar to some people's resistance to having their image "taken" by a photographer (cf. William M. Schniedewind, *How the Bible Became a Book: The Textualization of Ancient Israel* [Cambridge: Cambridge University Press, 2004], 27–31). Speculating further, perhaps they thought the claim being made on them by their ruler could come into conflict with the claim on them by their god, and so they made an offering to their god during the census.

5. In contrast, the son of David resists the temptation of kingly power offered by satan to usurp the worship of God (Matt. 4:8–10).

the king, all of them my lord's servants? Why then should my lord require this? Why should he bring guilt upon Israel?" (21:3). Given that censuses involve a claim of authority over those being numbered, the census of Emperor Augustus of "all the world" provides a dramatically charged background to Jesus's birth (Luke 2:1), the birth of the true king of Israel who will come into conflict with the power of Caesar, a conflict leading to his crucifixion (23:2–3). Finally, in Rev. 7:4–8, the numbering of the twelve tribes of Israel and the giving of their numbers tribe by tribe (totaling 144,000) goes hand in hand with the sealing of the people by an angel of God. In all these scriptural references, censuses involve a claim of a ruler over the people.

A common theological word for God's claiming of his people is "election." This word brings to mind the entire sweep of God's particular and unpredictable work in which God takes up and chooses—the world, a people, a remnant, his son—in order to bring about God's intentions for all of creation. These intentions are seen most clearly and realized most finally in Jesus Christ. The census of Num. 1 is an important moment within this larger history. Origen understood this as part of the import of this passage: the census was a figure for the electing and numbering of the elect, who are then formed and ordered in a particular way in the following chapters (1996–2001: 1.69–79).

In the history of Christian thought in the West, discussions of election became entangled with debates about the predestination from all eternity of elect individuals for salvation by an eternal decree of God. In the well-known section of the *Church Dogmatics* where he parts company with the emphases of Calvin on this particular doctrine, Karl Barth went far in disentangling these two issues: "But it is not men as private persons in the singular or plural. It is these men as a fellowship elected by God in Jesus Christ and determined from all eternity for a peculiar service, to be made capable of this service and to discharge it" (1936–77: 2/2.196).[6] Barth stresses that election in the Bible is not principally about the election of individuals for eternal salvation, but rather about God's eternal plan to bring salvation to the world in which a particular group of people, starting with Israel, is elected to play a special role.[7] Barth's understanding of election fits well with the election in the Num. 1 census.

But what kind of an entity is Israel? While in Num. 1 the boundaries of the community of Israel are quite clear—you were either counted or not—in Israel's later history what it meant to be part of Israel or to be a "true" Israelite was less

6. Lesslie Newbigin, *The Gospel in a Pluralist Society* (Grand Rapids: Eerdmans, 1989), 80–89, also stresses that the church is elected for mission.

7. Barth particularly emphasizes that Jesus Christ is the object (and subject) of God's eternal election. But within the perspective of human history, Israel is a crucial starting point of the way this election is played out in time. Subscribing to all the details of Barth's doctrine of election is not necessary for the point being made here. See also Carl E. Braaten and Robert W. Jenson, eds., *Jews and Christians: People of God* (Grand Rapids: Eerdmans, 2003), for discussion of the election of Israel.

clear. Israel might be thought of as a race. They are after all the "congregation of the sons of Israel" (e.g., 1:2). But while the literal phrase "sons of" refers to biological descendents, it is understood at the same time as a metaphor for those with similar traits or functions; so, while the biological descent of the people is important, it cannot be isolated as the primary thing that makes them a distinct group of people (Gottwald 1979: 239–44). This "people" (as in 23:9) is better seen as a political entity. They are united through their common allegiance to YHWH and through their political arrangements and shared cultic practices such as circumcision (Milgrom 1990: 335–36; cf. Gottwald 1979: 237–341). Later, given the breakdown of the united monarchy, the exile, and the Diaspora, what precisely marked one as part of Israel became a source of dispute—which continues to this day—and yet it is clear that Israel was at least intended to be a visible political community.

The census underscores that God is king of Israel, the political entity he rules. This model of political organization can most broadly be called theocracy, a term coined by Josephus to distinguish Israel from the monarchies, oligarchies, and republics of other peoples (*Against Apion* 2.165). While it helpfully points to what remains the same in Israel's polity over time, namely that the king of this "holy nation" is God himself, it is not specific as to how God's rule is mediated or what the details of the human political structure of Israel are.[8] These details change over time, from the tribal confederacy, through the judges to the monarchy and its breakdown, yet theocracy remains the basic political ideal evidenced in the Old and New Testaments. That theocratic ideal continued to form the basis for most Christian political thought until the modern period.[9] Numbers 1 is certainly part of this tradition.

Because God is spirit and transcendent, and thus unlike earthly kings, it is easy to spiritualize our understanding of this kingship of God. In the Old Testament, however, the continued understanding that "God is king" was not an ethereal theological claim, but one that had concrete political teeth. All political arrangements were subject to the will of God. God intended his people to be a community or society whose ways contrasted with the nations around them: "You shall be holy to me; for I the LORD am holy, and I have separated you from the other peoples to be mine" (Lev. 20:26). This understanding is evidenced in both the law and the

8. More specific terms are often used to describe the political system of the tribal structure, such as Martin Noth's amphictyonic league (*Das System der zwölf Stämme Israels* [Stuttgart: Kohlhammer, 1930]) or Gottwald's 1979 tribal confederacy.

9. I follow Allen Verhey, *Remembering Jesus: Christian Community, Scripture, and the Moral Life* (Grand Rapids: Eerdmans, 2002), 333–507; see also Barry A. Harvey, "Insanity, Theocracy, and the Public Realm: Public Theology, the Church, and the Politics of Liberal Democracy," *Modern Theology* 10 (1994): 27–57; and Oliver O'Donovan and Joan Lockwood O'Donovan, eds., *From Irenaeus to Grotius: A Sourcebook in Christian Political Thought* (Grand Rapids: Eerdmans, 1999). In Verhey's words: "The fundamental premise of theocracy . . . was that the cause we must serve politically and the cause the nations must serve is God's cause. Political authority derives from God and it is answerable to God!" (469).

prophets, not only during the tribal confederacy and monarchy, but also during the exile. This kingship of God had concrete impact on the way business, politics, and worship were to be conducted in Israel. Priests, kings, false prophets, judges, merchants, the privileged, the proud—all were critiqued for concrete actions out of line with the ways of life that God intended for Israel.[10] The expectation that the people of God should and will function as a contrastive people continues on, for example, in the prophecy of Isaiah that Israel will "shine": "Nations shall come to your light, and kings to the brightness of your dawn. . . . Your people shall all be righteous . . . so that I might be glorified" (60:1–3, 21).

The question often arises whether this aspect of God's relationship to Israel— God's marking Israel off as a visible and demarcated community that will shine in part through its contrastive practices—is a pattern that should inform the Christian church. At least for Jesus and his followers, the vision of God electing a community of people to be formed politically did not become spiritualized.[11] Their practical arrangements, form of community life, and united worship certainly mattered. Jesus called the twelve and told this renewed Israel that they were to be a "light," "a city . . . on a hill" (Matt. 5:14). Jesus's teachings about the kingdom of God include critiques of concrete political practices just like the Old Testament prophets. While Jesus teaches that the kingdom of God has different characteristics than the kingdom of Caesar and the nations, these differences should not be understood through a contrast between body/visible/political and spirit/invisible/apolitical. Instead, the greatest differences between these two kingdoms are their ways of life: "The kings of the Gentiles lord it over them; and those in authority over them are called benefactors. But not so with you; rather the greatest among you must become like the youngest, and the leader like one who serves" (Luke 22:25–26). Typical ways that power and authority function are turned upside down in this kingdom. Early followers of Christ understood themselves to be "citizens of heaven" yet still remained concerned with the ways that laws, authority, relationships, and power functioned both inside and outside the church. While early Christians understood that they should respect the governors and those in authority, and while they often had to negotiate multiple citizenships and loyalties, they clearly saw themselves as ultimately subject to God in all aspects of their lives: "We must obey God rather than any human authority" (Acts 5:29). Like Israel in Num. 1, they understood

10. Verhey, *Remembering Jesus*, 368.

11. Among the many twentieth-century works that sought to make this point in contrast to certain Protestant traditions, see esp. Dietrich Bonhoeffer, *Life Together; Prayerbook of the Bible*, trans. Daniel W. Bloesch and James H. Burtness, ed. Geffrey B. Kelly, Dietrich Bonhoeffer Works 5 (Minneapolis: Augsburg Fortress, 1996); idem, *Sanctorum communio: A Theological Study of the Sociology of the Church*, trans. Reinhard Krauss and Nancy Lukens, ed. Clifford J. Green, Dietrich Bonhoeffer Works 1 (Minneapolis: Fortress, 1998); Gerhard Lohfink, *Jesus and Community* (Minneapolis: Fortress, 1984); John Howard Yoder, *The Politics of Jesus: Vicit agnus noster* (Grand Rapids: Eerdmans, 1972); and Donald B. Kraybill, *The Upsidedown Kingdom* (Scottdale, PA: Herald, 1990).

themselves to be "a chosen race, a royal priesthood, a holy nation, God's own people" (1 Pet. 2:9).

The Numbers of Numbers: Theological Implications of a Question of History (1:46)

Numbers 1:46 says that 603,550 men were numbered in the census (cf. 2:32 and Exod. 38:26; about 600,000 in Exod. 12:37). Almost no contemporary scholar takes the number 603,550 to be historically probable, for many reasons: the difficulty of reconciling this number with (a) the best estimates of populations in Egypt and Canaan at that time, (b) historical reconstructions of the size of contemporary armies, and (c) the numbers implied by the description of the tabernacle construction in Exod. 38:21–31.[12]

Assuming that a rather important number recorded in scripture is not accurate is problematic. It, and many similar issues of historical fact, raises the question of the truth—here meaning historical accuracy—of Numbers and by extension the Bible. There are two basic ways to respond to such difficulties. One way is to understand that the biblical records were not attempting to be historical in the way we typically understand that word. The truth of these numbers is of a different nature: the text is making a theological rather than historical point.

In general, the observation that scriptures are not modern historical texts is very important.[13] The truth of scripture must not be reduced to questions of history. But why then would such *detailed* numbers be given? They may have been intentionally exaggerated for a theological reason; they may have been based on later censuses of Israel; it is even possible that the numbers were based on understandings of the tabernacle construction and the half-shekel tax recorded in Exod. 38 (Budd 1984: 6–9). Other theories have been developed for how these numbers were arrived at. Whatever their origin, such large numbers highlight the

12. This number of fighting men puts the total population of Israel conservatively at 3 million or more. The total population of Egypt at this time is estimated to be 3.5 million, and the Egyptian army at its height was only 20,000 men. Pharaoh dispatched only 600 chariots out of many more he apparently had available, which seems a small amount to send against a force of such superior numbers. In one of the largest battles recorded in the ancient Near East, the battle of Qarqar, eleven kings marshaled 53,000 troops against King Shalmaneser III of Assyrian in 853 BC. The population of the land of Canaan at the time of the wilderness wanderings is estimated at 140,000 to 150,000 people. The large numbers of Israelites dwarfs these numbers, and the dread that they had of both Pharaoh (Exod. 14:10–14) and the Canaanites (Num. 13:27–28) makes little sense, given these population estimates. See Hoffmeier 2005: 153–55.

13. Hans W. Frei's groundbreaking *The Eclipse of Biblical Narrative: A Study in Eighteenth and Nineteenth Century Hermeneutics* (New Haven: Yale University Press, 1974) did much to change the way that many theologians, biblical scholars, and readers of the Bible approach the text. He sought to free biblical narratives from the imposition of historical questions at the outset, and his work raised awareness that the expectation that the Bible should fit modern notions of history has had a detrimental effect on both Christian faith and on our ability to read the biblical narratives theologically.

blessing of God on the Israelites and the faithfulness of God to his promise to make Abraham's descendents great in number (Olson 1985: 78–81).

The other way to respond to such difficulties is to do further historical and textual work. In this case I find this way to be more promising.[14] The Hebrew word 'elep, translated "thousand" here, in other places indicates "clan, military unit, or subsection of a tribe," and this meaning might have been intended here (Hoffmeier 2005: 153–59, following earlier scholars). Given this broader meaning, the census count for the tribe of Reuben (1:21), for example, could be "forty-six units, five hundred fighting men," rather than "forty-six thousand, five hundred men." The grand total would thus be 598 units composed of 5,500 fighting men. This is a much more historically plausible number, and it also fits well with the images of Israel in its interactions with Egyptians and Canaanites.

One ramification of this reading is that, at some point in the writing process of the Hebrew text, the word 'elep came to be understood as "one thousand" and then parts of the text, including Num. 1:46 and Exod. 28, were written or adjusted accordingly.[15] However, this reading fits better with the understanding that the basic textual substructure of the wilderness traditions goes back quite early; it also fits well with the larger story of God's dealings with Israel in the wilderness (Hoffmeier 2005: 248–49).[16] Such numbers highlight the smallness of Israel and the power of God in electing and safeguarding such a small group of people through their encounters and battles with other peoples. Thus, instead of being artificial numbers highlighting the fulfillment of God's promises of a vast number of descendents, these smaller, potentially more historically accurate, numbers fit well with the larger biblical theme that God tends to elect and use what the world considers small and insignificant both to highlight God's glory and because God takes special care of the weak and lowly.[17]

14. On the one hand, one should not reduce one's hermeneutic for reading the biblical narratives to the questions and categories of modern history. On the other hand, the general assumption behind the many figural interpretations brought out in this commentary is that God did and does shape the people of God in similar ways throughout history. This requires some fit between the biblical narratives and the history of the relationship between God and Israel in the wilderness. One cannot claim that the biblical writers were not writing history in the modern sense, on this basis dismiss the need for a general fit between text and event, and then make claims about God working in similar ways throughout history. One should instead do the hard work of evaluating historical matters on a case-by-case basis.

15. At some point, probably during the monarchy, the word 'elep came to be associated with a military unit of one thousand soldiers, and this meaning was possibly superimposed by later readers and redactors on previous texts where the word meant "unit."

16. Hoffmeier is responding to a trend in historical scholarship that rejects any fit between the wilderness narratives and history—claiming instead that there never was an exodus from Egypt, that Israel as a people never was in Egypt, but rather the whole of the Pentateuch "is an artificial and theologically influenced literary construct" (Hoffmeier 2005: 6, quoting John Miller and John Hayes).

17. The story of Gideon (Judg. 7), the stories of the choosing of Saul and David as king (1 Sam. 9:21; 16:1–13), Jesus's selection of twelve fishermen and his ministry, including the parables of

Organization of Israel as a People (2:1–34)

In Num. 1 the community of God is chosen and numbered. The Levites are also specially marked off as a group (1:48–51), an indication that Israel is not merely a theocracy, but more specifically a priestly theocracy (→3:1–4:49). Numbers 2 gives in greater detail the specifics of the way this community is organized. The twelve tribes, with the exception of the Levites, are placed by the command of God in an order of encampment and marching. The text pays close attention to both the way the twelve tribes are organized in regard to each other and how they are positioned in relationship to the tabernacle.

The tribal order gives particular honor to certain tribes and structures the community so that there are recognizable roles and differences between them. Those at the front of the march are camped on the east side near the priests and the opening of the tabernacle, the place of honor. The marching order follows a roughly decreasing order of honor in clockwise fashion around the tabernacle:

> east: Judah, Issachar, Zebulun
> south: Reuben, Simeon, Gad
> west: Ephraim, Manasseh, Benjamin
> north: Dan, Asher, Naphtali

The sons of Joseph—Ephraim and Manasseh—have been elevated to equal status with the ten other sons in order to make twelve. This arrangement follows roughly the order of birth and status of the sons of Jacob. The five sons of Leah are placed first, but with Judah elevated to the first position and Reuben and Simeon demoted to reflect Gen. 49:2–27 and Deut. 33:2–29. After these, the sons of Rachael are placed together in the west. Finally, three of the four sons of Jacob's concubines are placed in the north, but with the firstborn of Leah's handmaid, Gad, promoted to the southern group, seemingly to maintain the symmetry of four groups of three while also keeping Rachael's offspring together (Budd 1984: 24–25).

While there is an order of honor to the tribes, the descripton stresses more strongly their relative equality and unity as a group. Each tribe forms one third of a side of the square. This picture well represents the movement toward a relative sociopolitical equality evidenced throughout the laws and precepts given at Sinai.[18] Throughout Numbers, the individual tribes are most often treated in a

---

the lost coin and lost sheep in the New Testament (Luke 15:1–8), are well-known examples of this theme.

18. "Relative equality" means constraints in the law against gross inequality and its related inequities. See Gottwald 1979: 611–21; Patrick Miller, "Property and Possession in Light of the Ten Commandments," in *Having: Property and Possession in Religious and Social Life*, ed. William Schweiker and Charles Mathewes (Grand Rapids: Eerdmans, 2004), 17–50; Herman Daly, *Beyond Growth* (Boston: Beacon, 1996), esp. 205–15.

relatively equal way. For example, the stylized and symmetrical description of each tribe's offerings in Num. 7 is markedly different from the distinctive treatment each son gets in Gen. 49:1–28 in both length and quality. Here the emphasis is on the contribution of each to the larger body.

Besides the positioning of the tribes, the other important feature of this picture of Israel is that the tabernacle, which represents and mediates the presence of God, is placed in the center of the camp and the march. And in Num. 3 the priests and the three Levite groups are placed between the tabernacle and the people on each of its four sides. The people are ordered and arranged around God and his priests.

The central place that God occupies in this iconic picture is even more striking when compared to similar portraits found in Egypt. Rameses II's temples contain artwork which portrays a similar, rectangular pattern for the Egyptian war camp at Kadesh with the larger-than-life tent of Rameses forming its center—an image quite similar to the picture painted by Numbers (Hoffmeier 2005: fig. 29 and 206–8). It is reasonable to think that the Israelites might have been aware of such artwork. Rather than having an earthly, yet godlike pharaoh at the center of their camp and lives, in Israel, God's presence as mediated through the tabernacle forms the center.

Similar images of the twelve tribes are found elsewhere in the Bible. In Ezek. 40–48, Ezekiel describes his vision of the temple, the surrounding holy district, and the territories of the tribes of Israel in which now the temple, rather than the tabernacle, is at the center of Israel. The twelve tribes are assigned territories surrounding the city (47:21–48:29), which has twelve gates in its walls, three on each side, each named after one of the twelve tribes (48:30–35). Instead of the camp, the people are pictured as a city, and the tribes are symbolically represented by the gates. Each tribe is assigned one territory and one gate, and the relative ranking of each is deemphasized; that they each are part of the larger whole is the point.

This "icon" of the people of God is also encountered in a different form in the Gospels, now embodied in the twelve disciples gathered around Jesus. While it is not clear that there are specific allusions back to Ezek. 40–48 or Num. 2, Jesus is portrayed as carrying on the functions of tabernacle and temple, and his disciples are clearly likened to the "city" of the people of God (Matt. 5:14). The image progresses from tabernacle to temple to Christ at the center—each surrounded by "the twelve."

Revelation makes clear allusions back to the Old Testament images in Numbers and Ezekiel. In John's vision of the new Jerusalem (Rev. 21:9–27), at the center of the city is no tabernacle or temple, "for its temple is the Lord God the Almighty and the Lamb" (21:22). The city contains twelve gates inscribed with the names of the twelve tribes, with twelve foundations representing the twelve apostles (21:12–14; cf. the twenty-four elders around the throne in 4:4). Here, the twelve apostles are given a similar role or status to the twelve tribes and their leaders. Importantly, they are added to the image rather than superceding the role of the twelve tribes.[19]

Three aspects of these images of the people of God, rooted in the description of the camp in Num. 2, stand out in particular and inform our understanding of God's intentions for his chosen people and put pressure on ecclesiology. Not surprisingly, they resonate well with three of the four Nicene marks of the church: one, holy, apostolic. The catholicity of the church (Greek *kat' holon*, "according to the totality"), understood as both the universality of the church and the impetus of the life of the church to be enfleshed in every ethnicity, is not yet a strong feature of the vision of the people of God in Numbers.[20]

First, in these images Israel is portrayed as a unified and interdependent whole that is at the same time composed of different individuals, tribes, and clans. They are totaled as a people (1:46) and called by one name. They form one camp, one city, one people. They are one. In their life together in the wilderness and later in Canaan, they formed a visible, political community, united by their common history, by their bloodlines, by their tribal structure and economy, and by their covenant relationship to God, which included the practices of circumcision, Sabbath keeping, and worship at the tabernacle or temple.

While many factors unite them as a people, the central factor in their unity and identity as a people is their covenant with God, in which their covenant-structured "horizontal" relationships to one another are intertwined with their "vertical" relationship to God. In Josh. 24:1–28 this identity is renewed at Shechem before Joshua sends them to their separate inheritances. Their commitment to God and their obedience to the "statutes and ordinances" (24:25) unify them and make them one. Such covenant obedience implies a certain visible and public way of life together—a life as a people, a body, in order that the ways of God might shine forth through their way of life as Israel.

This picture of the visible unity of Israel informs contemporary discussions of Christian ecclesiology. It at least suggests that the church, like Israel, should not merely be a collection of individuals who hold similar beliefs. Their unity came from being chosen by God as a visible people, whose commitment to God entails living in certain ways both individually and corporately.[21]

---

19. In later Christian tradition, these images are alluded to in the traditional Eastern Orthodox icon of Pentecost: the twelve disciples are arranged orderly and symmetrically around symbols of Father, Son, and Holy Spirit, with the background of city buildings. This suggests that Pentecost is the firstfruits of the coming of the new Jerusalem and the overcoming of the curse of Babel.

20. For this understanding of "catholic," see *Catechism of the Catholic Church* (Liguori, MO: Liguori, 1994), §830. Yet the promise that Israel will be a blessing to all nations (Gen. 12:1–3) strikes this theme.

21. Dietrich Bonhoeffer, *Life Together;* Lohfink, *Jesus and Community*; and Reinhard Hütter, *Suffering Divine Things: Theology as Church Practice* (Grand Rapids: Eerdmans, 2000) react against certain common Protestant interpretations of the church as "invisible" and call for a renewed emphasis on the church as a public, visible community.

However, the particular way that Israel was structured into a unified people—their tribal structure—cannot be understood as dictating a precise form of polity for the church. Israel and the church are organized into one body in a variety of ways throughout scripture, and a variety of images suggest such unity (e.g., "body of Christ"; Rom. 12:3–9; 1 Cor. 3:6–9; 12:4–31; 1 Pet. 2:5).[22] While one particular polity is not necessary, two extreme kinds of political structure do not fit well with the details of Israel's tribal structure. A structure that achieves unity through an erasure of individuality (via strictly enforced equality) or through the domination of one particular individual does not fit well with these pictures. On the one hand, with both the twelve tribes and the twelve disciples, the individual is honored and recognized for his or her particular contribution. A hierarchy is also apparent among both tribes and apostles—depending on how one defines that term. Unity is not achieved through the erasure of distinctions. On the other hand, in the Old Testament images of the people, the relative equality of each of the twelve is emphasized. In Ezekiel and Revelation, the gates, foundations, and inheritances are of equal size. While the twelve disciples are clearly named and seen in all their individuality, and while James, John, and Peter seem to have a higher status (Mark 9:2; 14:33), with Peter as the leader among even these (14:29, 37), Jesus explicitly undercuts typical ways that hierarchies of honor and position work in most social orders: "It will not be so among you" (Matt. 20:26; cf. 18:1–5). The phrase often used in Christian polity, "first among equals," does a good job of grasping these tensions.[23]

But even given a wide flexibility for the way that unity might be expressed, it is difficult not to read the later divisions within Israel and the schisms and denominations that eventually became part of the church as a falling away from the true nature and calling of the people of God. Ezekiel read the history of division within Israel as a punishment for its sins. In light of this fractured state, Ezekiel painted his image of a restored and unified people of God, an image of hope and a call to Israel to work and pray for such a restored unity. While Christians had mixed reactions to the twentieth-century ecumenical movement and the work of the World Council of Churches, there is little doubt that the impulse toward an organic unity that still protects the positive differences and individual contributions of the different "tribes" of Christianity is one that would move us toward greater conformance with these images of the people of God.[24]

22. Raymond Brown, *The Message of Numbers: Journey to the Promised Land* (Downers Grove, IL: InterVarsity, 2002), 30–31.

23. The Latin phrase *primus inter pares* ("first among equals") is used to describe the Patriarch of Constantinople in the Eastern Orthodox communion, the Archbishop of Canterbury in the Anglican communion, and the Dean of the College of Cardinals (but not the pope) in the Roman Catholic Church.

24. The different orders (such as the Benedictine) within the overall unity of the Roman Catholic Church is one form of polity that is analogous to the tribal structure of Israel in Num. 2.

A second important feature of this icon of Israel is the placement of the tabernacle at the center of the Israelite camp (2:2). God's presence, covenant commands, and worship represented by the tabernacle are at the center of Israel's life and identity (→7:1–10:10). Because God is in their midst, and in order that God will continue to be in their midst, they are and are to be a "holy" people (Exod. 19:6; Lev. 19:2).

For the Israelites, God is quintessentially holy (Milgrom 2000: 1711–26). This term designates and describes the nature of God, a characteristic that separates God from all other beings (1 Sam. 2:2; Milgrom 2000: 1712). Certain spaces, persons, and times are designated as holy, but only through a divine dispensation and dependent upon God's will. Typically, an object, place, person, or time must be "purified" or "consecrated" in order to bear a closer relationship to God. They are in this way set apart from the common and understood to bear a greater likeness to God through their clean or purified state (→7:1–88). This is reflected in the typical use and meanings of words based on the Hebraic root *qdš*, which expresses the idea of holiness. Adjectival forms of this word are translated "holy," while the verbal forms are translated "to purify, consecrate," that is, to make ready for proximity to and closer relationship to God.

Certain times, such as the fixed festivals of Num. 28–29, are called holy because work is prohibited during them (28:26; 29:1). Those times are thus like the Sabbath, set apart for God from common times and reflecting God's rest from work on the seventh day of creation (Gen. 2:2–3; Exod. 20:8–11). Certain individuals such as the Nazirite (Num. 6:5) are holy. The tabernacle is holy, as well as the items used in it. The term "holy" is also applied to the people of Israel: "You shall be holy, for I the LORD your God am holy" (Lev. 19:2). In the Gospels, Jesus makes a similar statement to his disciples: "Be perfect, therefore, as your heavenly Father is perfect" (Matt. 5:48). The people of God are set apart as a holy people by God and in certain ways are understood to participate in or reflect God's holiness.

The Holiness Code of Lev. 17–27 delineates more precisely what this holiness of the people consists of and forms the literary center of the Pentateuch. Through Moses, God addresses the people and gives them concrete instructions about their ethical behavior—both behaviors to refrain from (esp. Lev. 18) and behaviors to engage in (esp. Lev. 19) (Balentine 1999: 169). In and through these behaviors, Israel is to image God as a people, to reflect characteristics of him. This positive ethic can be summed up in two fundamental duties: "They are to love God exclusively . . . , and they are to manifest this commitment to God by engaging in acts of compassionate justice for all human beings" (Balentine 1999: 170).

The Holiness Code continues by listing and prohibiting "the practices of the nation that I am driving out before you" (20:23), suggesting that Israel's imaging of God's holiness in their practices will set them apart from the practices of other nations. Finally the code moves into positive prescriptions for worship and festival life (Lev. 21–25). This worship life mediates the holy presence of God to the people and builds a people with the faith and the vision of who God is and who they are to be in the world, enabling them to live into their calling to be a holy people.

Such holiness should also characterize the church. And just as Israel is who it is because of God's presence in its midst, symbolized and mediated through the tabernacle, similarly the church is the church because of the presence of God, most clearly mediated through the ministry of word and sacrament. This is why Luther and Calvin called word and sacrament the "marks of the church." Such holiness comes from the presence of Christ among the people: "Wherever we see the Word of God purely preached and heard, and the sacraments administered according to Christ's institution, there, it is not to be doubted, a church of God exists [cf. Eph. 2:20]. For his promise cannot fail: 'Wherever two or three are gathered in my name, there I am in the midst of them' [Matt. 18:20]" (Calvin 1960: §4.1.9).

Ephesians 2:20 mentions that the church is "built upon the foundation of the apostles and prophets, with Christ Jesus himself as the cornerstone." In the following sentences, the church is likened to the temple, "a dwelling place for God" (2:22). Calvin sees the worship life of the church as the means by which God shapes and forms the people of God into a people who are "unfeignedly holy" (§4.1.8), who are thus set apart in order to image God in the world. Similarly, Luther called practices surrounding word and sacrament *Heilthümer* ("holy things"), which make the church holy.[25]

These close connections between worship, ethics, and holiness are often lost in the practice and theology of Christianity. But they are reflected in this icon of the people of God in Num. 2 when interpreted in light of its Pentateuchal context. In fact, the first third of Numbers seems to intentionally connect the overall identity and structure of the people of God with its ethical life and its worship.

A third aspect of this icon of Israel is the emphasis on the twelve tribes with their twelve leaders. Both that there are tribes and that there are precisely twelve of them seem to matter. As the people of Israel are arranged, they are put "in their respective regiments, under ensigns by their ancestral houses" (2:2). In addition, when the tribe of Levi is devoted to God, care is taken to promote the sons of Joseph so that there would still be twelve tribes in total, as seen in the lists of the tribes (1:10, 32–34).

While these patterns tell us how Israel functioned as a political body at that time, the twelve tribes also had an enduring significance, part of which was the symbolic role they had in connecting one generation of Israel to the next and connecting Israel back to its origins. To say "I am of the tribe of Benjamin" connected one to a whole history, placing one in the context of

---

25. Luther recognized additional practices as marks in certain of his writings. His use of the word *Heilthümer* is in part a critique of contemporary practices surrounding relics, which had largely replaced the true things that made the church holy. See Martin Luther, *Church and Ministry*, vol. 3, ed. Eric W. Gritsch, Luther's Works 41 (Saint Louis: Concordia, 1966), 148–68.

those connections through time. The continuing importance of this number is seen throughout Israel's history and in the history of the church. Twelve tribes, twelve leaders in Num. 2, twelve disciples in the Gospels—all these twelves are signs of continuity with the origins of Israel. Even for scholars who doubt an actual historic continuity of bloodline from the sons of Jacob/Israel to the twelve tribes at the time of the Davidic monarchy (e.g., Gottwald 1979: 375), the use of the twelve-tribe system served to unite Israel around the "socioreligious foundations" of the kingdom even when in later times it ceased to have much political significance. It connected them to their roots. The most important part of these roots was the promises God made to Abraham and his descendents. These were promises not to humanity in general, but to a visible and continuous group of people.

That Jesus called twelve disciples suggests he understood his purposes to be in continuity with Israel's origins and the promises God made to the patriarchs and their descendents. The twelve disciples become a picture of a renewed and regathered remnant of Israel, led by Christ the Messiah.

As the Nicene Creed states, the church is also "apostolic." This stresses a historical continuity with the apostolic mission of the renewed Israel that Jesus called into being. Such apostolicity also points to continuity with the origins of Israel—a continuity symbolically represented in the image of the new Jerusalem in Rev. 21:12–14: "On the gates are inscribed the names of the twelve tribes of Israel. . . . And the wall of the city has twelve foundations, and on them are the twelve names of the twelve apostles." Within Christianity, connection to the apostles is traced not through bloodlines, but typically through the laying-on-of-hands from one bishop to the next. In light of the historic corruption of some church leaders, Luther and Calvin stressed that apostolicity should be understood rather as the church's continuity with the apostle's teaching and mission recorded in the Bible.[26] In either case, however, the pressure of Num. 2 on our understanding of apostolicity is to make Christians place importance on the continuity of the church as a people, in which continuity of both leadership and belief structure and mission are important and intricately related parts. While God is king and at the center of this people, this leadership of God does not undermine but rather uses human tribal and leadership structures to link the people of God through time.

26. The important ecumenical document *Baptism, Eucharist, and Ministry*, Faith and Order Paper 111 (Geneva: World Council of Churches, 1982) has a good discussion of this ecumenical issue: "Within the Church the ordained ministry has a particular task of preserving and actualizing the apostolic faith. The orderly transmission of the ordained ministry is therefore a powerful expression of the continuity of the Church throughout history; it also underlines the calling of the ordained minister as guardian of the faith. Where churches see little importance in orderly transmission, they should ask themselves whether they have not to change their conception of continuity in the apostolic tradition. On the other hand, where the ordained ministry does not adequately serve the proclamation of the apostolic faith, churches must ask themselves whether their ministerial structures are not in need of reform" ("Ministry," §35; cf. §§8–14).

Function of Priests and Levites in the Priestly Kingdom (3:1–4:49)

After the people are counted and organized according to tribes, the priestly classes within the people of God are organized. The sons of Aaron are named as the anointed priests of the people (3:1–4), the general duties of the Levites are outlined (3:5–13), a census of the three clans of the Levites is taken (3:14–39) and the number within those clans between thirty and fifty years old and thus able to work at the tabernacle is also reckoned (4:34–49), the firstborn of Israel are redeemed by the Levites (3:40–51), and the special duties of each Levitical clan—Kohathites, Gershonites, and Merarites—are outlined (4:1–33).

This section completes the overall organization of Israel, filling out the icon of the people of God. The separate censuses (1:48–54; 3:14–39; 4:34–49) and great detail concerning this priestly class highlights their crucial roles in this priestly kingdom. These roles have often been misunderstood and misused in later Jewish and Christian traditions—and as a result often underplayed, critiqued, or ignored.[27] Nonetheless their roles are critical parts of the identity and vocation of Israel.

The main functions of the priestly class of Israel can be grouped under four headings: to serve, to protect boundaries, to mediate across those boundaries, and to represent.[28]

The most frequent verbs used to describe the roles of the priests and Levites concern their service to the tabernacle and the people. The Levites are to "carry" the tabernacle (1:50), "tend" it (1:50), "set it up" and "take it down" (1:51). The

27. One difficulty in understanding the roles of the priests and Levites is that the Old Testament generally gives quite detailed descriptions of their duties and the ritual actions they are to perform, but little explanation of the meaning or theology of those actions or duties. Coupled with this, suspicion of priestly roles and practices has clouded reflection on them. Such suspicions come from a formidable list of sources: the prophetic critiques of temple practice in the Old Testament; Jesus's own critiques of Jewish leadership and his predictions of the destruction of the temple in the Gospels; Christian anti-Semitism and Marcionistic tendencies that created pressure toward supercessionist understandings of Old Testament worship and priesthood; Protestant suspicions of Old Testament priesthood and worship (they just seem so "Catholic") tied with certain theological understandings of Christ's high priesthood and the "priesthood of all believers," which undercut the need for or respect of priestly roles; modern critiques of authority and hierarchy; and major strands of modern historical scholarship that view priestly Pentateuchal materials as later degradations of earlier, purer forms of Israelite religion (Brueggemann 1997: 651–54; Balentine 1999: 3–36). Modern biblical scholarship and theology is currently rediscovering the importance of the roles of the priests and Levites in the worship life of Israel, how their role is deeply tied to the vocation and worship of Israel, and the great impact that priestly roles and larger worship life of Israel had on the theological vision and worship life of the early church.

28. I do not draw a strict distinction between the roles of the priests and Levites, but in general treat them together as a larger priestly class. In Num. 3 the two are well distinguished: lines between Aaronic priests and the Merarites, Gershonites, and Kohathites are clearly drawn. But in other parts of scripture, the roles of the priests and Levites are not carefully distinguished. There is continuing debate as to when the distinction between the roles of Aaronic priests and other Levites came about (Hutton 1994: 139–45; Levine 1993: 279–90). Moses and Aaron were from the tribe of Levi (Exod. 2:1), and so all Aaronic priests were Levites.

priests are to "minister" (3:3) and "attend" to their duties (3:10). The Levites are to "assist" (3:6) the priests, "perform duties for [Aaron] and for the whole congregation" (3:7), thus "do[ing] service at the tabernacle" (3:8). The Kohathites "do work related to the tent of meeting" (4:3; described in detail in 4:5–16), while the Gershonites and Merarites are given the task of "serving and bearing burdens" (4:24, 27, 49; described in 4:24–28, 31–33). The priests and Levites are separated from the rest of the people, and their proximity to God and the tabernacle gives them a certain status. But this separateness and election is to service, which is perhaps best epitomized by the regular physical labor of taking down and setting up the tabernacle.

The purpose of this service, which involves physical, interpersonal, and religious duties, was primarily to facilitate the regularized access to God centered on the tabernacle. They handled and cared for the physical objects associated with the tabernacle, and they performed ritual duties associated with the worship life of Israel centered at the tabernacle. But, as seen elsewhere in scripture, they also were the principal caretakers of the Torah, the covenant law of Israel, symbolized by the tablets contained in the ark in the holy of holies (Hutton 1994: 139). In contrast to the more intuitive and irregular world of the prophets in Israel, who communicated God's word in a more ad hoc fashion, the priests and Levites served by maintaining these ordinary and regular means of access to God.

The prophets of Israel have often been valorized by Christian interpreters, especially Protestants, and seen in opposition to the priests. Many have critiqued the regularized practices of organized religion that the priests represent. Certainly such service can lose sight of its purpose and end up serving its own institutionalized structure rather than providing a means of mediated access to God. Yet the prophets had their own pitfalls. The prophet ran the risk of reflecting his own mind or the mind of the people, rather than the word and mind of God, as the proliferation of false prophets in Israel attests. Each way of serving God—the bold speaking of God's word by the prophets and the careful study and teaching of God's word in the Torah by the priests—had its own strengths and dangers, but ideally the two could be complementary: "The fiery passion of the Word and the persistent reason of Torah complemented each other and corrected each other, but at the same time drew their strength from one another" (Hutton 1994: 171).[29]

Second, the Levites are appointed to protect the tabernacle and the people of God by making sure the boundary between tabernacle and camp is not wrongfully crossed. They are to "perform the guard duty of the tabernacle of the covenant"

29. Christ is seen in the New Testament as fulfilling the role of the high priest. While he does not explicitly connect service to his role as priest, Christ understands his vocation partially in terms of service, as reflected in these words he speaks about himself: "The Son of Man came not to be served but to serve" (Matt. 20:28). He tells his disciples to follow in his ways: "Whoever wishes to be great among you must be your servant" (20:26). This role of service is also built into the original calling of humanity—Adam was told to "serve" and "protect" the garden (an alternate translation of the Hebrew of Gen. 2:15).

(1:53; cf. 3:10, 38) and to "camp around the tabernacle" (1:50) in order that no one "encroaches" on the tabernacle space, in this way protecting the people from wrath. This duty of the Levites—guarding the boundaries of the holy area of the tabernacle from the common area of the camp—is representative of several ways the priestly class protected and kept the people of God out of harm's way by teaching and enforcing boundaries, both physical and other. They were also charged with teaching and making judgments concerning God's covenant patterns in the Torah, including distinctions between holy and common, between clean and unclean, and at a moral level between righteousness and sin. This maintaining of boundaries is summed up when the priests are told: "You are to distinguish between the holy and the common, and between the unclean and the clean; and you are to teach the people of Israel all the statutes that the LORD has spoken to them through Moses" (Lev. 10:10–11). These distinctions or boundaries are part of a larger worldview at the heart of the worship and ritual life of Israel.

Central to this larger worldview is the idea that God created the world with a certain pattern or "cosmic design" woven into it.[30] Creation is created good and ordered in such a way that there is a "harmonious interplay" between heaven and earth (Balentine 1999: 236). But this order and interplay are vulnerable. For this interplay to continue, careful boundaries and directives must be maintained; if they are not, life and goodness break down, and chaos and death result.[31]

The tabernacle and the rituals surrounding it become the one place in the world where these creational patterns of God regularly attain "visible, concrete, and effective representation" (Balentine 1999: 237).[32] This imaging of God's design and presence is what makes the tabernacle holy and sacred. It becomes a model for the restoration and completion of all creation. Thus a chief role of the priests and Levites is to serve the tabernacle, the people, and all creation by maintaining such a place and ritual activity. The Levites especially are to protect the physical boundaries around the tabernacle so that the holy does not get invaded by and broken down into the common. The priests and Levites are also to maintain the

---

30. Balentine 1999; Klawans 2000; Douglas 1993a; and Jon D. Levenson, *Sinai and Zion: An Entry into the Jewish Bible* (Minneapolis: Winston, 1985).

31. The distinction between clean and unclean indicates such order. Ritual uncleanness often has to do with the breakdown of boundaries or typical orders or patterns within creation. Ritual uncleanness in the body centers around instances where the body's boundaries have broken down (excretions, skin diseases, decaying corpses) (→5:1–4). Unclean creatures are in some way abnormal for their class or category (e.g., sea creatures without scales, animals without eyes, four-footed creatures without cloven hoofs). See Douglas 1993b.

32. For example, Balentine points to the correspondences between "the liturgy of creation" recorded in the creation narratives, which culminate on the Sabbath day, and the liturgies surrounding the construction of the tabernacle (Exod. 35–40): "Collectively, these parallels envision the construction of the tabernacle to be an intentional complement to God's creational designs for the cosmos." The completion of the tabernacle, given what it represents (a place where God's creational designs are realized in a fallen world) and the human work involved in it (part of God's intentions includes the activity of humans as cocreators with God), can be seen as the "completion of the work begun in creation" (1999: 140).

holiness of the people of God by teaching them the patterns of Torah. This is in part to prevent the boundaries between them and the nations from breaking down so they do not simply become another nation like the others.

This high view of the tabernacle and the worship conducted there is the background needed to understand the command to the Levites to kill those who intentionally encroach upon the boundaries of the tabernacle lest God's wrath break out.[33] The holiness of God and the tabernacle has a certain energy that personal categories cannot fully make sense of. Put plainly, God is envisioned like a person, but his presence is like the radioactive energy within a nuclear reactor (Hutton 1994: 147; for an alternate metaphor, →5:1–4). This energy of God is the source of life, but when it interacts with an unholy world it can be destructive. People who encroach on the tabernacle are like terrorists intent on breaking down the containment walls of a nuclear reactor—they must be stopped before they do their damage, otherwise the wrath of God, God's power and energy seen under their destructive aspect, will break out (Milgrom 1990: 342–43). While the Levites are charged only with keeping ritually unclean people away, in Korah's rebellion (→16:1–17:11), God's wrath breaks out in response to moral sin, the prideful and envious approach toward the holy things by Korah and the leaders of Israel.

Third, the priestly classes are called not only to protect such boundaries, but also to mediate across them, a role suggested by the physical position of the priests and Levites between the tabernacle and the rest of the people. They are to mediate or extend the holy into the common and help the common to move toward the holy. Balentine writes: "At the heart of priestly ministry, therefore, stands the abiding mandate *to secure a community of faith* in the midst of a fragile world, and by so doing *to build a world* evermore attuned to God's cosmic purposes" (1999: 175, emphasis original). In several ways they helped extend the holy presence of God outward across this porous boundary. Priests mediated the will of God outward most directly through Urim and Thummim (Exod. 28:30; Lev. 8:8; Deut. 33:8), special devices like lots that helped discern the will of God. But more regularly and importantly, they did so by teaching the Torah. They were to teach "all the statutes that the LORD has spoken . . . through Moses" (Lev. 10:11). While this teaching activity is not highlighted in Numbers, it is most clearly connected to the priests by the prophets (Hos. 4:1–6; 8:11–13; Mic. 3:11; Isa. 2:3; 51:4; Zeph. 3:4; Jer. 2:8; 18:18; Ezek. 7:26; 22:26; 44:23–24; Mal. 2:6–7; Hutton 1994: 145). They also had "charge of the rites within the sanctuary, whatever had to be done for the Israelites" (Num. 3:38; cf. 3:3) and thus oversaw and participated in the worship life of Israel, including its important system of offerings and sacrifices (→7:1–88). The priestly blessing (6:22–27) was another way that God's pres-

33. Jacob Milgrom, "Encroaching on the Sacred: Purity and Polity in Num. 1–10," *Interpretation* 51 (1997): 241–53, argues that what is envisioned in 1:51—"any outsider who comes near [Milgrom: "encroaches"] shall be put to death"—is an intentional attempt to break down and defile the tabernacle or sanctuary.

ence was mediated through the priests to the Israelites. In all these practices they facilitated the two-way connection between God and Israel.[34]

Fourth, not only did the priests mediate and facilitate others as they moved across these boundaries, they also had the role of substituting for and representing others before God. Words like "representation," "substitution," and "vicarious" can be understood in two distinct ways. First, in 3:11–13 and 3:40–57 the Levites and their livestock "substitute" for all the firstborn of Israel and of Israel's livestock. Since there were 273 more firstborn than Levites, "redemption" (*pidyôm*; cf. Exod. 21:30, where it is translated "ransom") money was required for those extra firstborn (→3:40–51). In this case, the Levites are substituting for others through the offering of their whole person or life. They are offered to God as priests in place of others.

But the priests also represent other Israelites or all Israel to God through certain particular acts, prayers, and sacrifices. When the priest sacrifices an animal for another Israelite, his own intentions and actions represent the intentions of another before God; they do not replace them. And in certain actions the priest represents the entire nation before God. The garments of the high priest symbolize this. Both the shoulder-pieces and the breastplate bear the names of the twelve tribes of Israel (Exod. 28:9–10, 29). On the Day of Atonement (Lev. 16), the high priest makes confession and sacrifices on behalf of the whole people of Israel, making atonement as representative of the whole nation. It is as if Israel was acting in and through the actions of the priest. Based on Jewish commentators, Jacob Neusner argues that the temple sacrifices were understood to be efficacious only if the intentions of the priest and the people coincided.[35] While one does not need to look hard to see that this ideal was not always realized in practice, these exceptions do not negate the ideal.

The distinction between substitution and representation is important for understanding the relationship between the priests and Levites and the rest of Israel. The priests do not undercut the calling of all the people to be a priestly kingdom, but represent it. And as the priest is to the people, so Israel is (ideally) to the nations.

Having these four priestly functions in mind helps us see how Israel might be called a priestly people (Exod. 19:6; Lev. 20:22–26). They are to serve God by keeping the worship life of Israel running through their own contributions. They are also to protect the holy from being broken down into the common by

34. Brueggemann 1997: 664 refers to this third function as he writes: "My impression is that the priests themselves do not mediate, but they supervise and attest the visual, material, physical acts of worship that do the mediation." But in their representative role, they do more than simply facilitate mediating practices.

35. Jacob Neusner, "Sacrifice and Temple in Rabbinic Judaism," in *The Encyclopedia of Judaism*, ed. Jacob Neusner, Alan J. Avery-Peck, and William Scott Green (New York: Continuum, 1999), 1290–1302. Neusner points out the importance of the question of how Jews who are not physically present might still participate in such offerings and sacrifices. The rabbinic answer was through the half-shekel tax specified in Exod. 30:11–16. The proper intention of the Israelite in giving the half-shekel was to participate in the offerings, and this was acceptable.

maintaining the stipulations of the covenant (20:25–26) and by protecting the purity and holiness of the nation. These two aspects of the priestly role are perhaps the easiest ones to associate with the holiness and priestly character of Israel. But they also perform functions vis-à-vis the nations that are analogous to the other two functions the Levitical priests performed for Israel.

The theme of Israel as mediator to and representative of the nations is found elsewhere in scripture. Israel is to teach the nations through its life lived in conformance to Torah. In this way it will be a light to the nations, drawing them to God (Isa. 42:1–9). It is to also be a mediator of blessing to the nations (Gen. 12:3). The construction of the temple, with its symbolically significant larger court of the Gentiles surrounding the much smaller court of Israel, suggests this role; Israel is to be priest to the Gentiles, who are also called to worship God.[36] And Israel's role as firstborn among the nations may hint at the priestly roles of representation and substitution. Certainly the deep meditations on the role of Israel as Suffering Servant reflect this. By bearing the iniquities of others and by making "intercession for the transgressors," Israel brings others to God (Isa. 43:12).

Such priestly functions are often taken on in part by smaller groups within Israel. The theme of the remnant or representative group of Israel that lives more fully into the calling of Israel is common in the prophets (e.g., Isa. 6:13), is reflected in the practice of the Nazirites (→6:1–21), and also informed the sense of vocation of later groups within Israel (e.g., Essenes and the Qumran community). This representation of the whole by the part is most fully seen in the vocation and work of Christ as representative of Israel and humanity. Christ as true Israelite and true human takes on the role of priest, teaching the ways of God and mediating God's presence to Israel, interceding for Israel to God, and most fully representing and fulfilling the sacrifice of obedience (Ps. 40:6–8; Heb. 10:5–10) that God desired of Israel and ultimately of all humanity.

Because of Christ's perfect fulfillment of this role of priest, it is sometimes thought that there is no place for priests in the church. Certainly our relationship to Christ's and God's presence in the church is different than in Israel, due to the gift of Christ's life, death, and resurrection; the end of the sacrificial system with the destruction of the temple; and the transformation of the worship of Israel into the life and sacraments of the church. The sacrifices and offerings we bring to God look different; however, much remains the same. Certainly there is a "once for all" and "final" aspect to the work of Christ. But while the priestly functions of teaching God's ways, protecting the holy from being broken down into the common, mediating God to the people, and representing the people to God are accomplished in Christ, we are also called to share in these. Christ fulfills the role of priest, yet we are still called to be "holy" and to be "a royal priesthood" (1 Pet. 1:16; 2:9). The key to understanding priesthood in general and the priesthood of

36. This theme in the architecture of the temple is picked up and transformed by Paul in Eph. 2:14.

Christ in particular is through the participatory notion of representation. Christ offered himself as a representative sacrifice not so that we don't have to make any offering or sacrifice, but in order that we may also be enabled to offer ourselves as "a living sacrifice, holy and acceptable to God, which is your spiritual worship" (Rom. 12:1–2). The representative role of priests within the church (and Israel) is similar. Certain members are set apart (in function or status, temporarily or more permanently) to represent and mediate—but in such a way that does not undercut the calling of all, individually and corporately, to also act in analogous ways.[37]

Levites, Firstborn, and Redemption (3:40–51)

The redemption of the firstborn, a significant subsection within the description of the priestly classes, raises several theologically rich questions. The idea that the Levites are to substitute for the firstborn and in this way "redeem" them is stressed in Num. 3:45–47 and 8:16–18. But why are the firstborn dedicated, and what principles underlie the redemption payment of the Levites' lives and money for the firstborn? The answers are tied to the larger sacrificial system of Israel and to the meaning of Passover.

In Exod. 22:29–30 God claims for himself the firstborn (*bkr*) of humans and animals, as well as the firstfruits of crops. Why? The firstborn and firstfruits are understood to be the best and most precious of the whole. Giving them to God is a thankful acknowledgement of God's prior gift of life and ongoing providence, as well as God's claim over his creatures as lord and god. "The Israelite father's offering to God of what is most beloved to him, his firstborn son, the firstfruit of his body presented lovingly to his Lord" formed the "ideal" gift back to God.[38] While YHWH directs Israel to give him such gifts, presenting firstborn and firstfruits was also a common practice in surrounding cultures. Such gifting or sacrifice to the Lord in the case of plants and animals took the form of bringing them to the priests to be sacrificed or redeemed. In surrounding cultures, "giving" of the human firstborn to God sometimes took the form of human sacrifice. In Israel it meant presenting the child to God for a life of service and devotion to God in a special, often priestly, capacity.[39] In such ideal sacrifice it is recognized that God does not delight in death, nor does God need sheep, goats, and other objects of sacrifice. Rather, God desires our obedient and faithful dedication as well as the acknowledgement of his claim over all aspects of our lives and possessions—even our firstborn.

---

37. *Baptism, Eucharist, and Ministry*, "Ministry," §17.

38. Jon D. Levenson, *The Death and Resurrection of the Beloved Son: The Transformation of Child Sacrifice in Judaism and Christianity* (New Haven: Yale University Press, 1993), 12.

39. The issue of whether the ideal or even the reality of child sacrifice was practiced at some point in Israel's history is a matter of debate (see Levenson's *Death and Resurrection of the Beloved Son* for one view). One's understanding of this affects the reading of esp. Gen. 22. Child sacrifice is condemned at least by the time of the prophets (Jer. 7:31), and the law states that the firstborn *must* be redeemed (Exod. 34:19–20).

Within Israel's history, notably in prophetic literature, this ideal sacrifice was challenged. Instead, the ideal gift to God was understood to be the dedication of oneself, which took the form of serving God wholeheartedly: "With what shall I come before the LORD? . . . Shall I give my firstborn for my transgression? . . . He has told you, O mortal, what is good; and what does the LORD require of you but to do justice, and to love kindness, and to walk humbly with your God?" (Mic. 6:6–8). Perhaps the dedication of one's firstborn male children and animals was understood as a real symbol of such dedication from the start. In that case, Micah's critique is that the symbol has become detached from its highest meanings and so does not represent what it should. It is not necessarily a criticism of sacrifice per se.

This general claim of God on all firstborn helps make sense of the reference to the exodus from Egypt in Num. 3:13 and, indeed, the entire celebration of Passover. But another Passover theme complicates matters: that of the contrasting fates of the Israelite and Egyptian firstborn. YHWH says: "When I killed all the firstborn in the land of Egypt, I consecrated for my own all the firstborn in Israel, both human and animal; they shall be mine." A similar reference in Exodus expands on this slightly: "Then you shall say to Pharaoh, 'Thus says the LORD: Israel is my firstborn son. I said to you, "Let my son go that he may worship me." But you refused to let him go; now I will kill your firstborn son'" (Exod. 4:22–23). In response to Pharaoh's refusal, God took the firstborn of Egypt by having them killed and in contrast saved Israel, his firstborn, in order that Israel might worship him.

The subsequent consecration of the firstborn of Israel, beasts and people alike, thus bears several meanings, including the more general one that it represents the ideal gift back to God for his providential mercies. The dedication of the firstborn is also a more specific symbol of the vocation of Israel as a chosen "firstborn" nation to serve God in a special way. Given the association of the firstborn with priestly duties, the firstborn of the nation represent in themselves the priestly vocation of the whole nation. Finally, the dedication of the firstborn has the more specific historical reference to Passover: "When Pharaoh stubbornly refused to let us go, the LORD killed all the firstborn in the land of Egypt, from human firstborn to the firstborn of animals. Therefore I sacrifice to the LORD every male that first opens the womb, but every firstborn of my sons I redeem" (Exod. 13:15). In thankfulness not only for God's providence in creation, in remembrance of its vocation as a nation, and now also in response to God's mercy in delivering Israel from Egypt, Israel gives its firstborn to God in response to God's command.

The Levites thus come to symbolize all of these meanings as they substitute for and redeem the firstborn. The idea of redemption or salvation expressed by *pdh* is an action, such as the payment of money, that frees one from a state of captivity, ownership, or a difficult situation. In these verses, the lives of the firstborn are paid for by money or substituted for by the lives of the Levites (Robert Hubbard in *NIDOTTE* 3.578–82). The money is not understood as equivalent in worth to the person, but is rather a token that acknowledges God's claim upon or ownership of the firstborn.

2

THE ETHICS OF GOD'S HOLY PEOPLE
(5:1–6:27)

Laws Representing Their Moral Vision

In Num. 1–4 we gain a bird's eye view of Israel, the priestly and holy people of God. Those chapters gave an overall vision of Israel's identity as a people, as they are counted, organized into tribes, and ordered around God, whose presence is mediated by the tabernacle and the priests. In the laws of Num. 5–6, we move from an encompassing picture into the details of their ethical life.

The five sections of lawlike material contained in these chapters at first seem to concern quite specific and rather disconnected matters.[1] While they can be read at this level, they also function in Numbers as five specially chosen laws that symbolically map important parts of the moral worldview of Israel (Douglas 1999: 144–50 interprets parts of these laws symbolically and figurally).

These laws map the moral universe of the Israelites in the sense that most of the key distinctions and terms through which the Israelites live in their world are referenced. As opposed to, say, a particular kind of Enlightenment utilitarianism that sees the world through calculations of overall well-being measured in terms of human pleasure and pain, Israel's moral vision is formed around the contrasts between holy and common, clean and unclean (5:1–4), sin and righteousness

---

1. This is a common view of many interpreters. For example, Levine 1993: 181 writes: "Chapter 5 is not a coherent unit but rather a collection of diverse laws and rituals. There are, to be sure, suggestive thematic links pertaining to such subjects as impurity and betrayal, but as a whole Numbers 5 is best seen as a repository of priestly legislation."

(5:5–10), faithfulness and unfaithfulness (5:11–31), and zealous dedication to God and apostasy (6:1–21).[2] In addition, the Israelites understand themselves to be part of a history in which God is moving all creation toward blessing and shalom (6:22–27), a state in which all the impurity, defilement, and sin that has infected the created order is cleansed. Each of these laws touches on one aspect of this larger composite moral vision.[3]

Furthermore, details of these laws foreshadow later parts of the narrative if interpreted figurally. By reading them figurally, the central subjects of each law—the unclean person, the person who has wronged another, the woman suspected of unfaithfulness, the Nazirite, and the congregation being blessed, perhaps even the Aaronic priest—can be read as figures of Israel. The issues touched on in each law are precisely those that confront Israel as it moves toward its vocation to be a holy people, faithful to God, among the nations. Will it maintain boundaries between clean and unclean? Will the individuals of the nation act correctly toward one another? Will Israel remain faithful to God? Will Israel move beyond a minimal obedience to a voluntary and zealous self-dedication to God? Will Israel accept the blessing of God and bear his name as a people and in this way be an avenue of blessing to others?

In seeing how these laws might be applied figurally to Israel and in seeing the larger ethical worldview that these laws are signs of, it becomes clear that this section of Numbers, rather than being a depository of unconnected laws with little contemporary relevance, informs us about the ethical calling of Israel and several issues within Christian ethics and spirituality.

Clean and Unclean, Holy and Common (5:1–4)

Israel is told that defiled and defiling people must be put outside the camp: "Put out of the camp everyone who is leprous, or has a discharge, and everyone who is

---

2. Richard B. Hays, *The Moral Vision of the New Testament: Community, Cross, New Creation: A Contemporary Introduction to New Testament Ethics* (San Francisco: Harper, 1996), 193–205, seeks to discern unity in the "moral visions" of the New Testament writings through the use of the "focal images" of community, cross, and new creation. Connections might be drawn between Hays's focal images and the vision we find here: clean and unclean resonate with the vision of a fully embodied new creation, holy/common and sin/righteousness specify what kind of community God is calling Israel to be, and the concern with faithfulness, self-dedication, and being a channel of blessing certainly resonates with Christian understandings of the cross.

3. Understood in this way, these laws also exhibit an ethical progression, moving step by step toward the highest potentials of human life as God intended. The distinction between clean and unclean (5:1–4) concerns being careful to observe certain ordered creational patterns. The discussion of wrongdoing and restitution (5:5–10) moves us up to moral concerns about correct relationships between humans. Issues of faithfulness (5:11–31) concern both longer-term commitments between people and especially Israel's covenant relationship to God. The voluntary self-dedication to God of the Nazirite (6:1–21) can be seen as an even higher form of relationship to God. Finally, receiving God's blessing and presence and being a channel of that blessing (6:22–27) are goals toward which Israel and humanity move both individually and corporately.

unclean through contact with a corpse" (5:2). This law introduces an important distinction within Israel's ethical worldview, the distinction between "clean" (*tāhôr*) and "unclean" (*tāmē'*). While this distinction is critical for understanding Israel's ethical worldview, the issues concerning Israel's purity laws, dietary laws, sins great and small, and the sacrifices connected with these are quite complex and often misunderstood. Out of the great amount of recent work on purity in ancient Judaism some consensus is emerging on central aspects of this vision.[4]

At the center of this ethical vision is the understanding that God is "holy," which means that God is separate—but separate from what? While as creator God is totally other than creatures (as Christian theologians rightly point out),[5] at least in the laws of Sinai the emphasis is that God's holiness is a separation from all corruption and chaos, from all moral impurity and sin. Persons, places, times, or objects that are set aside as "holy" (*qōdeš*) to God are separated from the "common" (*ḥōl*): "You are to distinguish between the holy and the common, and between the unclean and the clean" (Lev. 10:10). This is done not to separate *creatures* from God, but rather to create and preserve a holy sphere in the world where *physical corruption and sin* are excluded—so that God and creatures may, at least in one sense, draw near to one another. As reserved or separated for God, holy things gain a certain status simply because they are chosen for special service. And because they are chosen to be closely associated with God, they must also be holy. They must be sanctified, cleansed from contamination by corruption and sin in order to bear that closer proximity to God.

To explain why holiness is required for proximity to God, analogies are helpful, such as the image of vibrating musical strings and the attunement or dissonance between them (c.f., the analogy of the tabernacle as a nuclear reactor in →3:1–4:49). Musical strings, like those on a piano, are "sympathetic" to or harmonize with certain frequencies and are dissonant with others. The being of God might be thought of as having a certain frequency, harmony, or even rhythm to it.[6] These harmonies or patterns are reflected throughout creation, to the extent that creatures are capable of such harmonies, but they dwell in the tabernacle in a special way.[7] Only creatures that resonate with such tuning in both physical and moral ways can bear and come near God's presence. This creaturely holiness is

---

4. Balentine 1999; Klawans 2000; Douglas 1993a; Milgrom 1991. See also Nobuyoshi Kiuchi, *The Purification Offering in the Priestly Literature: Its Meaning and Function*, Journal for the Study of the Old Testament Supplement 56 (Sheffield: JSOT Press, 1987).

5. Robert Sokolowski, *The God of Faith and Reason: Foundations of Christian Theology* (Notre Dame, IN: University of Notre Dame Press, 1982), calls it the central Christian distinction.

6. This idea is a familiar concept in Hasidic Judaism. Madeleine L'Engle's 1973 novel *A Wrinkle in Time* and C. S. Lewis's 1965 novel *That Hideous Strength* illustrate evil having a physical and moral patterning rhythm to it. Karl Rahner's *Hearers of the Word* (trans. M. Richards; New York: Herder & Herder, 1969) makes much of the idea of attunement with God.

7. Citing Terrence Fretheim, Balentine 1999: 68 writes of such order in regard to the tabernacle: the tabernacle is "the one spot in the midst of a world of disorder where God's creative, ordering work is completed according to the divine intention just as it was in the beginning."

on a graduated scale—things can be more or less holy. Gradations of holiness are reflected throughout the architecture and laws concerning the tabernacle and the priests.[8] Creatures selected to be closer to God—for example, in the holy of holies as opposed to simply in the camp—must exhibit better attunement or holiness, otherwise the wrath of God might break out. God's wrath in certain passages is like the anger of a person, breaking out as a result of an intentional choice. But elsewhere, such as with an inappropriate entry into the tabernacle, God's wrath acts more like a physical field of power, like the unintentional dissonance and "beating" created when two out-of-tune strings vibrate near each other. The Levites thus must be careful to guard the boundaries of the holy so that wrath and plague do not strike the Israelites as a result of such encroachment on the sacred (1:53; 8:19; 17:12–13; 25:8–9; 31:16).[9]

Attunement or dissonance can occur at both a physical/biological level and the level of human thoughts, action, and intention (Klawans 2000: 3–20). A person may become "defiled," or move away from the purity of holiness, both physically and morally. Each way has different consequences and different means of moving back toward the holy.[10] It is common to draw a distinction between "ritual impurity" and "moral impurity" in reflecting on the different ways one can be unclean, even though such a distinction is not clearly made in the Torah.[11] The term "ritual purity" is an especially poor fit with the laws of Numbers. For example, in the law in 5:1–4, which focuses on the physical/biological way of being defiled, such impurity excludes one temporarily from the entire camp, not merely from rituals.

The logic that underlies the distinction between clean and unclean at the physical level involves two intertwined ideas: uncleanness is related to death, and death involves the breakdown of natural order and patterns.[12] The goodness, purity, or cleanness of creation depends in part upon its harmonious order and systems. This order and these systems are critical for life. This harmonious order is analogous to the systems studied in modern biology, such as the human skin. In nature as it

8. Philip Peter Jenson, *Graded Holiness: A Key to the Priestly Conception of the World*, Journal for the Study of the Old Testament Supplement 106 (Sheffield: JSOT Press, 1992).

9. For an analogy using disease or contagion, see Jacob Milgrom, "Encroaching on the Sacred: Purity and Polity in Num. 1–10," *Interpretation* 51 (1997): 243–44.

10. Klawans 2000: 11 writes: "Certain sins defile in their own distinct way."

11. Klawans 2000 draws a sharp distinction between ritual and moral impurity. He then shows how the relationship between the two kinds of impurity was understood in different parts of the Old Testament, later writers and schools in Judaism, and the New Testament. A difficulty he faces is that terms such as "clean" and "unclean" are used both precisely and more loosely or metaphorically through the Old Testament; thus the line between ritual and moral impurity is sometimes quite obvious, but in some cases much more difficult to draw (see 2000: 21–31). In contrast, Wenham 1979: 15–32 understands purity laws to form a much more integrated system.

12. Kiuchi, *Purification Offering*, 63; and Gordon J. Wenham, "Why Does Sexual Intercourse Defile (Lev 15:18)?" *Zeitschrift für die alttestamentliche Wissenschaft* 95 (1983): 432–34, represent many scholars who emphasize the association between uncleanness and death. Douglas's 1993a and 1999 books emphasize the connection between uncleanness and disorder.

was intended to be, the skin is whole, unblemished, and functions well. However, the goodness and life of creation are threatened by chaos and corruption, which break down this order, leading to death. Physically clean things exhibit the good order needed for life, while the unclean clearly exhibit some kind of breakdown of that order or blemish. Unclean things are in this way associated with death, or have the "aura of death."

The list of unclean items in 5:1–4 exemplifies this logic. Skin diseases very visibly represent the breakdown of the boundaries of the body, a breakdown that leads to death. The discharges of the body, especially those of blood and semen (Lev. 15), fluids of men and women that quite clearly represent life (cf. 17:11), can be understood as a leaking of life out of the body.[13] Corpses are obviously associated with death, and the corruption of the body after it is dead is perhaps the most visible breakdown of the order and boundaries of the skin and body required for life.[14] Skin diseases, certain emissions, and corpses are seen as making a person unclean or, better, simply *are* the uncleanness of a person. Such uncleanness is on a graded scale; some forms of uncleanness are more serious than others. Uncleanness is also understood to be "contagious" like a disease and can be transferred through contact. Other persons and even the tabernacle can become defiled through contact with the unclean. There is no moral culpability for this kind of physical uncleanness— but it keeps one from participating in the rites of the cult and even excludes one from the camp until the period of uncleanness is over.

The law in 5:1–4 is very similar to the wider set of laws covering physical impurity in Lev. 11–15, but it offers two additional details. The first is that contact with corpses makes one unclean. This detail points forward to Num. 19 and the red heifer ceremony, which remedies corpse contamination. It also calls attention to the association of physical impurity with death and the breakdown of natural order that leads to death.

13. Douglas 1993a: 156 writes: "In this system of taboos there is one unique possibility of defilement, the breach of the body's physical integrity. Emissions which are part of the normal bodily functioning do not defile. All the biblical emphasis is on the breakdown of the defences of the skin, the possible failure of the apertures to contain body fluids which should be contained, or to prevent entry through the mouth of the wrong foods." The specific animals and foods considered clean and unclean as listed in Lev. 11 may also correspond to such a conception of life-giving creational order. The prohibition against certain animals, which at first seems arbitrary, may refer to animals closely associated with corpses or to anomalous animals that do not seem to fit the regular patterns of nature (e.g., "everything in the waters that does not have fins and scales"; Lev. 11:9–12). Abstinence from some of these animals may be related to their anomalies making them weak and defenseless and hence exploitable. Abstinence thus may be both a sign of justice—i.e., respecting God-given order—and compassion. "In the blindness of worms, the vulnerability of fish without scales, the ceaseless labor of ants, there is perhaps an analogy to human counter-parts: the beggar, the defenseless widow and orphan, the laborer. . . . Holiness is incompatible with predatory behavior" (Samuel E. Balentine, *Leviticus*, Interpretation [Louisville: John Knox, 2002], 162, quoting Douglas 1993b: 22).

14. Acts 2:27, 31 and 13:34–37 lay great stress on Christ as Messiah not experiencing corruption, and Paul also stresses the imperishability of Christ's and our resurrection bodies (1 Cor. 15:50–57).

The other main difference with Lev. 11–15 is that for the cases mentioned here the unclean person must be "put … outside the camp" (Num. 5:3) rather than merely excluded from the tabernacle. This exclusion is only for a time, for unclean people can come back into the camp once the proper sin offerings (*ḥaṭṭā't*) are made. The rationale for excluding the ritually unclean from tabernacle service is given in Lev. 15:31: "Thus you shall keep the people of Israel separate from their uncleanness, so that they do not die in their uncleanness by defiling my tabernacle that is in their midst." The concern in Leviticus is with defiling the tabernacle by entering it in an unclean state; in Numbers the concern for purity is extended to the entire camp, because "I [the LORD] dwell among them" (5:3).[15] Leviticus is interested primarily in the tabernacle, while Numbers emphasizes that Israel as a people is to be holy.

At the foundation of this system of purity and impurity lies the recognition that God has constructed the world in certain ways that are good and that give life. God's presence is incompatible, at least in the long run, with breakdowns of that order. The sin offerings that must be presented when such boundaries have been broken show that, regardless of human intention, the breakdown of those boundaries and order is simply not pleasing to God.

How are Christians to receive this purity system? The way that purity laws are treated in the New Testament raises questions. In the Gospels, Jesus appears to have become unclean in every one of these ways. He touches lepers (e.g., Mark 1:40–45), "a woman who had been suffering from hemorrhages for twelve years" (5:25–34), and corpses (e.g., 5:21–24, 35–43). This direct contact has even more theological import when the same Gospels characterize Jesus as the new temple, the tabernacle enfleshed.[16] Such deliberate contact at first seems to suggest that Jesus is dispensing with or critiquing these laws.

But the logic of the impurity laws—that God and the breakdown of order and the powers of death cannot coexist in the same place—is upheld and fulfilled in a very important and surprising way. One might even say that in Jesus the wrath or the holy power of God breaks out and destroys that which is unclean as it comes near him. With Christ, however, such an exercise of destructive power takes the form of Christ healing what is broken. He destroys the uncleanness, not the person who is unclean. Christ heals lepers, heals the woman, and raises the dead. On even one occasion, this power breaks out from Christ unintentionally, simply through the contact of the woman with the holy hem of Christ's robe (Mark 5:30), after she intentionally "encroaches" into Christ's space and touches it. God as revealed in and through Christ is thus still opposed to all forms of uncleanness,

15. In contrast to Milgrom 1990: 33, who understands this as simply a way to keep those with more serious uncleanness further away from the tabernacle.

16. For example, in Mark 2:5–7 Jesus pronounces forgiveness of sins to the paralytic and is charged with blasphemy. N. T. Wright, *Jesus and the Victory of God*, vol. 2: *Christian Origins and the Question of God* (Minneapolis: Fortress, 1996), 489–527, argues that Jesus's relationship to the temple is at the heart of New Testament Christology.

but the way that such dissonance between the patterns of God and the patterns of sin and death is characterized and overcome takes a strikingly different form in the Gospels.

The lack of attention to and misunderstandings of the heart of Israelite ritual purity practices by most Western Christians seems to go hand in hand with the way the church is often ill equipped to respond carefully to issues having to do with the integrity of the body and the created order. Contemporary concerns about healthcare, environmental degradation, and genetic engineering show the need for ethical categories that include but are not reduced to human intention and choice. Many parts of the Protestant world easily swing between the extremes of a docetic lack of concern with such issues of the body and creation and a "health and wealth" gospel that has stepped into this vacuum and focuses principally upon them. Israelite priests were engaged in both physical and moral matters—unlike the unfortunate division common in the West where medical doctors get people's bodies while chaplains get their disembodied spirits.[17] To move forward in these issues, it would be wise to pay attention to Christian "priestly" practices that bear some connection to the principles behind Israelite purity practices. The contents of our prayers for physical healing and wholeness and the ritual practice of prayers said over communion elements that later will be brought to the sick and shut-in members of Christian congregations are good places to start.

Interpersonal Wrongs That Require Redemption (5:5–10)

The next law concerns what to do when one person wrongs another, particularly in situations where some kind of restitution of money or goods is possible. The concern with physical purity in 5:1–4 shifts here to the moral purity of the people in interpersonal relationships.[18]

In this passage the Hebrew word 'āšām is used. It typically refers to a specific kind of sacrifice, the "guilt offering," but here is used in two ways: the state of "guilt" that the person incurs as a result of wrongdoing (5:6) and the "restitution" (5:7) given to the offended party (literally, "they must return the 'āšām"), which is specified to be 120% of the value of the wrong. Guilt here might be thought of as a liability or debt. In addition to the 'āšām, the wrongdoer offers a ram of kippur ("expiation, atonement, covering") to God because they have also "broken faith" (5:6) with God.

17. A central theme in the work of Stanley Hauerwas, Paul Ramsey, and Gilbert Meilander in the area of Christian medical ethics is the breaking down of these modern divisions. See essays 27–31 in *The Hauerwas Reader*, ed. John Berkman and Michael Cartwright (Durham, NC: Duke University Press, 2001).

18. Three commentators note this deliberate movement from ritual/ceremonial purity to ethical concerns or, as I prefer, from physical to moral purity: de Vaulx 1972: 90–93; Budd 1984: 58–59; and John Sturdy, *Numbers* (Cambridge: Cambridge University Press, 1972), 41–42.

The fullest account of the "guilt offering" (*'āšām*) is found in the laws outlined in Lev. 5:14–6:7 (→7:1–88). Leviticus 4–6 systematically describes the main sacrifices, first the sin/purification offerings (*ḥaṭṭā't*), then the *'āšām*/guilt offerings. There is some debate about the logic that underlies them and that distinguishes them from the sin offerings, yet many scholars agree that the historical root of the *'āšām* offerings is that they are originally made in response to a violation or desecration of *sancta*, as Lev. 5:15 indicates. That the sin involves *sancta*, the holy things and places dedicated to God, creates the difference between this sacrifice and the sin/purification offerings. *Sancta* are desecrated by treating them as if they were common (Milgrom 1991: 339–78; Richard Averbeck in *NIDOTTE* 1.557–66). While concrete examples of such violations are not given, the damage of such desecrations must be measurable in some way, for such desecrations are to be compensated 120% (Lev. 5:16; 6:5). Potential cases include a common person eating a sacred offering by mistake or violating a sacred vow in matters of property (*NIDOTTE* 1.559).

In Num. 5:5–10, however, the guilt offering is presented as the proper response to general wrongdoings between Israelites. But why does a guilt offering rather than a sin offering need to be offered? Given the logic of the guilt offering, it is odd that this debt is to a person rather than to God.

Whatever the case may be for how the *'āšām* originated, it appears that in Num. 5:5–10 and Lev. 5:17–19 the concept of *sancta* comes to include more than simply sacred objects and places and vows. In response to this expansion Milgrom writes: "With the promulgation of 5:17–19 . . . , whereby the unwitting violation of any 'of the Lord's commandments' requires expiation for sancta desecration, the boundaries between the sacred and the profane are obliterated forever. . . . It embraces ethics as well as ritual, the relations between men and not just those between man and God" (1991: 363). It is not at all clear, however, that the boundaries between sacred and profane have been *obliterated* as much as *extended* to include the holy people of God. This extension goes hand in hand with the previous law (Num. 5:1–4), where certain cleanness and uncleanness rules are shown to concern not only the tabernacle, but now the entire camp. One can make sense of the law by understanding that it is the holy people who are being desecrated, necessitating the need for the guilt offering.

This extension of the law contains an important insight: God's presence is ultimately what makes something holy. It makes perfect sense that if God dwells in the camp, in the people of Israel, then they are holy. Treating another person wrongly can be seen as an offense not only against that individual, but also against God who dwells in them.

This is suggested by 5:6, where wronging another person is understood to be "breaking faith with the LORD." The phrase *lim'ōl mā'al* might be better translated "committing a sacrilege against the LORD" (Milgrom 1990: 35). Some commentators explain this by reference to Lev. 6:1–5, where the holy thing being infringed upon is a vow. They surmise that in Num. 5:5–10 a vow must have been broken.

But the text does not mention this, nor is this assumption needed. If the law is being extended to mean that whenever someone wrongs another they are desecrating the holy people, they would also be "committing sacrilege against YHWH" in their sin against another person. No further explanation is needed.

Such an extension of *sancta* from things and places and vows to people is familiar in New Testament thought. Jesus speaks of himself and his body as the new temple (John 2:18–22). By extension, those who are joined to Christ are also a holy temple in which the presence of God dwells (Eph. 2:21–22). Ambiguity about "holy things" is part of the Apostles' Creed: "I believe . . . in the communion of saints." The Latin phrase *sanctorum communionem* was regularly taken to mean a communion in and through the sacraments (i.e., holy things), which would create a holy people. Over time, the phrase was regularly understood to refer to the church as a communion of holy people.

Given the holiness of the people, it makes sense that a violation of relationships within the holy people of God is also an offense against God. Paul sees things this way as he writes to the church at Corinth concerning the divisions within them. The breakdown in their relationships is a "sacrilege" or "desecration" of holy things (1 Cor. 11:18, 22, 27); these divisions create a mockery of the Lord's Supper and are an offense against the body and blood of the Lord (cf. Acts 9:4).

The Numbers law points out how restoration of this offense against God's people involves a payment of one's guilt or debt against one's neighbor *before* one offers an atonement gift to God. Such an ordering is reflected in Jesus's statement in the Sermon on the Mount: "First be reconciled to your brother or sister, and then come and offer your gift [at the altar]" (Matt. 5:24).

In summary, the moral vision of Israel reflected in these verses considers the interpersonal relationships between the Israelites as part of the holiness of God's people. Tears or schisms in those relationships desecrates the holiness of the people and is an offense against God.

Ordeal for Suspected Unfaithfulness (5:11–31)

The third law raises the issue of faithfulness. Israel is called to live according to larger patterns of creational order that bring life (5:1–4) and to fulfill obligations and properly maintain its relationships in order to be a holy people (5:5–10). This law points to faithfulness within relationships as an important part of the moral world of Israel.

This law gives instructions for what is to be done when a man suspects his wife of "go[ing] astray" (5:12).[19] It outlines an ordeal that a jealous husband may put his wife through in order to test her faithfulness. Read at this literal level, this ordeal is filled with interpretational as well as theological and ethical difficulties.

19. The related Hebrew noun *śōṭâ* becomes the technical term in rabbinic literature for a woman convicted by the ordeal (Milgrom 1990: 37).

Unclear aspects of this law discussed in detail in rabbinic sources are the circumstances that could lead to such an ordeal (5:12–15, 29–30), the anticipated outcome of the ordeal (5:27–28), and the relationship between the woman's oath and the rest of the ritual (5:15–26; see Levine 1993: 200 for sources). But the overall sense of what is happening is clear. A man suspects his wife of going astray. The woman is brought to the priest in order to go through a ritual that involves presenting an offering, taking an oath, and ingesting "the water of bitterness that brings the curse" (5:18). As a result of taking the water, if she is guilty, the water will cause pain and apparently cause her to become barren. If she is innocent, the water will not cause pain and she will be able to conceive children.

This law presents several theological and ethical difficulties. The first is related to its unusual character. It is the only ordeal given as a law in the Bible, and it is the only biblical law whose outcome requires a miracle.[20]

Ordeals like this were used in both ancient Near Eastern cultures and the West through the Middle Ages to find out the truth and dispense justice in matters where the truth could not otherwise be known, such as when there were no witnesses. Since witnesses were an important part of Israel's judicial system, such cases fell outside typical judicial means. Ordeals are typically premised on the idea that God will miraculously intervene to protect the innocent and/or condemn the guilty, making make clear the truth of the matter. For example, the medieval Anglo-Saxon practice of "Corsned," current around 1000, was a trial by ingestion of a certain kind of barley bread.[21] Prayers were said over the bread, asking God to bring about different effects given the innocence or guilt of the accused. In some cultures, the premise for ordeals rests more on beliefs about the magical effect of the components than on the intervention of God. In Num. 5 the prescribed rituals with the water, dust, and oath share much in form with such magical practices.

The practice of this and other ordeals was eventually abandoned in both Judaism and Christianity. In rabbinic literature this particular law was abandoned sometime in the first century, at least by the time of the writing of the tractate *Sotah*, apparently for practical reasons (Babylonian Talmud, tractate *Sotah* 47a).[22] Within Western Christianity, priests were forbidden to take part in ordeals in 1215.[23] Aquinas gave a clear theological reason for the discontinuance of ordeals: Ordeal by hot iron or water is illicit because "a miraculous result is expected from God" (*Summa theologica* II–II Q95.8).

---

20. Milgrom 1990: 350. For parallels to ordeals in the Code of Hammurabi and at Mari, see Milgrom 1990: 346–48.

21. R. Bartlett, *Trial by Fire and Water: The Medieval Judicial Ordeal* (Oxford: Clarendon, 1986).

22. Since the ordeal was abandoned near the time the temple was destroyed, perhaps that was the reason. Rabbinic commentators suggest other reasons, such as the growth of male infidelity.

23. Adriana Destro, *The Law of Jealousy: Anthropology of Sotah* (Atlanta: Scholars Press, 1989), 2; Fourth Lateran Council, canon 18.

Can such a law, contained in Christian scripture, continue to shape Christian thought and practice? Applying it literally today is almost unthinkable. At the most basic level, there is no longer a working tabernacle or temple system. Theologically, Aquinas rightly critiques ordeals in general as impious since they force God's hand by requiring a miracle. This one in particular is also easily interpreted as relying on magic (i.e., the manipulation of forces of nature by unscientific means) or occult forces (and thus idolatrous). At an ethical level, the obvious double standard between men and women and the public shaming of the woman by the priest ("dishevel the woman's hair"; 5:18) flies in the face of Jesus's treatment of women (e.g., John 8:1–11; Matt. 19:8–9).

Many commentators, however, point out positive ramifications the law would have had for the lives of women at that point in Israel's history. Milgrom writes: "The priestly legislators made use of a pagan ordeal in order to protect a suspected but unproved adulteress from the vengeance of an irate husband or community by mandating that God will decide her case" (1990: 354). Thus while harsh, the law introduces a ritual that may provide some resolution to a potentially violent situation in a time when women had little power. Given such a charitable contextual reading, it could be said that Jesus upholds and extends the spirit that informs such a law. Jesus moves further away from a punitive patriarchal system in his teachings and practice, while still upholding the standard of marital faithfulness. This law—read literally, carefully, and charitably—could be interpreted as part of a larger movement of God within Israel toward having Israel be an example of mercy and equal justice for women among the nations—while still being a people who treat marital faithfulness with great respect (Calvin 1852: 3.87–90).

While a literal reading of the law might be understood in this way, several aspects of the text suggest that this law should also be read figurally, pointing to the important and powerful image of Israel as the bride of YHWH. Various aspects of the law link it quite closely with images and phrases used primarily about that relationship. For instance, the woman is accused not of "adultery" (*n'p*) but of "going astray" (*tiśṭeh*) and being "unfaithful to him" (*mā'ălâ bô mā'al*). The uses of these phrases brings to mind Israel's relationship to YHWH. The word *mā'al* ("to betray") is in every other Old Testament instance related to Israel's betrayal of God through idolatry. It is used in texts that liken Israel's apostasy to harlotry and marital unfaithfulness (Lev. 26:40; Num. 31:16; Hos. 2:2–20; Jer. 3:8–9; Ezek. 23:37; Milgrom 1990: 37; Douglas 1993a: 161). The word "goes astray" (more literally "turn aside") is an uncommon word in itself. Yet its opposite, *šûb* ("return"), is a very common call of the prophets to Israel after it strayed from the ways of God. The husband is said to be "jealous" (5:14). God likewise is said to be jealous of Israel, especially in connection with idolatry (e.g., Exod. 20:5; 34:14). Deuteronomy refers to the jealousy of God in reference to Israel's wilderness experience: "They made me jealous with what is no god, provoked me with their idols" (32:21; cf. 32:19; Milgrom 1990: 216; Douglas 1993a: 163). In Num. 25:11 Phineas is commended for his "zeal"—the same word in Hebrew is also translated "jealousy"—on behalf of God in response to the incident at Peor. Finally, the possible negative result of the ordeal, that the accused woman will become an "execration" (5:27) or curse among her people, is quite similar to the prophesied results, often in the form of curses, for Israel's unfaithfulness to God. She will become "an object of horror, a proverb, and a byword among all the peoples" (Deut. 28:37), "a disgrace, a byword, a taunt, and a curse" (Jer. 24:9; cf. 29:18, 22; 42:18), because she has forsaken God and his commands (Douglas 1993a: 168–69).

The basic image these allusions point to—Israel as YHWH's bride—tells us much about the moral vision of Israel. This image suggests that Israel's response to God should not merely be obedience to a law or covenant, but something much more personal and self-involving. Israel's faithfulness is ultimately a personal faithfulness to YHWH.[24] The covenant is not merely a political covenant between ruler and ruled, but also like the promise between husband and wife. Given a patriarchal setting, it is hard to know how much personal closeness is necessarily implied by this image of marriage. But the specific way this image of bride and bridegroom is developed throughout the Old Testament shows that YHWH and Israel's relationship certainly does (Hos. 2:14–20; Jer. 2:1–3; 3:1–20; Song of Songs). YHWH has a passion and love for his people and desires such a full response from them. While in this passage such faithfulness is not given a name, elsewhere the opposite of going astray is called *ḥesed* ("covenant faithfulness, devotion, loving-kindness"). Jeremiah writes in YHWH's voice: "I remember the devotion [*ḥesed*] of your youth, your love as a bride, how you followed me in the wilderness, in a land not sown. Israel was holy to the LORD, the first fruits of his harvest" (2:2–3). When Israel goes astray, God's response is not simply righteous anger, but more personal, like the jealousy of a husband who has been cheated on. While such an image of God is often difficult to receive and can be critiqued theologically as a metaphor that should be stripped of its projections of human emotions onto the transcendent and impassible God, scripture repeatedly affirms such an image.[25] God desires that his beloved human creatures, especially his chosen people, not only live within the life-giving boundaries of his creational order (Num. 5:1–4), not only deal justly with one another (5:5–10), but also be faithful to him—as well as to each other—with all their hearts, minds, and actions (5:11–31).[26]

24. In Rom. 1:5 Paul points to this with the phrase ὑπακοὴν πίστεως ("faith[ful]-obedience"), which he uses to describe the response to God that is made possible for the Gentiles through the work of Christ.

25. For discussion, see William C. Placher, *Narratives of a Vulnerable God: Christ, Theology, and Scripture* (Louisville: Westminster/John Knox, 1994).

26. In Hos. 6:6 and Mic. 6:8 such faithfulness is highlighted as part of the summative vision that YHWH has for his people—especially toward him, but also in human to human interactions. The people of Israel are sometimes called "the faithful" (*ḥāsîd*), a term that seems to capture both these dimensions: "He has raised up a horn for his people, praise for all his faithful, for the people of

Given a figural reading, the law suggests that all may not be well within this marriage relationship. If YHWH, the husband, becomes jealous of his wife, Israel, it is possible that she will be put through an ordeal to see if she has gone astray. Central to the ordeal is the "water of bitterness" that the woman must drink. For Israel, what is this "cup"? The law may foreshadow the difficulties and temptations that Israel will encounter on the journey to the promised land; these are the ordeal that tests Israel's faithfulness.

Israel's failure of the test drives the plot of the upcoming narrative. In Numbers 10:11–21:35 we see Israel fail YHWH seven times. While God has graciously offered a relationship to Israel through the gift of the law, through God's personal presence to Israel, and through the promise of the land that Israel spies out, Israel rejects it all. For YHWH, this is a personal refusal of him: "How long will this people despise me?" (14:11). One would expect that as a result Israel would be cut off and all the curses of the law would issue forth. But in spite of Israel's unfaithfulness, God still reaches out and brings blessing instead of cursing (as in the episode of Balaam). God's faithfulness and love for his bride rescues her from the logic of the ordeal. Even though Israel is unfaithful to him, God does not make her barren. God raises up the next generation, the literal children of the unfaithful generation, and gives them a new start as his people (Num. 26–36).

The themes of Israel's unfaithfulness and God's forgiveness and faithfulness in spite of it find their answer and fulfillment in the gospel of Christ. Christ is portrayed in the Gospels and throughout the New Testament as "the faithful one," the one who fulfills the righteousness, obedience, and faithfulness that Israel is called to. Christ undergoes a testing similar to Israel's, but remains faithful and obedient. By being faithful through his initial temptation (Matt. 4:1–11) and throughout his ministry and by remaining obedient "to the point of death—even death on a cross" (Phil. 2:8), Christ fulfilled the calling of Israel in his own person. The "cup" that Christ is said to drink (Matt. 20:22; 26:39) is arguably linked to the notion of a trial by ordeal, bringing to mind Num. 5 as well as many references to a cup of wrath and judgment in the prophets.[27] Christ drank the cup of the ordeal, but was proved faithful and righteous and vindicated by his resurrection.[28]

Israel who are close to him" (Ps. 148:14); "Sing to the LORD a new song, his praise in the assembly of the faithful" (149:1).

27. W. McKane, "Poison, Trial by Ordeal, and the Cup of Wrath," *Vetus Testamentum* 30 (1980): 491, writes: "The metaphor of the cup of wrath, like the figurative language in Jer. 8:4, 9:14, and 23:15, is founded on trial by ordeal procedure." Cf. Ezek. 23:31–33; Isa. 51:17. The mention in Jer. 8:14, 17 of a cup of poison and "letting snakes loose among you" might have connections to Num. 5 and Num. 21. See Douglas 1993a: 167–69.

28. Alternately, Christ drank the cup and took on the wrath itself—thus Christ's work becomes a vicarious punishment. But if this is the case, it is unclear why Christ would say that the sons of Zebedee would also drink his cup. Either way, this notion of the cup becomes tied to how we understand how Christ's life is "a ransom for many" (Matt. 20:28): either he dies and is punished for us or else he lives obediently for us—an obedience that is summed up and completed by his death on the cross (Phil. 2:8). While this is highly debated, the motifs of obedience and faithfulness more

Those who are "baptized into Christ" (Rom. 6:3) participate in his life and his righteousness (5:17–19). Through this union with Christ, we are more and more to become the "bride adorned for her husband" (Rev. 21:2, 9), the people of God who at the end of the age will finally fulfill our calling to be holy, spotless, and faithful to God.

Until that time, the church undergoes an ordeal similar to that of Israel. Just as the presence and law of God were the source of the testing of Israel's faithfulness, so too the presence of God through Spirit and word test the faithfulness of God's people today. As Heb. 6:4–8 indicates, the gospel of Christ does not mean that the church is now immune from failure—rather we have been presented with an even greater offer. In one sense this is an even stronger potion of testing, to use the image of Num. 5. The church, those who "have tasted the heavenly gift, and have shared in the Holy Spirit," are once more presented with the possibility of either "blessing from God" (Heb. 6:7) or being "on the verge of being cursed" (6:8).[29] The author of Hebrews speaks of "the heavenly gift," "the Holy Spirit," which as the presence of God among us perhaps might be figurally related to the holy dust of the tabernacle.[30] Our faithfulness is tested not only by our bitter trials, but also by the sheer offer of a relationship to God through his law, presence, and promises. This presence of God among us can bring either blessing or cursing depending on our reception of it. Bede thinks along these lines and explicitly likens the potion of Num. 5, composed in part of "words" added to the water, to the way that the words of scripture function within the church. Like the potion by which the faithfulness or unfaithfulness of the woman is made known, Christ speaks through scripture, condemning hypocrisy, and manifesting sin (Bede, *Patrologia latina* 91.361). Scripture—just as the law for Israel—cuts both ways; by presenting us with the path of life it makes us responsible to be faithful to those ways and thus to God. For those who are faithful, it contains the words of life (Ps.

---

faithfully communicate the central Christologies of the New Testament. Implicated in this is the related debate about how best to understand Paul's "faith of/in Christ" passages. See David Stubbs, "The Shape of Soteriology and the *pistis Christou* Debate," *Scottish Journal of Theology* 61 (2008): 137–57, for the theological ramifications of this debate.

29. On a more positive note, the author of Hebrews continues: "Even though we speak in this way, beloved, we are confident of better things in your case, things that belong to salvation" (6:9).

30. Certain features of the potion of testing are suggestive in this regard. The phrase describing the potion, "the water of bitterness that brings the curse," contains the key words "water," "bitterness," and "curse"—which are central to the Marah ("bitterness") incident (Exod. 15:22–27). Israel encounters bitter water there, and this is where "the LORD . . . put them to the test." The allusions to this incident could indicate that Israel's ordeal is simply the difficult experiences it must go through in the wilderness. But the potion is created from holy water, the dust of the tabernacle—the symbol of God's presence in Israel—and from the words of the scroll with curses on it. The "oath" with its curse and "amens" (Num. 5:21–22) bears a striking resemblance to the curses and the twelve "amens" of Deut. 27. These two passages are the only two places the word "amen" is used in the Pentateuch. This might suggest that the woman, and figuratively Israel, is tested through contact not only with bitter hardships, but more fundamentally, by God's presence and law.

119:1; Deut. 27:1–10; Matt. 7:24; John 15:10); but for those who "turn aside," it is the means by which they are judged.

Self-Dedication of the Nazirite (6:1–21)

The fourth law in this section concerns the vow and sacrifices of the Nazirite. Nazirites were people who took on the specific vow outlined here for either a restricted period of time or for their entire lives (Milgrom 1990: 43, 355–58).[31] The ideals and motivations of the Nazirite further fill out the moral universe inhabited by the Israelites.

The vows the Nazirite takes and the sacrifices he or she makes indicate the ideal underlying this practice: a great zeal for God and dedication to God's law. Those vows and sacrifices bear a close relationship to laws and sacrifices involved with the consecration of priests.[32] The Nazirite is thus a priestlike figure, set apart and holy to God. However, unlike the priest—whose primary role is to be a mediator between God and the people, offering sacrifices on behalf of others—Nazirites offer themselves to God. And unlike the priest—who is conscripted into the role— Nazirites offer themselves voluntarily (at least according to this law). Since being a Nazirite is open to all Israelites, men and women of any tribe, it is an especially apt symbol for the calling of all Israel. Israel is called to be a priestly people and holy nation, zealous for God, willingly dedicating itself as a holy offering to God.

If the laws in Num. 5–6 form a progressive picture of key aspects of Israel's ethical vision, perhaps this willing self-offering is in some way higher than the fidelity between husband and wife that underlies the law in 5:11–31, or is the highest expression of that faithfulness. Viewed from the perspective of Christian faith and theology, the Nazirite image touches upon some of the deepest and most difficult truths of Israel's calling and Christian discipleship.[33] "If any want to be my followers, let them deny themselves and take up their cross daily and follow me. For those who want to save their life will lose it, and those who lose their life for my sake will save it" (Luke 9:23–24; cf. John 15:13). Paul writes that "even

31. Samson, Samuel, and John the Baptist—the lifelong Nazirites recorded in scripture (Judg. 13:7; 1 Sam. 1:11, 28; Luke 1:7, 15)—were possibly all dedicated by their previously barren mothers as a thanksgiving offering (this is explicit in the case of Samuel). Rabbinic literature attests that the temporary Nazirite vow, often taken for a thirty-day period, was a common practice in Israel near the close of the Second Temple period. Some early Christians were Nazirites (Acts 21:23–24).
32. In especially three ways—abstention from wine (Lev. 10:9), abstention from corpse impurity even of their own immediate family (21:11 versus 21:1–4), and the wearing of a special symbol that marks their consecration and anointing (Exod. 29:6)—the Nazirite acts similarly to the high priest. The sacrifices that mark the conclusion of the vow of the Nazirite are similar to those of the consecration of a priest (Lev. 8).
33. This calling of Israel is captured in Isaiah's image of Israel, or a representative of Israel, as the Servant who "make[s] his life an offering for sin" and who "poured out himself to death" (Isa. 53:10–12).

if I am being poured out as a libation over the sacrifice and the offering of your faith, I am glad" (Phil. 2:17). Such a calling to self-offering is grounded upon Christ's and thus God's own self-offering (1 Tim. 2:5–6), a mystery that Christian theology has often seen grounded in the continual self-offering that characterizes the inner life of the Trinity.

This passage is the only law that explicitly outlines the vows and sacrifices of Nazirites in scripture. The word for Nazirite (*nāzîr*) is related to both the verb *nāzar* ("to dedicate" oneself or an object to the Lord) and noun *nēzer* ("ordination, consecration"). This noun refers to certain symbols of consecration that were worn on the head by kings (2 Sam. 1:10; 2 Kgs. 11:12; Ps. 89:39; 132:18) and priests (Exod. 29:6; cf. 28:36; 39:30), possibly a crown, diadem, or inscribed metal strip (Jackie Naudé in *NIDOTTE* 3.73–74). The hair of the Nazirite, "the consecrated head" (Num. 6:9), is a similar symbol of their consecration.[34]

This law may be divided into several sections. The first outlines the three things the Nazirite must abstain from during the period of the vow (6:1–8), procedures for what to do if the "consecrated head" is defiled during that period (6:9–12), the ritual for the completion of the vow (6:13–20), and the colophon or concluding summative statement (6:21).

First, the vow itself is "to separate themselves to the LORD" (6:2); it is a period of special dedication to God. The three abstentions associated with the vow can be seen as symbols of this overarching goal and of the great zeal that motivates and accompanies it. Abstention from contact with corpses (6:6–8) is necessary because everyone who comes into contact with a corpse becomes ritually unclean (5:1–4). Ritual purity laws imply a great respect for God's creational order and have an implied recognition that breakdowns in that order are opposed to God's ways and intentions. As such, ritually unclean things and people are not allowed to come near God. By taking on this abstention from ritual impurity, Nazirites show great dedication to God by allowing desire to be near God to trump obligations even to family, should a family member die. This does not imply that family obligations are not good. Rather, such obligations are commanded by God (Exod. 20:12) and are usually passionately and meticulously observed. For a time, however, Nazirite obligation and dedication to God must be even greater.

Abstention from wine can be interpreted in a similar fashion. Some interpreters reason that this abstention is because wine is often an occasion for sin, since one's usual inhibitions might become dulled. Being extra holy, the Nazirite abstains from drinking wine or any grape products as a way to avoid sin and to avoid even the symbols of unfettered desires.[35] Whatever truth there is in this, wine is also associated with great zeal and boldness. Great passion is sometimes mistaken for drunkenness, and abstention from wine is arguably not for the purpose of

---

34. Perhaps Jeremiah has this image in mind when he tells the nation to "cut off your hair and throw it away," because the Lord has rejected Israel (Jer. 7:29).

35. Markus Bockmuehl, "Let the Dead Bury Their Dead (Matt 8:22/Luke 9:60): Jesus and the Halakhah," *Journal of Theological Studies* 49 (1998): 575n76.

avoiding sin, but rather for making clear to others that the boldness and zeal of those abstaining come from God rather than from wine.[36] Wine, just as one's family obligations, is not seen as a negative thing.

Finally, the unshaven hair of the Nazirite is certainly a multivalent symbol, but includes the ideas of consecration, anointing, zeal, and strength. Hair was often seen as "the seat of man's vitality and life-force" (Milgrom 1990: 356). It is a natural symbol of power and virility, since hair grows in new ways at puberty, but ceases to grow as fast, turns grey, thins, and falls out as one passes one's prime. It is also a symbol of life itself since it grows throughout life and even after death. It thus can be seen as a symbol of one's own life force and vitality. Sacrifices of hair are attested in many cultures (Milgrom 1990: 357). The culminating sacrifices that complete the period of the vow include a burnt offering sacrifice of the Nazirite's hair—symbolizing the gift and dedication of one's life. During the time of the vow, the unshaven head of the Nazirite is a visible symbol of dedication to God. The heads of the kings and priests of Israel were also marked, anointed with oil, to symbolize their consecration to God and their related authority to mediate the rule and presence of God. Kings and high priests wore a *nēzer* on their head as a symbol of this. For the high priest, this was a "rosette" (Exod. 28:36–38) with the words "Holy to the LORD" engraved on it. For the Nazirite, the unshaven head was a similar symbol.

The connections between dedication, consecration, anointing, and zeal should be traced through carefully. Nazirites seek to dedicate or consecrate themselves to God. They offer their life and vitality over to God, an offering symbolized particularly by their hair. It is as if a simultaneous two-way gift occurs: from humans to God, a giving over or setting apart of a life to God, and from God to humans, God's gift of his spirit, presence, and power to the one offering the gift.[37] In the cases of the Nazirite Samson and Kings Jehu and Jehonadab, this anointing was tied to their zeal. Their zeal is the outward activity resulting from God's anointing them with his spirit of life, an anointing also symbolized by their particular *nēzer*, their unshaven hair.

In sum, the Nazirite represents the highest ideals of Israel: holy people who voluntarily dedicate themselves, all their strength, vitality, and passion, in the zealous service of God. The Nazirite represents the calling of all Israel to be a holy and priestly people.

Given this emphasis on what the Nazirite is and represents, it is no surprise that Jesus is often seen as fulfilling the figure of the Nazirite. The Gospel of Matthew records that Jesus comes from Nazareth "so that, what had been spoken through the prophets might be fulfilled, 'He will be called a Nazorean'" (2:23). It is unclear what passage Matthew is referring to, but Judg. 13:5 is suggested by many

36. For example, Jehu and Jehonadab (2 Kgs. 9–10; Jer. 35), Hannah (1 Sam. 1:14–15), John the Baptist (Luke 1:15), Pentecost (Acts 2:4, 13), and Paul's instructions (Eph. 5:18).

37. In the cases of barren women—Hannah, the mother of Samuel (1 Sam. 1:9–11), and Manoah's wife, the mother of Samson (Judg. 13:3–5)—there seems to be an exchange of life (the Nazirite dedication) for life (the pregnancy itself, not yet the anointing of God's spirit on the Nazirite).

throughout the Christian tradition: "The boy shall be a nazirite to God from birth. It is he who shall begin to deliver Israel from the hand of the Philistines."[38] If this is the scriptural connection, then Matthew understood Jesus to be connected in some way to the Nazirite tradition.

Jesus's practice connects with all three Nazirite abstentions. As for corpse contamination, Jesus regularly breaks ritual purity rules and exposes himself to many dead bodies, but he does so in a way that affirms rather than breaks the concerns behind the purity rules (→5:1–4). His difficult statement, "Let the dead bury their dead," made in the context of his call for radical discipleship, may be an oblique reference to a kind of quasi-Nazirite dedication he calls his disciples to.[39] As for the abstention from wine, Jesus was criticized throughout his ministry for his eating and drinking practices, and he is even accused of being a drunkard. However, he says some intriguing things about "new wine" in response (Luke 7:33–34; 5:33–39) and says that when he is gone his disciples will in fact fast and abstain. Moreover, both the vow he makes during the Last Supper with his disciples—"I will never again drink of the fruit of the vine until that day when I drink it new in the kingdom of God" (Mark 14:25; Matt. 26:29; Luke 22:18)—and his refusal to take wine and/ or vinegar while on the cross arguably take the form of a Nazirite vow.[40]

Whether or not Jesus is intentionally portrayed as a quasi-Nazirite in the Gospels, he certainly fulfills the impulse to offer oneself wholeheartedly to God. John 2:17 explains that his disciples, in watching Jesus's cleansing of the temple, remembered Ps. 69:9: "Zeal for your house will consume me." Hebrews portrays Jesus as the fulfillment of the long line of Old Testament faithful who strove with great passion and went through great suffering on account of their faith in God.

The cross, with its own crown of thorns, is the great symbol of faithful discipleship in the face of suffering (Heb. 12:1–2). The hymn attributed to Bernard of Clairvaux, "O Sacred Head," speaks of the holy head of Christ crowned with thorns:

> O sacred Head, now wounded,
> with grief and shame weighed down,
> now scornfully surrounded
> with thorns, thine only crown.

The crown of thorns, like the hair of the Nazirite and the crowns and rosettes of Israel's kings and priests, fittingly symbolizes both the anointing of God and the

---

38. John Calvin, *A Harmony of the Gospels: Matthew, Mark, and Luke*, ed. T. F. Torrance and D. T. Torrance (Edinburgh: Saint Andrew Press, 1972), 1.104–6, argues against Chrysostom's position that the quotation must be from a lost book of scripture and agrees with Bucer that it refers to Judg. 13:5. But Calvin thinks it also alludes back to Joseph, who in Gen. 49:26 and Deut. 33:16 is called a Nazirite, one "separated" from his brothers, and who also bears a blessing on his brow. Calvin calls Samson and Joseph "antitypes" of Christ.

39. Bockmuehl, "Let the Dead Bury Their Dead," 553–81.

40. Ibid., 571–72. Possible allusions to Ps. 69:21 and the Nazirite vow may explain variations in the Gospel accounts of his words on the cross.

zealous dedication of Jesus. But the crown of thorns more than any of these other symbols strongly suggests the great personal sacrifice such anointing may require.

Priestly Blessing (6:22–27)

The fifth law in this section of Numbers fittingly brings us to the final end of Israel's moral universe: the blessing of God that results in shalom. The priestly blessing related here is one of the most familiar texts in Numbers. It is and has been recited regularly in temple, synagogue, and church, and for Christians who follow standard lectionaries it is one of the few passages from Numbers regularly read as a lesson in worship.[41]

Its familiarity is happily matched by its importance. Not only is this passage a crucial text for understanding Numbers, but it also touches on several themes—blessing, shalom, and the placing of God's name upon Israel—that are important for understanding the biblical account of human history in its entirety. The laws of Num. 5–6 progress toward this law. This progression foreshadows the movement of the people of Israel toward blessing in their spiritual pilgrimage through the wilderness, a blessing given to Israel through Balaam (Num. 22–24). And yet it also points beyond that particular act of blessing. Given the way the blessing was used in the later worship life of the tabernacle and temple, and given the content of the blessing and the instructions concerning it in our passage, this blessing seems to call not only for God's favor now, but also evokes an eschatological longing for the full revelation and presence of God on earth, a presence that ultimately brings the fullness of God's grace and a final Sabbath peace.

The Centrality of Blessing in the Pentateuch, the Bible, and Numbers

"Blessing" is a central organizing image within both the Pentateuch and the overarching story of the Bible.[42] The Bible begins with the accounts of God blessing humanity (Gen. 1:28) and the Sabbath (2:3) at the creation of the world; continues with the call of Abram, who is blessed by God to be a blessing (12:1–3); and ends with tidings of blessing for humanity: "Blessed are those who are invited to

41. The priestly blessing is read at the Feast of Holy Name, the celebration of Jesus's naming, which occurs soon after Christmas. Numbers 6:22–27 is paired in the Revised Common Lectionary with Ps. 8; Gal. 4:4–7 or Phil. 2:5–12; and Luke 2:15–21. These passages emphasize the placing of God's name on Israel through the act of blessing.

42. In the Documentary Hypothesis, the Yahwist (J) narrative strand within the Pentateuch arguably centers on the blessing of Abraham in Gen. 12:1–3, and the ensuing narrative is driven by the question, How will God's blessing reach the peoples through Abraham? Similarly, a major theme of the Priestly (P) materials of the Pentateuch is the unfolding of the fivefold blessing given to humanity in 1:28; see Walter Brueggemann and Hans Walter Wolff, *The Vitality of Old Testament Traditions* (Atlanta: John Knox, 1975). As for the claim blessing is a driving motif within the overarching story of the Bible, see Richard Bauckham, *Bible and Mission: Christian Witness in a Postmodern World* (Grand Rapids: Baker, 2003), for an argument that the Bible has an overarching story.

the marriage supper of the Lamb. . . . See, I am coming soon! Blessed is the one who keeps the words of the prophecy of this book" (Rev. 19:9; 22:7). This final blessing is pronounced by the "bright morning star" (22:16), the one who will finally fulfill the fourth blessing of Balaam on Israel (Num. 24:17: "A star shall come out of Jacob"). This same one, Jesus, began his Sermon on the Mount with a deeper interpretation of what it meant for the people of God to be blessed (Matt. 5:1–12; cf. Luke 6:20–26) and reminded them that they should be a blessing to others (Matt. 5:13–16; cf. Rev. 21:22–27). He was pronounced "blessed" during his triumphal entry into Jerusalem (Matt. 21:9; Mark 11:9–10; Luke 19:38; John 12:13). He in turn blessed his disciples with the gift of the Spirit (John 20:19–23) and shared himself with his disciples through the blessed bread and wine of the meal in the upper room (Matt. 26:26–29; Mark 14:22–25; Luke 22:14–23; cf. Eph. 1:3). Blessing is a crucial notion for understanding the intentions behind God's relationship to his chosen people and all of humanity.

The theme of blessing plays an important role in Numbers as well. These verses conclude the group of laws that foreshadow the later experience of Israel in the wilderness. Their placement in the structure of the book suggests that blessing is the final goal of their difficult time in the wilderness. The final words of the law in 6:27, "So they shall put my name on the Israelites, and I will bless them," suggests why that journey is so difficult for them. Being blessed as a people certainly involves physical safety and prosperity (cf. 23:21–24; 24:5–9; Deut. 28:9–10), but it is more than that. Just as they physically bear the ark and tabernacle through the wilderness toward life with God in the promised land, their spiritual journey toward blessing is a movement that involves bearing the name of God as a people—a phrase suggestive of both the presence of God and the holiness of the people required to bear that presence. The central dramatic tension in the book stems from God's people not being ready for this blessing or willing to accept it. Similar to their inability to bear the full presence of God on the mountain, fearing that they would die (Exod. 20:18–21), in Num. 13:32 the Israelites reject the promised land, calling it a land that "devours its inhabitants." Numbers makes a contribution to this biblical theme by stressing that such blessing and presence is not easily borne by a sinful people.

Given this movement toward blessing in Numbers, it comes as a bit of a shock that later in the narrative the blessing of God is mediated through Balaam in Num. 22–24. Balaam is not a priest of Israel, but rather an outsider and potential enemy. In this way, the priesthood of Israel—the established Aaronic priesthood and the priesthood of the people—is both established and also relativized. God's blessing is to be regularly mediated through "Aaron and his sons" (6:23), but God's presence and blessing are not limited to this regular means. This is a second contribution of Numbers to this larger biblical theme. God's intentions to bless his people and show his glory in and through them will happen through the work of his chosen priests, at times will need to occur in spite of the failings of his priests and leaders (20:12), and may even be mediated through the enemies of God and his people (Num. 22–24). God's plan to fill the earth "with the glory of the LORD" (14:21;

cf. Rev. 21:22–27) will be accomplished both through and in spite of his chosen priestly people (Exod. 19:5–6; Num. 14:22–24).

The Meaning of Blessing and Its Relationship to Putting on God's Name

In Num. 6:23 YHWH tells Moses to tell Aaron, "Thus you shall bless [*tĕbārăkû*] the Israelites." What is this action of blessing, and what expectations and meanings are attached to it?[43]

In these verses, the action of blessing is distinguished from any kind of magical activity where humans seek to control the future by manipulating spiritual forces. It is God who blesses. In each of the three main clauses of the blessing, "the LORD," YHWH, is the subject of the clause and the action. This threefold repetition hammers home that God, not the priest, is the ultimate source of this blessing. While the priests are holy and intimate with God, the formula here, as well as the interpretation in 6:27, "*I* will bless them," makes it clear that the priests are strictly channels or mediators of blessing.[44]

---

43. Scholars posit several meanings of the Hebrew root *brk* ("bless, blessing, blessed"). Claus Westermann's influential works make a strong distinction between blessing, which "denotes God's continuous action," and God's saving activity: "Blessing is a work of God which is different than saving insofar as it is not experienced as the latter in individual events or in a sequence of events" (*Elements of Old Testament Theology*, trans. Douglas W. Stott [Richmond: John Knox, 1982], 113; cf. 103; and *Blessing in the Bible and in the Life of the Church*, trans. Keith Crim [Minneapolis: Fortress, 1978]). It follows that the content of such blessing is likewise tied to these general processes. For Westermann, expectations concerning blessing thus had to do with "growth, prosperity, and success" in the larger, regular processes of life that Israel shared with all cultures. Patrick D. Miller, "Blessing of God: An Interpretation of Num. 6:22–27," *Interpretation* 29 (1975): 240–51, helpfully interprets the Aaronic blessing based in part on Westermann's work, but pays little attention to Num. 6:27. While Westermann's distinctions helpfully highlight tensions that Israel might have sensed between God as savior and as lord of creation, limiting blessing to only the sphere of regular processes does not accurately describe how blessing functions in Numbers or in the larger trajectory of the Bible and the Christian tradition. While it is true that God's blessing is manifest in these regular occurrences, blessings are often given in specific historical moments when "the mediation of God's favor" was needed or expected (William J. Urbrock, "Blessings and Curses," in *Anchor Bible Dictionary*, ed. D. N. Freedman et al. [New York: Doubleday, 1992], 1.756). Furthermore, the distinction between general blessing versus special saving does not reflect how salvation and blessing are tied together in the history of election in the patriarchal narratives, the larger history of Israel, and certainly the Gospels. Rather than distinguishing salvation and blessing according to God's general versus special activity, they are more helpfully distinguished by understanding salvation as God's action to free someone from some evil, while seeing blessing as God's pouring out his good toward someone. Blessing by God in the Bible often signals something about the quality of relationship between God and the recipient. J. McKeown, "Blessings and Curses," in *Dictionary of the Old Testament: Pentateuch*, ed. T. D. Alexander and D. W. Baker (Downers Grove, IL: InterVarsity, 2003), 84–86, points out that "God bestows blessing on those who are in harmony with him," the effects of which include "fertility, prosperity, authority and security." While such harmony could be interpreted in a more general sense as being in harmony with nature (or God's natural law), many passages in the Bible, such as Mary's Magnificat (Luke 1:46–55), reflect the understanding that being blessed is tied to a very specific harmony, relational favor, and action of God.

44. Milgrom 1990: 51; Miller, "Blessing of God," 244.

That only the priests bless is suggestive. In their activities connected with the tabernacle and temple, priests mediate the presence of God, not merely the favor of God. The interpretation in 6:27, that in this act of blessing "the name" of God is put on the people, also suggests that God's presence, not merely favor, is being mediated.[45]

The name of God is an idea related to Hebraic understandings of God's presence. The phrases "name of God" and "glory of God" are ways that the Israelites articulated that God was specially present in and attentive to the tabernacle and temple, while not limited to those places.[46] Given this, what might the phrase "so they shall put my name on the Israelites" mean? Several explanations are possible.

Perhaps all that is being implied is God's ownership of Israel. This view is seen in Deut. 28:10: "All . . . shall see that you are called by the name of the LORD" (Milgrom 1990: 52).

Another possibility is that the priest would first bless the people, then write the name of God, YHWH, on their hand or forehead.[47] Such a concrete, ritual way of taking on God's name certainly would imply a stronger connection between God and Israel than mere ownership. It implies that Israel is supposed to behave in a way that corresponds to the character and ways of God. This practice of concretely taking on the name also lies behind the commandment "you shall not take the name of the LORD your God in vain" (Exod. 20:7 RSV; Deut. 5:11) in which not "taking" or "bearing" the name in vain would be a commandment against misbehaving rather than taking a false oath or cursing with God's name.[48]

45. The Septuagint retains this emphasis of placing the name "on" the people by using the word *epi* rather than *pros* both in the interpretation of the blessing and in the phrase "make his face shine on [*not* toward] you."

46. For example, the phrase "the place that the LORD your God will choose as a dwelling for his name" (Deut. 12:11) suggests that God's presence and attention are especially associated with the temple, while at the same time holding that YHWH still dwells in heaven and is not contained by the temple (cf. 12:5, 21; 14:23–24; 16:2, 6, 11). The consensus of much biblical scholarship is that in the wake of the destruction of the temple in 587 BC, the Israelites, who had trusted in the real presence of the God in the temple, now attempted to better understand how God was both in the temple and yet not limited to it (Tryggve N. D. Mettinger, *The Dethronement of Sabaoth: Studies in the Shem and Kabod Theologies*, Coniectanea biblica: Old Testament 18 [Lund: Gleerup, 1982], 38–134; Brueggemann 1997: 670–74). Two primary theological trajectories developed out of this. The Priestly trajectory (e.g., Exod. 40:34–35 and Ezekiel) spoke of God's presence in terms of the *glory* of God dwelling or present in the temple/tabernacle "without making a claim that is flat, one-dimensional, or crassly material" (Brueggemann 1997: 671). The Deuteronomist tradition, however, spoke of God's immanent presence by referring to the *name* of God.

47. Bar-Ilan Meir, "'They Shall Put My Name upon the People of Israel' (Num. 6:27)," *Hebrew Union College Annual* 60 (1989): 19–31. A similar symbolism occurs in Rev. 14:1 and 20:4. In Jerusalem in the sixth or seventh century, the priestly benediction was "worn on the body in the form of amulets" (Milgrom 1990: 52). In a similar concrete way, the high priest bore the names of the tribes before God: they are carved on two stones placed on the high priest's right and left shoulders (Exod. 28:9–10).

48. This connection between bearing God's name and an implied behavior is seen in Leviticus, where the Israelites are warned against "profaning" the name of the Lord by their unholy or unethical behavior

But given the association of God's name and presence, putting God's name *on* the Israelites arguably further implies calling on God to be specially on, in, or among them. Samuel Terrien suggests that "the reality of the presence of God stands at the center of Biblical faith" and even claims that "the distinctiveness of the Hebraic theology of presence rather than the ideology of the covenant . . . provides a key to understanding the Bible." "The history of biblical religion hinges upon the growth and transformation of the Hebraic theology of presence."[49] In Israel's theology of the name of God, Terrien argues that the name does not suggest merely a kind of hypostasized presence in the temple.[50] Rather, "the word 'name' appears to have been a device for designating YHWH's will to create a holy people within the history of mankind and at the same time Israel's acceptance of this election."[51] Such holiness suggests a presence of God in and on human beings that is instantiated in the activity of divine initiative and human response.[52] In this covenantal communion between God and Israel, God's presence on his people looks like obedience but cannot be reduced to it.

This presence of God results not only in obedience, but also ultimately blessings and shalom. The following narrative of Numbers, however, shows that in order for a sinful people to fully bear the name of God and fully experience blessing and shalom, atonement, cleansing, and obedience are required. The prophets Jeremiah and Ezekiel make similar connections. In Jeremiah's vision of the new covenant, the law and knowledge of God would be intimately present in Israel, in their hearts. But because God is holy and they are not fully so, this presence and knowledge of God in them requires God's forgiveness (Jer. 31:31–34). In Ezekiel the final blessing involves God dwelling among them, a renewed covenant of peace in which God will cleanse them, and they will "be careful to observe my statutes" (36:25–30; 37:24–28).

Thus the author(s) of Numbers, in tying the blessing with putting the name of God on Israel, makes several theological insights that are borne out throughout scripture: blessing is most fundamentally a function of divine presence, and God's presence, while it painfully burns away impurity, ultimately brings blessing and shalom. The wilderness experience of Israel can in this way be seen as a deep meditation on what it means to bear the name and presence of God as a people.[53]

(18:21; 19:12; 20:3; 21:6; 22:2, 32). Profaning the name through unholy actions is distinguished from blaspheming the name, which involves using the name directly in a curse (24:11, 16).

49. Samuel L. Terrien, *The Elusive Presence: Toward a New Biblical Theology* (San Francisco: Harper & Row, 1978), xxvii, xxviii, 31.

50. Ibid., 200.

51. Ibid.

52. Ibid., 200–203.

53. The Hollywood movie *Raiders of the Lost Ark* arrives at similar insights. The presence of God, tied to the ark, was desired by the Nazis as a magical means of blessing, a guarantee of victory in battle. However, by the end of the movie, the presence of God is seen to be a burning fire, a presence that eradicates evil and cannot be controlled by humans. The British government decides

Structure and Content of the Blessing

The words of the blessing suggest what this presence and blessing of God mean for Israel. The blessing is often interpreted merely as a calling on God's favor to bless Israel in its settled life from day to day, from season to season. "May God help the corn grow and protect us from our enemies," it might be interpreted as saying. However, given the suggestive images of God's face and peace, as well as the blessing's relationship to the Psalms of Ascent, one can also sense within it a deep eschatological longing for the revelation of God's final purposes and the entry of Israel in a fuller way into the promised land of Sabbath rest and peace.

The blessing consists of three parts, and the subject of each part is "the LORD," YHWH. The repetition of "the LORD" as the subject of the activity within the blessing and the statement "I will bless them" stress that blessing comes from the activity of God.

The three clauses crescendo in length: from 3 to 5 to 7 words, from 15 to 20 to 25 consonants, and from 12 to 14 to 16 syllables (Milgrom 1990: 51), a striking progression that suggests its careful construction. The lengthening of each phrase moves one expectantly toward the final and seventh word of the final line, shalom ("peace"), suggesting the movement toward the seventh day of Sabbath peace.[54]

All three lines have two verbal phrases: "bless" and "keep," "make his face to shine" and "be gracious," and "lift up his countenance" and "give you peace." The structural logic or relationship between these verbs may be understood in several ways.[55] However, the similarities between "bless" and "be gracious" and between "keep" and "give you peace" make a strong case for seeing a twofold structure to the blessing. The first line announces the two themes: blessing and keeping. "Bless" points to YHWH's giving good to Israel; "keep" draws attention to God's protection of Israel against evil. The second line is an elaboration of "bless" and calls upon YHWH to shine his face upon Israel, a request concerning the relationship of God to Israel. This leads to or is tied to YHWH being gracious to them—a result of this relational favor. Similarly, the third line is an elaboration of "keep." The first part is a prayer for a certain relational stance of God toward Israel, that of God "lifting his face" toward them, and this issues in the result of giving them shalom (Ashley 1993: 152).

This twofold structure—announced in the first line and elaborated in the second and third lines—fits well with two ways the blessing was taken up in Israelite and Christian tradition. The blessing was probably the impetus behind the

---

that such a presence is dangerous and unbearable and hides the ark where it can do no damage—an action similar to Israel's turning away from the promised land in Num. 11–21.

54. This interpretation is supported by noting how sevenfold repetitions are used as a structural feature in Num. 3–4, 9, 19, 32. See Milgrom 1990: xxxi.

55. Milgrom 1990: 51; Ashley 1993: 151–53; Olson 1996: 40–43; Miller, "Blessing of God," 243–44.

formation of the Psalms of Ascent[56] and possibly the common New Testament salutation "grace and peace."[57]

The first part of the first line, "the LORD bless you," is echoed and extended by the second line: "The LORD make his face to shine upon you, and be gracious to you." The phrase "the LORD make his face shine upon you" suggests the granting of general favor, like a smile. Indeed, in several psalms, God making his face shine is seen as the reversal of ill fortune and paired with the saving action of God that causes visible goodness to be bestowed on an individual or the people (Ps. 4:6; 31:16; 44:3; 80:3, 7). Along with this, however, is the recurring theme that God's shining also causes God's elect people to shine. God's glory and way will be known on earth as people look at the embodied life of Israel: "May God be gracious to us and bless us and make his face to shine upon us, that your way may be known upon earth, your saving power among all nations" (Ps. 67:1–2; cf. 89:15; 119:135; Isa. 60:1, 19; Ezek. 43:2; Dan. 9:17; Deut. 28:9–10). Being exposed to the shining face of God causes one's own face to shine.

The connections between Moses's encounter with God on Sinai and this blessing are too many to ignore.[58] The face-to-face encounter with God (Exod. 33:11; cf. 33:20), the shining of Moses's face after his encounter (34:29), the mention of God's graciousness (33:19), God's self-revelation by speaking his name (33:18–20), and God's promise to be present to Israel and "give you rest" (33:14)—all seem to connect the theophany on Sinai with the blessing. The connection—whether to

---

56. The Psalms of Ascent, Ps. 120–34, are fifteen psalms used liturgically in Israel during the three pilgrim feasts (David Barker, "Voices for the Pilgrimage: A Study of the Psalms of Ascent," *Expository Times* 116 [2005]: 109–16; Leong Liebreich, "The Songs of Ascent and the Priestly Blessing," *Journal of Biblical Literature* 74 [1955]: 33–36). "Ascent" refers both to going up toward the temple mount and to ascending the fifteen steps leading up into the temple. According to Jewish tradition, a psalm was sung for each step as the priests and ministers ascended into the temple (Mishnah, tractates *Middot* 2.5 and *Sukkah* 5.4). There are several links between these psalms and the Aaronic blessing. The blessing is composed of fifteen words, and there are fifteen psalms and fifteen steps. Given the apparently ancient origins of the blessing (Milgrom 1990: 52), perhaps the number of temple steps was constructed with the blessing in mind, or maybe three psalms were added to the twelve that draw most directly from the blessing in order to round out the collection to fifteen (Liebreich, "Songs of Ascent," 36). Aaron's anointing as a priest is alluded to in Ps. 133:2 (cf. Exod. 29:7). Most important, these psalms are related to four key words in the blessing: "bless" (*bārak*), "keep" (*šāmar*), "be gracious" (*ḥānan*), and "peace" (*šālôm*) (Ashley 1993: 151; Liebreich, "Songs of Ascent," 33–34; Barker, "Voices for the Pilgrimage," 110). These four words are the stress points of the blessing since the first parts of the second and third lines move toward "grace" and "peace" as their results.

57. The possibility that the common New Testament blessing "grace and peace" is a shorthand reference to the Aaronic blessing is quite enticing, for the phrase serves to summarize the results of Christ's life and work for some New Testament writers (Rom. 1:7; 16:20; 2 Cor. 1:2; Gal. 1:3; Eph. 1:2; Phil. 1:2; Col. 1:2; 1 Thess. 1:1; 2 Thess. 1:2; Phlm. 3; 1 Pet. 1:2; 2 Pet. 1:2; Rev. 1:4). The gospel of Christ in this way would be seen as an extension and fulfillment of the blessings of the Aaronic blessing.

58. Contra Gray 1903: 73: "With Ex. 34:29f. (P)—the effect of the fiery glory of Yahweh on Moses' face—the expression has no connection."

the Sinai narrative or to theophany in general—seems to suggest that the blessing is an extension of the presence of God to the people.

The Hebrew word for "be gracious," *ḥānan*, is used "exclusively in connection with God's mercy and grace."[59] God being gracious means "that God will temper His justice by His mercy" (Milgrom 1990: 52). Following the call for the shining presence of God, such graciousness is desperately needed if God's presence will ultimately result in good and blessing for his sinful people. The tension between God's holy justice and God's graciousness is certainly pronounced in the following narrative of Numbers and is clear in God's statement in 14:20–21: "I do forgive, . . . nevertheless . . ." (cf. Exod. 34:5–7). As in Numbers, this combination of ideas is often found in the Psalms. The psalmist recognizes that blessing and justice come from God and his presence, but because of the sinfulness of God's people, this coming near to bless and to bring justice must also involve God's graciousness. In later Christian tradition, such a call for the graciousness or mercy of God finds its way most prominently into Christian liturgy in the *Kyrie Eleison*: "Lord, have mercy upon us." Any movement by a sinful human toward God's blessing and shining presence requires God's grace.

In the second group of ideas in the blessing, the final part of the first line, "keep you," is extended and deepened in the third line: "Lift up his countenance upon you, and give you peace." The Hebrew word *šāmar* ("to keep") has connotations of watching over, guarding, and preserving from harm. God protects his people from physical enemies (1 Sam. 30:23) and from every kind of evil (Ps. 91:11; Ps. 121).

The phrase "lift up his face" can mean several things when used with human subjects: "to look" or "to regard favorably" (Milgrom 1990: 52). The only other occurrence of this phrase with God as the subject in the Bible has this meaning (Gray 1903: 73). However, the phrase makes better sense when viewed as the opposite of a common and suggestive phrase used in regard to God's relationship to a person or Israel: God "hiding" (*sātar*) his face. This hiding of God's face is almost always linked with disaster, oppression, and affliction, which in the majority of cases is seen as the result of Israel's sin and unfaithfulness. It is as if God has hidden his face because of Israel's sin and shame, and as a result of the absence of God's presence, evil fills the vacuum. It sums up the state of Israel in exile: "We have all become like one who is unclean, and all our righteous deeds are like a filthy cloth. We all fade like a leaf, and our iniquities, like the wind, take us away. There is no one who calls on your name, or attempts to take hold of you; for you have hidden your face from us, and have delivered us into the hand of our iniquity" (Isa. 64:6–7). "My anger will be kindled against them in that day. I will forsake them and hide my face from them; they will become easy prey, and many terrible troubles will come upon them" (Deut. 31:17). When God hides his face, removing his protective presence from Israel (31:18) or an individual

---

59. *Ḥānan* is not found elsewhere in texts associated with the Priestly tradition (Milgrom 1990: 52).

(Gen. 4:14; cf. Ps. 51:9), disaster strikes. In this way, the blessing of God "lifting up his face" on an individual or Israel is the reversal or avoidance of such a state of disaster and vulnerability to evil. It has a similar sense to the Jewish and Christian prayer: "Deliver us from evil."

The word "shalom" (*šālôm*), like the English word "peace," can mean simply the lack of strife, disaster, and fear (Ps. 120:7; 125:5; Lev. 26:6; Job 21:9). As such it is the result of God's keeping and guarding work and is a fitting end of the third line. But this rich word is also used more broadly for a general sense of well-being—hence the translation of *šĕlāmîm* as "well-being offerings." As the word becomes closely associated with God's covenant purposes, it is a wonderful one-word summary of the end toward which God is moving Israel and all of creation. Similar to the idea of Sabbath, it becomes a key descriptor of Israel at rest and in prosperity with its God in its midst (Ps. 128; Ezek. 37:26). It is used as an explanatory adjective of Israel's covenant with God, a covenant of shalom (Num. 25:12; Isa. 54:10; Ezek. 34:25). It describes the kingdom of God ruled by righteousness and justice (Isa. 9:1–7; 32:16–20). In this way, this final word is the goal toward which the entire blessing moves. In fact, it is the goal toward which God moves all of history.

The blessings coming to Israel summarized in this verse are described more fully in the lists of blessings in Deut. 7:12–14; 8:7–10; 28:1–14. God's gracious presence among the people in the promised land and Israel's keeping of the covenant result in blessings of prosperity, peace, and fruitfulness. But given that Numbers was written in the context of an Israel that has known exile from that land, one can sense an eschatological longing built into this blessing. Certainly, there is a sense in which shalom in the here and now is wished for and channeled to the individuals or people of God corporately as they receive this blessing. But there is also something quite bittersweet about the blessing. The final rest, the return to the garden, the eternal Sabbath, life in the promised land, the peaceable kingdom—all of which are alluded to with the word "shalom"—have not been realized yet in the lives of the priest or the people receiving the blessing. This absence of God's full presence and ultimate blessing is quite poignant whenever the blessing is given. Yet for both the ancient Israelite and the contemporary Christian, the blessing is not merely a wish for some future realization. God is with his people to bless them in this "thin" moment when God's presence and name are at hand, when the peace from above is extended to earth.[60]

Blessing in Israelite and Christian Practice

This blessing had its roots in the worship life of the tabernacle (Lev. 9:22–24). Later it was said at the temple in Jerusalem in connection with the daily sacrifices and the worship services connected with the great pilgrim feasts. As part of the

---

60. In *Midrash Sifre Num.* 42 (commenting on Job 35:2), peace is seen to be the highest good of heaven. A foretaste of this heavenly peace is understood to be asked for in the blessing.

liturgy, after the sacrifices, the priest would then lift up his hands and bless the people. It was an act that mediated the presence of God and the benefits of the sacrifices. In the synagogues, the blessing was also said daily, but the name YHWH was not pronounced (Adonai was substituted instead; Gray 1903: 72; *Midrash Sifre Num.* 39).

For the Israelites, the blessing of God was at the center of their liturgical life and helped form their identity as God's chosen people. In this way the blessing of the high priest played a similar role to the blessings of the patriarchs on their children. While the blessing looked forward to material blessings, at its heart it continued Israel's relationship to YHWH as God's children of the covenant promises. As Karl Barth puts it: "Nor should it be forgotten that while the good thing, the benefit, the gift which the person giving the blessing passes on to the person he blesses, includes a whole wealth of external salvation, its kernel and substance lies in the fact that the people blessed derive from YHWH and may live in the light of His countenance and under His grace" (1936–77: 3/2.580). Through the act of blessing they participate in this blessing of their relationship to God and look forward to its fulfillment.

Given that Christ is the fulfillment of the covenantal relationship between God and Israel, the meaning of such a blessing is different for Christians (Barth 1936–77: 3/2.581). Such a blessing does not simply pass along a particular relationship to God with a promised future goal. Because Christ represents Israel and took on and fulfilled the call of Israel, the goal of the relationship between God and Israel has been realized in the person of Christ. As a result, Christ is the source and content of blessing.[61] The goal of this blessing, this life of shalom, is extended to Christians through union with him by the work of the Holy Spirit (Chrysostom, *Patrologia graeca* 58.514–16). Given this, the act of blessing in the mouth of a Christian calls for the blessing of union with Christ, the one in whom the promises of the promised land are fulfilled.

Christians commonly trace the sign of the cross in the air or on one's forehead as they give and receive the benediction at the end of a liturgical service as an enacted prayer for this deepening relationship to Christ. Such liturgical acts of placing the name or mark of Christ on Christians are taken quite seriously by contemporary Eastern Orthodox and Roman Catholics. Roman Catholics consider such acts "sacramentals," seeing in them both a remembrance of God's

---

61. Theodoret of Cyr makes similar connections between the Aaronic blessing and the life of Christians in their relationship to Christ (*Patrologia graeca* 80.363–64). As he examines each line of the blessing, he notes how the hopes of God's blessing of Israel were finally fulfilled in the person of Christ. In the incarnation, the grace and mercy of God are most fully lavished on human flesh, and "he is our peace" (Eph. 2:14–15). Theodoret also connects the life of the Christian to the way the Nazirite vow (Num. 6:1–21) leads toward blessing (6:22–27); it is through the struggle of sanctification that we come to have the divine name sealed on us, to have Christ formed in us (Gal. 4:19). William Kelly, *Lectures Introductory to the Study of the Pentateuch* (London: Broom, 1871), 338, also sees a movement from the conclusion of the Nazirite vow to blessing.

blessings given in creation and in the economy of redemption and also a prayerful means of further effecting the personal salvation of an individual and building up the body of Christ.[62]

While Luther and Calvin continued the practice of blessings at the end of every service, in fact recovering the use of the Aaronic blessing as one of a few possible biblical options,[63] many Protestants have been uncomfortable with such acts of mediation. The discomfort stems both from a Zwinglian reinterpretation of sacraments as acts of remembrance rather than places of encountering the presence of God and the understanding that Christ's high priesthood supersedes all human priestly activity in such a way that makes such actions incoherent. Since Vatican II, there has been a great rethinking of such acts intended to "give humans access to God" among Catholics, Protestants, and Eastern Orthodox—both in the most central of these acts, baptism and Eucharist, but also less central acts such as the act of blessing.[64] Reformed theologian J. J. von Allmen, building on the strong sacramental theology of Calvin, calls Protestants to reembrace these acts of blessing and understands backing away from them as an act of cowardice.[65]

This fuller reading of the Aaronic blessing supports such a robust sacramental theology. In such a blessing, the name or presence of Christ (through the work of the Holy Spirit to the glory of the Father) encountered most fully in the sacramental act of the Eucharist is being recalled or further mediated through the act of blessing. God intends to communicate his presence and life to us for our salvation. In such places and times, God is especially present to encounter his children, connecting us to the life of Christ in, under, and through our recommitment to him in our enacted prayers and through the work of the Holy Spirit that puts God's name onto our hearts and lives.

---

62. Anscar J. Chupungco, *Handbook for Liturgical Studies*, vol. 4: *Sacraments and Sacramentals* (Collegeville, MN: Liturgical Press, 2000), 394; cf. Kevin W. Irwin, "The Constitution on the Sacred Liturgy *Sacrosanctum concilium* (4 December 1963)," in *Vatican II and Its Documents* (Wilmington, DE: Glazier, 1986), 59.

63. Nathan MacDonald, "The Purity of the Camp (Num. 5:1–6:27)," paper read at Seminar on Scriptural Exegesis, St. Andrews University, November 2006.

64. James F. White, *Introduction to Christian Worship* (Nashville: Abingdon, 1980), 163. Robert Webber, *Ancient-Future Worship: A Model for the 21st Century* (Wheaton, IL: Institute for Worship Studies, 1999), indicates that some evangelicals are also rethinking sacramental practice, moving in directions similar to the renewal of worship theology and practice since Vatican II. Among Eastern Orthodox, Alexander Schmemann (*The Eucharist: Sacrament of the Kingdom*, trans. P. Kachur [Crestwood, NY: St. Vladimir's Seminary Press, 1987]) and others have worked to thin out excesses in this tradition. Elena Velkova Velkovska carefully critiques the preponderance of blessings in Eastern Orthodox practice, saying that blessings can be easily misunderstood and "twisted into a kind of magico-ritual consecration" (in Chupungco, *Handbook for Liturgical Studies*, 4.389). Her solution to this problem is to reconnect the act of priestly blessing with the celebration of the Eucharist.

65. Jean-Jacques von Allmen, *Worship: Its Theology and Practice* (London: Lutterworth, 1965).

3

HOLY PLACES, HOLY PEOPLE, HOLY TIMES (7:1–10:10)

Setting into Motion the Worship Life of God's Holy People

In Num. 7–10 we move from narratives and laws that concern the identity and vocation of Israel (Num. 1–4) and its ethical vision (Num. 5–6) to aspects of Israel's life of worship. These chapters treat the sacramental ways the relationship between Israel and YHWH is mediated: its holy places, holy people, and holy times. Offerings, the ark, lamps, ordinations, the Feast of Passover, the pillar of cloud and fire, and silver trumpets—all of these are sacramental signs and practices in, under, and through which the ongoing relationship between God and his people is sustained and deepened.

These narratives and laws set forth an overall vision of Israel's worship life and also record the final events in Israel's life in the wilderness of Sinai before they set out for the promised land. In two ways these events provide a fitting conclusion to Israel's time at the holy mountain.

First, these events and laws tie up loose ends and complete all the processes needed for Israel to leave Sinai and begin its journey and so provide a fitting narrative conclusion to Israel's year at Sinai. The offerings of the tribes, the final adjustments to the holy place's lampstand (the menorah), and the consecration of the Levites completes and sets into motion all the aspects of the worship life of the tabernacle (Num. 7–8). This moveable place of meeting in a sense replaces Sinai just as it will eventually be replaced by the temple in Jerusalem (1 Kgs. 8). With its worship and rituals put into motion, Israel is ready to leave. The celebration of Passover one year after the initial Passover (Num. 9:1–14; cf. Exod. 12:1–20) recalls their redemption from Egypt and the beginning of their new life as a people. The reappearance of the cloud and fire over the tabernacle recalls their guidance toward the holy mountain of the covenant (Num. 9:15–23; cf. Exod. 13:21–22); it is also the means by which God will now lead them toward the promised land. The making of the trumpets (Num. 10:1–10) points even more clearly to the future, suggesting the need of the people to draw together to face difficulties and enemies on their way to Canaan.

Second, similar to the section concerning the ethics of Israel in Num. 5–6, these four chapters touch briefly on all the important aspects of Israel's corporate worship life—holy places, holy people, holy times—and in this way complete the comprehensive sketch of the life of Israel in the first part of the book (1:1–10:10). The three sections of 7:1–8:4 concern the three main parts of the tabernacle: outer court with its important sacrificial system, holy of holies, and holy place. In 8:5–26 the Levites—the holy people within this holy people—are consecrated and made ready to begin their service. And the three sections of 9:1–10:10 have ties to the holy times of Israel—the three great pilgrimage feasts that structure its year: Passover, Weeks, and Booths.

One striking feature of the life of worship outlined in these chapters is its sacramental character. YHWH, the holy God of Israel, gives to Israel certain means by which his presence and reality come into contact with it. While YHWH has direct encounters with individuals in highly significant and powerful moments of revelation, God makes his presence most regularly available to Israel through certain "modes of mediation" or "sacramental" rituals and times (Brueggemann 1997: 568–72). In, under, and through these practices, Israel comes into contact with God. Different aspects of God's character and will are made known to Israel through them, and different aspects of Israel's relationship to God are transacted among them. "In worship, Israel is dealing with the person, character, will, purpose, and presence of Yahweh. While this presence is *mediated* by ritual and sacramental practice, it is the *real presence* of Yahweh that is mediated" (Brueggemann 1997: 650, emphasis original). Reflections on how God is present in these sacramental places, people, and times can be an important resource in reflecting further on the Christian sacraments.[1]

In 7:1–8:4 Israel completes the preparations for making and sanctifying the tabernacle and inaugurates the worship life of Israel that is centered there. Each

---

1. For example, some argue that Christian sacramental theology took an unhelpful direction as a result of a ninth-century dispute that focused Western eucharistic theology on debates about God's action vis-à-vis the bread and wine rather than understanding God's action in the Eucharist and in worship in a much wider fashion. See Alexander Schmemann's critique of "western scholastic models" in *The Eucharist: Sacrament of the Kingdom*, trans. P. Kachur (Crestwood, NY: St. Vladimir's Seminary Press, 1987), 13–14. Looking afresh at Old Testament sacramental practices tends to push Christian eucharistic theology in directions similar to Schmemann's.

of the three natural divisions of this section focus on an activity that takes place in each of the three main zones of the tabernacle: outer court (7:1–88), holy of holies (7:89), and holy place (8:1–4).

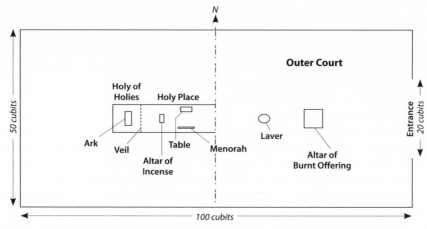

The Tabernacle

The tabernacle's architecture is a wonderful symbol of Israelite theology.[2] As detailed in Exod. 25–30, the tabernacle enclosure is a large rectangle composed of two abutting squares, each fifty cubits square. At the center of one square, the outer court, is the altar of burnt offerings. At the center of the other square is the ark of the covenant, the throne of God. These fittingly portray the encounter between God and Israel: "From the Ark in the Holy of Holies, God reaches out to Israel; from the altar of sacrifice, the Israelites reach out to God."[3] The holy place has two main items—the menorah (Exod. 27:20–21; Lev. 24:1–4) and the table for the twelve loaves of bread (Exod. 25:30; Lev. 24:5–9)—that are symbols of the result of this encounter: the enlightenment and prosperous life of God's people.[4] Given this, the order of the three narratives—from outer court to holy of holies to holy place—makes sense: Israel approaches God and then encounters God. The results of that encounter are symbolized by the menorah and table in the holy place.

Israel's Sacrificial System (7:1–88)

All Israel, as represented by the leaders from each of the twelve tribes, "made offerings" (7:2). The twelve-day-long procession of gifts to the tabernacle from

2. See Nahum M. Sarna, *Exodus*, JPS Torah Commentary (Philadelphia: Jewish Publication Society, 1991), 155, for a more detailed diagram.
3. Ibid., 156.
4. Samson Raphael Hirsch, *Collected Writings* (New York: Feldheim, 1984), 3.1209–12.

each tribe is a striking image of the people of God dedicating themselves and their possessions to God. These offerings were "used in doing the service of the tent of meeting" (7:5). Each tribe first brought oxen and wagons for carrying all the equipment and furnishings of the tabernacle (7:3–9) and then offered silver plates, silver basins, golden dishes filled with incense, choice flour mixed with oil, and a variety of animals: bulls, rams, male lambs, male goats, and oxen (7:10–88).

Used for the "dedication," or better "initiation," of the altar and the tabernacle services centered on the altar (7:10, 84, 88),[5] all these offerings were connected to the communal services and sacrifices of the tabernacle (Milgrom 1990: 55). The great amount of materials and animals mentioned in this chapter were not all sacrificed and used during this inaugural period but instead given to stock the tabernacle stores (Milgrom 1990: 362–64). The sacrificial system given as law in Leviticus is now put into practice for the first time, with great fanfare and repetition. It is an important event in the life of God's people.

All the main types of sacrifices described in Lev. 1–5 are represented here, with the exception of the *ʾāšām* ("guilt offering"), which is probably not included because it is the only one performed exclusively on behalf of an individual—it is never an offering of the community (→5:5–10). The summary section in 7:84–88 lists the animals offered and connects them to the main types of sacrifices: *ʿōlâ* ("burnt offering"), *minḥâ* ("grain offering"), *ḥaṭṭāʾt* ("sin offering"), and *šĕlāmîm* ("sacrifices of well-being").

The great quantity of offerings and the great detail and repetition in their description show the high importance of sacrifice in the worship life of Israel and in its relationship to God. The importance of sacrifice is matched by the importance of the theological questions surrounding the central meanings of the sacrifices represented here. Difficulties arise, however, in assessing the meanings of these sacrifices because in Numbers, Leviticus, and the Old Testament as a whole, typically only the details or rubrics of the sacrifices are described while the theological understandings that surround the practices are left unstated. There has been much recent debate concerning the meaning of Israel's sacrifices. The positions in these debates are often tied to basic questions concerning the best method for unpacking those meanings.[6] In what follows, I put much more weight on the meanings attached to these sacrifices in the later biblical writings and the traditions of Judaism and Christianity than on comparative studies of sacrifice in the cultures neighboring Israel. This "effective history" of these practices, rather than a synchronic study of sacrifice in general, gives a much better indication of what *God* intended for Israel, as God, through the leaders and prophets of Israel, uniquely shaped and formed this kind of ritual action.

---

5. A distinction can be drawn between the anointing or dedication of the altar and the initiation of the worship life at the altar. The word used here is *ḥănûkkâ*. Hanukkah celebrates the temple's cleansing and initiation back into use during the time of the Maccabees.

6. For a critique of recent theological work on sacrifice based on the sociological methods employed, see John Milbank, "Stories of Sacrifice," *Modern Theology* 12 (1996): 27–56.

Why Does God Desire Sacrifices?

A basic theological question concerning these sacrifices is, Why would God have commanded any sacrifices at all? The general goal of all the sacrifices is to interact with God in a way that improves one's individual or corporate relationship to God. The Hebrew word for sacrifice is derived from the verb meaning "to bring near."[7] But why would God either set up or commandeer this particular cultural practice of offering sacrifices in order for all Israel to come nearer to him?

Christians often try to make sense of this by placing the act of sacrifice within a larger "covering law" that requires it. The problem is that this "basic law" is then understood to determine God's act and in this way explain it. For example, Heb. 9:22 ("without the shedding of blood there is no forgiveness of sins") is sometimes used to explain why God *must* require blood sacrifice in order to forgive his people.[8] It is as if this primordial law required God to set up the system of Old Testament sacrifices in the first place—a deeply problematic way of thinking. Rather we must reflect on how God acts and use scriptural metaphors and motifs to describe what is happening. The most we can claim is that the sacrificial system fits well with the picture of God's character gained from the larger biblical narrative.

One part of the picture found in biblical stories and practices is that God, in his mercy, accepts something partial or representative in place of the whole. Such symbols or parts-of-the-whole or deposits-of-the-future are often acts of righteousness accepted in place of the total righteousness that God desires from a person or group of people. For example, in the story of Abraham and the city of Sodom, God is convinced by Abraham not to destroy the city "for the sake of ten" people who are righteous (Gen. 18:22–33). Similarly, the zealous and righteous act of Phineas is accepted as "atonement for the Israelites" (Num. 25:13).

The larger resonances of the word *kippur* ("atonement") help to deepen our understanding of God's merciful acceptance of such a token act. The Hebrew root *kpr* points to the action of "covering" something. While the word is also connected with "ransoming" or "wiping clean," on linguistic and narrative grounds "covering" is the most basic sense.[9] The presupposed idea is that God cannot bear sin and that sin and sinful creatures cannot bear the holy presence of God;

7. Jacob Milgrom, *Leviticus: A Book of Ritual and Ethics* (Minneapolis: Fortress, 2004), 17–20; Kiuchi 2007: 54.

8. Colin E. Gunton, *The Actuality of Atonement: A Study of Metaphor, Rationality, and the Christian Tradition* (Grand Rapids: Eerdmans, 1989), exposes problems with certain versions and understandings of Christian atonement theories.

9. For a helpful overview of arguments about its meaning, see Richard Averbeck in *NIDOTTE* 2.689–710. The meaning of *kpr* as "covering" can easily be extended analogically to interpersonal relationships; for example, covering over a wrong could also be extended to a sacrificial act that ransoms a person or thing from a state of debt or slavery: the sacrifice covers over or hides the debt.

in order to come near, they need some kind of protection that hides or covers over their sin. That sacrifice provides a covering for sin fits well with several foundational narratives of Israel.

For example, in the garden of Eden, as a result of their sin, Adam and Eve "hid themselves from the presence of the LORD God" (Gen. 3:8). They could not bear his presence in their state of sin, and in that state they were "exposed to danger and expulsion."[10] They attempt to cover themselves, but God in his mercy comes to them and makes "garments of skin" (3:21) to cover them. Similarly, when Jacob is about to meet the angry Esau, he sends offerings ahead of him and says, "I may appease him [*kpr*; literally, "cover his face"] with the present that goes ahead of me, and afterwards I shall see his face" (32:20). In the middle of this story is the story of Jacob wrestling with the angel in order to gain a blessing. Through that event, he gains his new name, Israel—"for you have striven with God and with humans"—and he is blessed by the angel. He then says, "I have seen God face to face, and yet my life is preserved" (32:30). The intertwining of the two stories highlights several analogies between the two kinds of interactions. It suggests that God's face might be covered by offerings, similar to the impact the offerings had on Esau, but eventually God will be seen face to face. The idea of sacrificial blood being a covering also makes sense of Passover. While the word is not used in the Passover account in Exodus, the blood of Passover lambs provides some kind of protection or cover for Israel. Because of the blood, God will "pass over" them (Exod. 12:13).[11] In sum, these texts suggest that God, by commanding the system of sacrifices, provides an atonement or covering for their sin, so that they can bear the presence of God in their midst and come near him.

This meaning of atonement informs us theologically of several things. First of all, it indicates that the final goal of the relationship between God and Israel is that Israel and God can be intimately present to one another; to be "uncovered" in a reversal of the fall, to see one another "face to face." The goal is for humanity, represented by Israel, to be able to stand in God's presence without shame, to be reconciled with God as Jacob and Esau were. The sinfulness and uncleanness of Israel disallows this, and yet God in his mercy provides a means of atonement or covering so Israel can draw near. This is reflected in the architecture of the tabernacle: offerings are made in the outer court so that God can be approached in the holy of holies.

But this image also shows that this act of covering is not a final solution; guilt or impurity is overlooked, but a greater work must be done so that the sin of Israel is not merely covered, but dealt with at a deeper level. It is precisely this situation that Paul speaks of in Rom. 3:21–31, where he writes that "in his divine

10. See Douglas 1999: 246. Kiuchi 2007: 36–37 works extensively with the related notion of sin as "self-hiding."

11. This interpretation does not depend upon the meaning of the word *pesah*. The popular meaning of this Hebrew word as "pass over" is disputed.

forbearance he had passed over the sins previously committed," but now, through the work of Christ, the goal of the law has been achieved. In the person of Christ, the human is healed and purified so that God can fully dwell in humanity without a covering. Christ is the new temple where God dwells fully, and no further sacrifice for sin is needed. Using the terms of Paul, as we are united to Christ, we too become part of his body and God can dwell in us more fully.

A final question is, Why is it fitting that God would accept *these particular symbols and acts* often involving animal sacrifice as such a covering? Further consideration of each major type of sacrifice in Num. 7 shows that they are fitting symbols of what God desires of Israel.

Burnt Offering

The burnt offering (*ʿōlâ*) is usually first in lists of offerings and is often the first sacrifice to be offered in practice. It is probably the oldest type of Israelite sacrifice (cf. Gen. 8:20). The distinguishing mark of the ritual is that the thing being offered is totally consumed by fire on the altar.

What would it mean for an Israelite to offer such a sacrifice? "The purpose of the whole burnt offering was probably originally to express homage to God and to win his favour by a costly gift."[12] But the typical act of the offerer laying their hand on the animal's head for most of the sacrifices (Lev. 1:4; 3:2, 8, 13; 4:4, 15, 24, 29, 33; 8:14; 16:21) suggests something more—that the offerer is identifying with what is offered (Kiuchi 2007: 56, following H. H. Rowley and Hans-Joachim Kraus). The blood and then all the rest of the animal is offered. These acts indicate the life of the animal (cf. 17:11) is being offered to God. This life somehow represents or substitutes for the life of the worshiper. This may seem to solve the issue, but there are two major ways of interpreting even this.[13] First, one could understand the life of the animal given to God as a representation of *an obedient and faithful life* being offered up to God by the worshiper. The implication would thus be that this is an act of wholeheartedly dedicating oneself to God—through this act symbolically giving oneself over to God. Second, one could understand that the animal's death is being substituted for the offerer's own death—and that this substitutionary *death* appeases the wrath of God.

12. H. H. Rowley, *Worship in Ancient Israel: Its Forms and Meanings* (London: SPCK, 1967), 120.

13. Milgrom suggests a third alternative for the logic of sacrifices, centered on the cleansing of the *sancta*, especially the tabernacle and altar, accomplished through the sacrifices and blood manipulation; see Milgrom 1990: 444–47; *Studies in Cultic Theology and Terminology,* Studies in Judaism in Late Antiquity 36 (Leiden: Brill, 1983); "Further on the Expiatory Sacrifices," *Journal of Biblical Literature* 115 (1996): 511–14; "Encroaching on the Sacred: Purity and Polity in Num. 1–10," *Interpretation* 51 (1997): 241–53. While aspects of Milgrom's understanding are especially relevant to the sin offerings, this emphasis is best understood as part of a larger whole. The cleansing function of some sacrifices can be derived from the central meaning of the *ʿōlâ*.

Wenham opts for this latter theme: "Thus the burnt offering does not remove sin or change man's sinful nature, but it makes fellowship between sinful man and a holy God possible. It propitiates God's wrath against sin" (1979: 57).[14] In a slightly different vein, Kiuchi suggests that the punishment of the worshiper is not what is being substituted for, but rather the sacrifice represents "the death of one's sinful and worldly desires (a forsaking of this world)" (2007: 61).[15] The death of the animal thus substitutes for the death or punishment of the worshiper (Wenham) or represents the death of the worldly desires of the worshiper (Kiuchi), and it is this that is a "pleasing odor" to God.

Instead, I hold what is most centrally pleasing to God is an *obedient life*, not death, and God intended the burnt offerings to symbolize precisely an obedient life given freely to God. The life of the animal, represented by its body and its blood, is being offered to God in the burnt offerings as a token, substitute, or representation of the worshiper's self-dedication to an obedient and faithful life.[16]

I am convinced of this basic direction for several reasons. First of all, the biblical passages and rituals seem to suggest that the point of killing and then burning the animals or other items was not to destroy, torture, or punish them but rather to "turn the whole into smoke on the altar" (Lev. 1:9). Smoke and fire are common biblical symbols that recall God's presence on Mount Sinai: it is a presence not easily grasped, one that is high and elusive yet nonetheless powerful and real. The point of turning them into smoke is to transfer them to the realm or presence of God.[17] The killing is thus part of the offering of the gift of the animal; the point is not their death per se.

This emphasis on the animal as a token of an obedient life is more coherent with later prophetic and New Testament statements about sacrifices. They critique

14. Wenham appears to understand that the wrath is placed on the animal instead of the offerer. Elsewhere he writes: "Here it suffices to say that *make atonement* literally means 'pay a ransom' or 'ransom,' and 11c could be paraphrased 'the blood ransoms at the price of life.' In other words the ransom price for man's life is not a monetary payment (as in Exod. 21:30) but the life of an animal represented by its blood splashed over the altar" (1979: 245). Thus the price for human sin is not precisely life, but rather the end of that life, or death, and this price is paid by the death of the animal.

15. Kiuchi stresses that this act and other such sacrifices symbolize the "annihilation of the offerer's worldly desires" (2007: 60). But given the stress of the symbolism of burning and smoke on transference to God rather than destruction, this act is better understood in terms of wholehearted self-dedication to God.

16. Milbank also follows this general direction. While there is a place for expiation and suffering in his understanding ("Stories of Sacrifice," 52–53), he *contrasts* notions of sacrifice in many ancient and modern cultures and theories of religion with the central thrusts of biblical religion: "In the case of the biblical religions, by contrast, creative giving is not loss but a self-emptying *in order* to be, and sacrificial response is, in return, a total giving back which is the only possible mode of continuing to participate in Being" (52).

17. Jacob Neusner, "Sacrifice and Temple in Rabbinic Judaism," in *The Encyclopedia of Judaism*, ed. Jacob Neusner, Alan J. Avery-Peck, and William Scott Green (New York: Continuum, 1999), 1292.

misunderstandings of the sacrificial system, often specifically burnt offerings, and also offer examples of positive appropriations of the sacrificial system, in essence calling Israel back to the true purposes of sacrifice rather than suggesting what sacrifice should have been but was not.

For example, Hos. 6:6 and Mic. 6:6–8 critique the insincere burnt offerings of the people. These critiques imply what the sacrifices should and potentially do represent: the desire to live in communion with God and according to his ways. Repentance, sorrow, and the eradication of sin are certainly part of this (as means to an end), but the central goal is the positive, obedient life of justice, kindness, and walking humbly with God. The burnt offering represents one aspect of this: a wholehearted devotion and self-offering to God. This understanding fits well with the first mention of burnt offering in the Bible: Noah's sacrifice after the flood was a burnt offering with a "pleasing odor" to God (Gen. 8:20–21). While the narrative does not explicitly say what about the sacrifice God is pleased with, the surrounding narrative contrasts the evil "inclination of the human heart" with the obedience, wholeheartedness, and blamelessness of Noah (6:9). There is little hint of this sacrifice being an offering of a substitutionary death in payment for Noah's sins, but good cause to see it associated with Noah's thankfulness and wholehearted and faithful obedience, major themes in that story.[18]

Loyalty Offering

The second offering mentioned in Num. 7 is the "grain offering" (*minḥâ*). The components of this offering are suggestive of the exodus and the covenant made then between God and Israel. It consists of choice flour mixed with oil, incense, and "the salt of the covenant" (Lev. 2:13; cf. Num. 18:19), while leaven and honey are specifically forbidden (Lev. 2:11). The unleavened cakes or wafers created with the grain and oil recall the unleavened bread of the exodus. The proscription against leaven and honey also makes sense in light of the exodus, when the people ate unleavened bread as they left Egypt. Honey is a key description of the promised land, and so its omission would recall the time in the wilderness. Kiuchi writes that the symbolism of the elements "appears to signify that the offerer ought to revert to the initial covenant allegiance exhibited by Israel in the exodus" (2007: 71). For this offering, part of the wafers are burnt and offered up to God, while the other part of the offering is eaten by "Aaron and his sons" (2:10). This sharing of elements further suggests that

---

18. Another example is Ps. 50:12–13, which critiques the understanding that God is somehow fed in a literal way by burnt offerings: "If I were hungry, I would not tell you, for the world and all that is in it is mine. Do I eat the flesh of bulls, or drink the blood of goats?" Instead, God is pleased with sacrifices that are sincere indications of making a covenant with God (50:5) or that are part of a thanksgiving or fulfillment of vows to God (50:14). While these themes are also related to the loyalty offerings and the sacrifices of well-being and not simply the burnt offerings, this psalm stresses that God is pleased with the commitment and thankfulness of the worshiper as motives for the sacrifice—not because God desires food or requires a substitutionary death.

it is symbolic of their covenant relationship. Accordingly, Kiuchi suggests that *minḥâ* is better translated "loyalty offering"; "grain offering" merely focuses on the main ingredient.[19]

Given this interpretation, this sacrifice, made both individually and communally, is a way in which the wholehearted devotion to God symbolized in the burnt offering gains greater specificity. Israel communally and individually makes this offering to God as a way of rededicating themselves to their initial covenant with God.

Sin Offering

The third offering mentioned in Num. 7 is the "sin offering" (*ḥaṭṭāʾt*), which deals with the negative effects of sin. Only the male goat sin offering—male goats are used for communal rather than individual sin offerings (Lev. 4:1–5:13)—is represented in Num. 7, further suggesting that these tribal offerings are intended to stock the Levites with material for the regular corporate sacrifices and festivals (Num. 28:15, 22). The Hebrew word is also used for the act of sinning, hence the usual name of this offering.

This sacrifice is distinguished in part by the way the blood of the sacrifice is manipulated. For sin offerings related to the sins of the priests and the people (Lev. 4:1–21; 16:1–34)[20] the blood of the animal is brought into either the holy place or the holy of holies and some of it is sprinkled on the altar of incense (4:7, 18) and before the curtain (4:6, 17). On the Day of Atonement, it is sprinkled on the mercy seat itself (16:15).

There is no scholarly consensus about the details of the meaning of this sacrifice. Milgrom's influential theory argues that the negative effects of sin do not so much defile the person or people sinning, but instead defile the temple (or tabernacle). Impurity caused by sin is like a physical substance that is attracted to the sanctuary. The sanctuary thus needs to be cleansed or purified by the sacrifices. The blood acts like a cleansing agent or "ritual detergent" (1991: 253–60). This suggests that *ḥaṭṭāʾt* might be better translated "purification offering."[21] Sprinkling the blood

---

19. Wenham also points out that the word *minḥâ* in nonsacrificial settings often means "'tribute,' the money paid by a vassal king to his overlord" (1979: 69). For Israel, a token that recalls the exodus event in which YHWH became Israel's king is fitting. That this loyalty offering also plays a part in the ordeal of the woman suspected of adultery (Num. 5) makes sense on both the literal level (faithfulness promised to one's spouse is part of God's covenant law) and the figurative level (Israel's faithfulness to the covenant is being tested in the wilderness).

20. Baruch A. Levine, *In the Presence of the Lord: A Study of Cult and Some Cultic Terms in Ancient Israel* (Leiden: Brill, 1974), 103, understands that the sin offering has a slightly different meaning and effect for the unintentional sins of tribal leaders and individual Israelites (Lev. 4:22–5:13).

21. Klawans 2000: 14–15; Jacob Milgrom, "Israel's Sanctuary: The Priestly 'Picture of Dorian Gray,'" *Revue biblique* 83 (1976): 390–99; Wenham 1979: 89; Levine, *In the Presence of the Lord*, 101–4.

of the animal is not meant to purify the people directly, but the sanctuary so that God in his holiness will continue to dwell in it (Lev. 16:16).

Milgrom's view is called into question by many scholars. A central argument against it is that people are forgiven as a result of the sacrifice (Lev. 4:26, 31, 35; Num. 15:25, 28).[22] The texts indicate that sin offerings directly dealt with the guilt and separation of individuals and the community from God.

While I disagree with Milgrom that the central meaning of the sin offering is the purification of the sanctuary, his understanding helpfully points to a theme evidenced in scripture: sin has a defiling or contaminating effect, which might be thought of as the long-term effects of sin on places and people. While aspects of this are difficult to understand or translate into modern categories, a possible analogy is the idea of the character of a person, community, or place being degraded over time through the effects of sin and uncleanness. Given the repeated breakdown of natural patterns of life and health in certain places, environmental degradation sets in. Given recurrent moral sin, a person's or community's character becomes warped or filled with vice.

So, while God is ever ready to forgive sin and allow impurity to be atoned for, if sin is not confessed and dealt with, the eventual result of the buildup of its effects is that God might abandon the tabernacle or temple, places in which the sacramental presence of God dwells. For example, Ezekiel says that the coming wrath of God will result finally in the removal of God's presence from the temple, its destruction, and the exile of Israel: "Therefore, as I live, says the Lord GOD, surely, because you have defiled my sanctuary with all your detestable things and with all your abominations—therefore I will cut you down" (Ezek. 5:11). "He said to me, 'Mortal, do you see what they are doing, the great abominations that the house of Israel are committing here, to drive me far from my sanctuary?'" (8:6). Whether the sin offering is intended to deal with this buildup is another question.

At the very least, the meaning of the sin offerings should not be reduced to sanctuary purification, for it is clear that sin causes an interpersonal disruption and that part of the effects of the sacrifice is to help heal this relationship. In this regard, the symbolism of the blood of the animal in the sin offerings may be different than in the case of the burnt offering. There, the blood and body of the animal represented that the life of the animal is given to God as a substitutionary representation of the obedient and faithful life of the worshiper. Here, however, the sin offering is a sacrifice of confession, a cry to God that the effects of sin be taken away. One could still make the claim that the offering of a token of the dedication of one's life to God would be a fitting "covering" for one's sin. But the blood in this case might instead represent a substitutionary death—either a death of punishment (Wenham) or a death of sinful desires (Kiuchi). Either of

---

22. David Janzen, "Priestly Sacrifice in the Hebrew Bible: A Summary of Recent Scholarship and a Narrative Reading," *Religion Compass* 2/1 (2008): 43–46.

these understandings may in fact fit better with the rituals of the Day of Atonement. Whatever the case may be, the sin offering is an action on Israel's part that recognizes the seriousness of sin and its effects. God in mercy accepts the sacrifice as a covering so that he might continue to dwell among Israel.

Sacrifice of Well-Being

The final offering mentioned in Num. 7 is the "sacrifice of well-being" (šĕlāmîm). The ritual for this sacrifice was different from the other sacrifices. The animal was sacrificed, and then only certain fatty portions of the animal were burned, turned "into smoke," and offered "as a food offering by fire to the LORD" (Lev. 3:11). The other portions were eaten by the priests, the offerer, and other invited guests (Deut. 12:7; 1 Sam. 1; 1 Kgs. 8:62–66). This offering was typically not one of the regular corporate sacrifices of the people (Num. 28–29). However, it was celebrated at Pentecost (Lev. 23:19) and formed an important part of national celebrations, such as the temple dedication (1 Kgs. 8). Passover shares much in common with what is eventually called the šĕlāmîm.[23] Most often the sacrifice was made in response to events in an individual's life, such as a public profession of "thanksgiving" (tôdâ; Lev. 7:12), out of "free will" (nĕdābâ; 7:16), or in response to a "vow" one has made (neder; 7:16), such as the Nazirite vow (Num. 6:17).

The meaning of this offering is tied to its name, which shares the same root with the word "shalom" ("peace, completeness, well-being"). While there are different opinions about how the offering might be related to the idea of peace or completeness, the best explanation is that the offering celebrates an event where the shalom of God is particularly experienced. Perhaps the ritual might best be translated "the shalom celebration sacrifice." It afforded "worshipers the experience of joining together with the priests in a sacred meal at which God Himself was perceived to be an honored guest."[24] This meal celebrated an occasion when the blessings of God and the longed-for harmony between God, humans, and all creation are partially experienced here and now.[25] Using Christian theological words, it was "a foretaste of the feast to come." This sacrificial meal was regularly held at harvest, at Shavuot, at the inauguration of the temple, at celebrations of the blessings of the promised land (Deut. 12:5–7), or at the birth of a child given in response to a vow (1 Sam. 1:24–25). As the final sacrifice listed and celebrated within larger celebrations, it fittingly symbolizes a foretaste of the goal toward which God is bringing his people and all of creation.

23. Baruch A. Levine, *Leviticus*, JPS Torah Commentary (Philadelphia: Jewish Publication Society, 1989), 14.

24. Ibid.

25. Wenham writes: "It was a meal in which God's presence was recognized as specially near" (1979: 81). True, but more particularly this is a meal in which God's kingdom in all its aspects was recognized as specially near.

Sacrifices in Relationship to Christ and the Eucharist

All of these sacrifices inform the New Testament understanding of Christ, the Eucharist, and the Christian life. Language used of these sacrifices, especially the burnt and sin offerings, is applied first of all to the life and death of Christ.

For example, in Eph. 5:1–4 Paul applies burnt offering imagery to Jesus: "Therefore be imitators of God, as beloved children, and live in love, as Christ loved us and gave himself up for us, a fragrant offering and sacrifice to God." His love, self-offering, and imitation of God are Christ's sacrifice, pointing again to the self-offering of one's life as the central significance of the burnt offering. Humble obedience to God's ways in a warped and sinful world will surely involve suffering and death. But it is the life, not the death per se, that is most centrally pleasing to God, as the Christ hymn suggests: "He became obedient to the point of death. . . . Therefore God also highly exalted him" (Phil. 2:8–9).

In the letter to the Hebrews, the imagery of both burnt and sin offering is applied to Christ (10:6). The important phrase "see, I have come to do your will" (10:7, 9) indicates that Christ came to fulfill the law by offering to God the true human life that the law pointed to (10:16). In this way Christ's sacrifice is like a burnt offering. But Christ is also said to be a sin offering: "Christ . . . offered for all time a single sacrifice for sins" (10:12). As a result of his sin offering, God "will remember their sins and their lawless deeds no more" (10:17).

John also draws upon the sin offering imagery: "If we walk in the light as he himself is in the light, we have fellowship with one another, and the blood of Jesus his Son cleanses us from all sin. . . . If we confess our sins, he who is faithful and just will forgive us our sins and cleanse us from all unrighteousness" (1 John 1:7, 9). Our confession of sin is likened to the sin offering with Christ as the sacrifice.

The double stress on Christ's obedience and self-offering that brings forgiveness, rooted in a fuller understanding of the Old Testament sacrificial system, guards against the reduction of Christ's work to a single theme, as some modern atonement theories do. We benefit from Christ's multifaceted sacrifice by participating in his own righteous life, as the burnt offering imagery represents. But we also experience forgiveness because of the self-giving of God in Christ, as the sin offering imagery represents.[26]

While the New Testament primarily uses burnt and sin offerings in reference to the work of Christ, the themes and images of all four main sacrifices are used in reference to the Last Supper and the Lord's Supper. Christian understandings of the Eucharist are greatly enhanced when its relationship to the Old Testament sacrifices is better understood and highlighted. The offerings in Num. 7 can even be likened to the offerings of Christians in worship and the eucharistic feast. The burnt offering, a sacrifice symbolizing a person's total self-dedication to God, finds

---

26. The creation of a new humanity in Christ through his obedience as true human ("The Servant as Lord") and the self-giving of God in Christ ("The Lord as Servant") are two principal themes in Barth's doctrine of reconciliation (1936–77: 4/1–2).

its true type in Christ's self-offering and obedience, obedience even to the point of death on the cross. As they eat the bread and drink the cup, Christians are united with Christ and renew their pledge to take up their own crosses in obedience to God, an obedience that might also lead to their own suffering. Just as Christ was a "fragrant offering" to God, so too we present ourselves to God as "living sacrifices" (Rom. 12:1–2) as we approach the table.[27] The grain/loyalty offerings resonate with the covenantal aspects of the Eucharist. The often unleavened eucharistic wafers draw from the same well of meaning as the unleavened cakes of the grain offering. By eating them and drinking Christ's "blood of the covenant" (Mark 14:24; Matt. 26:28) or "the new covenant in my blood" (Luke 22:20; 1 Cor. 11:25), we renew our baptismal vows as people of the new covenant.[28] The sin offerings, which find their highest form in the Day of Atonement, also find their highest type in the sacrifice of Christ: "For if the blood of goats and bulls, with the sprinkling of the ashes of a heifer, sanctifies those who have been defiled so that their flesh is purified, how much more will the blood of Christ, who through the eternal Spirit offered himself without blemish to God, purify our conscience from dead works to worship the living God!" (Heb. 9:13–14). As we drink Christ's blood, "shed for the forgiveness of sins," we too are purified individually and corporately. And finally, just as the shalom celebration sacrifice celebrates not only what God has done, but also looks forward to the fullness of God's shalom, so too the Eucharist is a foretaste of the feast to come.[29] Christ's statement that he will not "drink of this fruit of the vine until that day when I drink it new with you in my Father's kingdom" (Matt. 26:29) highlights the joyful dimension of celebrating God's blessings and goodness that the wine and the sometimes leavened bread of the Eucharist represents. By noting several aspects of this sacrifice—its celebratory aspect, the distribution of the meat of the šĕlāmîm (and the leavened bread and wine associated with it; see Lev. 7:13; Num. 15:1–10), and the image of eating a meal together with God—one can draw bold lines of meaning between this meal of the Old Covenant and the eucharistic meal of the New.

27. "The Lord's Supper, as Calvin presents it, is thus the occasion of a twofold self-offering: in it Christ gives his crucified body to his people, and they in turn present their bodies as a living sacrifice to God, which is their spiritual worship" (Brian Gerrish, *Grace and Gratitude: The Eucharistic Theology of John Calvin* [Minneapolis: Augsburg Fortress, 1993], 126–27). This is true, but the different Old Testament sacrifices do a better job of further identifying the more complicated transactions occurring and remembered in the two-directional gift-giving of the Eucharist. The burnt offerings find their type in Christ's offering of obedience to God, which we are called to as we are joined to Christ; that is part of the gift. The loyalty, sin, and shalom celebration offerings specify additional aspects of God's gift to us in Christ and our offerings to God.

28. See John Witvliet's *Worship Seeking Understanding* (Grand Rapids: Baker, 2003), 67–89, for an excellent discussion of covenantal themes of the Lord's Supper that are often underemphasized in ecumenical discussions and documents such as *Baptism, Eucharist, and Ministry*, Faith and Order Paper 111 (Geneva: World Council of Churches, 1982).

29. This emphasis is highlighted especially by Eastern Orthodoxy; see Schmemann, *Eucharist*; and Geoffrey Wainwright, *Eucharist and Eschatology* (New York: Oxford University Press, 1981).

Listening to YHWH in the Holy of Holies (7:89)

In 7:89 Moses enters the holy of holies, speaks with the Lord, and hears God's "voice speaking to him from above the mercy seat." In this important moment comes the fulfillment of the promise by God concerning the tabernacle in Exod. 25:22: "There I will meet with you, and . . . I will deliver to you all my commands for the Israelites." Just as the offerings of Num. 7:10–88 inaugurate the system of sacrifices in the outer court, so here is narrated the inaugural event of the holy of holies. It follows naturally upon the reception of the gifts for the sacrifices. Those sacrifices were intended in part so that sin would be dealt with and Moses, Aaron, or a representative of Israel could draw near and enter into the presence of God.

This meeting between Moses and God has many parallels to the earlier encounter between God, Moses, and the people on Mount Sinai. In Exod. 19 the people are consecrated, and God descends upon the mountain on the third day (19:11). The mountain is "wrapped in smoke" (19:18), and God finally spoke the words of the covenant to Moses (20:1–2). Later in the tent (33:7–11) and on the mountain (33:12–23), Moses hears and speaks with God and experiences an amazingly intimate meeting with God in which he even speaks with God "face to face" (33:11) as with a friend. Alternately, he is able to see God's glory and hear God's name (33:19).[30] Moses in these moments secures the promise of God's continuing presence with Israel (33:15), while also receiving God's commands and law (34:1–2).

Now in the tabernacle, Moses has similar experiences. He approaches the presence of God through the smoke of the incense burning outside the holy of holies (as detailed in Exod. 30:6–8) and enters God's presence, who is enthroned above the cherubim of the ark, and he hears God's voice. The similarities suggest that the tabernacle is like a portable Sinai.

Being in God's presence in such an intimate way and receiving God's law and direction are two central purposes for drawing near the holy of holies. In addition, Moses draws near in order to boldly make intercessions for the people. He does so at Sinai (Exod. 33:12–16; 34:9) and "at the tent of meeting" (Num. 12:5; 14:10–19; 16:19) after Israel's rebellions at Sinai and during their sojourn through the wilderness. Thus at the center of Israel's worship life is God, who not only graciously speaks and directs Israel through Moses, who not only offers himself to be intimately known, but who also allows Moses to speak to him and who listens to his intercessions.

These aspects of human encounter with God at the center of the holiest place of Israelite worship find their fulfillment in Jesus Christ. Christ fulfills this encounter from the side of Israel and Moses, offering up prayers and supplications during

---

30. Samuel L. Terrien, *The Elusive Presence: Toward a New Biblical Theology* (San Francisco: Harper & Row, 1978), 106–60.

"the days of his flesh" (Heb. 5:7), making God's word, glory, and name known to the disciples (John 17:14, 22, 26). But even more, in Christ's own person the most intimate union of God and humans occurs. He is the fulfillment of that which the tabernacle and temple point to (Col. 2:9, 17).

But through Christ's work and through the sending of the Spirit, the veil of the temple is torn, and Christ, also in the role of God, makes the presence of God available to us. This presence is spoken of in the New Testament as being "in Christ" or "in the Spirit." In Christian worship, especially in the sacrament of the Lord's Supper, such images and themes are also encountered. In certain traditions, the use of incense around the sanctuary and altar recalls the incense of the tabernacle and the smoke of Sinai. We come to the table not only to re-call Christ's sacrifice and the forgiveness of sins. Certainly his sacrifice opened the way into the holy place (Heb. 9:12) by covering our sins. But even more, by offering us "his flesh" (10:10), at the Lord's Supper we intimately come into contact with God through Christ by the Holy Spirit. We also are to be formed into the patterns of his life through receiving his body and taking into us the blood of the new covenant. In this way we hear the words of the covenant and take those words and patterns of being into us, so that the covenant will be heard by us and also received and written on our hearts and minds (10:16). We are thus enabled through Christ and the Spirit to live lives that follow in the ways of Jesus (12:1–2).[31]

In this way Christians individually and communally may be thought of as following in the steps of Moses—both as he ascends the holy mountain and as he enters into the holy of holies in the tabernacle. Such a spiritual reading of the ascent of Moses into the cloud and the problems he encounters after that ascent can provide a model for the Christian life, as seen in Gregory of Nyssa's *The Life of Moses*, which speaks of the goal of the Christian life: "We regard . . . becoming God's friend the only thing worthy of honor and desire."[32] Such a friendship involves intimacy, which results in our reflecting God's character: "He who has truly come to be in the image of God and who has in no way turned aside from the divine character bears in himself its distinguishing marks."[33] This then is the longed-for result of the entry into the holy of holies—a personal intimacy and encounter with God that results in us bearing forth God's law and word and character not only on our lips, but in our being. Such at least we find in Christ, the fulfillment of this figure of Moses.

---

31. The movement from encounter with God made possible through Christ to the call to lead lives in conformance with Christ is also seen in Ephesians. Explicit temple imagery (Eph. 2:14–21) leads naturally into parenesis (4:1–2), which calls us to live into the pattern of Christ: "Be imitators of God . . . and live in love, as Christ loved us and gave himself up for us, a fragrant offering and sacrifice to God" (5:1).

32. Gregory of Nyssa, *The Life of Moses*, trans. A. J. Malherbe and E. F. Ferguson, Classics of Western Spirituality (New York: Paulist Press, 1978), 137.

33. Ibid., 136.

Lighting the Menorah in the Holy Place (8:1–4)

Another act represents the inauguration of the life of the tabernacle, this time in the holy place. Aaron sets up the seven lamps of the lampstand so that they would "give light in front of the lampstand" (8:3). Placing this brief narrative after description of the holy of holies is fitting, for this symbolic "lighting of the menorah" is the result of the encounter between God and Israel. The menorah itself can be a symbol of Israel lit on fire, but not consumed, by the spirit of God. Israel as a people is to "give light," a light that comes from God's presence in and among them.

Within the holy place were two main symbols: the table and the lampstand or menorah (*měnôrâ*).[34] While the functional purpose of the lampstand was to give light, it also had a theological meaning, just as the table did. Their symbolic meanings are not explicitly stated in scripture, but both Jewish and Christian traditions drew reasonable conclusions about these images:

> The meaning of the menorah in the Sanctuary would seem obvious. Light symbol-izes knowledge, and the candlestick, especially by virtue of its place opposite the table in front of the Ark of the Covenant would signify that spiritual enlightenment which, together with the table, the symbol of material prosperity, would symbol-ize the Jewish national life that stems from God's Law and remains consecrated to the Law forever.[35]

As described in Exod. 25:23–30, twelve loaves of bread, called "the bread of *pānîm*," were to be regularly placed on the table located on the north side of the holy place. *Pānîm* typically means "presence, face, interior." The loaves symbolize the prosperity of Israel given the presence of God and their obedience to the law (Deut. 11:14–15). The Gospels make no direct connection, but bread symbolism appears in crucial places, such as the temptation accounts (Matt. 4:3) and the feeding of the five thousand, when twelve baskets of bread are collected (14:20). In both cases, bread is suggestive of prosperity or material blessing.

Each component of the menorah—lampstand, flames, and resulting light—can be connected to common symbols associated with Israel and its calling. The lampstand itself is constructed and decorated in ways suggestive of a tree or bush. The tree is often used as a symbol of Israel or more generally for righteous Israelites who follow the law of the Lord (Ps. 1). Placed together, the symbols of tree and

---

34. While the altar of incense is also in the holy place, it seems to be symbolically connected more to the holy of holies, imaging the cloud within which YHWH dwells.

35. Hirsch, *Collected Writings*, 1.211. Martin Selman in *NIDOTTE* 2.977–78 suggests a con-nection between later models of the lampstand and the garden of Eden, while also pointing out that the lamps in Zech. 4:2, 10 symbolize the eyes of God. Sarna (*Exodus*, 162–65) suggests that the twelve loaves of bread symbolize the twelve tribes of Israel and that the construction of the lamp is suggestive of a tree (probably the tree of life) and its light linked to God's presence. The menorah is now a symbol of the modern nation of Israel.

light are suggestive of the calling to be filled with God's spirit in such a way that they shine as a people and give light to the nations. In many places in scripture not necessarily connected with the menorah, light rests on or shines through the people of Israel. Like the burning bush that Moses saw, Israel is aflame with God's spirit yet not consumed.

The most direct references to the menorah in the prophets are in prophesies by Isaiah and Zechariah. In Zech. 4:2–10 the seven lamps are "the eyes of the LORD, which range through the whole earth" and represent God's "spirit" (4:6). In Isa. 11:2 God's sevenfold spirit is said to rest on a remnant of Israel that will grow out of the stump of Jesse. And in 42:6 the servant of the Lord is called to be "a covenant to the people, a light to the nations." These prophecies connect the menorah to Israel, God's presence in it, and God's intentions for it to be a light to the nations. In Revelation a connection is made between the light of the people of God and the lampstand in the temple. Many of John's symbols are related to different parts of the temple. In Rev. 1:12–20 "seven golden lampstands" symbolize the churches among whom Christ walks and the angels of God associated with the churches. These symbolisms lend credence to Hirsch's interpretation that the menorah is a symbol particularly of Israel, called to be bright like a lamp, lit by God's spirit, and shining before the nations. This brightness is a result of the presence of God among them, the enlightenment they gain through the knowledge of God and his law, and their just and compassionate way of life as they put into practice the ways of God. Such a way of being is a beacon of hope among the nations. As Israel shines, God's name is glorified among the peoples.

Table and menorah are primary symbols of the end or goal of Israel's worship and life lived in the presence of God. This life of prosperity and light is also the goal of Israel's journey from the mountain of God into the land of Canaan. Just as the Sinai experience is not the end of the story for Israel, so too the ordering of these chapters is suggestive: it is a movement from outer court to holy of holies and *then* to holy place. This vision of the end is quite unlike parts of Christianity that have an almost Gnostic view of the goal of the Christian journey, namely a goal of the "escape" of the human soul from the destruction of the world, "saved" for a disembodied existence of the individual soul with God. Rather, this vision of the goal or end of God's work with his people is quite embodied. Arguably it corresponds better to visions of renewal of all creation, of heaven coming down to earth: "See, the home [tabernacle] of God is among mortals. He will dwell [tabernacle] with them as their God; they will be his peoples, and God himself will be with them" (Rev. 21:3).

Holy People: Consecrating the Levites (8:5–26)

When the worship life of Israel is set on its course, not only is the tabernacle inaugurated, but also the Levites are "cleanse[d]" (8:6) and "purified . . . from sin" (8:21) in order that they might serve in the work of the tabernacle and be offered as a representative offering (8:11, 15). This representative role of the Levites gives greater insight into the part they are to play in the life of Israel and into the "spirituality of Levitism" (de Vaulx 1972: 121–23). As representatives of Israel, they become role models for the purity, self-offering, and service that Israel is called to.

The Levites are first purified (8:5–13). They are to be in close proximity to God and so must be ritually cleansed. The rite here is different from that of the ordination of the priest described in Lev. 8–9. While the priests are first cleansed and then anointed with blood and oil and given special vestments (8:6, 30), the Levites are cleansed in a detailed manner that conjures up a variety of associations. They are sprinkled with "the water of purification" (Num. 8:7; cf. 19:1–22), and they shave and wash their clothes, actions recalling the cleansing of a leper (Lev. 14:8; cf. Exod. 19:14). This great attention to cleansing draws attention to the contrast between the purity of God and the sinfulness and uncleanness of humanity. The desire to be clean before God is reflected in the prayer of Ps. 51: "Purge me with hyssop, and I shall be clean; wash me, and I shall be whiter than snow. . . . Create in me a clean heart, O God, and put a new and right spirit within me" (51:7, 10).

After this, they are "unreservedly given" (*nětunîm nětunîm*) over to God (Num. 8:16). The people lay their hands on the Levites, and the Levites lay their hands on the two bulls. The first bull is sacrificed as a sin offering, the second as a burnt offering, and then the Levites are in some way ritually shown to the people, showing that they are given to the Lord (8:12–13). As discussed in →7:1–88, the sin offering provides an atonement for sin, and the burnt offering represents a positive gift and self-giving to God. These sacrifices are typical of the ordinations of priests and the offering of the Nazirite (Lev. 8:14, 18; Num. 6:16). After the sacrifices, the Lord says, "Have the Levites stand before Aaron and his sons, and you shall present them as an elevation offering to the LORD" (8:13). Such an elevation or wave offering is some kind of formal presentation. In the case of grain or other such gifts, those gifts are lifted up before God; this is similar to how the offering plates are lifted up in some Christian churches in order to show that they are being dedicated to God. But here, it is the Levites themselves who are given to God; they are to be living sacrifices for Israel.

That the Levites are a sacrifice for Israel is underlined by their replacing the firstborn as an offering (Num. 8:16). Instead of their firstborn, Israel presents the Levites to God. The Levites thus are a perpetual reminder of the redemption of Israel by God from the land of Egypt (8:17–18) and of their national calling as the firstborn of YHWH (Exod. 4:22–23), to be a holy people and royal priesthood (19:6). Just as the firstborn of Israel become a symbol and substitute, the Levites become a substitute or representative of the calling and vocation of the nation. They "make atonement" for the firstborn, covering their debt.

The Levites, both through their service and by being offered to God, are one more reminder of Israel's calling to be a holy people.

Holy Times: Redemption, Guidance, and Call to Judgment (9:1–10:10)

The final aspect of the worship life of Israel is its liturgical calendar, revolving around the three central feasts of Pesach, Shavuot, and Sukkot. The full calendar is detailed in →Num. 28–29, including the regulations for daily offerings, the Sabbath, monthly sacrifices, and the three yearly feasts. Here, however, representative elements of the three yearly pilgrim festivals are touched upon, and events associated with the historical foundations of each festival are retold. As with the laws in Num. 5–6, there is no stress here on interpretation, nor does the text explicitly point out that these sections are structured according to the pilgrimage feasts. Yet putting narrative and law together in this way forms an overall map of Israel's festivals, showing their importance in Israel's life of worship and their orientation as a people.

Numbers 9:1–14 records the first anniversary of Passover or Pesach, giving additional regulations for its celebration. In 9:15–23 the pillar of cloud and fire are described. While the celebration of Shavuot is not explicitly mentioned, a crucial theme of that festival is God's faithful guidance of and care for Israel. God does this both through the pillar of cloud and fire and also through the gift of his law and covenant. This care and guidance are evidenced by the harvest and prosperity of the promised land (cf. Deut. 26:8–10). The pillar of cloud and fire can be understood as a key historical event linked to the themes of the later festival. Finally, in Num. 10:1–10 the making of the silver trumpets is commanded. These trumpets were used in several ways during Israel's forty-year journey through the wilderness and also gained importance through their use in and association with the opening convocation, the Festival of Trumpets, that began the third great pilgrimage feast of Israel, Sukkot (Lev. 23:24; Num. 29:1–6).

The importance of these festivals in the ongoing life of Israel is difficult to exaggerate. Samson Raphael Hirsch remarks: "The Jew's calendar is his catechism."[36] It was chiefly through the festivals and great pilgrim feasts of Israel that most Israelites learned about the determining events of their history and came to understand the central ideas of their faith.

Thus in Num. 9–10 at least two levels of meaning are at play. First, events linked to the themes of the feasts are in fact happening. Israel has recently been redeemed through God's action in Passover, God is guiding Israel through the pillar of cloud and fire to the promised land, and the silver trumpets are being made that will summon Israel forward in its journey and to encounters with its enemies.

36. Quoted in Harold Kushner's foreword to Hayyim Schauss, *The Jewish Festivals: A Guide to Their History and Observance*, trans. S. Jaffe (New York: Schocken, 1962).

Second, the material placed together here suggests the ongoing importance of the worship celebrations in Israel's life for orienting it theologically and preparing it for the journey toward the fulfillment of its vocation as a people.

Celebrating Passover (9:1–14)

The first Passover meal, celebrated during Israel's exodus from Egypt, marked the foundation of their life as a nation: the redemption by God of Israel out of the bitterness of Egyptian slavery. While this gracious act of God is the historical foundation of the nation of Israel, it is also its theological foundation. It told them what kind of god YHWH is and who they were in relationship to God. God reached down to his people in their bitterness and provided a new life for them, rescuing them from a situation in which they were powerless to free themselves. But God does not merely free them: he also claimed them as his own people, his firstborn. The regular celebration of Passover and Unleavened Bread oriented Israel in its life as a people both then and through the years. The celebration of this feast directly before the departure from Sinai is thus quite fitting.

This section has three main parts: the record of Israel's second celebration of Passover (9:1–5), questions posed to Moses by some unclean people whether they could present Passover offerings (9:6–8), and God's reply to the questions, which allowed another Passover celebration for the exceptional case of corpse contamination and guaranteed the resident alien equal opportunity to celebrate (9:9–14; →15:1–41).

The narration of the celebration notes that the Lord spoke to Moses in the first month of the second year (9:1). But this presents a chronological problem, because the events of Num. 1–10 in general are said to take place in the *second* month of the second year after they had come out of Egypt (1:1; 10:11). However, God's reply to Moses in 9:11 says that those unclean through corpse contamination or on a journey can celebrate Passover on the *fourteenth* day of the *second* month. Reading between the lines, it appears that Israel or at least some people are celebrating Passover here during the second allowable time because of corpse contamination (Milgrom 1990: 67).

The presentation of the exceptional case concerning corpse contamination is the main focus of this episode. Numbers often supplements the Levitical laws with mention of corpse contamination (e.g., Num. 5:2; 6:6; 19:11–16). Given the logic concerning ritual purity, namely that the distinction between clean and unclean concerns respecting the God-given natural order that leads to life (→5:1–4), the human corpse is a fitting summative symbol for all that is unclean. A corpse's normal boundaries and systems, most obviously its skin, have broken down, and as a result all life is gone. Perhaps the author(s) of Numbers is simply adding these laws and concerns here rather than editing or adding material to Leviticus out of respect for earlier material. But this concern with corpses also finds resonance with the larger rebellion narrative. As a result of Israel's rebellion against the ways of God, God declares that Israel "shall suffer for your faithlessness, until the last of your dead bodies lies in the wilderness" (14:33).

At one level this Passover celebration simply records that Israel was obedient in celebrating Passover and also gives legal information about exceptional cases. However, it also points to the importance of this feast for the larger orientation of Israel. By remembering, Israel knows who it is and where it is going as a nation. It remembers that its identity is based on a specific and gracious act of redemption by God. Its identity as a people is not the result of a human revolution or a rationally constructed social contract—Israel is instead a people born in grace and called by God to be his firstborn. All the key symbols of Passover—blood of the lamb, unleavened bread, bitter herbs—point to a specific event: the exodus from Egypt, in which Israel was born as a people (→28:16–25).

Following the Cloud and Fire (9:15–23)

"On the day the tabernacle was set up, the cloud covered the tabernacle, the tent of the covenant; and from evening until morning it was over the tabernacle, having the appearance of fire" (9:15). After nearly a year at Mount Sinai, the reappearance of the fiery cloud in the narrative signals that God is ready to continue leading and guiding his people toward the promised land. The pillar of cloud and fire is first encountered right after Passover (Exod. 13:21–22) as a sign of God's presence, and it travels "in front of the people," "to lead them along the way." In 33:7–11 God's presence in the pillar of cloud becomes associated with the tent of meeting. But apparently due to Israel's sin with the golden calf, the tent at that point was placed "far off from the camp." But after the tabernacle was constructed, and it, the people, and Levites were consecrated, the pillar of cloud and fire once again rested above the tabernacle or filled it (40:34–38). Now in Num. 9, the pillar of cloud with "the appearance of fire" is mentioned again, showing that God is ready to lead the people on their journey.

While these verses signal that the next chapter in the journey of Israel is beginning, their placement in this part of Numbers also alludes to the second important pilgrimage festival in Israel's yearly calendar: Shavuot (Weeks). While the connection with Shavuot is not explicitly made in these verses, Israel being guided by God through the wilderness is arguably one of the historical events that provides the background to and is celebrated in this festival.

Shavuot is associated with God's providence in giving his people food and successful harvest on a yearly basis, and it also celebrates significant events of God's guidance of his people, especially God's covenants (→28:26–31). While the connection between these themes in this festival may have been coincidental, there is reason to see a closer connection. Namely, through and because of God's guidance and commands and the people's obedience, successful harvest and the prosperity of the people in the promised land come about. The liturgy recorded in

Deut. 26:1–11, probably associated with this festival,[37] celebrates the first harvest in Israel and recalls that "the LORD brought us out of Egypt with a mighty hand and an outstretched arm, with a terrifying display of power, and with signs and wonders; and he brought us into this place and gave us this land, a land flowing with milk and honey" (26:8–9). God not only told Moses that he had "come down to deliver them from the Egyptians," but also that he would also "bring them up out of that land to a good and broad land, a land flowing with milk and honey" (Exod. 3:8). Thus as Passover is associated with the initial delivery from Egypt, Shavuot is associated with God's power and guidance in bringing them into their present state of settled existence and plenty.[38]

This guidance of God is characterized in terms of command and obedience. There is a sevenfold repetition of the phrase "at the command of the LORD" (9:18 [twice], 20 [twice], 23 [three times]). Great detail is given to all the possible circumstances of Israel's camping and setting out—in all these circumstances, Israel obeyed God. This repetition and detail paint a clear picture of the right relationship between God and Israel: God commands and Israel listens and obeys, whatever the circumstances. Israel does obey God—at first. But it is precisely Israel's disobedience and rebellion against the commands of God that provides the dramatic engine and pathos of the middle part of the book.

Making Silver Trumpets (10:1–10)

The making of the two silver trumpets completes the preparations of Israel for the journey. This section describes both how the trumpets (*ḥăṣôṣĕrâ*) are to be made (10:2) and their principal uses: to summon the congregation (10:2) and the leaders (10:4), as a signal for breaking camp and setting out (10:2, 5–6), as Israel goes to war (10:9), and on certain festival days (10:10). Only the priests shall blow these trumpets (10:8).[39]

At the level of the historic narrative, mentioning the trumpets here naturally follows the mention of the fiery cloud in the previous verses. As the Lord commands the people to camp and set out through the fiery cloud, the priests of the

---

37. Rowley, *Worship in Ancient Israel*, 89; J. G. McConville, *Deuteronomy*, Apollos Old Testament Commentary 5 (Downers Grove, IL: InterVarsity, 2002), 377–80.

38. The liturgy emphasizes coming and being brought by YHWH; McConville, *Deuteronomy*, 378.

39. This is the crucial distinction between these silver trumpets and the shofar, horns made of animal horn. Shofar and trumpets often overlap, and throughout most of the Bible (outside the Priestly sources according to Milgrom 1990: 372–73) these two horns remain undistinguished; the term "shofar" is used for horns or trumpets in general, including the silver trumpets. In many circumstances, horn trumpets and silver trumpets would likely be used at the same time. Thus the key difference is not meaning or circumstance of use, but rather who is allowed to blow them. According to some rabbinic traditions, these silver trumpets were used only by Moses and hidden by him just before his death (Rashi on Num. 10:2; cf. Deut. 31:28; *Sifre Num.* 75). These instructions for the trumpets were then carried out using other kinds of horns.

Lord would respond, signaling the people to do so by the trumpets. The trumpets supply the details of how the Israelites would concretely follow the guidance of God through the wilderness.

On another level, the trumpets round out this section by alluding to the third of the three pilgrim feasts of Israel: Sukkot. By subtly pointing to this festival, the larger overview of the major aspects of Israel's worship life in 7:1–10:10, and more specifically these "holy times" in 9:1–10:10, is complete. At Mount Sinai, Israel is prepared and oriented for its spiritual journey to life in the promised land by its worship life and these major pilgrimage festivals.

The allusion here is rather straightforward: the first of three celebrations within the Festival of Sukkot is called the Day of Trumpets (later Rosh Hashanah, the Jewish New Year; →29:1–40). This section of Numbers is explicitly tied to various aspects of this celebration as developed in the Jewish tradition. The specific blasts of the trumpets outlined in 10:3–7 are duplicated in the festival as a call to the people to assemble. In addition, 10:10 is understood to structure the three main sections of the central prayer of the Rosh Hashanah service (Milgrom 1990: 75).

A major theme of this celebration is the judgment of Israel by God. The three parts of the Rosh Hashanah prayer focus on the kingship of God, his favorable and merciful remembrance of his creatures and their deeds, and his future gathering of the exiles and rebuilding of the temple. The overall movement of the day is that the trumpets sound, the people gather before God, God pronounces judgment, followed by the hope and prayer that God will finally bring his purposes to pass for Israel.

The theme of sounding trumpets is also strikingly found in the vision of John in Revelation. Seven angels blow seven trumpets (8:2–11:15). While the first six involve the "wrath" of God and the "judging of the dead" (11:18), at the seventh trumpet, we finally see the purposes of God coming to pass and the "mystery of God . . . fulfilled" (10:7)—a fulfillment that is announced with a triumphant statement: "The kingdom of the world has become the kingdom of our Lord and of his Messiah, and he will reign forever and ever" (11:15).

In Numbers the trumpets seem at first to serve merely a utilitarian purpose: the sound signals Israel to assemble before the tent of meeting or to set out in their march (10:3–7). But the trumpets gain more significance in their other uses. They are blown to signal God in battles against those who "oppress" (*ṣrr*) Israel, "so that [Israel] may be remembered before the LORD your God and be saved from [its] enemies" (10:9). They are calls or prayers to God to bring judgment on Israel's enemies. This indeed happens in the war against the Midianites (who "harassed" [*ṣrr*] Israel; 25:18), the only time the trumpets are specifically mentioned as being blown (31:6). They are also blown over the burnt offerings and shalom celebration sacrifices (10:10) as a call to God to come near. But this time, God will come near in order to be with Israel, to accept their burnt offerings and to be present in the *šĕlāmîm* feast, which is a foretaste of the final shalom prayed for in the Rosh Hashanah prayer and seen in John's vision.

The trumpets may have a final meaning within the larger narrative. They call God or announce that God has come to judge—but in the following narrative God's judgment takes an unexpected form. While at first there is confidence that God's presence will bring Israel victory over their enemies—as Moses's saying in 10:35 suggests: "Arise, O LORD, let your enemies be scattered"—the tone of narrative shifts dramatically in 11:1. As Israel moves into the wilderness, the most difficult enemy Israel faces is within itself. The trumpets do announce judgment, but instead of this judgment falling primarily on its enemies, it falls on Israel itself. In the central section of the book (10:11–25:18), it is the evil within Israel that must be done away with. The trumpets announce the coming judgment in the wilderness.

PART 2

THE LONG JOURNEY (10:11–25:18)

The Struggles of God and Israel in the Wilderness

"In the second year, in the second month, on the twentieth day of the month, the cloud lifted from over the tabernacle of the covenant" (10:11). By the lifting of the cloud, God signals the beginning of the journey of the Israelites away from Sinai to the promised land. It is an important and historic moment, the inauguration of a new phase in the life of Israel. They have been redeemed by God from the bitter slavery of Egypt. God has tenderly cared for them in their newborn vulnerability in the wilderness. They have been instructed and taught who they are to be as a people through their dramatic encounter with God on Sinai. There at the mountain, they entered into covenant with YHWH and through this became a "treasured possession" of God, "a priestly kingdom" (Exod. 19:5–6). Specifics of what this would mean for them are elaborated in the final parts of Exodus and in Leviticus. An "executive summary" of this covenantal strategic plan for Israel is given in Num. 1:1–10:10. In their next stage as a people, they need to follow God's guidance into the promised land and begin to put into practice those covenantal patterns. Their obedience to those precepts will make them prosper as a holy people and make them a light to the nations.

But as we know, Israel's journey through the wilderness toward implementing this glorious vision does not go well. T. S. Eliot's 1925 poem *The Hollow Men* may aptly be applied to Israel:

> Between the idea
> And the reality
> Between the motion
> And the act
> Falls the Shadow
> > *For Thine is the Kingdom*
>
> Between the conception
> And the creation
> Between the emotion
> And the response
> Falls the Shadow
> > *Life is very long*

The falling of shadow on the light of Israel is portrayed clearly and honestly in Numbers. Israel's vows of obedience to the covenantal vision at Mount Sinai (Exod. 24:7; cf. Deut. 27:15–26; Num. 5:22) quickly turn into the murmurings and complaints of the wilderness. While in this middle part of Numbers Israel battles with other nations, it becomes clear that the chief obstacles to the achievement of its vision and calling are not the surrounding nations but the shadows within. Because of this, the wilderness not only is a place of redemption, care, and covenant; it also becomes a place of testing and purgation, punishment, and forgiveness.

These chapters record the sevenfold rebellion and final apostasy of Israel in the wilderness. This rebellion narrative is a carefully structured piece of writing. The laws and other material that are placed in the context of this larger narrative contribute to the themes of the whole. This display of the sins of Israel and the response of God is not only of historical or literary interest, however. Read as Christian scripture, the rebellions of Israel have much to tell us about the constant struggle of God's people with sin and the ways that God works to overcome it.

4

A GOOD BEGINNING (10:11–36)

Images of Obedience, Blessing Others, and Confidence in God's Power

In the three opening sections of Israel's journey, all begins well. In 10:11–28 the companies of Israel set off "at the command of the LORD." The details of their marching order show that all is according to God's instruction, highlighting the obedience of Israel. In 10:29–32 the interaction between Moses and his father-in-law Hobab is an offer to extend the blessings of God given to Israel to other peoples: "Whatever good the LORD does for us, the same we will do for you," recalling the promise that other nations will be blessed through Israel (Gen. 12:1–3). Finally, in Num. 10:33–36 Moses's saying concerning the ark shows his and Israel's confidence that YHWH will guide and lead it to victory over all foes and enemies. These three sections together indicate how Israel's journey through the wilderness should have gone in its entirety.

Obedience of Israel to the Command of God (10:11–28)

Israel begins the journey toward the promised land in accordance with the directions and commands of the Lord. The two main features of this section (breaking camp and setting out) show in detail Israel's exact obedience. Israel breaks camp and begins its journey at the signal of God—the lifting of the cloud over the tabernacle (10:11). The phrase "at the command of the LORD" is used seven times in 9:18–23 to highlight the link between the cloud and the command of God. Israel, in response to "the command of the LORD" (10:13), obediently follows. The following verses give a detailed description of the order of the march (10:14–28), showing that Israel does indeed put into practice the directions of God given in 2:1–34 and 4:1–20.

The primary descriptor of the righteous response to God that is given here and echoed through much of scripture is obedience to "the command of the LORD." The Hebrew term for "obedience" stems from the verb "to hear." Obedience is a hearing that is receptive and active. Israel is to hear and obey God, as in the phrase "Hear, O Israel" (Deut. 6:4). Obedience to the word of God is at the core of Israelite religion and a cornerstone of its ethics, as Samuel later reminded Saul: "To obey is better than sacrifice, and to heed than the fat of rams" (1 Sam. 15:22; cf. Isa. 1:11–17; Hos. 6:6).

Israel's obedience to the Lord can and should be a model for Christians. Unquestioning obedience to authority can be quite dangerous, but Israel's righteous obedience is not simply a free-floating characteristic of those who love obeying authority as opposed to those who are more comfortable displaying a "Question Authority" bumper sticker. Israel's obedience is always obedience to the command of God. This qualifies our understanding of and enthusiasm for obedience in at least two ways.

First of all, given that the word of God always comes in mediated ways, we must temper our passion for obedience to the extent to which authorities speak the word of God. Given that in Num. 10:11, 13 the pillar of cloud and Moses mediated the word and will of God precisely and transparently, the immediate and unqualified obedience of Israel to those signals and commands is appropriate. Christians typically understand that God has put into place authorities and governments for our benefit and that they to a certain extent mediate the authority of God. Based on this reasoning Paul writes: "Let every person be subject to the governing authorities" (Rom. 13:1). However, given that the word and will of God is not always reliably mediated through these authorities, discernment is required for proper Christian obedience. Thus the words of Peter in Acts 5:29—"we must obey God rather than any human authority"—also express a proper Christian attitude. Christians have a responsibility to discern the extent to which church authorities, Christian tradition, governing authorities, our understanding of the internal witness of the Holy Spirit, and our interpretations of scriptural passages correspond to or mediate the word and will of God.

Second, enthusiasm for obedience should be qualified by asking, To what extent is obedience to God's word the goal of the Christian life? The answer depends on how one understands what obedience is. Obedience can be understood as merely obeying certain laws and prescribed behaviors. But the vision of who Israel is to be, seen in the images of the faithful wife and zealous Nazirite (→Num. 5–6), shows that God desires much more from Israel than outward obedience to law. As we move to the New Testament, the mystery of the calling of humanity in response to the word of God is shown to be much deeper than an outward obedience. In Jesus Christ the word of God becomes flesh (John 1:14). Thus obeying the word of God becomes discipleship to Christ enabled through the power of the Holy Spirit. Deeper still is the mystery that through the Holy Spirit, Christians come to participate in the life of Christ: "When Christ who is your life is revealed, then you also will be revealed with him in glory" (Col. 3:4). Obedience to Christ is ultimately an aspect of participation in the divine nature (2 Pet. 1:4). At this level Christian obedience is quite different from the lack of will and initiative of slaves who obey the commands of their master. It is rather the outward expression of friendship with and enjoyment of God.[1]

Interaction with Hobab of Midian (10:29–32)

The interaction between Moses and his father-in-law Hobab (called Jethro and perhaps Reuel in Exod. 2:16–18; 3:1; 18:1–27) might be interpreted in several ways (Milgrom 1990: 78–79). Moses seems to be asking Hobab to be their guide through the wilderness: "Do not leave us, for you know where we should camp in the wilderness, and you will serve as eyes for us" (Num. 10:31). This raises a theological problem, for the previous section indicates that YHWH, through the mediation of the cloud, will be their guide. Perhaps Moses is hedging his bets by getting his trusty father-in-law to come along just in case something goes wrong with the cloud. While possible, the overall positive tone of this section and further positive references to Hobab and his descendents, the Kenites, do not fit well with this interpretation.

One solution to this problem is that Numbers preserves two narrative lines or traditions: one that highlights the action of God, and one that highlights the human means by which God acts (Milgrom 1990: 79). Such "double agency" is seen preeminently in the story of Joseph, where the same outcome is attributed by Joseph to both human agents and the agency of God: "Do not be distressed, or angry with yourselves, because you sold me here; for God sent me before you to preserve life. . . . Even though you intended to do harm to me, God intended it for good, in order to preserve a numerous people" (Gen. 45:5; 50:20). While double agency is an important theological principle,[2] the contrast here is not between divine agency and creaturely agency, but rather two different types of creaturely agency—God's guidance mediated through the cloud or through Hobab. The analogy to Joseph is tenuous at best and creates tension in the text.

1. Aquinas understands charity to be "friendship with God" and as the highest virtue of human life (*Summa theologica* II-II Q23.3). The Westminster Shorter Catechism says: "Man's chief end is to glorify God, and to enjoy him forever" (Q1). Obedience per se is not the highest good, but concomitant with it.

2. Austin Marsden Farrer, *Faith and Speculation: An Essay in Philosophical Theology*, Deems Lectures 1964 (New York: New York University Press, 1967).

Another possibility is to understand that Moses is not primarily asking for guidance but is offering a religious alliance or pact of mutual aid and nonaggression between Moses's people and Hobab's. Moses's original offer (10:29) is to have Hobab join in on the "good" that YHWH promised to Israel; Moses's last statement also concerns sharing in the good (10:32). This possibility is strengthened by translating the Hebrew perfect verb *yāda'tā* (usually "you know") as "you have known." Many ancient translations understood the text this way (Milgrom 1990: 79), which means that Moses is simply pointing out that this offer is partly in recognition of the good that Hobab had previously done for Israel (de Vaulx 1972: 146).

Given this, the text is about Moses's offer to share the good with Hobab. This section highlights the good beginning of Israel's journey to the promised land, and such a mutual sharing of good might be seen as an ideal type of the interactions Israel should have with its neighbors. While the text is silent about Hobab's final response, Hobab's people—the Kenites (probably a subset of the Midianites)—are given favorable treatment by Israel over the years (Num. 24:21; Judg. 1:16; 4:11; 1 Sam. 15:6). Several medieval commentators took this episode as a symbolic appeal to other nations to benefit from God's blessing of Israel (de Vaulx 1972: 145). This mutual benefit does happen for the Kenites, but not in later episodes with Edom (Num. 20:14–21), King Sihon and the Amorites (21:21–32), and King Og (21:33–35). Just as Israel falls short of obedience, so too the ideal of the nations benefiting from the blessing of Israel is not fully realized in Numbers or in Israel's later history.

The Ark and Confidence in God's Victory (10:33–36)

The sayings that Moses would proclaim when the ark set out and came to rest in Israel's journeys appear to be part of an ancient song with strong parallels to Ps. 68 and Ps. 132 (Milgrom 1990: 81).

Especially intriguing are the parallels of Num. 10:36 and Ps. 68:17, which explicitly mention the journey of Israel from Sinai to Zion: "With mighty chariotry, twice ten thousand, thousands upon thousands, the Lord came from Sinai into the holy place." Psalm 68:1 and Num. 10:35 are also very similar, and the issue of finding a resting place is mentioned in both Num. 10:33 and Ps. 68:10, 16. The result of this powerful and victorious movement of God is that all the nations of the earth, even those that rebel against God (68:18), will finally bring gifts to and worship him (68:32). This journey to Zion is likened to the pilgrimage feasts of Israel, where the tribes of Israel come in a liturgical procession to the holy hill of Jerusalem (68:24–27).

The words of Moses in Num. 10:35, "Arise, O Lord," are poetic expressions of confidence in God's presence. God will guide and protect Israel and defeat all his foes. If the spirit of Ps. 68 also informs Moses's words, the goal is not simply the defeat of other nations and their subservience to Israel, but that the kingdoms of earth worship God. These songs of confidence in God, while associated with the ark, make clear that the ark is not seen as a kind of Greek palladium or magical device that assures the victory of Israel; instead it is a symbol of the presence of God.

In the later narratives, Israel's confidence in God falters in two different ways. In Num. 13:30–14:10 the people, with the exception of Joshua and Caleb, are fearful of the inhabitants of the promised land. Such fear is clearly lack of faith in the power of God to scatter his enemies. And in 14:44 the presumption and misplaced confidence of the Israelites to defeat their foes without the ark of God and Moses led to their downfall in a different way. In contrast to these negative examples, these verses exemplify a proper confidence in God's power and leadership.

These three passages combine to create a picture of the proper course that Israel takes at the beginning of its journey—one that lasts for only three days.

5

THE SEVENFOLD TESTING
OF UNFAITHFUL ISRAEL
(11:1–21:35)

While Israel begins its journey well—obedient to God, willing to share the good that God will give, and confident in the Lord's leadership and power—the journey quickly turns sour. Like Abraham (Gen. 22:4), Israel journeys three days into the wilderness (Num. 10:33); but unlike Abraham it fails the test of faithfulness. In seven separate episodes, the unfaithfulness and wickedness of Israel is revealed. As a result of sin, God delays Israel's entrance into the promised land until forty years is completed (14:33–35). These forty years can rightly be characterized as punishment for Israel's wickedness, and yet punishment is not the only purpose: the time in the wilderness is also intended to purge Israel of sinfulness. This vision of sanctification is at least partially realized (→21:4–9). However, the subsequent apostasy at Peor (25:1–18) shows that the older generation has not grown much since the golden calf incident at Mount Sinai (Exod. 32); instead, Israel's sanctification as a people occurs primarily through the death of the old generation and the rise of the new.

While "unfaithfulness" is an encompassing reference to Israel's sin and failure, the poor performance of Israel in the wilderness is described in a variety of ways. YHWH comments on his people's sinfulness in the central rebellion of Israel in Num. 13–14. The people have "despised" YHWH (14:11, 23) and the promised land (14:31), "refused to believe in" YHWH (14:11), "tested" YHWH (14:22), "not obeyed [YHWH's] voice" (14:22), "complained against" YHWH (14:29,

36), shown "faithlessness" (14:33; cf. Exod. 34:16–17; Num. 15:39), and "continue to transgress the command of the LORD" (14:41). These different descriptions involve both the people's disposition toward YHWH and their related actions. They suggest that Israel's most fundamental sin is distrust in and rejection of YHWH and his ways. The opposite is seen in Caleb, who is said to have "followed [YHWH] wholeheartedly" (14:24).

Later descriptions are similar. In Num. 32 Israel has "not unreservedly followed" YHWH (32:11; cf. 1 Kgs. 11:4, 6) and thus has "done evil" (Num. 32:13). Moses warns the Gadites and Reubenites not to "turn away from following him" (32:15) as their fathers did. In Deuteronomy they are said to have "no trust" (Deut. 1:32) and "no faithfulness" (32:20; cf. Isa. 26:2). Psalm 95 similarly describes that generation as a people "whose hearts go astray" and that "do not regard my ways" (95:10) and whose hearts have been hardened so that they do not listen to God's voice (95:7–8). These summative descriptions show Israel's sin is a combination of disposition and action: a lack of faith and trust in God (a disposition) leading to their hearts going astray (a disposition) as seen in their concrete rebellions against the ways and voice of God (their actions).

While summative descriptions are helpful, part of the power of this section is that the sinfulness of Israel is seen in its variety rather than just pointed to generally. The carefully crafted chiastic structure puts the episodes of Israel's unfaithfulness in a specific order that creates a miniature breviary of sin:[1]

Passage	People's Complaint	Moses's Action	YHWH's Action
A (11:1–3)	misfortunes	intercedes	sends fire
B (11:4–34)	food	lacks faith	gives food (plague)
C (11:35–12:16)	leadership (Moses)	intercedes	sends leprosy
D (13:1–14:45)	promised land	intercedes	delays forty years
C′ (16:1–17:11)	leadership (Moses and Aaron)	intercedes (with Aaron)	sends earthquake and plague
B′ (20:2–13)	water	lacks faith (with Aaron)	gives water (punishment)
A′ (21:4–9)	various misfortunes	intercedes	sends fiery serpents

Given that chiasms generally stress the central element, the sins of Israel move up a kind of "ladder of being" from general circumstances (complaints about outward circumstances in A and A′), to bodily desires (complaints about food and body in B and B′), to interpersonal relationships (complaints about leadership and social problems in C and C′), to culminate in issues of faith and trust in

1. Pope Gregory I's well-known list of the seven deadly sins performs a similar function; see Aquinas, *Summa theologica* I-II Q72. For contemporary discussions of sin, see Cornelius Plantinga Jr., *Not the Way It's Supposed to Be: A Breviary of Sin* (Grand Rapids: Eerdmans, 1995); and Robert W. Jenson, *Systematic Theology* (New York: Oxford University Press, 1999), 2.133–53.

God (rejection of God's plan for bringing them to the promised land in D)—a refusal that YHWH interprets as despising of and unbelief in him (14:11). The temptations in B-C-D also bear some analogy to the temptations that Jesus Christ resists and overcomes (Matt. 4:1–11; Luke 4:1–13).[2]

While each historic episode contains many specific points of interest, they might also figure the struggles of God's people in many times and places. Because of this, they can be placed in conversation with other descriptions of sin throughout the Bible and Christian theology. The careful structuring of these episodes suggests that the author was communicating that these continue to be common or "besetting" sins of God's people.

Various laws and subnarratives are introduced after the last four rebellions (15:1–41; 17:12–20:1; 20:14–21:3; and 21:10–35). Each of these sections responds in different ways to the themes and problems of the previous rebellion. The relationship of these laws and narratives to the larger sequence of rebellions will partially guide their interpretation.

Rebellion 1: The Problem of Evil and Misfortune (11:1–3)

The first rebellion, like the final one (21:4–9), is recounted quite briefly and succinctly. Its compact form makes it a good introduction to the rebellions that follow, in that it quickly outlines the dynamic between God and Israel that happens repeatedly throughout the narrative. It consists of four main parts: sin of the people, punishment by God, prayer to God, and salvation. These four movements are stereotypical for the rebellions to follow and can also be seen in many narratives in scripture. This pattern is especially clear in the stories of the judges (e.g., Othniel in Judg. 3:7–11; de Vaulx 1972: 151). Like other incidents in Numbers, the event is remembered by naming the place where it happened after the episode—here Taberah ("burning").

The offense of Israel is "complaining in the hearing of the LORD about their misfortunes" (11:1). The Hebrew word *ra'* ("misfortunes") is the typical word for "evil, bad." While the phrase might be translated "the people took to complaining *bitterly*" (Milgrom 1990: 82; Levine 1993: 320; but "misfortune" in Gray 1903: 99; Ashley 1993: 201; Budd 1984: 120), rendering the word as an adverb, the NRSV seems to fit better with the general, stereotypical format of the few verses and also parallels the more general complaints of the seventh rebellion about the misfortunes or bad things they had encountered.

2. Matthew and Luke record the same temptations, but the second and third are reversed. In Matthew the order bread-temple-nations could be seen as movement from sins concerning bodily needs, to spiritual presumption in order to gain social standing, to rejection of God's way of being the people of God and becoming instead like the nations—corresponding to the order B-C-D in Numbers. Luke's ordering might also correspond to Numbers by giving a different emphasis to the second (personal power over others) and third (tempting God) temptations.

This complaint, as well as the later complaints about water (20:2–13) and food (11:4–34), is similar to the complaints Israel made on the way to Mount Sinai (water in Exod. 15:22–26 and 17:1–7; food in Exod. 16), but now the results are quite different. Before they reached Sinai, God simply sends water and food in response to their complaints. But in the incidents related in Numbers, God also punishes the people.

Why has God's response changed so dramatically? One possibility is that the complaints and murmurings have gotten worse. Or perhaps God is simply loosing his patience. These complaints are occurring on the other side of the golden calf incident (Exod. 32), a rejection of YHWH that almost led to God's rejection of them. They are certainly testing the patience of God through their continued complaining.

But that they are on the other side of Mount Sinai may be the central reason for this different reaction of God to their complaints. They have received a dramatic revelation of God's power and glory on Mount Sinai and have entered into a covenant relationship with YHWH. It makes sense that God expects better faithfulness and dedication from them. While before Sinai they were like a "newly adopted child" who is tenderly taken care of, they now have come to a position of greater responsibility (Olson 1996: 63). While evil things happening to God's people is bad in one sense, oftentimes one must go through difficult circumstances in order to reach a good goal. "There are no gains without pains," as Benjamin Franklin said in his 1758 *Way to Wealth*. A particular form of this general lesson for God's chosen people is repeated throughout scripture. God's people, in order to become holy, must sometimes go through difficulties of various kinds and must develop patience and longsuffering. The writer of Hebrews puts it this way: "Endure trials for the sake of discipline. God is treating you as children; for what child is there whom a parent does not discipline?" (Heb. 12:7). This is a principal lesson of the wilderness, but one that Israel is resisting from the outset.

But does patient endurance mean not complaining or lamenting to God about one's troubles? The question is pressed home most forcefully by considering the similarities and contrasts between Israel's complaints in this episode and Christ's complaint on the cross. Christ overcomes the temptations that beset Israel, yet he also complains to God: "My God, my God, why have you forsaken me?" What is the difference between the bitter complaint of Christ and the bitter complaints of the Israelites in Num. 11:1–3? Certainly God viewed them quite differently. He vindicates the righteousness of Christ by raising Christ from the dead, and yet he sends fire on the Israelites. While both were complaints to God about his treatment of them, the tremendous difference between them emerged from very different states of heart in Israel and Christ. The complaint of Christ came from a heart paradigmatic of human willingness to follow God; Christ was on the cross in part because of his willingness to become "obedient to the point of death" (Phil. 2:8) and because of his desire to have his will conformed to that of God's (Matt.

26:39). Righteous lament or complaint can still come from such a character. The will of Israel on the other hand is conformed to its own comforts; in response to real but less serious suffering on the way to the promised land, it is ready to reject God at the first instance where God's will seemed to involve discomfort. This lack of faithfulness, patience, or longsuffering on Israel's part is what its complaining represents. It is this that draws forth God's wrath.[3]

Put another way, Israel had its own particular "problem of evil."[4] It apparently thought that following after God should result in God not allowing difficulties or misfortunes to come its way. When they came, Israel was ready to go back to Egypt and its gods, as becomes more apparent in the rebellions to come.

Rebellion 2: Meat and the Seventy Elders (11:4–34)

The second episode is a double rebellion—both the people and their leader fall short. The people, at least "the rabble among them," have "a strong craving" for meat rather than just the manna God is providing for them.[5] As a result they complain and weep and compare their lot with God in the wilderness to their life in Egypt, where they had fish, cucumbers, melons, leeks, onions, and garlic (11:5). Intertwined with this story of the people's rebellion is Moses's complaint that God has given him too great a burden (11:10–15); Moses doubts that all these people can be properly fed (11:22–23). God responds first to Moses's problem (11:16–20) and then to the people's (11:31–34).

These incidents are similar to events recorded in Exodus. There, the people complain about their lack of food, a legitimate need, and God responds by sending them manna and quail (Exod. 16). In addition, after Jethro, Moses's father-in-law, sees the many responsibilities that Moses has, he tells Moses that "the task is too heavy for you" (18:18). As a result, Moses sets up a system of additional officers

---

3. Calvin makes a similar point about the wills and emotions that motivate our complaints and requests in prayer: "For even though he bids us pour out our hearts before him [Ps. 62:8; cf. Ps. 145:19], he still does not indiscriminately slacken the reins to stupid and wicked emotions; and while he promises that he will act according to the will of the godly, his gentleness does not go so far that he yields to their willfulness. Yet in both, men commonly sin gravely; for many rashly, shamelessly, and irreverently dare importune God with their improprieties and impudently present before his throne whatever in dreams has struck their fancy" (1960: §3.20.5). One must distinguish between complaints about evils and misfortunes that come one's way while seeking to humbly follow God and complaints about the ways, plans, and leadership of God offered up in a prideful, unconcerned, and challenging spirit. See Don Postema, *Space for God: The Study and Practice of Prayer and Spirituality* (Grand Rapids: Bible Way, 1983), 131–49.

4. The modern problem of evil is the apparent philosophical problem of how God can be all good and all powerful and yet still allow evil to exist. Israel's problem is more specific: "Should I still follow this God who allows evil and misfortune to come my way?"

5. The "rabble" or "riffraff" are the "mixed crowd" that also went out from Egypt with the people of Israel (Exod. 12:38), a detail that may show that the rebellion against God starts on the edges of the camp and moves inward into the heart of the people; Milgrom 1990: 83; Olson 1996: 64.

---

who will help judge the people (18:13–27). Here in Numbers, we encounter similar stories, but they have a much more negative tone to them. There are several options for interpreting what these similar stories might mean in terms of the composition history of the text.[6] However, in the text as we have it, the change in tone is best understood as an intentional highlighting of developments in the relationship between YHWH and Israel, especially in light of Israel's new status as a covenant partner after its time on Mount Sinai.

These incidents also have parallels to the sixth rebellion (20:2–13), which involves a similar double problem: the people desire water and so want to go back to Egypt, and Moses and Aaron act in such a way that shows their lack of "trust" (20:12) in YHWH. Given this intentional pairing, the two episodes can help interpret each other.

This passage does not comment on what precisely Israel's sin was, what was wrong with their craving and weeping. However, Deut. 8:3 is explicit: "He [YHWH] humbled you by letting you hunger, then by feeding you with manna, with which neither you nor your ancestors were acquainted, in order to make you understand that one does not live by bread alone, but by every word that comes from the mouth of the LORD." The phrase "one does not live by bread alone" means that humanity—and specifically Israel—is called to something higher than simply meeting their basic needs. The phrase "every word" refers to "this entire commandment that I command you today" (8:1)—it is the covenantal way that leads to life. The sin of Israel is that they worry too much about their daily bread. Their worry and lack of trust in God's providence causes them to think fondly of Egypt, and eventually they begin making plans to abandon God's plan and elect a leader who will take them back (Num. 14:4). They allow a legitimate need and desire, the desire for good and tasty food, to become a craving that gets in the way of their calling as a people. Their faithfulness to God's purposes is choked by their desire for material and bodily comfort, a desire that becomes a roadblock in their journey to the fullness of the life God intends for them.

Using the terminology of virtue theory, the people of Israel lack temperance, which is the virtue of being able to say no to the desires of one's body—whether

---

6. The older scholarly consensus was that an original single tradition, most likely positive, about Israel's wilderness experiences highlighted God's care and providence for Israel, but later writers doubled these stories and reworked them to highlight Israel's sin and God's punishment and forgiveness in order to serve theological purposes of their own time (e.g., George W. Coats, *Rebellion in the Wilderness: The Murmuring Motif in the Wilderness Traditions of the Old Testament* [Nashville: Abingdon, 1968], 16–17). More persuasive are arguments that the earliest traditions had both negative and positive elements and that later writers and prophets simply emphasized different aspects of this originally complex story given the issues they confronted in their own contexts: "There is not sufficient evidence to suggest that an election tradition with just a positive interpretation of the wilderness ever existed by itself"; "the negative interpretation of Israel in the wilderness was equally part of the oldest tradition and not a later transformation of an earlier stage of the tradition which was completely positive in character" (Brevard S. Childs, *The Book of Exodus*, Old Testament Library [Philadelphia: Westminster, 1974], 263, 259).

good or bad—insofar as they get in the way of the pursuit of higher goods (the classic Christian exposition is Aquinas *Summa theologica* I-II Q61.2–3).

This specific sin is one aspect of their lack of faith in God and lack of trust in God's power to sustain them. In referring back to this particular incident, Ps. 78 says that the anger of God "mounted against Israel, because they had no faith in God, and did not trust his saving power," and "did not believe in his wonders." The psalm says that "their heart was not steadfast toward him; they were not true to his covenant" (78:21–22, 32, 37). If they had more faith in God and faith that God would soon lead them to the promised land, they might have been able to stave off or be content to delay the gratification of their cravings. In Numbers, the stress is on the specific sin of inordinate bodily cravings that made the people falter in their dedication to God and his purposes. That it involves or leads to a rejection of God is clear in Num. 11:20: "You have rejected the LORD."

God's punishment of Israel fits this understanding of their crime. In response to their untempered desire, God sends them so many quails it makes them sick, along with a plague that itself seems related to the great quantity of quail.[7] The Septuagint renders the Hebrew word "loathsome" in 11:20 as "cholera," a disease that results in vomiting and nausea (Milgrom 1990: 88, 92). In the earlier episode, God sends a plentiful amount of quail and manna; here God sends them so much it becomes their punishment.

That focusing on lower bodily goods can get in the way of God's higher purposes for us is commented on by Jesus in the Sermon on the Mount. "Strive first for the kingdom of God . . . , and all these things will be given to you as well" (Matt. 6:33) is precisely the lesson Israel needed to learn in the wilderness.

Jesus himself overcomes a similar temptation in the Gospels, when the tempter comes to him and tempts him to turn stones into bread. Jesus refuses and replies: "One does not live by bread alone, but by every word that comes from the mouth of God" (Matt. 4:3–4; Luke 4:3–4). By citing Deut. 8:3 Jesus indicates he is resisting the temptation that Israel failed to resist, and he shows that he would not lead the people by pandering to their lower needs. Yet later on in the Gospels he *does* miraculously provide bread for the people. One way to make sense of this apparent tension is to understand that in his later actions, he takes on the role of YHWH or YHWH's representative and provides their "daily bread." Thus, it is not the material goods and well-being per se that is the earlier temptation, but rather the prioritizing of this over the higher goods and vocations of Israel. Jesus's response to the tempter describes this very principle.

Moses's temptation and sin are different from those of the people: whereas the sin of the people falls into the general category of intemperance, a wrong ordering of the passions, Moses falls short in his leadership of the people in a different way.

7. Rabbinic interpreters are divided as to whether the plague is strictly supernaturally caused or related to the quail.

As the focus of the story turns from the people to Moses, it develops somewhat surprisingly. Moses is "displeased" in response to the weeping of the people: "Then the LORD became very angry, *and* Moses was displeased" (Num. 11:10). Usually Moses displays more concern for the people. He often steps "in the gap" between God and the murmuring people and intercedes for them. Here Moses fails to intercede and rather adds his complaint to that of the people. Furthermore, one finds out that his displeasure or complaint is not the same as the Lord's. While God's displeasure is with the people, Moses is displeased with God. He complains that God's expectation of him to care for and feed the people is too much. It is possible that Moses lacks fortitude, among other things. Fortitude is the virtue that strengthens the soul to carry on toward what is good in spite of danger, tiredness, and other passions telling one to stop and give up (Aquinas, *Summa theologica* I-II Q61.3). While Moses's longwinded complaint covers several issues (11:11–15), the solution that God brings—the sharing of the burden of leadership among the seventy elders—puts the focus on his complaint about "the burden of all this people" (11:11). Even though he had the spirit of God, for whatever reason— natural human limitations, lack of trust in God, lack of fortitude—Moses was buckling under the burden of leadership.

The passage does not suggest that Moses is culpable for needing to share the burden of leadership with others, however. The end result of sharing the spirit with the elders is a good thing, for God says the elders will "bear the burden of the people along with you" (11:17). Moses's limitation is not necessarily the problem, as can be seen by comparing this episode to the one with Jethro in Exod. 18:13–26.

The problem is that his own limitation leads him to question not only his own strength but also God's: "Where am I to get meat to give to all this people?" (Num. 11:13); "are there enough fish in the sea to catch for them?" (11:22–23). He lacks faith in God's power and providence. The quail ad nauseam is an answer to both the craving of the people and Moses's lack of faith.

Christ's ministry fulfills the qualities of leadership that Moses lacks—concern and love for his people, sufficient fortitude, and faith in God. Christ calls himself the good shepherd, who loves and cares for those who follow him, even to the point of laying down his life for them (John 10:1–18), in contrast to the shepherds of Israel during his own day. Instead of needing to unload his own burdens, Christ says: "Come to me, all you that are weary and are carrying heavy burdens, and I will give you rest" (Matt. 11:28). Christ also displays the providence of God in the face of the lack of understanding and faith of those appointed as leaders. His disciples, faced with hungry multitudes, ask, "How can one feed these people with bread here in the desert?" (Mark 8:4). Jesus himself provides more than enough, using the bread and fish at hand. While Christ perfectly fulfills these roles, those who lead the church are also called to be like him and increase in love, fortitude (Heb. 12:12), and faith. "Do you love me? . . . Feed my sheep," Christ tells Peter and those who are called to lead the people of God (John 21:15–17).

The division of the spirit on Moses among the seventy elders is a final detail of theological import. In response to Moses's need for help, God takes "some of the spirit that was on him and put it on the seventy elders" (Num. 11:25). In light of 11:29, this spirit is not Moses's spirit per se, but rather the spirit of God. While God's spirit is in all of creation, sustaining it and providing life and power, it works in different ways and to different extents. In the Pentateuch, God's spirit is closely tied with the idea of anointing, by which certain people are specially endowed for special service. Like the flame on the burning bush or the flame of the menorah, God's spirit rests on or dwells within Moses.[8] And as a candle's flame may light other wicks, the seventy others are "lit" by God through Moses. This complex image shows that this distribution of the spirit comes from God directly, but it does not override or ignore the institutional framework and authority of Moses. The elders are inspired by God, but are also subject in part to the authority of Moses.

The pouring out of the spirit on Eldad and Medad, the two who remained in the camp,[9] shows that the regular process of transmission also allows for the working of the spirit outside regular institutional frameworks. Joshua's response is to stop this unauthorized spreading of the spirit, but Moses's response is exemplary: "Are you jealous for my sake? Would that all the LORD's people were prophets, and that the LORD would put his spirit on them!" (11:29).[10] Moses is not afraid to share his leadership and is even open to works of God outside his control. It is quite fitting that Moses is recorded as being "very humble, more so than anyone else on the face of the earth" (12:3) in the following episode.

A similar balance between honoring the spirit's regular movement and being open to the work of the spirit outside standard channels is found in the Gospels. The orderly passing on of the spirit is exemplified in Jesus's commissioning of the seventy in Luke 10:1–17, where his disciples are given power so that "even the demons submit" to them. The spirit and spiritual power and authority is then passed to subsequent leaders within the church through the laying on of hands at ordination and also to all of God's people through baptism.[11] But an instance

8. Combating an interpretation of this passage that sees the spirit here as coming from Moses and as a thing that can be divided into parts, like pieces of a pie, Origen 1996–2001: 1.124 writes that this is the Holy Spirit, which is like a lamp or flame that lights those around it so that they also become sources or hosts of the spirit.

9. Whether Eldad and Medad were part of or in addition to the seventy is unclear. Manuscripts of Luke 10:1–17 are evenly divided as to whether the disciples numbered seventy or seventy-two, reflecting the uncertainty of whether Eldad and Medad should also be counted; J. H. Crehan, "Theology and Rite, A.D. 200–400," in *The Study of the Liturgy*, ed. Cheslyn Jones, Geoffrey Wainwright, and Edward Yarnold (London: SPCK, 1978), 306–7. See Milgrom 1990: 90 for various ways this is understood in rabbinic literature.

10. Moses's hope for a more general outpouring of the spirit on all of God's people—a hope foreseen by the prophets (Joel 2:28–29)—begins to come to fruition at Pentecost (Acts 2:1–21).

11. See Crehan, "Theology and Rite," 306–7. The figure of these elders influenced discussions about the relationship of bishops to presbyters. The thinking was that as Moses was to the seventy,

of the spirit's work outside regular means is also recorded when the disciples report that they "saw someone casting out demons in your name." Like Joshua, they were suspicious of someone who was not part of their group, but Jesus, like Moses, told them not to stop this activity (9:49–50).

Throughout scripture and Christian history, while the spirit and the word of God are mediated through the regular means of God's grace for his people, most typically in the various ministries of word and sacrament, it is also common for special works of God to come from the margins. The lives of many prophets, Christ's being born in a manger and coming from Nazareth, the ministry of Paul the zealous persecutor of the church turned apostle to the Gentiles, and various reform movements in the church—all bear witness to this. Honoring regular institutional patterns while being open to the spirit working and speaking in unexpected places continues to be a difficult task for the church, one that requires humility and discernment.

Rebellion 3: Jealousy, Presumption, and Friendship with God (11:35–12:16)

In the third rebellion, Israel's unfaithfulness is not simply located at the fringes of the people, "the rabble," but it also infects two central leaders, Miriam and Aaron. The chiastic structure of the rebellions leads us to expect the third one to be similar to the fifth one, and indeed it is. Both episodes center on the sin of the leaders of the people, their jealousy of other leaders, and their presumption before God. Compared with the second and sixth rebellions, which involve food and drink, the locus of this sin moves inward and upward. It moves inward to the central leadership of the people from the fringes and upward into the higher parts of the human. The sins in this episode involve Aaron's and Miriam's identity, worth, and desire for status.

Miriam and Aaron, the protagonists of this rebellion, are typically seen as exemplary leaders of Israel, though the faults of each are also recorded. Aaron, the elder brother of Moses and from the tribe of Levi (Exod. 6:20; 7:7), was chosen by God at the very beginning of Israel's delivery from Egypt to be the mouthpiece of Moses (4:14–16). He accompanied Moses throughout the confrontation with Pharaoh and the exodus from Egypt. Aaron was appointed as high priest of Israel, and his descendents continue the priestly line (Num. 3:38). Aaron is unfortunately known for several major sins: making the golden calf (Exod. 32), rebelling (here), and a final mistake (Num. 20:2–13). His death, recorded in 20:22–29, is a key marker of the death of the exodus generation of Israel, the generation not allowed to enter the promised land.

---

so are the twelve to the seventy in Luke, and so are bishops to presbyters in the church—they all have the same spirit, but Moses/the twelve/bishops also have been given a *principalis Spiritus*, often understood as the power to command with authority (Hippolytus, *Apostolic Tradition* 3.3).

Miriam, sister to Aaron and Moses, is also an important leader within Israel. She is remembered alongside Moses and Aaron in Mic. 6:4 as part of the leadership God sent to bring Israel out of Egypt. Traditionally she is identified as the sister of Moses who watched over Moses's papyrus basket as it is rescued by Pharaoh's daughter. Then in an act of great bravery, Miriam convinces her to use Moses's mother as a nurse for Moses (Exod. 2:5–9). She is also remembered as a prophet and a musician, singing the song of victory after Israel crosses the Red Sea (15:20–21). Her death is recorded in Num. 20:1. Remarkably for a patriarchal society, her leadership and importance are clearly marked, suggesting her exceptional character and activity. Her recognition is also part of the great attention paid to women and their roles in Numbers, as seen in the later laws concerning women (esp. 27:1–11; 36:1–12). That the sins as well as the accomplishments of these important leaders within Israel are so candidly treated is a hallmark of scripture; there are no illusions about the perfection of Israel's leaders.

In this episode, the interpersonal dynamics between the people and between Israel and God are complex. But even so, one can readily see that there are two basic parts of Miriam and Aaron's sin: their jealousy of Moses and their presumption about their own status before God.

At first, their complaint against Moses is "because of the Cushite woman whom he had married" (12:1). This phrase is ambiguous: was it something the Cushite woman did, or simply because Moses had married a Cushite? Some interpreters suggest that Miriam and Aaron are upset because Moses married someone other than Zipporah (Levine 1993: 328). If, however, Cush is a region or subgroup within Midian (i.e., if "Cush" and "Cushan" in Hab. 3:7 refer to the same place), then perhaps this woman is Zipporah (de Vaulx 1972: 159). Perhaps, Miriam and Aaron feel their own power threatened by her influence over Moses (Olson 1996: 71). The traditional interpretation (found in the Septuagint) understands that they are upset because Moses married someone from Cush, a region in the Sudan or Nubia, perhaps even Ethiopia. If so, then this woman cannot be Zipporah, who is a Midianite. Since the people of that area have dark skin (Jer. 13:23), some suggest that Miriam and Aaron were upset because of her race. Even though modern racism simply did not exist at that time (Milgrom 1990: 93; Sakenfeld 1995: 80–81), the emphasis on her as a Cushite might suggest that her ethnicity (rather than race) is at issue.

If such prejudice against an ethnic outsider underlies their complaint, the way Miriam is publicly shamed and pushed to the outside is poetic justice. She is marked by leprosy and put outside the camp for seven days, temporarily becoming an outsider. God's rejection of their complaint suggests that he accepts Moses's marriage to the Cushite. At the very least, the marriage of Moses to an ethnic outsider or foreigner is not explicitly mentioned as a problem by God. But whatever the background to 12:1, their primary complaint and ultimately their sin are tied to their questions in 12:2: "Has the LORD spoken only through Moses? Has he not spoken through us also?"

The implied answers to these questions are technically correct—God has spoken through people other than Moses, including Aaron and Miriam—but these questions challenge Moses's unique status and authority. Such a challenge is understandable in light of the spirit that had rested on Moses being taken and distributed among the seventy elders (11:25). Miriam was also called a prophet, and part of Aaron's role as high priest was to consult the Urim and Thummim—which was a way God spoke to the people through Aaron. All these might call into question Moses's unique status as prophet; combined with the problem of the Cushite woman, they provide an opportunity for Miriam and Aaron to "speak against Moses"—a phrase that suggests "rebellion or advocacy of the same" (Levine 1993: 328).

At the interpersonal level, Miriam and Aaron are jealous of Moses's status within Israel and before God. They apparently want to use their presumed status before God in order to increase their standing among the Israelites. This desire for position, the desire to be on the inside or at the top, is at the root of much conflict within communities and groups of people throughout human history. While this particular jealous desire is an instance of pride, a sin often associated with original sin in at least the West, C. S. Lewis's phrase "the quest for the inner ring" does an even better job of getting to the heart of the matter in the case of Miriam and Aaron.

In his memorable essay "The Inner Ring," Lewis makes the claim that the desire to be on the inside of certain groups or "rings" is "one of the great mainsprings of human action."[12] The desire to experience the "secret intimacy" of those on the inside often looks like pride or ambition, but it does not necessarily coincide with higher status or power. A standard feature of human society, the existence of social systems or hierarchies is not necessarily a bad thing. However, the desire to penetrate them seldom leads to good action and often turns an otherwise good person into a "scoundrel."[13] Lewis's crucial insight is that the *desire* to have the status and perquisites that a certain place in a group offers (i.e., its external goods) is different from and often in tension with the *desires* that are proper to that position (i.e., its internal goods and goals).

Seen in relation to Israel's history, the desire to be inside and the (seldom stated) delight at others being outside are attitudes that Israel experiences and that color its understanding of what it means to be a chosen people. Israel is chosen to be a peculiar people, and in order to maintain its identity and purity, certain boundaries are absolutely necessary. But the desire to maintain and enforce those boundaries for the wrong reasons—to exclude others and to keep the gifts of God for itself—is a constant and subtle temptation for the people of God that obscures the call to be blessed and to bless others. Similarly, for Israel's leaders, the delight and pride in their outward status and appearance often causes them to forget their true role

---

12. C. S. Lewis, "The Inner Ring," in *The Weight of Glory* (New York: Macmillan, 1949), 100.
13. Ibid., 103.

as servants and shepherds of the people. This is a sin that the prophets and Jesus often criticize (Luke 11:43; 12:1; 20:45–47).

Miriam and Aaron have fallen into this temptation. Their jealous desire leads them to speak against their brother and their leader, harming their relationship with him. In addition, Miriam and Aaron also presume a certain kind of intimacy and status before God and attempt to use that relationship in order to further their social position. In response, God's anger is kindled against them both, and Miriam is stuck with leprosy (Num. 12:9–10).[14]

Miriam's leprosy forced her outside the camp (5:1–4). Even after she is healed, she had to go through a seven-day purification ritual (Lev. 14:1–20). However, the whiteness of the leprosy seems to indicate that it was noncontagious (13:13, 17; Milgrom 1990: 98). Given this, her punishment meant that she was marked by the disease and made uncomfortable by it rather than being made ritually unclean. Since spitting in one's face is an act of shaming (Deut. 25:9; Isa. 50:6), the statement "if her father had but spit in her face, would she not bear her shame for seven days?" (Num. 12:14) suggests that Miriam is being publicly disgraced and excluded due to norms of shame (Milgrom 1990: 98). Whatever the case, as a result of her and Aaron's actions, rather than becoming like Moses in his intimacy with God and status before Israel, Miriam is being thrust away. Rather than being exalted and allowed into the inner ring, she is humbled.

Why was only Miriam and not also Aaron struck with leprosy? The feminine singular Hebrew verb "spoke against" in Num. 12:1 seems to indicate that Miriam was the instigator and thus fairly bears a stronger punishment (Milgrom 1990: 93). Or perhaps Miriam was treated unfairly in a way that "preserves the androcentrism of the culture that preserved the story" (Sakenfeld 1995: 82–84). Either way, she is shamed in front of the community, while Aaron is humbled in a different way. He pleads with Moses to plead with God to heal her. Instead of directly addressing God, Aaron is made to realize that Moses has a unique relationship with God and calls Moses "my lord" (12:11).

In contrast to the jealousy and presumption of Miriam and Aaron, the humility of Moses is pointed out: "Now the man Moses was very humble, more so than anyone else on the face of the earth" (12:3). Moses's humility is exhibited here by his not responding directly or angrily to the murmurings of Miriam and Aaron. While Miriam and Aaron want to use their intimacy with God in order to increase their status among the people, Moses enjoys the greater good of such intimacy—friendship with God: "Moses . . . is entrusted with all my house. With him I speak face to face—clearly, not in riddles; and he beholds the form of the LORD" (12:7–8). Moses elsewhere is said to speak with YHWH "face to face, as one speaks to a friend" (Exod. 33:11). There are limits to this

---

14. Most scholars suggest that the skin diseases commonly translated "leprosy" do not typically include modern leprosy, known as Hanson's disease. The symptoms seem to suggest that they were skin diseases like psoriasis or vitiligo. For relevant literature, see Ashley 1993: 110n7.

intimacy, for Moses cannot *see* God's face (33:20), but is allowed to see the "form" (Num. 12:8) or "back" (Exod. 33:23) of God. This unique intimacy between God and Moses is attested in the words that record his death: "Never since has there arisen a prophet in Israel like Moses, whom the LORD knew face to face" (Deut. 34:10).

These issues of intimacy with God, humility, and presumption find resonance in the life of Jesus. In Jesus's temptations at the beginning of his ministry, he resists throwing himself off the temple and having God save him with his angels (Matt. 4:5–7). While this could have been a temptation to prove to himself that he was the Son of God,[15] it also might have been a temptation to use his intimacy with God to prove to others who he was, exploiting his intimacy with God to increase his status in the view of the people of Israel. In contrast, Jesus is humble like Moses: "Let the same mind be in you that was in Christ Jesus, who, though he was in the form of God, did not regard equality with God as something to be exploited, but emptied himself, . . . [and] humbled himself" (Phil. 2:5–8).

Jesus's disciples faced similar temptations. Their question concerning who is the greatest among them is sternly rebuked by Jesus (Matt. 18:1–5; Mark 9:33–37; Luke 9:46–48). In Corinth, Paul ran up against certain members of the congregation, the "super-apostles" (2 Cor. 11:5; 12:11), who were critiquing Paul's leadership apparently in an analogous way to how Miriam and Aaron critiqued Moses. Paul's defense of his ministry and leadership took the form of an exhibition of his humility and humbleness: "I myself, Paul, appeal to you by the meekness and gentleness of Christ—I who am humble" (10:1). Paul does not commend himself (10:12) and ironically boasts "of the things that show my weakness" (11:30). The goal of his leadership and the use of his authority and status is not to raise himself up, but rather to be transparent to Christ, who dwells in him (12:9), and to build up the church at Corinth rather than himself (10:8; 13:9–10).

Temptations to use one's chosen status, authority, and religious connections in order to secure power and position is a constant temptation for the people of God and their leaders. God has chosen to redeem and heal the world not by an instantaneous decree, but in great part through a slower process, by choosing and electing a people—Israel, Jesus, the church—and using these mediators in the world to bring blessing and healing to the nations. Within the people of God, certain representatives, leaders, or parts of the body are used for special purposes; within Israel the prophets, priests, kings, patriarchs and matriarchs, and sages are the typical examples. The call for such leaders is to be humble, to be a transparent and willing channel of God's work. But the ever-present temptation is to use one's position and authority as a means for self-aggrandizement.

15. So Austin Marsden Farrer, *The Triple Victory: Christ's Temptations according to Saint Matthew* (London: Faith Press, 1965), 45–60.

Rebellion 4: Fear, Despair, and Rejection of the Promised Land (13:1–14:45)

"The LORD said to Moses, 'Send men to spy out the land of Canaan, which I am giving to the Israelites'" (Num. 13:1). Israel is on the edge of the promised land, ready to finally enter into the blessings God has in store for it and to live into its calling to be a nation whose ways will be a light to all other nations. But instead of being the prelude to a story of celebration, the glimpse of the promised land given to the spies leads to another rebellion of the people against God.

This fourth rebellion is the crux of Israel's rebellions in the wilderness. It forms the center of the sevenfold pattern of Israel's unfaithfulness toward God in Numbers, it is the longest of the rebellions, and it is the most serious, both in terms of the offense against God and the punishment given in response to it. It is Israel's darkest hour. When Deuteronomy looks back on Israel's time in the wilderness, two sins serve as summative reminders of its sin toward God: the golden calf incident in Exod. 32 and this incident (Deut. 9:7–24; cf. 1:19–45). It is because of this that Israel had to stay in the wilderness a full forty years before being allowed to enter the promised land.

Given the centrality of this rebellion in the story of God's people, it is fascinating to realize that the sin that stops Israel from entering the promised land is not pride, the primal sin of Adam and Eve that lost them their home in the garden. Nor is it sexual sin, envy, or greed. It is despair. Despair stemming from lies and fear leads the people to reject the whole promised land project—the goal that God's work in Israel has been leading up to since God called Abram in Gen. 12:1–3. It is a rejection of the entire covenant relationship between Israel and YHWH.

This incident thus sheds light on the dynamics of sin, especially in relationship to the calling of the people of God. Two additional important themes can be drawn from the narrative: the pivotal role played by the leaders of Israel, and the judgment and mercy of God in response to the sin of Israel.

Structurally, the story consists of five scenes, probably woven together from earlier traditions. At the center of each scene are the good actions of several of Israel's leaders, which are often contrasted with the lying, despair, and rejection of God's purposes by the people. The narrative seems to have been carefully constructed to give a clear picture of the sin of Israel, the calling of Israel's leaders, and the relationship between God's judgment and mercy (I follow Milgrom 1990: 387–90 but I'm not convinced by his claim that the five scenes form a chiasm):

Scene 1: Forty days to spy out the land
    God's command (13:1–2)
    Moses's sending of the spies (13:3–20)
    exploration of the land (13:21–24)

Scene 2: Report of the spies
   initial report (13:25–29)
   Caleb's plea (13:30)
   subsequent lies (13:31–33)
Scene 3: The people's rebellion
   rebellion (14:1–4)
   leaders' prayers and pleas (14:5–9)
   people's response (14:10a)
Scene 4: God's response and Moses's intercession
   God's proposed rejection (14:10b–12)
   Moses's threefold plea for forgiveness (14:13–19)
   God's forgiveness and judgment (14:20–35)
Scene 5: Beginning of judgment
   death of spies, plan of the people (14:36–40)
   Moses's plea to the people (14:41–43)
   unsuccessful battle (14:44–45)

Scene 1: Forty Days to Spy the Land (13:1–24)

In the first scene, God directs Moses to send out representatives of Israel to look over the land. Moses does just that: he selects representatives and instructs them what they are to do.

The story is told slightly differently in Deut. 1:22–25, where the people get the idea to scout out the land, and the purpose is chiefly to find the best route into the land. In Num. 13:1 the impetus comes from the Lord. However, the Hebrew verb "send" is not like most other direct commands of YHWH in Numbers; it is best translated "send for yourself" and can be interpreted as God distancing himself from the selection of the scouts and the project. God is giving reluctant permission. If Moses wants to send scouts, then he should pick them for himself (Milgrom 1990: 100, following rabbinic interpretation). This view both harmonizes the two accounts and makes sense of the problems to come. Yet it is not the most natural reading of the narrative.

The leaders Moses selects are different from the tribal leaders listed earlier (1:5–15; 7:12–83). It makes sense that these leaders would not be the heads of their ancestral tribes, but rather younger men who could readily take on the rigors of such a journey. Moses instructs them (13:17–20) not only to check on the military aspects of the people in the promised land, but also to investigate the land itself and "bring some of the fruit of the land."

The mission is in part a reconnaissance for route-finding and military purposes. But given the representative nature of the twelve leaders and Moses's instructions concerning the land, the more central purpose seems to be to send witnesses who can come back and bear testimony that God's promises about the land are true. The twelve are to be witnesses to the goodness of the land and the faithfulness of God (cf. Ps. 34:8). This would reassure the people and give them the hope, courage, and trust in God needed for the final and potentially most dangerous part of their journey.

The scouts do fulfill at least part of their mission. They journey the entire length of the promised land[16] and go into the hill country of the south, bringing back pomegranates, figs, and a cluster of grapes from Wadi Eshcol ("cluster"). The image of the scouts bringing back a cluster of grapes so large that it is hung on a pole supported by two men is a wonderful symbol of the fruitfulness of the promised land. Grapes, pomegranates, and figs may have been mentioned simply as part of the historical difference between the crops of Canaan and Egypt (see 11:5 for the fruit that the people missed). Or these luscious and celebratory fruits of Canaan might be a subtle indication that God's purposes are even better than what the people imagined in their unfaithfulness. The cluster of grapes and other fruit become a symbol of the faithfulness of God to his covenant promises. The land is indeed a good land; and the faithful God has brought them to a good place of not simply manna and water, but of grapes, wine, celebration, and feasting.

The images of fruit are often inverted by the prophets as symbols for the faithfulness of Israel that God desires, instead of God's faithfulness to them. The fruit that manifests Israel's faithfulness is their love of God and their just and compassionate actions toward one another. While Israel found good fruit in the promised land, the prophets say that YHWH searches for fruit among his people but often does not find any. YHWH laments: "Woe is me! For I have become like one who, after the summer fruit has been gathered, after the vintage has been gleaned, finds no cluster to eat; there is no first-ripe fig for which I hunger. The faithful have disappeared from the land" (Mic. 7:1–2; cf. Hos. 9:10; Isa. 5:1–7; Ps. 80:8–19). Jesus similarly looks for fruit on a fig tree that represents Israel and the temple leadership but does not find any (Luke 13:6–9; Matt. 21:18–22; Mark 11:12–24). The image of God's people bearing fruit is further taken up in Jesus's parable of the sower (Matt. 13:3–9), his teaching about the vine and branches (John 15:1–11), and Paul's discussion of the fruit of the Spirit (Gal. 5:14–26). All these passages make the point that the fruitfulness of the people of God is dependant upon their faithfulness to God.

Scene 2: Report of the Spies (13:25–33)

The scouts return and give their report. They show the people the fruit of the land, and their first words are that the land indeed "flows with milk and honey"

16. The wilderness of Zin is the southern boundary of the promised land (Num. 34:3–4; Josh. 15:1–4), just north of the wilderness of Paran. Lebo-hamath is the northernmost tip of the land, on the north boundary of Israel during the reigns of David and Solomon (Num. 34:7–9; 1 Kgs. 8:65; 2 Kgs. 14:25; Ezek. 48:1; Amos 6:14).

(13:27)—that is, excellent for grazing milk-giving animals and filled with bees: a perfect land for people like the Israelites. But their concern and anxiety quickly overshadow their initial positive vision, as is apparent in their lengthy rehearsal of the inhabitants of the land—a traditional list of the peoples who lived in Canaan. Of special note are the descendents of Anak (13:28; cf. 13:22; Josh. 15:14), over-sized humans who are mentioned in the conquest stories (Deut. 1:28–33; Josh. 14:12–15; 15:13–19) and the encounter between David and Goliath (1 Sam. 17).[17] While the scouts are impressed with the land, they are even more afraid of the inhabitants.

Caleb then speaks up and quiets the people (Num. 13:30). The report of the spies, which was beginning to tend toward the negative, must have created a murmuring among the people. Caleb tries to intervene and give courage and hope to the people. Contrasting his faith with the fear and faithlessness of the major-ity, Caleb's statement could be taken as one of shear optimism in the strength of Israel—optimism that stems from his trust in the leadership of YHWH (14:8).

The majority of the scouting leaders, however, respond to Caleb by embellishing their original story, making both the land and the people in it much worse than they really were. The Hebrew word *dibbâ* ("unfavorable report"; 13:32) is mostly used for slanderous or untrue statements (BDB 179; Milgrom 1990: 106). That the scouts are lying or stretching the truth is clear in 14:37, where "evil" further qualifies the report. First, they say that the land "devours its inhabitants" (13:32). While there are several ways to understand this phrase (Ashley 1993: 242–43), it is ironic that God later causes the wilderness, not the promised land, to devour Korah and his followers as the earth literally opens up and they "go down alive into Sheol" (16:30, 33). The spies themselves might be comparing the promised land to Sheol, the subterranean dwelling of departed souls, which is often imaged as opening its mouth and devouring people (Job 24:19; Prov. 1:12; 27:20; Isa. 5:14; Jonah 2:2; Hab. 2:5). Second, the inhabitants are now said to be Nephilim, the products of the mythological marriages between the gods and humans (Gen. 6:4). The scouts lie in order to frighten the Israelites, and it works. The scouts fail in their purpose of bearing witness to the goodness and faithfulness of God; rather than giving courage to the people, they cultivate fear, which leads to despair.

Scene 3: The People's Rebellion (14:1–10a)

Upon hearing the evil report of the majority of the scouts, the Israelites weep, complain, imply that God has evil motives, and desire to change leadership in order to go back to Egypt.

The sin of the people is multifaceted. One might first find fault with their gullibility. They are quite willing to believe the exaggerated claims of the ten. The

---

17. Given the link between the Anakites and the Rephaim in Deut. 2:20–23, King Og of Bashan provides a good example of their size. His bed—apparently saved as a museum piece—was 9 cubits (13 feet) long (3:11).

counterreport of Caleb and later Joshua and the previous providential care and promises by God should have led to a different reaction. But instead, they fail to trust in God's good intentions for them, they do not remember God's faithful care for them, nor do they trust that he will give them the promised land. They cry, weep, and complain (14:1–2). Their fear leads to despair.

In addition, they begin to skeptically suspect God of evil intentions: "Why is the LORD bringing us into this land to fall by the sword?" (14:3). Their skepticism distorts their vision so that the slavery of Egypt looks better than following after God. And so they begin to formulate a plan to return to Egypt: "Let us choose a captain, and go back to Egypt" (14:4). They have in their hearts already rejected God's plan for them, God's appointed leaders, and ultimately YHWH.

The central rebellion, and thus the central sin, of Israel in Numbers is this anxious fear, which leads them finally to reject God and his plan for them. It is not a prideful rejection of God, but something else. The sin in the garden of Eden is often interpreted to be a form of pride. Adam and Eve sin in response to the serpent's lies ("you will not die," "you will be like God") and his implication that God did not have their best interests in mind when he forbade them to eat the fruit of the tree of knowledge of good and evil (Gen. 3:4–5). Lack of trust and pride went hand in hand in the garden.

But the sin of Israel in Numbers, while sharing many features with the sin of Adam and Eve, is different. God is leading his people back to a place that has many analogies to the garden. Like the garden, the promised land is a fruitful place, a place where God and Israel will dwell again together in harmony. And like the garden, lies poison that harmony, but now, it is the scouts who lie, and the lie is not "you will not die" but "you will die." Because of their resulting lack of trust in God's care, purposes, and providence for them and their related anxious fear, they are unwilling to possess the land and take hold of its fruit. And yet, while they despair of God's plan for them, they do not do nothing; instead they think that their own plan to return to Egypt will be better.

Even though their plan involves elements of pride and apostasy in exchanging Egyptian gods for YHWH, Israel rejects God not because they want to be more, but rather because they are willing to settle for less. For this reason, Israel's sin is best named sloth or even despair.[18] Aquinas writes that sloth is "the negligence of

18. Barth's analysis of one form of sin is similar: "The direction of God, given in the resurrection of Jesus Christ who was crucified for us, discloses who is overcome in His death. It is the man who would not make use of his freedom, but was content with the low level of a self-enclosed being, thus being irremediably and radically and totally subject to his own stupidity, inhumanity, dissipation and anxiety, and delivered up to his own death" (1936–77: 4/2.378). Barth sums up the refusal and nonuse of God's offer as the "sloth and misery" of humanity—an apt description of what we find in Num. 13–14 (1936–77: 4/2.478–83). For a good summary of the important contribution of feminist theology to the renewed attention to the sins of sloth and despair in the twentieth century, see Serene Jones, *Feminist Theory and Christian Theology: Cartographies of Grace* (Minneapolis: Fortress, 2000), 94–125. The classical terminology for "despair" is *acedia*; see Evagrius, *Praktikos* 12.

a man who declines to acquire spiritual goods on account of the attendant labor" (*Summa theologica* I-II Q84.4). Israel exhibits sloth in its unwillingness to go up against the inhabitants of the land. But because negligence is combined with a lack of hope and skepticism that the future is even a good one, perhaps despair is a better title. As a result of their unfaithful sloth/despair, Israel turns back from entering the promised land and chooses the path of Egyptian slavery and misery over the path of courage, effort, and hope leading toward the promised land.

In contrast to this failure of Israel, and in light of the constant temptations of fear, sloth, and despair that plague the people of God, the New Testament calls the people of God to the hard work of sanctification in a variety of ways. "Do not worry about your life, what you will eat or what you will drink," but rather "strive first for the kingdom of God and his righteousness," says Jesus (Matt. 6:25, 33). "Forgetting what lies behind and straining forward to what lies ahead, I press on toward the goal" (Phil. 3:13–14), writes Paul. And the author of Hebrews rightly calls us to follow in the ways of Jesus, who had the courage, faith, and faithfulness that Israel did not and who as such is the "pioneer and perfecter of our faith. . . . Consider him who endured such hostility against himself from sinners, so that you may not grow weary or lose heart" (Heb. 12:2–3). The cross itself is the symbolic center of the faithfulness that eluded Israel. Instead of fearing for his life and avoiding and rejecting the call of God, Christ entered into his own place of rest at the right hand of God through enduring the cross: "Who for the sake of the joy that was set before him endured the cross, disregarding its shame, and has taken his seat at the right hand of the throne of God" (12:2). Christ's obedience to the point of death on the cross is the antithesis of sloth and despair and pride and—at the root of them all—unfaithfulness (e.g., Phil. 3:9, "the faith of Christ").

In response to Israel's rejection of God (Num. 14:1–4), Moses and Aaron fell on their faces before the congregation (14:5). This act may be interpreted as an appeal to either the congregation or, more likely, God to intercede for the people (contra 1 Sam. 20:41 and Gen. 50:18; see Ashley 1993: 247). Whatever the case, the narrative shifts focus to Joshua and Caleb as foil to the sin of Israel.

Joshua and Caleb counter the negative portrayal of the land, the fear of the people of Canaan, and the rebellion against YHWH. They first of all act as trustworthy and faithful witnesses to the goodness of God. They tell the people that the goal of their journey, the land in which they will live as God's people, is "exceedingly good" (14:7). They also rightly declare their trust in the power and care of God. The inhabitants, though they might be powerful, are not an obstacle. "The LORD is with us," and with his leadership they "are no more than bread" and so easily devoured (14:9). And they rightly see that the actions of Israel are a rebellion against God. Their trust in God helps them to see the good of the future that God intends for them and also gives them the courage, energy, and hope to confront the obstacles that lay in their path. They are exemplary in their leadership and witness.

The people respond by threatening to stone them (14:10a). Determined to go back to Egypt, they reject even the suggestion of any other course of action and "set in stone" their verdict on the way proposed by Joshua and Caleb, a verdict also on God and his ways and covenant purposes for them.

In the New Testament, the Gospel of John portrays the rejection of Christ by both Rome and the Jewish leaders in a similar way: "The Jews took up stones again to stone him" (John 10:31). Their rejection of Christ is their own verdict on God, a verdict that ironically becomes the evidence by which they themselves are judged: "This is the judgment, that the light has come into the world, and the people loved darkness rather than light" (3:19).

Scene 4: God's Response and Moses's Intercession (14:10b–35)

The Lord's appearance interrupts the people's intention to stone their leaders. God first laments this action, which reveals the people's "despising" of him and their ignoring "all the signs that I have done among them" (Num. 14:11). Then God offers to Moses his plan to destroy the people and create a new nation from Moses alone. This in effect would be the end of God's covenantal history with Israel.

This drastic solution was once carried out by God in the story of Noah (Gen. 6). God threatens such a drastic action only one other time: right after Israel's apostasy in the golden calf incident. YHWH says to Moses, "Now let me alone, so that my wrath may burn hot against them and I may consume them; and of you I will make a great nation" (Exod. 32:10). In Num. 14:12 YHWH's words "I will strike them . . . , I will make of you a nation" are better translated "let me strike them . . . , let me make of you a nation" (Milgrom 1990: 109). They have a similar sense to "let me alone" in Exod. 32:10: God dialogues with Moses and opens himself up to Moses's response. It is as if God is testing Moses, or opening the possibility for Moses to intercede, which he does. God's threat, however, shows the seriousness of the people's sin. As in the golden calf incident, they are rejecting the leadership of God, and God would be just to also reject them as a people.

But God's justice is tempered by his "forgiveness" (*sālaḥ*). After Moses intercedes for the people (14:13–19) YHWH's actual response involves both a poetic (or retributive) justice and forgiveness. In order to see how these fit together, the content of both this forgiveness and God's judgment must be examined more closely.

God's response is first of all a word of grace: "I do forgive" (14:20). Rather than rejecting Israel as a nation, God forgives, "just as you [Moses] have asked." This forgiveness requires the suffering patience of God and consists of the extension of God's covenant with Israel even though Israel has rejected and despised God. Forgiveness is the continuance of the covenant relationship with the community of Israel in spite of its rebellion and sinfulness. God will bring Israel into the promised land and in the future will come to Israel in the person of Jesus. Forgiveness here has nothing to do with forgetting—there is no mention of wiping the score clean. God's forgiveness is a gritty patience and willingness to continue on in relationship in spite of the past.

The prophets later speak of forgiveness as a complete wiping away or healing of sin (Isa. 1:18; 6:7; 43:25; 44:22; Jer. 18:23; Hos. 14:4; Mic. 7:9). But for now, sin is covered, bypassed, and overlooked (Milgrom 1990: 392–96). Interplay between justification and sanctification—to use Christian terminology—creates difficulty for some Christians in defining these terms and understanding their relationship. Forgiveness in Num. 13–14 means at least the willingness of God to remain with Israel, even in its sin. Ultimately, however, sin itself must be cleansed, blotted out, made white; the sanctification of Israel eventually must be made complete.

Forgiveness is not the only word God speaks in Num. 14. Just as the revelation of God's character on Mount Sinai to Moses in Exod. 34:5–6 includes both forgiveness and retribution (which Moses quotes in his intercession), God's forgiveness and grace is accompanied by a "nevertheless" (Num. 14:21). Even though God forgives Israel as a people, he also pronounces judgment upon the individuals of the generation who have "seen my glory and the signs I did" yet have still "not obeyed my voice" (14:22) and have been faithless (14:33). That generation, with the exception of Caleb and Joshua (14:24, 30) will not be allowed to see the promised land, but will instead die in the wilderness. The judgment is not death per se, but a delay until the fortieth year, when the generation of the exodus will have died out. The judgments pronounced in 14:28–34 are retributive: they correspond creatively to the offenses.

When one considers the individuals involved, God's sentence is a punishment. The individuals of the generation that rejected and despised God and his covenant purposes due to their fear and faithlessness will no longer be able to enter and taste the goodness of the promised land.

But when one considers Israel as a people, this delay is a kind of cleansing, discipline, or surgery; it is the painful molding and shaping of a people who are called to be holy. The unfaithful and murmuring elements of Israel are excised or cleansed from Israel by keeping them out of the promised land until they die, mainly by old age. This is both because they rebelled and also for the sake of God's purposes for this people. God's first response to Moses—"I will make of you a nation greater and mightier than they" (14:12)—suggests that God's purpose is not merely or mainly to punish, but to create an alternate strategy. God's judgment is painful. Even the children of that older generation will "suffer" (14:33). But Num. 26–36 shows the rise of that next generation and casts a hopeful look forward to the promised land. God's good purposes for humanity ultimately cannot coexist with sin, so for God to forgive and continue in relationship to Israel, sanctification in its negative aspect of eradicating and/or healing sin is also needed.

This passage can help form our understanding of the continuing work of God with the people of God as a community and individually. Perhaps the individual aspect of this journey of sanctification is most familiar to Christians. Israel's cleansing as a people, the death of the old generation, can be seen as a type of the death of the old self: "You have stripped off the old self with its practices and have clothed yourself with the new self, which is being renewed in knowledge according to the image of its creator" (Col. 3:9–10; cf. Rom. 6:6; Eph. 4:22).

But at the level of the community, this story of Israel also pushes us to reflect on how God might be creating a holy people in the church in, under, and through the instrument of church discipline—an important, yet very delicate and difficult issue. Church discipline is extremely difficult for many to discuss, yet it appears to be an implication of God being forgiving and holy and his calling out a people to be a "holy nation."[19] Similarly, Paul calls on the Corinthians to remove from among them the man living with his father's wife (1 Cor. 5:1–2) and in this way to "clean out the old yeast" so that it does not leaven "the whole batch of dough" (5:6–7). Paul's actions correspond well to the action of God here in Numbers. Parts of the people of God are being cut away—perhaps just for a time—so that the people can bear the presence of God in the church, especially in the Eucharist. Luther understands that justification—God's acceptance of us while still sinners—also involves sanctification, both individually and as a church community. This is certainly true at the individual level: "Christ lives, works, and rules *per redemptionem*, through grace and the forgiveness of sins, and the Holy Spirit *per vivificationem et sanctificationem*, through daily cleansing of sins and renewal of life, so that we do not remain in sins, but can and should lead a new life in all kinds of good works and not in the old, evil works."[20] At the communal and public level, the church, according to Luther, has been given the power to discipline public sins, for "the church or people of God does not tolerate public sinners in its midst."[21] Recognizing that such a practice needs to find a middle course between "arrogance and faintheartedness," Luther nevertheless sees such judgment and discipline within the community of the church both as a means of the work of the Holy Spirit to sanctify us and for the sake of the mission of the church to be a holy people among the nations.

Turning finally to Moses's intercession (Num. 14:13–19), three aspects of this fascinating passage raise theological issues: the example of Moses's leadership, his successful intercession/deliberation with God, and his three arguments to convince God not to disinherit Israel.

Moses shows himself to be an exemplary leader in his response to God's initial reaction. Moses is given an offer from God that is very similar to the promise given to Abram (Gen. 12:1–3), that God would raise a great nation from his offspring. For Moses, this nation would be even greater than Israel. Given the way that much of Israel rebelled against his leadership as well as God's, such an offer

19. David Yeago, "The Office of the Keys: On the Disappearance of Discipline in Protestant Modernity," in *Marks of the Body of Christ*, ed. Carl E. Braaten and Robert W. Jenson (Grand Rapids: Eerdmans, 1999).
20. Cited in ibid., 99.
21. Ibid., 104.

would have been tempting. But Moses—out of his humility, love for the people, and concern for God's glory—instead boldly intercedes with God to save Israel. Such a pattern is seen also in Christ, who did not use his equality with God for his own sake (Phil. 2:6), but rather offered his own life for the sake of others and now intercedes for rather than condemns "those who approach God through him" (Rom. 8:34; Heb. 7:25). While Christ perfects this priestly role of Moses, the church is also called to join in this role: church leaders should intercede for the people, and the people for each other and for the world.[22] Rather than using their role of intimacy with God as a point of privilege, leaders should follow the example of Moses and use whatever status or intimacy they have with God by praying for others.

Moses's entering into deliberation with God here and in other passages—such as Exod. 32 (golden calf) and Exod. 3 (burning bush)—also raises many theological questions about divine action in response to prayer, whether God changes his mind, and how God is related to time. These are questions of great importance and great complexity and require that one simultaneously juggle many assumptions about biblical interpretation, metaphysics, and theology. The reigning opinion of the Western theological tradition has treated this and similar passages nonliterally. The understanding is that while God is portrayed in this passage as forming his course of action partially in response to the intercession of Moses, this is not in fact the case. Rather, God is timeless and eternal and consequently does not change his mind in history or as the result of human intercession. "Changing God's mind" in response to human intercession, at least in the commonsense understanding of that phrase, seems to run afoul of God's atemporality, aseity (underived or unconditioned), and perhaps even foreknowledge—all typical attributes of God in classical Western Christian theology. In the tradition that holds to common understandings of those attributes of God, a story about a deliberation in time between God and Moses is interpreted as an accommodation to typical ways of viewing God and is thus a representation of something else (there are many possibilities). In response, however, the timelessness of God is being questioned by many contemporary theologians and philosophers, including evangelicals and conservatives. Such scholars call into question the received understanding of many traditional divine attributes, typically for the reason that they run afoul of much of the biblical witness, which seems to indicate that God is part of an ongoing, responsive history with Israel.[23] For example, Wolterstorff argues that even though scriptural passages such as this one and Exod. 3 portray God highly

22. This is one of the three offices of Christ that can become models for the ministries of the church and its leaders; see Geoffrey Wainwright, *For Our Salvation: Two Approaches to the Work of Christ* (Grand Rapids: Eerdmans, 1997). For the intercessory office of Christ, see Leanne Van Dyk, *The Desire of Divine Love: John McLeod Campbell's Doctrine of the Atonement*, Studies in Church History 4 (New York: Peter Lang, 1995).

23. A few examples are Gregory Ganssle, ed., *God and Time: Four Views* (Downers Grove, IL: InterVarsity, 2001); Robert W. Jenson, *Systematic Theology* (New York: Oxford University Press,

anthropomorphically, "this is not a good reason for concluding that *everything* in them is *purely* anthropomorphic"; rather, such passages portray God "as having a history of action, knowledge, and response" in time. He remains unconvinced by typical and traditional biblical and philosophical arguments for taking those aspects of the portrayal of God nonliterally.[24] The interaction in this chapter certainly portrays God as an actor in time and as responsive to Moses.

Finally, the arguments that Moses uses to convince God not to abandon Israel reveal something of the character and motivations of God. Moses argues first that God's reputation and glory in the sight of "the nations" (Num. 14:15) will be compromised if he abandons Israel. He also implicitly holds God to his "promise" (14:17) and appeals to God's "steadfast love" (14:19). This is similar to Moses's intercession after the golden calf incident, when Moses first appeals to God on the basis of his reputation (Exod. 32:11–12) and then on the basis of his promise to Abraham, Isaac, and Israel (32:13). The difference is that Moses now makes a stronger appeal to God's steadfast love than he did in Exodus. God's *ḥesed* is not simply kindness, but "steadfast love" or "covenant faithfulness." It is the aspect of God that makes God willing to stick with Israel and not abandon the covenant even though Israel time after time is unfaithful. Moses understands that about God. It is this aspect of God that motivates him to forgive his sinful people.

While God's character is the ultimate basis of God's forgiveness of Israel, Moses's first argument is important as well. The people of God are of crucial importance for God's plan of salvation and in the history of God's glory in the world. The glory of God—the manifestation of who God is and of his sovereignty over the world—will be fully revealed only through the salvation and sanctification of God's people. What was true for Israel was also true for the early church. Summary descriptions of the early church in Acts 2:43–47 and 4:32–37 indicate that the life and embodied witness of the community of believers was of great importance for the spread of the gospel of Christ. In much twentieth-century theology, the importance of the public nature of the church as a light to the nations has been recovered and emphasized (→1:1–54). As in Numbers, the life of the people who are called by God's name matters for the glory of God.

Scene 5: Beginning of Judgment (14:36–45)

Immediately after God pronounces his forgiveness and judgment on the people, the repercussions of the sin of the people begin to be felt. First of all, all the scouts who spied out the land and gave the "bad report" "die by a plague." What God

1999), 1.46–50; and Eberhard Jungel, *God's Being Is in Becoming: The Trinitarian Being of God in the Theology of Karl Barth*, trans. John Webster (Grand Rapids: Eerdmans, 2004).

24. Especially given Nicholas Wolterstorff's methodological principle: "An implication of one's accepting Scripture as canonical is that one will affirm as literally true Scripture's representation of God unless one has good reason not to do so"; see "Unqualified Divine Temporality," in *God and Time*, 188.

had originally threatened for the whole people (14:12) happens now only to these leaders.

The rest of the people, in response to God's judgment, begin to move toward the promised land to take it by force, on their way offering to Moses a confession that "we have sinned" (14:40). Their confession does not change their fate or seem to have any effect. Moses does not even respond to it, but rather responds to their intention to enter the promised land. The confession of the people in the seventh rebellion, however, is effective: "We have sinned by speaking against the LORD and against you; pray to the LORD to take away the serpents from us" (21:7). The difference could be simply that in Num. 14 they confessed their sin *after* God pronounced judgment, while in Num. 21 they confessed their sin *before* judgment was pronounced (so Milgrom 1990: 116). But the nature of the confession is also different. In Num. 21 they confess their sin against God; in Num. 14 they confess their error in judgment. The people, rather than turning from their sin against God, seem to be simply saying that they were wrong to be afraid of attacking the Canaanites. The threat of dying in the wilderness might have even contributed to their courage and resolve. But they lack something crucial: faithfulness to God and his presence in their midst. They rely on their own strength, attacking without either the ark or Moses. As a result they are routed in their first military encounter in Numbers.

Dealing with Ingratitude, Rejection, and Unfaithfulness: Laws concerning Thankfulness, Sin, and Remembrance (15:1–41)

Directly following the climactic account of Israel's great rejection of God and the promised land in Num. 13–14, it might seem puzzling to find the narrative interrupted by a section of lawlike material. Some interpreters are unable to see any connection of this material to the surrounding narrative.[25] However, these laws do comment on the preceding narrative of Israel's rebellion in Num. 13–14, just as the lawlike material in Num. 18–19, following the narrative of the rebellion of Korah in Num. 16–17, will comment on it. These laws and short narratives are linked to the preceding narrative through common words, themes, and catchphrases (see Olson 1996: 97–101 for connections), but even more substantially, the laws respond to Israel's rebellion by directing how Israel might deal with the kind of sins it has committed, through counterexamples, direct laws, and preventative practices.

More specifically, the chapter begins with laws concerning sacrifices (15:1–21). In the rebellion of Num. 13–14, Israel rejects God and his gifts of the land and the rest that Israel might enter into if it obediently follows his leadership and

25. The comments of Noth 1968: 114 are often cited in recent commentaries: "It is not clear why this rather unsystematically arranged collection of various cultic-ritual ordinances should have found a place at all at this point in the Pentateuch narrative."

laws. These laws concerning sacrifices help the reader step back and consider what Israel's response to God's gifts *should have been*. They paint a positive picture of how the people of God should thankfully respond to the blessings they will encounter in the promised land. The phrase "when you come into the land" (15:2) also underscores the promise that, even though Israel has rejected the land, God will be faithful to bring at least some of their descendents into it. These sacrificial laws are then followed by laws concerning what to do if the Israelites fail to do as they should (15:22–31), a brief case study concerning both unintentional and intentional sins (15:32–36), and a law concerning fringes on one's garments (15:37–41). Through this very concrete practice, the Israelites will have a constant reminder to be faithful to God and to their high calling to be a priestly people and holy nation.

The first part of the chapter contains laws concerning sacrifices of both animals (15:1–16) and dough (15:17–21). Numbers 15:1–16 expands upon laws already encountered in Lev. 1 for the *ʿōlâ* ("burnt offering") and in Lev. 3 for the *šĕlāmîm* ("sacrifice of well-being"). As discussed in →7:1–88, the *ʿōlâ* is an act of devotion to God in which one symbolically gives oneself over to God. *Zebaḥ* (15:3) is common shorthand for *zebaḥ šĕlāmîm* ("sacrifice of well-being"), a joyous sacrifice in which a meal was shared between worshipers and God, usually marking an event in which the shalom of the world made right was tasted in part and celebrated with thanksgiving and joy.

The vision painted of Israel offering both sacrifices "when you come into the land" (15:2) stands in marked contrast to the reactions of the ten spies when they encountered the land and reported on it. Rather than offering themselves to God in total devotion, they rejected God and desired to go back to Egypt. And rather than celebrating the goodness of God in giving them a good land with wonderful produce, they brought "a bad report about the land" (14:36). The self-dedication and celebration of God's goodness represented here provides both a counterexample and tonic to the sloth and despair of the spies and the people.

These laws also add three new features to these sacrifices. First, details are added for a "grain offering" of flour and oil and a "drink offering" of wine (15:4–12), details reflected in Num. 28–29. These add to the imagery of presenting a full meal to God. The elements also represent the three principal harvests of Israel: grain in May–June, grapes in August–September, and olives for oil in October (cf. Ps. 104:15). These sacrifices thus represent an offering to God for the fullness of the land in thankfulness for God's providence—again a meaning that contrasts with Israel's previous rejection of the land.

The second addition is that a "dough offering" must also be given (Num. 15:17–21) when they come into the land. It is another symbol of thanksgiving to God for the bounty of the land as well as a symbol of the dedication of the fruit of human labor to God. It makes sense that these statutes would be added to the sacrificial laws when settled agricultural life in the promised land was envisioned.

The third addition concerns the "alien" or "resident alien" (*gēr*). In early Israel, these people were landless and so, often, poor—usually day laborers or artisans. The Pentateuch frequently mentions them, and Numbers is no exception (9:14; 15:14, 15, 16, 26, 29, 30; 19:10; 35:15). Almost always laws mentioning the alien show a concern to protect and include them. They are allowed but not required to participate in most of the worship practices of Israel, such as the sacrifices mentioned in Num. 15. They are required to obey the prohibitive requirements of the law so as not to pollute the land or the sanctuary (with the exception of certain dietary laws; Milgrom 1990: 398–402). It is often stated that there is to be "a single statute" (15:15) for both full members of Israel and aliens. This recognizes—but speaks firmly against—the tendency for a double standard in matters of justice and business. In Deuteronomy the alien is listed alongside the orphan and the widow (e.g., Deut. 14:29; 16:11; 24:17), the stereotypical categories of those without power who are easily preyed upon in Israelite society. They all come under special mention and protection by the law because God in his justice loves them, and Israel should remember that it too was a stranger in Egypt (10:18–19). God is a God of justice, love, and compassion, and Israel should act similarly, remembering that it was once in such a powerless position as a people.

Current debates about immigration policy and undocumented residents in the United States and the treatment of Palestinian Christians and Muslims (some of whom are Israeli citizens) by Israeli Jews in Israel bear many analogies to the situations addressed by this ancient law. While the contemporary situations are admittedly complex, this piece of Christian scripture pushes Christians toward supporting actions that would create justice and hospitality in our time for people analogous to Israel's "resident aliens."

The next section (15:22–31) speaks of sacrifices that must be made if Israel as a people (15:24–26) fails to observe "all these commandments" without direct intention, or if an individual sins unintentionally (15:27–29). It also speaks of the consequences for someone who sins "high-handedly" (15:30–31).

There is some confusion about how the law concerning sacrifices for unintentional sins differs from similar laws in Lev. 4 and why additional laws are given here.[26] In the first situation (Num. 15:24–26) both a bull and a male goat are sacrificed, which correspond to the sin offerings of the congregation and the ruler of the people in Lev. 4:14 and 4:23. Perhaps what is imagined is both congregation and king forgetting "all the commandments" of the Torah and thus sinning, as happened during the reigns of wicked kings. Perhaps the same kind of situation is in view for the individual, such as Israelite children being taken into captivity and thus unaware of their origins. Such examples of Israelites simply forgetting about the covenant might seem far-fetched but for the fact that they repeatedly happened!

---

26. The narrative supports an interpretation that the law closes a loophole in Lev. 4 by putting both sins of commission and sins of omission, "all the commands," into view.

It is clear that Israel did not sin unintentionally in Num. 13–14; they consciously rejected "all the commands" and desired to go back to Egypt. As a people, they were in a very different situation than Israel in times when the Torah had been forgotten by the people. Rather they fit much more closely with the description in 15:30–31 of those who sin "high-handedly."

The phrase "whoever acts high-handedly" (15:30) can be best understood within the context of the ancient Near East in which statues and depictions of deities were often constructed with the deity's right hand raised high in a threatening gesture, often holding a weapon such as a hammer, spear, or lightning bolt (Milgrom 1990: 125). This phrase is used of Israelites defying the Egyptians during the exodus (Num. 33:3; Exod. 14:8); a similar phrase, "an outstretched arm," is used when YHWH defies all other powers (Deut. 4:34; 5:15; 26:8). This threatening gesture symbolizes a brazen or open defiance of God. Such an attitude is seen in both the rejection of God's leadership by the people (Num. 14:4) and the people gathering together against God's leaders (16:11).

The punishment of a high-handed sin is that "such a person shall be utterly cut off [*hikkārēt tikkārēt*] and bear the guilt" (15:31). Commentators are divided about what exactly this punishment entails.[27] The word *kārat* indicates that God cuts off the person from the covenant people (9:13; 15:31; 18:3; 19:13, 20). As a result, they are also cut off from God's protection and covenant (Ashley 1993: 180, 288–89). Since they are not considered part of the covenant community by God, they will not benefit from the atonement offered to Israel by God through its sacrificial practices. They will not be "covered" by God's mercy, his wrath will not pass over them (9:13), and they will "bear the guilt" (15:31) of their sin.

While the connection is not explicit, the short narrative of the man who gathered sticks on the Sabbath (15:32–26) is likely meant to illustrate high-handed sin (Ashley 1993: 291). The hesitancy of the Israelites about what to do with this man can be understood better in light of the relevant Sabbath laws that he was breaking (Exod. 20:10–11). Death is prescribed as the punishment for profanation of the Sabbath (31:14–15), and kindling domestic fires is included in what might constitute this (35:2–3). In light of these laws, the people's hesitancy could likely have been that the man was gathering sticks in order to light a domestic fire, and he was intending to do so in a high-handed fashion, but he had not actually done so yet.

Israel was in the same position: they were high-handedly rejecting the leadership of God—almost to the point of selecting another leader—but had not actually committed apostasy yet. Perhaps one could say that they had already switched their orientation, had already high-handedly committed apostasy in their hearts, and had already turned. As a result, God forgives Israel as a people, but those

---

27. Milgrom 1990: 405–8, lists the nineteen cases of *kārat* in the Torah and convincingly shows that this penalty is exacted by God for sins against God. Rabbinic interpretations range from one's progeny being cut off to one being cut off from life with one's progeny in the life hereafter.

who had rejected God "shall fall in this very wilderness" (14:29). The man who gathered sticks was among the first.

The ruling from God is that the man should be punished, even though he has not yet lit a domestic fire. Given this reconstruction, the ruling shows that God is just as interested in a person turning away from him in their heart as in the final crossing of the legal line. Jesus's teachings in the Sermon on the Mount follow a similar trajectory: "You have heard that it was said . . . , 'You shall not murder.' . . . But I say to you that if you are angry with a brother or sister, you will be liable to judgment. . . . You have heard that it was said, 'You shall not commit adultery.' But I say to you that everyone who looks at a woman with lust has already committed adultery with her in his heart" (Matt. 5:21–27). Following God does not merely consist in staying on the correct side of a legal boundary; it is also a matter of the heart and the directions of a person's will and activity.

The commandment concerning the "fringes" (*ṣîṣit*) or tassels that are part of Israelite garments (Num. 15:37–41) is a stunning law with great consequence for the Jewish people. Its main purpose is to very practically remind the Israelites who they are—that they are to be "a royal priesthood" and a "holy nation." It is one of the three passages (with Deut. 6:4–9; 11:13–21) that compose the Shema, the prayer said twice daily in current Jewish piety. The law has several connections to the preceding narratives and laws and provides a fitting ending to this section.

The purpose of the tassels is given in Num. 15:39: "So that, when you see it, you will remember all the commandments of the Lord and do them, and not follow the lust of your heart and of your own eyes." The phrase "all the commandments" was encountered in 15:22, where it was imagined that Israel might forget all the commandments of God, thus forgetting its covenant and identity altogether. To combat such forgetfulness, these tassels are to be a perpetual visual reminder of Israel's identity. The words translated "follow the lust of your heart and of your eyes" could more literally be translated "so that you are not spying out [*tûr*] after your own heart and after your own eyes as you are whoring [*zānâ*] after them" (Olson 1996: 98). The same Hebrew words are used in 14:33–34, where God condemns Israel for faithlessness or "whoring" after it spies out the land.

Such tassels had at least two cultural resonances. First, the tassels or fringes in the hem of a garment were typically the most elaborate decorations of the outer garments worn at that time. Nobility and royalty wore tassels or fringes longer than other people; those fringes were considered symbols of the extension of their authority and person.[28] That all the Israelites were to wear tassels symbolized the elevation of all the people to the status of royalty: they were a royal people. The blue thread that was to be part of the four tassels on the corners of the outer garments had a priestly connotation. Blue or purple was created from the dye of a

---

28. See discussion and sources in Milgrom 1990: 410–14. These connotations make sense of the otherwise obscure story about the interactions between David and Saul after David secretly cuts the hem from Saul's robe while Saul is in a cave relieving himself (1 Sam. 24).

snail and was extremely expensive. It was the color of the curtain placed in front of the ark (Exod. 26:31), parts of the high priests' vestments (28:31), and the cord binding the high priest's turban (28:37). In addition, the oldest rabbinic traditions (e.g., Septuagint and Targum Jonathan on Deut. 22:12; see Milgrom 1990: 413) understand that these tassels were a mixture of linen and wool, a mixture that is prescribed for the high priest to wear but is ordinarily forbidden to Israelites (Lev. 19:19; Deut. 22:11). By wearing such materials, the Israelites understood that all of them took on priestly privileges and responsibilities: they were a priestly people.

Tassels on the corner of modern Jewish prayer shawls or tallith remind Israel of its identity and high calling.[29] Instead of running after the desires of the heart, seeking gods and ways of life that promise security, comfort, and a life of ease, as Israel did in Num. 13–14, Israel is reminded that it is God's royal and priestly people, an identity and task spelled out in "all the commandments" of the Lord.

The implications of this "high egalitarianism"—that all Israel is called to royal and priestly status—are misunderstood in the very next chapter.

Rebellion 5: Korah's Revolt, Aaron's Censer, and Aaron's Staff (16:1–17:11)

Few narratives in scripture are more dramatic and gripping than the rebellion of Korah. From the audacity of Korah and the other leaders (16:3, 12–15), to the ground opening and swallowing the household of Korah (16:31–34), to the fire consuming the 250 men offering the incense (16:35)—this is a story of mythic proportions. This rebellion is immediately followed by two other memorable events: the atonement accomplished by Aaron as he carries his censer of incense into the middle of a plague and the miraculous budding of Aaron's staff.

Perhaps the most famous representation of this episode in European culture is the Sistine Chapel fresco commissioned by Pope Sixtus IV in 1480 and painted by Sandro Botticelli. While the Sistine Chapel is better known for Michelangelo's ceiling paintings, Botticelli's fresco depicting the punishment of Korah is more relevant to the key function of the chapel: since 1492 it has been the site where the College of Cardinals elects the pope. The fresco depicts Aaron wearing the triple-ringed tiara of the pope, swinging his censer, while Korah and other rebels begin to fall into the earth. In the fresco's background is the arch of triumph of Constantine, who gave the pope temporal power over the Roman world. The meaning conveyed by the fresco is quite clear: the pope is the successor to Aaron and those who would challenge his authority should think twice. It also serves as a

---

29. Later traditions added even more meaning to the tassels as they were tied in certain ways to symbolize the name of God. This innovation further highlights that part of Israel's royal and priestly calling was to bear the name of God among the nations. Over time, the way the tassels were worn changed, but they have remained part of Jewish practice until today.

warning to those seeking the papal office to question their own motives and calling (the inscription on the arch quotes Heb. 5:4: "And one does not presume to take this honor, but takes it only when called by God, just as Aaron was"). This artistic application of the images of Num. 16–17 to the office of pope highlights some of the central theological issues raised by these stories: What are God's intentions for priestly leadership within the people of God? How should those who are not as high in status or role behave toward leadership of the church? What analogies and distinctions should be drawn between Aaron and those in priestly roles in the church? A closer look shows that the narrative suggests principles helpful in answering these questions.

The sevenfold rebellion of Israel in Num. 11–21 provides a compendium of sins that regularly test the people of God. At the center is the people's rejection of the promised land (Num. 13–14), a rejection involving sloth, despair, and apostasy. But on either side of this central rebellion are stories concerning leadership, power, and envy. While the rebellion of Num. 12 centers around the *prophetic* office of Moses, that in Num. 16 clearly focuses on the office of Aaron as *priest* and the people as a priestly people.

The three main scenes in these chapters form a coherent narrative whole about the rebellion against the priestly leadership of Israel. They provide insight into the nature of priestly leadership, showcasing both sins to be avoided and positive models. These chapters can guide Christians singled out for similar leadership within the people of God and can also inform the people of God as a priestly community how they should engage the surrounding world.

Scene 1: Revolt of Korah and Others and Their Punishment (16:1–40)

The first scene relates the rebellion led by Korah, Dathan, and Abiram (16:1–11). Its canonical form seems to have been composed from materials that have had a lengthy history (Milgrom 1990: 414–23). While there are many fascinating aspects of this carefully constructed, subtle, and ironic text, the central theological issues of the narrative center on the sin of the leaders of Israel and the response of Moses and God to this sin. The narrative is easily subdivided into three parts: the interactions between Moses and those who were rebelling against his and Aaron's authority (16:12–19), the interactions between God and his people about their sin (16:20–35), and the creation of the bronze covering on the altar to serve as a visible warning not to follow in the ways of Korah and his company (16:36–40).[30]

What then is the central sin or failure of Korah and those leaders of Israel? While the story makes quite clear that Korah and others were wrong to challenge the role of Aaron, it is less clear what the reasons for this challenge were, and even less clear how this message should be more generally applied to the people of God.

---

30. Num. 16:36–40 in English Bibles is numbered 17:1–5 in the Masoretic Text.

Two central reasons are put forward for challenging the status of Aaron. The first argument is advanced by the group led by Korah the Levite (16:3), the second by "Dathan and Abiram sons of Eliab" (16:12–14). In 16:3 the challenge is framed in terms of holiness: since all Israel is holy, why should Aaron (and Moses) be "exalted" above the rest? Reading between the lines, Korah and his followers seem to be motivated by envy and a desire for exaltation and high status. And yet their challenge is based on a central truth about Israel—that it is called to be a holy people. Why should some be given greater status and access to God? This is a serious question, one that is similar to many debates about the status of priests and clergy within the church given the affirmation of the "priesthood of all believers."

There are two main ways to read the text's answer to this question. The first is to focus on God's choice: what separates Aaron from Korah is simply God's choice and call, as Moses says in 16:7: "The man whom the LORD chooses shall be the holy one." Given this, the sin of Korah and his followers is refusing to submit to God's choice. But an additional possibility focuses on the nature of holiness: what separates Aaron from Korah is that Aaron *is* holier, as Moses says in 16:5: "In the morning the LORD will make known who is his, and who is holy." Given the theme of holiness in Numbers—namely that God is attempting to form a holy people to reflect the ways of God to the nations—it is fitting to find an emphasis on holiness of character and not mere chosenness.

These two possibilities are not necessarily opposed. Korah and company are not satisfied with God's decision concerning their status and role as Levites. Their seeking the priesthood (16:10) not only goes against God's choice, but also stems from blameworthy motives. It is evident that they are envious of Aaron, and their envy itself is a result of their understanding of the priesthood in terms of social power and exaltation (16:3). In essence they are buying into a system of envy, power, and privilege that is opposed to the ways of God and to the purpose of the priesthood. It is in this way that they "gather . . . against the LORD" (16:11).

Ambrose recognizes this double sin: "They were willing to exercise the priesthood unworthily, and for that reason they dissented. Moreover, they murmured and disapproved of the judgment of God in their election of their priests" (cited in Lienhard 2001: 229).

The censer, the first of the two symbols of Aaron's priesthood highlighted in these chapters, represents the holy calling of the priest. The action of Korah and others in grasping for and using the censer in order to improve their status and privilege exhibits a fundamental misunderstanding of what priesthood and holiness are. Perhaps Moses's question, "What is Aaron that you rail against him?" (16:11), in part implies that Korah and company misunderstand what Aaron is—that is, they misunderstand the office of the priest. Aaron's action with the censer in making "atonement for the people" and standing "between the dead and the living" (16:48–49) contrasts sharply with the actions of Korah and company. Aaron's use of the censer shows that the priesthood is not primarily about exaltation and privilege, but rather service and prayerful mediation for the benefit of others. Priestly actions formed with these intentions are part of what makes a priest holy.

The arguments of Dathan and Abiram move in a slightly different direction (16:12–14). They oppose Moses and Aaron, saying that they have led them out of a good situation to a bad one. They accuse them of in fact wanting "to kill" and "lord it over" the people (16:13), simply wanting power and not caring at all about them, even desiring their ill rather than good. Moses denies their charges. His response, "I have not taken one donkey from them, and I have not harmed any one of them" (16:15), makes sense in light of these accusations.

Dathan and Abiram are in one sense right: the leaders should guide the people toward good, to "a land flowing with milk and honey." Priests should lead in the paths of life, rather than the ways of death. Furthermore, leaders of the people of God should not "lord it over" people for the love of power or material gain. This purpose of true priestly leadership is aptly symbolized by Aaron's budding staff and by Moses's prayer to God to save the people from death (16:22). But Dathan and Abiram grossly misperceive what is good and what is evil for the people. By mistaking Egypt for the promised land, calling it "a land flowing with milk and honey," and the life-giving leadership of Moses and Aaron for one that leads toward death, they fundamentally misunderstand the ways of God. Or perhaps they are simply lying. Whatever the case, their misrepresentation of the situation unmasks the envy and ambition that most likely motives them and shows them to be opposed to the ways of God and "assembled against" God's chosen leaders (16:19). They are blinded by their own desire for power and see Moses and Aaron as leaders with similar intentions to their own—a classic case of projection. Like Korah, they fundamentally misunderstand what priestly leadership should be.

The second part of the story tells the responses of Moses and God to these rebellions (16:19b–35). Moses proposed a test in which all who wanted to lead Israel were to fill their censers and perform priestly duties at the tabernacle (16:16–17), presumably to see which leaders God would accept. Moses later states the terms of this ordeal-like ritual: "If these people die a natural death, or if a natural fate comes on them, then the LORD has not sent me. But if the LORD creates something new, and the ground opens its mouth and swallows them up, . . . then you shall know that these men have despised the LORD" (16:29–30). The result is well known: the earth opened up and swallowed the rebellious leaders, their households, and all their goods, and then 250 other leaders who went along with Korah, Dathan, and Abiram were consumed in fire.

Two things should be said in response to such a horrific event. First, the abhorrence of God for the sins of Korah, Dathan, and Abiram must not be missed. They are symbols of a type of religious leadership that is in stark contrast to the ways of God. These leaders of Israel use language and arguments that are partially true—the people *are* holy, and the leaders *should* lead the people in the ways of life. Likewise, they take up a key symbol of the priest's role, the censer. But they use these truths and that symbol to disguise that they really have rejected the ways of God and instead subscribed to a style and understanding of leadership that is ultimately about power, position, and envious desire for them. It is frightening how easily disguised such intentions can be and how difficult it is for leaders, especially leaders of the people of God, to sift through even their own intentions.

A similar situation is seen in the temptation of Christ at the beginning of his ministry. As recorded in Matthew and Luke, the temptations of Christ seem to be precisely about what kind of Messiah he would be. The temptation involving the temple—"if you are the Son of God, throw yourself down" (Matt. 4:6)—concerns whether Christ would use his status before God in order to serve his own ends or would resist the temptation and instead follow the difficult priestly way of the cross, offering his life for the sake of others.

The difficulty in discerning the motives of leaders can even be seen in the way that this text has been used throughout church history. In early controversies about the leadership within the church, Num. 16 was used to suppress bishops and leaders considered heretical. For example, Cyprian uses this passage to argue that people should separate themselves "from a sinful leader and should not take part in the sacrifices of a sacrilegious bishop" (cited in Lienhard 2001: 230). Whether this is an appropriate application of the text depends in part upon Cyprian's motives. Is he using religious language in order to bolster his own position and power, and so ironically acting more like Korah, Dathan, and Abiram than like Aaron? Or is he a true shepherd of the flock, interested in leading the people in the ways of life? Similarly, Botticelli's fresco points to the same temptations that leaders of the Roman Catholic Church must face. Does the fresco use religious imagery in order to stop questioning of absolute papal power, or is it a warning to all church leaders, even the pope, to avoid the errors of Korah and company?

A related issue is the historical background of this text itself. Much discussion is devoted to the way this episode functioned in the context of later priestly conflicts in Israel.[31] One historical reconstruction of this text sees a power struggle between the descendents of Aaron and the descendents of Korah. The Aaronites sought to secure their priestly power and status over the Korahites by forming this story in such a way as to show that God wanted them, and not the Korahites, to be high priests. By putting this story in the sacred texts, the Aaronites secured their power. The ironic thing about this reconstruction is that the final form of the text clearly speaks against such motives for power and status and against the understanding that the priesthood is essentially about high status, power, and privilege. If there was such a conflict between Aaronites and Korahites, the providential hand of God in the construction of the final form of the text clearly subverted the bad intentions of its redactors. Perhaps there are better ways to reconstruct the history of these texts.

31. Hutton 1994: 35; Budd 1984: 181–86; Milgrom 1990: 414–23; and Coats, *Rebellion in the Wilderness*, 165–84.

A second response to the punishment of Korah and company might be ventured. The scenes of destruction as whole tents and families are swallowed by the earth and images of the charred remains of the 250 leaders are disturbing. One might question the harshness of God's punishment and the justice of his punishing all the households of rebellious leaders. Moses and Aaron themselves set a precedent for such questioning. They begged God to limit his wrath in the face of sin: "O God, the God of the spirits of all flesh, shall one person sin and you become angry with the whole congregation?" (16:22). But they do not question God based on a notion of justice derived independently of God's law. For how could such a notion of justice be properly grounded? Instead, they first mention a characteristic of God—that God is the creator of "the spirits of all flesh"—to appeal to God's concern and love for all that he created, not to a separate standard of justice. Similarly, Christians might also humbly question the aptness of this punishment by referring to another action of God, the giving of his son for the salvation of sinners, that at first seems incongruous with God's pouring out of his wrath on so many people in Israel. God's justice in this passage seems closer to the form it takes in the story of Noah than to the form "the righteousness of God" (cf. Rom. 1:17) takes in God's activity in Christ. But rather than driving a wedge between the New Testament mercy of God and the Old Testament justice of God, in Christ both mercy and righteousness meet. In Christ the righteousness that Israel was called to is fulfilled and the wrath of God against sin is simultaneously expressed. God's mercy and justice are seen and fulfilled in Christ.[32]

Scene 2: Revolt of the People and Aaron's Censer (16:41–50)

After the punishment of Korah, his family, and the 250 men who offered incense, the censers of the rebels are taken and beaten into "a covering for the altar" (16:36–40). This covering becomes "a sign" (16:38) for the Israelites that they should not follow in the ways of Korah, that "no outsider, who is not of the descendants of Aaron, shall approach to offer incense before the LORD" (16:40). The censers are beaten into a symbol that is a reminder to the priests of how not to act.

But immediately after this, the whole congregation wrongly blames Moses and Aaron for what happened to Korah and the others. This second part of this larger rebellion (16:41–50) highlights the people acting in a way quite opposite to how they should act as a priestly people.[33]

One might have expected that in response to the punishment of Korah the people would have mourned for their complicity in the rebellion. But instead of repentance and mourning and confession, the people blame Moses and Aaron: "You have killed the people of the LORD" (16:41–42). Instead of cleansing themselves of their own sin (→19:1–22), they sought to blame others. It is clear that

32. Barth's treatment (1936–77: 2/1.322–677) of the perfections of God is a classic exposition of the way God's justice and mercy should be understood in light of each other.
33. Num. 16:41–50 in English Bibles is numbered 17:6–15 in the Masoretic Text.

they are in error—Moses and Aaron neither killed them nor asked God to. Instead, Moses and Aaron pleaded with God to not consume the entire congregation along with the instigators. The people's response, both their accusation and their "assembling" against Moses and Aaron (16:42), shows that they too are rebelling against the leaders God has chosen and refusing to follow the Lord's direction. Korah's rebellion was premised on their being holy and called to be priests. Their actions show that they have far to go to live up to such a vision.

In response, God is once again ready to consume them: "Get away from this congregation, so that I may consume them in a moment" (16:45). Hearing this, Moses and Aaron again work together to avert disaster. At Moses's direction, Aaron takes fire from the altar and offers incense in order to "make atonement" (16:46) for the people. In contrast to the way that Korah and the leaders took up the censer, Aaron uses it in a way that shows what it means to be a true priest. He "stood between the dead and the living" (16:48), offered incense to God, and in this way "made atonement for the people" (16:47).

Offering incense to God is often associated with burnt offerings and is understood throughout scripture as a ritual of worship and dedication to God. The sweet smell of incense symbolizes something pleasing to God, the prayers of the saints (Ps. 141:2; Rev. 5:8; 8:3–4). While burnt offerings are tokens of the dedication of one's whole self to God, incense is more closely associated with the offering of our "mouths" to God—our thoughts and words in prayer. Such prayer is kindled by the fire of love for God.

While Moses and Aaron earlier prayed before God on behalf of the people (16:22), Aaron now shows his priestly zeal in a more visible way. Just as some kind of "plague" breaks out from God as an extension of his wrath, Aaron apparently steps into its path, standing "between the dead and the living," risking himself while praying and censing to God in order to keep the plague from advancing. In so doing, he shows great love for those he is priest to. Just as the sweet smell of incense is pleasing to God, so too is that which the incense symbolizes: Aaron's zeal and prayers of intercession for the people. Aaron's actions atone for the people's sins because they are worthy tokens of the dedication and service God desires of all his priestly people (→7:1–88). Aaron's act of priestly zeal is accepted by God in such a way that it covers over the sin of the people. On account of Aaron's prayer and zealous action on behalf of the people, God's wrath is stopped—it passes over the people. Aaron's action with the censer both atones for the sin of the people and provides a wonderful symbol of the calling of priestly leaders.

Scene 3: Aaron's Budding Staff (17:1–11)

The final scene in the rebellion against the priestly leadership of Moses and Aaron is the story of the budding of Aaron's staff.[34] A second ordeal-like test is

---

34. Num. 17:1–11 in English Bibles is numbered 17:16–26 in the Masoretic Text.

now commanded by God, a test intended to put an end to the people's questioning and challenging of Aaron and Moses. The initial rebellion of Korah questioned whether Moses, rather than God, had chosen Aaron to be high priest over the priests and Levites. Both the authority of Moses and Aaron were being challenged. To put an end to this, the leaders of the tribes were now instructed to bring a staff with their name written on it,[35] and they as well as Aaron were to place their staves in front of the covenant in the tabernacle (17:2–4). The staff that sprouted would be a sign from God about "who is his, and who is holy, and who will be allowed to approach him" (16:5). The next day, Aaron's staff had sprouted: "It put forth buds, produced blossoms, and bore ripe almonds" (17:8). Given the lack of any further direct challenges to the authority of Moses and Aaron until their deaths, the test and the staff's placement in the tabernacle as "a warning to rebels" (17:10) served their purpose.

Both the test and the symbols involved in it inform us about the nature of Aaron's priesthood and the nature of priestly roles within the people of God. That such a test was conducted at all shows that not just anyone could fill the role of high priest; its miraculous nature suggests that a special calling or anointing was required, at least in the case of Aaron. Serving in this capacity was not left to the will of the individual or based on the holiness of the people or even the special status of the tribe of the Levites. Out of all the people, God desired one person, Aaron, to be priest before him, and from him, his family, as is written in Heb. 5:4: "One does not presume to take this honor, but takes it only when called by God, just as Aaron was." Just as the staff symbolizes authority, its miraculous budding is a sign of the special call and anointing by God.

So while Korah was right to say that "all the congregation are holy, everyone of them, and the LORD is among them" (16:3), a more specific calling and further initiative of God is required for certain tasks and callings of the people of God.[36] Christian theology often calls such Old Testament callings "offices," roles within the larger people of God that came about by a special anointing and calling by God.[37] While not all priests required miraculous proofs that they were individually chosen by God, the priestly calling to cross the boundary between creatures and God can be made effective only through the work and initiative of God, who calls, equips, and works in and through the actions of the priest. Such work

35. There is debate whether there were twelve or thirteen staves. Since most lists of the tribes in Numbers do *not* count Levi as one of the twelve (e.g., 1:5–15; 26:5–50), it is likely that there were thirteen in total.

36. These statements are consciously in contrast to the typical Weberian distinction between prophets and priests, that the priests' authority rested upon an institutionalized type of authority while the prophetic authority was more charismatic. See discussion and critique of such common assumptions in Hutton 1994.

37. See Wainwright, *For Our Salvation*, 109–17, for discussion of the three offices of prophet, priest, and king in church writings. The application of these three titles or offices to Christ and the people of God is found in the New Testament and systematically used as early as the fourth century.

of God is well symbolized by the anointing of the priest with oil and the rites of investiture (Lev. 8–9).

The stress in Numbers that all the people are called to be holy, however, shows that the relationship between Aaron's role and that of the people is not as simple as Aaron being holy while the Levites and people are not; rather, the role of the people is in some way specially focused and/or intensified in the priest. He represents the people in a participative way. The priest's garments bear the names of the tribes, suggesting his representation of all the people. Conversely, the blue thread in the tassels that all the people wear bears a resemblance to the garments of the priests, suggesting that all the people are like priests (→15:37–41). Yet, that only Aaron and his sons are invested with certain responsibilities shows a gradation in the holiness of different classes of people within Israel.

The difficulty in precisely naming the relationship between the holiness of the Old Testament priest and the holiness of the rest of the people is mirrored in Christian debate about the meaning of ordained ministry, a debate complicated by Christ fulfilling the role of high priest (Heb. 5:5–10). One pole of the debate is well represented by Josiah Tidwell: "As Christians, we are all priests alike. Christians, through the virtue of the blood of Christ, occupy the same position before God. . . . The New Testament knows no such thing as a certain class of men—a certain privileged caste—being brought into higher position, or a nearer position, to God than their brethren. All such teaching is flatly opposed by the teaching of the New Testament and is subversive of the first and finest principles of Christianity."[38] On the other hand, the official teaching of the Roman Catholic Church since the sixteenth century has generally emphasized the unique calling of its priests and bishops. In recent times, however, it has more warmly embraced the notion that the people of God as a whole participate in these offices of Christ, while still holding on to the special status of the "apostles and their successors."[39] Conversely, many Protestant traditions are reclaiming richer notions of pastoral ordination, notions that more closely reflect the status of the priestly classes in Numbers.[40]

However one understands the precise relationship between the calling of ordained ministers and the priesthood of all believers in the church, the details of the test in Num. 17—that rods or staves were used, that the sign of selection is the staff budding and blossoming—suggest deeper meanings about the nature of the priestly calling. Many allegorical interpretations of Aaron's budding rod have been suggested. Jewish kabalistic interpretations correlated the bare staff, buds, blossoms, and ripe almonds to the four letters of the divine name.

38. Josiah Blake Tidwell, *Christ in the Pentateuch; or, Spiritual Values in the Books of Moses* (repr., Grand Rapids: Zondervan, 1940), 331.
39. For this understanding of "catholic," see *Catechism of the Catholic Church* (Liguori, MO: Liguori, 1994), §§436, 783–86, 871–73.
40. Wainwright, *For Our Salvation*, 107; *Baptism, Eucharist, and Ministry*, Faith and Order Paper 111 (Geneva: World Council of Churches, 1982).

Christians often see the rod as the stem of Jesse, or Mary, out of which springs Christ. Others note that the almond is one of the first trees to blossom in spring and so symbolizes new life. Some point out that the Hebrew word for "almond" (*šāqēd*) is related to the word for "watch" (*šāqad*; cf. Jer. 1:11–12) or is a play on the root for "holy" (*qdš*), which suggests that the role of the priest is to be watchful or to create holiness in the people. Finally, some understand that the new life springing out of bare wood is a symbol of Christ's resurrection.[41]

While all these are possible, perhaps the basic and obvious interpretations are most helpful. The rod is a symbol of authority, and its budding and sprouting is a symbol of life. The rod thus symbolizes proper priestly authority and leadership that brings life. The besetting sin of many leaders is seeking or using authority and power for their own benefit and prestige. Instead, the role of leadership in the people of God is to bring life to the people, to guide them in the paths of life, and to use discipline and authority for the health and life of the community. In Ps. 23, the rod and staff are used by the good shepherd, the Lord, to guide the people of God "in right paths" (23:3). Leaders of the people of God should use their authority and power similarly. Thus while the rod itself may or may not be a direct type of Christ, certainly Christ's leadership, priesthood, and authority fulfill the image of proper leadership and use of power that Aaron's rod represents (→27:12–23).

Dealing with Unworthy Approaches to God: Laws concerning Levites and Priests, the Red Heifer Ceremony, and Death of Miriam (17:12–20:1)

In the aftermath of the rebellion led by Dathan, Korah, and Abiram, many Israelites died through the action of God, both the 250 who offered incense (16:35) and 14,700 from the larger congregation (16:49). While Israel is called to be a people with God in their midst, a people called to approach God in worship and receive God's blessing (6:22–27), because of their sin and rebellion, approaching God appears instead to be bringing judgment and death. It is not without reason that the congregation said, "Everyone who approaches the tabernacle of the LORD will die" (17:13).[42]

These chapters offer pragmatic solutions to the problem raised in 17:13 (Ashley 1993: 336). They set down laws for the priests and Levites and for the people to help prevent unworthy approaches in the future and to minimize the negative impact when they do happen. They consist first of laws about the service of the

---

41. Calvin's interpretation is classic Calvin: "I pass by the frivolous allegories in which others take delight," but then he proceeds to allegorize. He argues that the rod is a symbol of Christ, for he is the "sprout from the stem of Jesse," and that "by His resurrection He was separated from the whole human race" (1852: 4.127).

42. Num. 17:12–13 in English Bibles is numbered 17:27–28 in the Masoretic Text.

Levites and priests (18:1–7) and the tithes and offerings that support this service (18:8–32). The priests and Levites are told that they will "bear responsibility" (18:1) for the sins of others. Their heightened responsibility for guarding the tabernacle will help prevent the kind of mass destruction of the people just seen in Num. 16.

Similarly, the laws of 19:1–22 concerning the cleansing water made from the ashes of the red heifer are certainly practical. Given that so many people of Israel had died in the rebellion, there were many corpses throughout the camp, inevitably causing the entire people to be ritually unclean and thus unable to approach the tabernacle. These rituals provide a way for the people to be free of uncleanness from corpses and enemies (→31:19–24). The gift of these laws highlights God's continuing provision of ways that Israel might approach him even in their uncleanness.

But all these laws are more than pragmatic responses to problems. Just as the laws of Num. 15 contrast with the behavior of Israel in Num. 13–14, so too these laws set forth patterns of life and worship for the priests, Levites, and the people that contrast with the leaders' rebellious approach to God in 16:1–17:11.

These practices undercut the envy, pride, and desire for power that motivated Dathan, Korah, and the other leaders. The priests and Levites will have "no allotment in their land" (18:20), but rather will exist through the tithes of those they serve (18:8–19). Furthermore, the Levites are instructed to give a tithe of the tithes that they receive (18:25–32). Rather than bringing only privilege, this "honour, conjoined as it was with so much difficulty and danger, was by no means to be envied" (Calvin 1852: 2.253). These practices have the potential to form attitudes of service, humility, and responsibility in these priestly leaders of Israel. So too the practices by which the people purify themselves will help them to live into the vision of who they are to be in the promised land.

Responsibility of Priests and Levites for Holy Things (18:1–7)

The main duties of the priests and Levites were presented in Num. 1, 4, 3, where an important function of those priestly classes was to guard the holy places and things against encroachment by outsiders (1:50–53; 3:10, 38). Now laws are given that stipulate the chain of responsibility when such order is broken down, when there are "offenses connected with the sanctuary" (18:1).[43]

If the holy things are improperly approached, these laws say that God's wrath will not break out on the entire people of Israel as it did in 16:45. Instead, the priestly classes—not the entire congregation—will "bear responsibility." The Hebrew word *ʿăwôn* ("responsibility") can mean either guilt or penalty. Given that the reason for these duties is "so that wrath may never again come upon the

---

43. The chain of responsibility is that the priests and Kohathites will be responsible for offenses by lay Israelites (18:1a), the priests for offenses by other priests (18:1b), and the priests and all the Levites for offenses by Levites (18:3) (Ashley 1993: 337; Milgrom 1990: 145).

Israelites" (18:5), this most likely means bearing the penalty or wrath of God for these offenses.

The assignment of responsibility serves two purposes in this context. It first reassures all the Israelites that their fear expressed in 17:12–13 will not come to pass. They can approach the tabernacle to worship and offer sacrifices without fear of death. It also reminds the priests and Levites that their election and call to service is not an election to privilege and power, but rather to an important service that has grave responsibilities attached to it. Its importance is seen in the words "the LORD said to Aaron" (18:1). The Lord spoke directly with Aaron only here (18:1, 8, 20) and in Lev. 10:8. These speeches concern central aspects of the duties of priests and Levites, including dire warnings for improperly carrying them out.

The great responsibility attached to priestly leadership within the people of God is not limited to ancient Israel. The admonition of James concerning leadership within the people of God is similar: "Not many of you should become teachers, my brothers and sisters, for you know that we who teach will be judged with greater strictness" (Jas. 3:1). The task of priestly leaders to keep out those who would approach the holy things of God unworthily also resonates with Paul's description of church leaders as "stewards of God's mysteries" (1 Cor. 4:1). His instructions about church discipline and the Lord's Supper (11:27–34) highlight that such stewardship involves discernment and discipline within the people of God—for their own good: "Examine yourselves. . . . For all who eat and drink without discerning the body, eat and drink judgment against themselves. For this reason many of you are weak and ill, and some have died" (11:29–30). Recent scholarship on these verses argues that the sins of the Corinthian church, manifested in their unworthy celebration of the Lord's Supper, were quite similar to the sins of the Israelites, manifested in their approach of the tabernacle: class and leadership conflict, pride, envy, and spiritual presumption.[44] The form that discipline should take in the church and issues of who should come to the Lord's Supper continue to be difficult issues for Christians. But this section of Numbers suggests that discernment and cleansing are the responsibility not only of church leaders (Num. 18) but also of the people (Num. 19).

The question of what defines a worthy or unworthy approach is another matter. An example of an unworthy encroachment on the tabernacle would be a person who willfully desired to physically desecrate the holy places and things (→3:1–4:49). But in the previous rebellion, it was Korah and the leaders' presumptive spiritual pride and desire for power that made them unworthy and that caused the wrath of God to break out. Yet one need not be entirely holy to approach the tabernacle. Instead, humility before God, proper desire for God, sorrow for sin

---

44. Gordon D. Fee, *The First Epistle to the Corinthians*, New International Commentary on the New Testament (Grand Rapids: Eerdmans, 1987), 531–69.

as symbolized in the sacrifices, willingness to recognize God's order in the observance of the proper boundaries between clean and unclean and in one's place in the community—it is these that make an approach worthy.

Portions for Priests and Levites; Tithing of Tithes (18:8–32)

Following the responsibility placed on the priestly classes, the people of Israel are given laws concerning the tithes and sacrifices due to priests (18:8–19) and Levites (18:20–24). The portions for the priests are divided into two kinds: those from the "most holy" sacrifices (18:9–10) and those from the other "holy" sacrifices (18:11–19). The first group must be eaten only by the priests, while the second group can be shared by those who are ritually clean in the priest's household (18:11, 13). The Levites are to receive the regular tithes for their portion and support (cf. Lev. 27:30–31; Deut. 14:23).

This section groups together regulations scattered in different parts of the Pentateuch and also emphasizes that these offerings are given to the priests and Levites in exchange for their valuable service at the sanctuary. As Num. 18:20, 21, 24 states, the priests and Levites are to receive no land and no allotment. "I am your share and your possession among the Israelites," God tells the priests (18:20). The landlessness of this class means that they are dependent upon other Israelites for support. Their need and dependence is a living reminder of what is true of all Israelites: that they live because of God's gift and providence. The system of tithing and support serves practical purposes, but the way that Israel is structured economically also points beyond themselves to their relationship to God.

That the Levites must also tithe from the tithes received (18:25–32) shows that tithes in general are not merely taxes, mandatory payments for centralized services, but are also gifts given back to God. "It shall be reckoned to you as your gift" (18:27)—in the same way that tithes of other Israelites were portions of their means of support and gifts back to God. Tithing by Levites is a way to recognize that the tithes they receive are gifts from God.

The Old Testament idea of supporting priests and Levites through the tithes and offerings of the people continued in New Testament church practices: "Do you not know that those who are employed in the temple service get their food from the temple, and those who serve at the altar share in what is sacrificed on the altar? In the same way, the Lord commanded that those who proclaim the gospel should get their living by the gospel" (1 Cor. 9:13–14).

It is easy for those in capitalist economies to view this pattern of tithing through the reductive logic of an exchange of payment for services. Many have critiqued the support of clergy through the offerings of the people as problematic on many grounds, one of which is its great potential to distort their character. It could create an incentive for hypocrisy (since clergy must feign devotion to God in order to eat), sloth, or working hard for the wrong reasons, such as the desire for larger or more affluent congregations so that their own income will be greater.[45]

While there is always danger of abuse in any system—as Num. 16 certainly reminds us—the system of tithing, if done in the right way with the right intentions, can be understood as a solution to such abuses.[46] The tithing of the Levites themselves resists the logic of simple exchange of services, and the whole system can be understood as an exchange of gifts that recognizes and reflects the great generosity of God. John Milbank and other contemporary theologians argue that the very triune nature of God is one of an eternal gift exchange.[47] This self-giving should be reflected in our own horizontal economies and patterns of relationship, in this way manifesting the inner life of God. In Numbers, the system of tithing and the motivations that should underlie it contrast with, and are a partial solution to, the unworthy motivations of Dathan, Korah, and others concerning the priesthood. Rather than critiquing the system itself, the contemporary church could well benefit from paying closer attention to tithing and support of clergy, which if rightly practiced bring us closer to the heart of our worship of God.

Corpse Contamination and the Red Heifer Ceremony: Responsibility of Israelites to Purify Themselves (19:1–22)

In the aftermath of the rebellion of Dathan, Korah, and others, nearly 15,000 Israelites died. The issue of corpse contamination would thus be of great concern to the Israelites at this point, and it is likely that the entire congregation would have been unclean because of the many dead bodies. Laws describing the rituals to perform in order to rectify corpse contamination naturally follow the rebellion and provide a practical solution to a serious problem that Israel faces as a result.

On a deeper level, these laws also provide a different kind of solution to Israel's problems caused by Korah's rebellion. The ceremonies envisioned here could be practiced by any clean person in Israel. Indeed, one of the emphases of the chapter is the responsibility of the average Israelite to "purify themselves" (19:13, 20). This stress on the responsibility of nonpriests or non-Levites to maintain their own ritual purity balances the grave responsibilities of priests and Levites to protect purity in worship (18:1–7). In combination, all Israel—priests and nonpriests—is responsible to keep ritually clean and pure in order to worship God. It is a purity

---

45. David Hume's trenchant critique of the character of clergy is in part tied to their monetary support by their congregations; *Writings on Religion*, ed. A. Flew (La Salle, IL: Open Court, 1993), 11–14.

46. See Olson 1996: 117–19 for a healthy critique of the potential and actual abuses of the priesthood included in this portion of Numbers and elsewhere in the Old Testament.

47. John Milbank, "Can a Gift Be Given? Prolegomena to a Future Trinitarian Metaphysic," *Modern Theology* 11 (1995): 119–61. Todd Billings argues that Calvin's theology is more amenable to such an understanding of the gift nature of God's character and economy than Milbank and others acknowledge; *Calvin, Participation, and the Gift: The Activity of Believers in Union with Christ* (Oxford: Oxford University Press, 2007).

that resists and disowns death and corruption—both of which are associated with the breakdown of God's life-giving order in the world. It is a purity that takes time, patience, and effort. A people formed by such practices would have a different character than that of Korah and the other leaders.

Three rituals are described: making the ashes of the red heifer or cow (19:1–10), cleansing someone who touches a dead body (19:11–13), and cleansing people who come into contact with tents where people died, graves, human bones, and those slain in battle (19:14–20), plus the detail that the person who sprinkles the water or touches it is unclean until evening (19:21–22).

The entire ceremony is considered a purification or sin offering: "It is a purification [*ḥaṭṭāʾt*] offering" (19:9). Sin offerings rectify the contaminating aspect of sin and the broken relationship between God and sinner (→7:1–88). While some sin offerings directly cleanse the sanctuary, especially on the Day of Atonement (Lev. 16:16), by sprinkling blood on it, here the people themselves are sprinkled. The holiness of the people is tied to that of the tabernacle: "All who touch a corpse . . . and do not purify themselves defile the tabernacle of the LORD" (Num. 19:13). Concern about the tabernacle's holiness moves outward to include the camp and the people.

The red elements of the sacrifice—the red cow, cedarwood, and "crimson material" (19:6)—are significant because they are the color of blood, a symbol of the power of life.[48]

Similar materials are used in the ritual for cleansing leprous persons: the priest "shall take the living bird with the cedarwood and the crimson yarn and the hyssop, and dip them and the living bird in the blood of the bird that was slaughtered over the fresh water" (Lev. 14:6).[49] The two ceremonies are similar because of the connection between death and leprosy: both manifest the breakdown of the body, and leprosy is a kind of social death that removes one from the community. Miriam was earlier punished by God with leprosy, and her state was likened to a stillborn child (Num. 12:10–12).

The cleansing ritual itself is rather simple: special ashes are mixed with "running water" (19:17) and sprinkled on the contaminated people and objects using hyssop (a reedlike plant with a hairy surface that retains liquid and is ideal for ritual sprinkling), once on the third day and again on the seventh day. As a result, they are purified. The prominence of the number seven—"purifying them on the seventh day" (19:12, 19)—is suggestive of the seven days of creation.[50]

Given all this symbolism, the purpose of the cleansing ritual apparently is to move people and things from a deathlike state where corruption reigns to a renewed life, to a new creation. This new beginning allows the people of God to

48. Samuel E. Balentine, *Leviticus*, Interpretation (Louisville: Westminster John Knox, 2002), 110.

49. The only other specific rite that explicitly mentions hyssop is that of the placing of blood on the doorposts and lintels during Passover (Exod. 12:22).

50. Balentine, *Leviticus*, 109.

participate again in the worship and sacrifices of the tabernacle. For the people of Israel in the wilderness, this cleansing was certainly needed in order for them to worship God without offense.

But as the rebellions of Israel also showed, Israel needed to be cleansed not only on the outside, because of their contact with corpses, but also at the moral level. The concern with clean and unclean is in part a concern to live within the life-giving order of God at all levels (→5:1–4). The obedient practice of this rite would involve the people, not only the priests and Levites, in the concern to shun death and corruption and all ways of being that run against the ways and order of God.

In, under, and through this rite, God provided a way for the people to approach him in a worthy manner. Performed with the connection in mind between outer and inner purity, the ceremony could also be an embodied prayer in which the ways of death were rejected and God implored for forgiveness. The writer of Hebrews makes this connection explicit for Christians, for he understands that the ashes of the red heifer find their true type in the sacrifice of Christ (9:11–14), arguing "how much more" will the blood of Christ "purify our conscience from dead works to worship the living God!" The psalmist also makes explicit connections between outer and inner cleansing: "Wash me thoroughly from my iniquity, and cleanse me from my sin. . . . Purge me with hyssop, and I shall be clean; wash me, and I shall be whiter than snow. . . . Hide your face from my sin, and blot out all my iniquities. Create in me a clean heart, O God" (Ps. 51:2, 7, 9–10).

Death of Miriam (20:1)

After the rebellion of Korah and the laws given in its aftermath, the people of Israel continue on their journey. As they reach Kadesh, Miriam's death is recorded simply: "Miriam died there, and was buried there" (20:1).

While mentioned without much fanfare, this notice of her death is significant. It underlines that Miriam, a woman, is considered one of the most important leaders of the exodus generation of Israel next to Moses and Aaron. She is recognized as a prophet (Exod. 15:20–21) and leads the people in the victory song after their passage through the Red Sea. She is an important example that women are considered capable of and called to positions of leadership in the people of God.

In Numbers, however, she is also an example—along with Moses and Aaron—of how even exemplary leaders can fall short of who they are called to be. Miriam, with Aaron, challenged the prophetic status of Moses in the third rebellion. Similar to the fifth rebellion of Korah and the other leaders, it was a challenge to the leadership of Israel that God had instituted. Miriam's death marks a significant point in the death of the exodus generation. Given the response of God to the central rebellion—"in this wilderness they shall come to a full end" (14:35)—the death of that generation had to happen before Israel could enter the promised land. Seen also as a spiritual journey, Israel's progress involves the "death" of the sins that older generation embodies and symbolizes. Miriam's sin, similar to that of Korah, was one of envy, pride, and the pursuit of leadership status for the wrong reasons, a sin that led to its own uncleanness (12:14–15). Like Miriam, that uncleanness had to die in order for Israel to make progress toward its goal. It was a costly and difficult journey.

Rebellion 6: Waters of Meribah; Moses and Aaron's Sin (20:2–13)

In the sixth rebellion in the wilderness, it is once again the congregation who complains: "Now there was no water for the congregation; so they gathered together against Moses and against Aaron" (20:2). Like the second rebellion, the matter concerns the basic physical needs of the people: in 11:4–34 it was food, here the concern is water. And similar to that earlier episode, the leaders of the people, Moses and Aaron, also falter. As a result of their sinful response to the people and God's instructions, they are punished: "You shall not bring this assembly into the land that I have given them" (20:12).

While the action is fairly straightforward, several intriguing and ambiguous details in the episode raise questions about how to interpret the action: Were the Israelites wrong to complain since God does not punish them? What precisely was Moses and Aaron's sin? How should one interpret Moses's question, "Shall we bring water for you out of the rock?" Is there any significance to the rock? the staff? the two strikes? What does "showing God's holiness" mean? Interpreters through the centuries have given a range of answers to these questions (Milgrom 1990: 448–56; Olson 1996: 126–28). One's interpretation should be guided by paying close attention not only to the episode itself but also to the parallel account in Exod. 17:1–7 and to this episode's place within the carefully structured rebellion narrative of Numbers.[51] Given that the middle section of Numbers focuses on the failures of Israel to live up to its calling, the key interpretive challenge is to understand both the sin of the people and the sin of Moses and Aaron.

The narrative first highlights that the congregation "gathered together against" Moses and Aaron (20:2) and "quarreled with" Moses (20:3) in response to the lack of water. Their full complaint is stated in 20:3–5. Even though much of the narrative focuses on the sin of Moses and Aaron, the conclusion in 20:13 bookends the episode by pointing again to the problems of the people: "These are the waters of Meribah, where the people of Israel quarreled with the LORD." This clearly highlights the failure of the people and not merely the sin of Israel's leaders,

51. Since the two episodes are similar, their differences help interpret them. But it is not helpful to find a theoretically reconstructed "original" single narrative as Gray 1903: 260–64 does, who then concludes: "The truth is, the story is mutilated; and as any attempt to reconstruct it must be tentative, the exact nature of the sin of the leaders must remain doubtful" (262). Ashley 1993: 377–79, 386 is rightly unconvinced that these two separate narratives refer to a single incident, told twice in different ways. Whatever the historical case, the final author(s) of Numbers was clearly aware of Exod. 17:1–7 and intentionally portrayed this as a similar, yet distinct, episode in the travels of Israel, as shown by the mention of both in Num. 33:14, 37.

just as in the second rebellion. Their complaint is quite similar to the people's complaint in the second and fourth rebellions. The people remember their life in Egypt as better than their circumstances now: "Why have you brought us up out of Egypt, to bring us to this wretched place? It is no place for grain, or figs, or vines, or pomegranates; and there is no water to drink" (20:5; cf. 11:5; 14:2–3). Their complaint about the figs, vines, and pomegranates drips with irony, for those are the very foods that the scouts brought back from the promised land (13:23–24). They forget that their own rejection of the land, their own refusal to believe (14:11) and obey (14:22) God, is the reason they are not enjoying those foods.

As in the second rebellion, the people's sin is their almost willful forgetfulness and lack of gratitude for what God has done for them, their lack of seeing their own sin as part of the reason for their problems, combined with their lack of trust in God's ability and desire to provide for their basic needs. While they are not punished for their sin, the tone and word choice of the text and the parallels to previous rebellions indicate they are blameworthy.[52] The lack of punishment should be seen as a sign of God's compassion and merciful restraint (as Ps. 78:38 claims) rather than their innocence. Lacking water, they should have asked Moses and God for it, rather than ungratefully and unfaithfully quarrelling and desiring to go back to Egypt. Positive counterexamples of what Israel should have done can be seen in the Nazirite, who voluntarily forgoes the fruit of the vine for a time out of zealous dedication to God (Num. 6:1–4), and in the practices in the yearly festival calendar, in which Israel remembers God's goodness in delivering from Egypt, providential guidance, and promises for the future and recommits itself to being God's covenant partner (Num. 28–29). Instead, Israel, at the first sign of creaturely discomfort and potential trouble, is willing to turn away from God and forget all that God had done.

While the people are blameworthy, the climax of the narrative is the sin of Moses and Aaron. The response of the Lord to their actions makes clear that they have done something seriously wrong: "Because you did not trust in me, to show my holiness before the eyes of the Israelites, therefore you shall not bring this assembly into the land that I have given them" (20:12). The key issue is that they do not "trust" God (*lō' he'ĕmantem bî*), or they were not faithful to him (cf. 14:11). The full phrase suggests that their lack of trust or faithfulness involved not "sanctifying" God or "showing God's holiness" in the eyes of the people.

A clue to how their actions did not sanctify God is seen in 20:13. It says that even though Moses and Aaron did not show God's holiness, through these events God "showed his holiness." God's holiness was manifest in two ways: through judging the sin of Moses and Aaron and "by giving water to his thirsty people and their animals" (Ashley 1993: 386). If Moses and Aaron had strictly obeyed God's instructions, they would have shown forth God's holiness through their

---

52. Contra Thomas B. Dozeman, "The Book of Numbers," in *The New Interpreter's Bible*, ed. L. Keck (Nashville: Abingdon, 1998), 2.160; Olson 1996: 129.

obedience and trust and by manifesting God's mercy and power to provide for his people. Based on this, Moses's sin may have been the double sin of lacking faith in God's trustworthiness to provide and assuming that God lacked mercy and care for the people.

Moses's question in 20:10—"listen, you rebels, shall we bring water for you out of this rock?"—can be reasonably interpreted in several ways (Olson 1996: 126–27). It may be a manifestation of the impatience of Moses with the people ("you rebels!") combined with his desperate doubt of God's power and/or trustworthiness to bring forth water from the rock (Olson paraphrases: "Do you really think we can bring water for you out of this rock?"). Moses's culpability was compounded by doing so publicly in front of the Israelites. While other explanations are just as convincing if only this verse is taken into account,[53] this interpretation fits better with the larger structure of the rebellion narratives. Given Moses's doubt and lack of faith in God's providence, Moses's attitude would be quite similar to his questions in the second rebellion: "Where am I to get meat to give to all this people?" (11:13); "are there enough flocks and herds to slaughter for them?" (11:22). His lack of trust is similar to the people's lack of trust in the central rebellion: "We are not able to go up against this people, for they are stronger than we" (13:31). Thus in the second, fourth, and sixth rebellions, the leaders and the people show a lack of faith in God's power and providence, while in the third and fifth, the leaders are too prideful and self-promoting.[54]

Compounding this lack of trust in God was Moses's anger and lack of care for the people, as suggested by Ps. 106:32–33: "They angered the LORD at the waters of Meribah, and it went ill with Moses on their account; for they made his spirit bitter, and he spoke words that were rash." Moses did not sanctify God by not exhibiting God's mercy and care in his role as God's representative to the people (contra Milgrom 1990: 448–49).

Moses's double strike of the rock with the rod can be seen as manifesting his lack of faith in God—one strike should have been enough—and also as an expression of anger and frustration with the people (as Ibn Ezra and Maimonides suggest). Again, the parallels to the second rebellion convince me that part of Moses's sin is his lack of concern for and frustration with the people. Moses's questions in 11:12—"Did I conceive all this people? Did I give birth to them?"—suggests that this was part of Moses's failure in that episode. The chiastic structure of the rebellions suggests it is also part of his sin here.

53. Milgrom 1990: 451–56 suggests that the question was a prideful and idolatrous decree that Moses and Aaron had the power to bring water out of the rock and that this was their sin rather than lacking faith in God's power. By saying "shall *we*" rather than "shall *God*," they put themselves in God's place.

54. Jerome and Basil the Great interpret the sin of Moses and Aaron similarly as lack of trust. Jerome writes: "Priests also must take care lest they be insincere, lest they doubt the power of God" (cited in Lienhard 2001: 239).

The double sin of Moses, and by implication Aaron, can be understood most fundamentally as their failure as leaders to be transparent to the leadership of God. They were called to show forth God's holiness, to represent his power, providence, care, and concern for the people in and through their words and actions. Through both their public doubt in God's power and care and their anger toward the people, they became opaque to God's leadership. Throughout Numbers, the issue of proper leadership emerges as a difficult matter for the people of God. A leader of God's people can become opaque either through doubt and lack of trust in God (second, fourth, and sixth rebellions), lack of care and concern for the people (second and sixth rebellions), or prideful self-promotion and self-interest (third and fifth rebellions). The deeply resonant phrase in 20:12, "to show my holiness before the eyes of the Israelites," suggests the incredibly high calling of a leader of God's people. The tradition in Christian art of painting halos around the heads of saints reflects such an understanding. Within Protestantism, the phrase "the priesthood of all believers," which is intended to highlight the high calling of all Christians—not simply the ordained clergy or religious—has often had the opposite result and lowered expectations and understandings of the church's leadership. Rather than being representatives of God's holiness to the people—an understanding highlighted more in Roman Catholicism and Eastern Orthodoxy—pastors are sometimes understood as little more than therapists or business managers. Numbers pushes back on this tendency.

Dealing with Desire: Encounter with Edom, Death of Aaron, and Vow at Hormah (20:14–21:3)

Between the sixth and seventh rebellions are three episodes: the encounter with Edom (20:14–21), the death of Aaron at Mount Hor (20:22–29), and the vow and war against the Canaanite king of Arad (21:1–3). The fourth and fifth rebellions were both followed by narratives and laws that provide positive counterexamples to the sins of Israel. We find something similar here.

Israel's sixth rebellion consists in part of their complaint about food and water (20:5). Their progress toward the promised land was stalled by their bodily desires. Because of the way they dealt with their physical longings, they were ready to abandon the journey. Here, the positive counterexample consists in Moses's offer to the king of Edom: "We will not pass through field or vineyard, or drink water from any well; we will go along the King's Highway, not turning aside to the right hand or to the left until we have passed through your territory" (20:17). In order to move through this obstacle, Israel is willing to go without grain, wine, or water—or at least not use any of Edom's—for a period of time. In the encounter with the king of Arad, Israel vows to forgo all the spoils of war, dedicating them to God. Both episodes provide positive images of how Israel might deal with its penchant for sins of the body: a kind of voluntary fast from certain desires in order to move forward. In these encounters, Israel exhibits a newfound patience, an increasing ability to deal with its bodily desires, and an increasing dedication. The tone of the journey begins to change as Israel starts its positive turn toward living into its calling to be a holy and priestly people by abstention and self-dedication to God (cf. the Nazirite vow in Num. 6).

Encounter with Edom (20:14–21)

In the encounter with Edom, Moses sends messengers to the king of Edom and asks permission to pass through his land (20:14–17). Moses appeals first to Edom's sympathy for its oppression and hardships (20:14–16) and then argues that Israel will not be a burden on Edom (20:17). Israel vows to pass through without using any of Edom's resources. In Moses's second negotiation, he even promises to pay for anything they might use (20:19). But Edom refuses and blocks Israel's way.

The people of Edom are the descendants of Esau, the brother of Jacob/Israel. So, while the phrase "your brother Israel" (20:14) may be typical diplomatic language, it also contains a deeper truth. While there are other layers to Israel's encounters with Edom here and in later scripture, given that this encounter occurs directly after a rebellion about food and water, one might expect that a main theme of this encounter would relate to that, and indeed food and drink play a prominent role in this meeting of Edom and Israel. The original tension between these brothers also had to do with food. Famished from his time in the field hunting, Esau "despised" and sold his birthright in exchange for Jacob's food (Gen. 25:29–34). Israel's temptations in the wilderness similarly twice included the willingness to abandon the journey to their promised inheritance because of their desire for food and water (Num. 11:4–6; 20:3–5). But now Israel, instead of letting go of higher goods for the sake of bodily cravings, is acting differently. Israel is setting its eye on the promised land and agreeing to go without or limit its food and drink in order to make progress on its way. Israel "fasts" in order to make progress toward its goal.

Fasting is common to all religions. While it has several related meanings, the center of the practice is controlling bodily desires to better achieve the higher purposes of life. "The intention of fasting is to purify the body by abstaining from eating and drinking in excess in order to control our 'appetites' and 'desires.'"[55] Jesus began his own ministry with fasting (Matt. 4:2) and resisted the temptation to be a Messiah who would appeal simply to the physical needs and desires of his followers: "One does not live by bread alone, but by every word that comes from the mouth of God" (4:4). Similarly, Israel begins to move more positively toward the promised land by its own willingness to deal with bodily desires. Even though the way is still blocked by Edom, Israel's actions for once do not result in punishment.

55. Susie Hayward, "Food," in *The New Westminster Dictionary of Christian Spirituality*, ed. P. Sheldrake (Louisville: Westminster John Knox, 2005), 307.

Death of Aaron at Mount Hor (20:22–29)

The encounter with Edom is followed by Aaron's death. Miriam, Aaron, and Moses are the main leaders of the exodus generation, and they all die near the end of Israel's forty years in the wilderness. Miriam died following the fifth rebellion (20:1), and now Aaron dies at the end of the sixth rebellion. The priestly leadership is passed on to the next generation, his son Eleazar. The death of the first high priest of Israel is marked with great mourning, as is befitting such an important leader: "All the house of Israel mourned for Aaron thirty days" (20:29). Normally, mourning lasts only seven days (Gen. 50:10; 1 Sam. 31:13), but this lengthy period indicates Aaron's great importance. Yet the account of his death is marred by the remembrance of his sin: "He shall not enter the land that I have given to the Israelites, because you rebelled against my command at the waters of Meribah" (Num. 20:24). While at times Aaron was an exemplary leader and priest—a high point is his standing "between the dead and the living" in the aftermath of the rebellion of Korah (16:48)—his sin at Meribah kept him from leading the next generation into the promised land. Like Miriam's death, Aaron's death marks again the painfulness of Israel's journey toward its goal.

Aaron's death is clearly a sign to all of the seriousness of their sin: "For it must needs have suggested itself to them, that God was no longer to be trifled with, before whom not even this sacred dignity could escape punishment" (Calvin 1852: 4.145). But the passing on of the priesthood to Eleazar is also a sign of hope. As Israel saw Moses and Eleazar come down from Mount Hor (20:28–29), they realized both that Aaron had died and that God would not utterly abandon them, for he was providing continuity of leadership as they traveled forward.

Israel's Vow at Hormah (21:1–3)

The scenes of battle and victory for Israel in this chapter mark a turning point in the narrative (21:1–3, 10–35). After Israel's first complaint in the wilderness (11:1), Israel's journey to the promised land has been full of misfortune. During the central rebellion, God declared that it would "bear [its] iniquity, forty years." Not believing God and not desiring to wait, Israel attempted to take the promised land without God's blessing. As a result, it suffered defeat in the first military encounter at Hormah (14:39–45).

Thirty-eight years later, Israel finds itself once more at Hormah (21:1–3). But now, its fortunes are reversed, and instead of Israel being "utterly destroyed" as the name Hormah suggests, the Canaanites are. This first military success, the travel itinerary from Hormah to Moab (21:10–20), and the victorious battles against King Sihon (21:21–32) and King Og (21:33–35) all suggest that God "lifted up his countenance" upon Israel. Israel's time in the wilderness will soon be over.

That the fortunes of Israel changed directly after Aaron's death at Mount Hor is significant. In the later extensive travel itinerary, both Aaron's death and the episode with "the Canaanite, the king of Arad," are given extra attention (33:38–40).

Aaron's death is a significant marker of the end of the exodus generation, but is this change of fortune simply the end of the old generation, or does a positive change in Israel also accompany the rise of the new generation? Positive change is indicated by the vow that Israel takes (21:2–3) and the actions of confession, intercession, and forgiveness involving Israel, Moses, and God following the seventh rebellion (→21:4–9).

That Israel takes a vow is important: "Then Israel made a vow to the LORD. . . . The LORD listened to the voice of Israel, and handed over the Canaanites." The first mention of a "vow" (*neder*) was in the section on the Nazirite (6:2, 5, 21). The Nazirite who takes a vow becomes a positive image of what Israel is called to be: the nation is like the Nazirite dedicated wholeheartedly and zealously to God. Vows are also mentioned in 15:3, 8 in a section outlining sacrifices associated with vows and freewill offerings. These sacrifices contrast with the actions of Israel in the central rebellion; they seem to symbolize what Israel should have done, but did not do.[56] In light of these images, this vow that Israel now takes is an indication that it is finally beginning to dedicate itself to God. And God takes notice.

The content of the vow is important. Israel does not vow to dedicate itself (as a Nazirite) or to offer a sacrifice of livestock or food (as in Num. 15). Rather, the vow is one of *ḥerem*, vowing to "utterly destroy" all the people, livestock, and things in the town, rather than taking them as war booty. The dedication or sacrifice of these things to God by destroying them also takes place in the encounters with Sihon and Og (21:34–35). The notion of *ḥerem* is not unique to Israel, nor is it easy to identify one particular practice or understanding of it in the Old Testament. *Ḥerem* is sometimes understood as necessary for justice, sometimes for assuring purity. The practice also represented a great sacrifice, for the value of booty taken in battle can be substantial (Wood 1998: 20–27; Niditch 1993: 28–89; and →31:1–54). The utter destruction of the Canaanites was considered a great sacrifice to God, offered in thanks for or in exchange for the blessing of God on their military enterprise.

Reflecting a newfound courage, self-sacrificial dedication, and zeal in the Israelites, the vow is a turning point in Israel's journey. The self-sacrificial dedication and zeal that Israel manifested in its vow is a clear change from how it acted in Num. 11–20.

This zealous dedication and self-sacrificial attitude is certainly praiseworthy and finds its true exemplar in Christ (→6:1–21). However, that it also involved the slaughter of whole populations—not to mention animals (cf. Jonah 4:11)—is extremely disturbing. These passages fostered an understanding of God and Christian participation in war throughout history that runs counter to other images of God's love and concern for sinners and animals throughout the scriptures. But

---

56. Num. 29:39 speaks of sacrifices associated with vows, and the vows of women are limited several times in Num. 30. Vows are mentioned more in Numbers than in any other book of the Old Testament, including the Psalms.

this passage too is part of Christian scripture. How should it and other holy-war passages (e.g., Num. 31:1–54) be read in order to best shape our faith and practice concerning war? This important question will be further examined in →21:10–35 (see Wood 1998 and Niditch 1993).

Rebellion 7: Misfortunes and the Bronze Serpent: Victory over Evil and Acknowledgement of Sin (21:4–9)

A beautiful and elaborately carved cross, dating from 1148, is on display at the Cloisters Museum in New York City. At the center of the cross is a medallion depicting the central image of this passage: Moses holding a pole with a serpent hanging from its crook.[57] Given its place on the cross, this event is seen as a "type," a shadow or prediction, of Christ's passion. This typology was common in medieval art. But such typological interpretation raises several questions: In what way is this event a type of the crucifixion? And what is the significance of this image and the mysterious events surrounding it in the wilderness journey of Israel?

The raising of the bronze serpent occurs at a turning point in Numbers—the seventh and final rebellion of Israel before they reach the plain of Moab. While the entire incident is presented quickly and without explicit interpretation, both the fiery serpents and the raising of the bronze serpent are picked up elsewhere in scripture as important and representative. The serpents are representative of the trials and hardships of Israel in the wilderness (Deut. 8:15; Wisdom of Solomon 16:5, 10), and the bronze serpent itself was apparently preserved by the people and later placed in the Jerusalem temple (2 Kgs. 18:4). The image of the raising of the serpent is taken up by Christ himself as a figure for his own "lifting up" (John 3:14; cf. 8:28; 12:32; 19:37), commented on with great frequency by patristic interpreters, and became an important typological image in Christian art. This is also one of the only three Numbers passages in the Revised Common Lectionary; it is read in Lent and paired with John 3:14.[58]

The high importance of the passage is matched only by the high level of bewilderment experienced by most modern interpreters in trying to make sense of it. However, if one trusts the typological tradition that draws analogies between Christ's crucifixion and this event, one finds interpretive possibilities of this event that also fit well with the surrounding narrative. But this involves rejecting modern interpretations of the serpent based on comparison with other ancient Near Eastern religions. And more surprisingly, this typological interpretation calls into question certain understandings of the cross of Christ firmly held by many

57. Elizabeth C. Parker and Charles T. Little, *The Cloisters Cross: Its Art and Meaning* (New York: MMA/Abrams, 1994).

58. The other two are the Aaronic blessing (6:22–27) and the passing of Moses's spirit to the seventy elders (11:4–30). See Andrew Langford, *The Revised Common Lectionary* (Nashville: Abingdon, 1992).

contemporary evangelicals. At the center of this interpretational puzzle is this question: what was the bronze serpent a symbol of?

Bronze Serpent as Symbol of Judgment, Victory, and Call to Difficult Obedience

Many modern interpreters understand the bronze serpent to be a kind of healing idol or cultic symbol fashioned by Moses in the wilderness in response to attacks by snakes, probably drawing from Egyptian practices of "sympathetic magic" or else drawing upon association of the serpent with gods of healing.[59]

Alternately, given that the serpent was revered among many ancient Near Eastern peoples as "a potent symbol of life and death," other interpreters reason that, at the command of God, Israel coopted this symbol of life and death and used it as a symbol for YHWH or YHWH's power, the God who holds both life and death in his hands.[60]

In contrast to these modern interpretations, serpent imagery elsewhere in the Bible leads one to see the serpent as a symbol associated with evil and sin.[61] Thus the sending of the serpents and the lifting up of the bronze serpent become revelations or symbols of Israel's sin. This basic meaning opens up the episode in a different way, ultimately showing that God's healing occurs in conjunction with the people's confession and repentance of their sinful ways.

The account of the rebellion is quite brief, but has several components. First, "the people became impatient" (21:4). The phrase *tqṣr npš h'm* literally means

---

59. Karen R. Joines, "The Bronze Serpent in the Israelite Cult," *Journal of Biblical Literature* 87 (1968): 245–56, argues that in Egypt the serpent was associated with several gods and that images of serpents were often used as objects of sympathetic magic: "Repelling serpents by a serpent image was very common to" Egyptians (253). In Mesopotamia and Canaan, however, bronze serpents were associated with fertility cults. The most likely reconstruction of Num. 21 is that Moses constructed a bronze serpent in the wilderness in an act similar to Egyptian practices of sympathetic magic, but another serpent was constructed for the temple in David or Solomon's time, "to affirm the agricultural powers of YHWH," drawing from Canaanite practices (255; cf. Noth 1968: 155–58). Other commentators agree with the Numbers and 2 Kings accounts and think that Moses's serpent was placed in the temple and that the idolatrous practice surrounding it was a later development. See Ashley 1993: 403.

60. Olson 1996: 137–38 develops the symbol along these lines and shows how Christ's cross then symbolizes "the poison of death as well as the life-giving power of God." The chief problem with a cooption theory is that the serpent image was often associated with Egypt. Since the serpent worn on the pharaoh's headdress represented "the patron cobra-goddess of Lower Egypt" (Nahum M. Sarna, *Exodus*, JPS Torah Commentary [Philadelphia: Jewish Publication Society, 1991], 20; cf. Ezek 29:3), this would make a serpent an unusual choice by YHWH as a symbol for himself or for healing.

61. In the Old Testament, the word "serpent" never carries a positive connotation, nor can it be a symbol of life or healing other than in this passage. Rather, the serpent symbolizes wicked people who speak lies (Ps. 58:4; 140:3); wine, a tempting drink that "sparkles . . . and goes down smoothly," but can bite like a serpent (Prov. 23:31–32); people sent to punish Israel (Isa. 14:29; 27:1; Jer. 8:17; cf. Amos 5:19; 9:3); or people who have done evil, yet are themselves punished (Jer. 46:22; Isa. 65:25; Mic. 7:17).

"the souls of the people were shortened." In Prov. 14:29 the phrase is translated "hasty temper," the opposite of slow to anger or long-suffering. Another alternate translation is "discouraged." Whatever the translation, the people "lacked the soul" for bearing their long and difficult journey.[62] The phrase "on the way" might be translated "because of the way," that is, they were impatient or discouraged because of yet one more detour and difficulty (Milgrom 1990: 173, following Rashi). The source of this discouragement is further seen in their question—"why have you brought us up out of Egypt to die in the wilderness?" (21:5)—showing again their lack of faith that God was leading them toward the promised land and doing so to give them life, not death. Their contradictory comment—"there is no food and no water, and we detest this miserable food"—reveals more about their mental state than their actual circumstances. They lacked faith in the goodness and wisdom of God. More specifically, they lacked faith that God's good plan for them might come through difficulty and suffering.

In response to this lack of faith, God sends serpents that bite and poison the Israelites. While the serpents could simply be a convenient method of punishment for YHWH, ready at hand in the wilderness, given the attention to the symbol in the passage, one might expect there to be a symbolic appropriateness to this punishment.[63] At the most literal level, the serpents are agents of suffering and death. Their description as *hnḥšym hśrpym* (NRSV margin: "fiery serpents") most likely draws attention to the burning of their poisonous bite (Gray 1903: 277).[64] They are, and also come to represent, the physical difficulties of the journey to the promised land. As Deut. 8:15 suggests, the "poisonous snakes and scorpions" of the "terrible wilderness" were, along with hunger and thirst, part of the actual physical trials of the people.

Elsewhere in the Pentateuch, serpents appear in two other crucial passages, both of which give the serpent a more-than-physical sense. In the confrontation between Moses and Pharaoh (Exod. 4:3; 7:9, 10, 15), the serpent likely symbolized Egypt and its gods. In that episode, the power of God triumphs over the power of the gods of Egypt. In our passage, then, perhaps snakes represented God's punishment of Israel by a symbol of the object of their desires—life back in Egypt under the rule of the snake, Pharaoh, and the gods of Egypt. "Why have you brought us up out of Egypt?" is part of the people's complaint. They seem to prefer life under the power of Egypt, the serpent, rather than life under YHWH.

---

62. The Septuagint uses the verb ὀλιγοψυκέω ("discouraged, fainthearted"); John William Wevers, *Notes on the Greek Text of Numbers*, Society of Biblical Literature Septuagint and Cognate Studies 46 (Atlanta: Scholars Press, 1998), 341; cf. Gray 1903: 277.

63. Gray 1903: 275 rejects the story as an actual experience of the people of Israel in the desert because (1) it lacks an adequate explanation for the "choice of this particular kind of miracle" and (2) Israel could not have manufactured such an object in the wilderness. But the choice for recording this episode is reasonable, and this generation of Israelites certainly had learned some building skills in Egypt.

64. The description of the serpents as "fiery" may intentionally parallel the first rebellion, where God punished the people with fire, so that the place was called Taberah, "burning" (11:3).

There, their freedom, vocation, and worship of God were prevented, but at least their stomachs were filled.

The other key reference in the Pentateuch is to "the serpent [who] was more crafty than any other wild animal," who tempts Adam and Eve in the garden of Eden (Gen. 3:1, 2, 4, 13, 14). God's judgment and punishment of Adam and Eve is a result of their failure to resist the temptation of the serpent. The punishment of Israel by God in Numbers might also reveal that they have succumbed to the poisonous lies of the deceiver, who tempts them to both doubt that God's provision and ordering are really for their good (as seen in this passage) and creates envy in them for the power of God to morally order the world (as evidenced in the other rebellions).[65]

The Gospels implicitly suggest the interpretation that Israel succumbed to temptation by the devil in the wilderness (Matt. 4:1–11; Mark 1:12–13; Luke 4:1–13). Later Jewish tradition reinforces the tie with seduction and deception and sees such serpentine tempting occurring in the wilderness, during the "youth" of Israel: "I was a pure virgin and did not go outside my father's house; but I guarded the rib from which woman was made. No seducer corrupted me on a desert plain, nor did the destroyer, the deceitful serpent, defile the purity of my virginity" (4 Macc. 18:7–8).[66]

In sum, the serpents can be seen to be a judgment upon Israel that reveals and symbolizes their sin.[67] The souls of the Israelites have been poisoned by the deceiver so that they do not trust in the goodness of God and his provision and plan for them. The people who committed themselves to the covenant with God instead adulterously follow after Egypt and the way of life it represents—a life where their immediate desires are fed yet they are enslaved, a life that falls short of what God intends for them in the promised land. The serpents' venom, like bitter water, has entered into the people and caused bitter pain, showing that they have indeed gone astray. As with Adam and Eve, the venom of doubt about the words, ways, and goodness of God had taken hold of Israel and was leading to their "spiritual death."

In response to the serpents, Israel is moved to confession: "We have sinned by speaking against the LORD and against you; pray to the LORD to take away the serpents from us" (Num. 21:7). As a result of this confession, God does relent. He does

65. Given their recent deliverance from Egypt and the possibility that oral traditions of the serpent in the garden were in circulation among the Israelites even then, either or both of those symbolic resonances are possible for the Israelites in the desert; they certainly were for the final writer or writers of Numbers.

66. Wisdom of Solomon 2:24 also equates the devil with the serpent; the devil's sin is seen as "envy," and one can belong to the "company" of the devil.

67. It is an act of poetic justice that reveals their poisoned spiritual state. Like the inhabitants of Greek mythology's Tartarus or in Dante's *Inferno*, they are judged and punished in a way appropriate and representative of their sin. More pertinent to the context of the Israelites is Hammurabi's "eye for eye" (Exod. 21:24; Lev. 24:20; Deut. 19:21; Matt. 5:38), where again there is a just relation between crime and punishment.

not simply forgive them of their sin and heal them outright, but rather commands Moses to construct a "fiery serpent"[68] and set it on a *nas* ("standard").[69]

The bronze serpent represents to the people all that the fiery serpents represent. In it they can see the sufferings of their journey. But in it they also can see the judgment of God about them. Like the raising of a battle standard, this action ironically represents who the people are truly following: the serpent, rather than God. This people, this generation, have rejected God and his ways, and are following instead the ways of the serpent, the envious desire for power, the lust for the easy comforts of Egypt that makes them turn back from entering the land. It is a fitting symbol for all the rebellions of the people.

But the raised serpent is more than a sign of judgment. It is also a sign of God's victory over the serpent. Like the head of an enemy placed on the tip of a spear and shown to the people, the serpent lifted up shows that God is more powerful than the serpent. God is able to cure the physical effects of the serpents' poison. By offering to the people this symbol of victory over the serpent, it also becomes a symbol of God's compassion and desire to heal them and to do them good. It is a symbol that God did not send Moses to his people in Egypt to condemn them, but to save them and bring them life.

The Israelites' act of turning and looking at the bronze serpent thus takes on deeper meaning when God tells Moses that "everyone who is bitten shall look at it and live" (21:8). The act of turning and looking at a symbol recognized *as* a symbol of their sin and God's judgment on them amounts to a confession or acknowledgement of their sin. Furthermore, turning to this symbol of sin and judgment in order to live required faith in God, in God's mercy and desire for their good. Such an act was tantamount to a recommitment to God's way, even if it involved the difficulties and purgative trials they had been experiencing.

In these ways, the symbol of God's judgment was at the same time a symbol of God's victory. God's life and goodness is made available to them through the curing of their poisoned desires and devotion to the serpent. The bronze serpent lifted up suggests that, for those bitten by the serpent in the wilderness, the way to the promised land is one of confession, repentance, faith, and recommitment to God's difficult yet healing ways.

This episode thus becomes a fitting ending of the sevenfold rejection of the ways of God. Furthermore, the bronze serpent is a fitting liturgical symbol for the entry courts of the temple, where it was placed in later years (2 Kgs. 18:4). It could be seen as a symbol calling for confession and summarizing the way of difficult yet purgative obedience that the rituals of cleansing and many of the sacrifices also pointed to. The later misunderstanding and idolization of the bronze serpent is

---

68. God commands Moses to make a "fiery serpent" (*śrp*), and Moses makes a *nḥš nḥšt* ("a serpent of bronze or copper, a brazen serpent"). This wordplay between "serpent" and "bronze" continues in 2 Kgs. 18:4, where the serpent is called "Nehushtan" (Milgrom 1990: 174).

69. The Hebrew word is used for a conspicuous high place around which warriors gather, hence a standard or banner (Gray 1903: 278).

also easily understood—especially as one compares it to similar uses of the symbol of the cross in Christianity.

Did Israel see all this in the bronze serpent?[70] We are told that they were healed physically (21:9). And the surrounding narratives (→20:14–21; →21:1–3) show that the younger generation is beginning to act in ways befitting such repentance and renewed dedication to God and the difficult journey to the promised land.

The Cross of Christ and Christian Practice in Light of the Bronze Serpent

Because of Jesus's explicit use of this image as revealing some of the meaning of his own being "lifted up" in John 3:14, the bronze serpent should be seen as a type of Christ's passion. "And as Moses lifted up the serpent in the wilderness, so must the Son of Man be lifted up [*hypsōthēnai*; also 8:28; 12:32], that whoever believes in him may have eternal life. For God so loved the world that he gave his only Son, so that everyone who believes in him may not perish but have eternal life. Indeed, God did not send the Son into the world to condemn the world, but in order that the world might be saved through him" (3:14–17). Given the aptness of this typology, the meanings associated with the bronze serpent in Numbers create pressure on Christian understandings of how to view Christ, his work, and the cross.

The Israelites in the wilderness were judged by their reactions to the signs and wonders of God's guidance and goodness. The bronze serpent was a symbol of their rejection of God and their following of the serpent. Just as the lifting up of the bronze serpent was a symbol of the sin of Israel, so too is the lifting up of Jesus the Messiah. This meaning of the cross is especially stressed in the Gospel of John, when Jesus takes upon himself this symbol of bronze serpent: Jesus explains that he will be the cause of judgment: he comes into the world as light (John 1, 3, 8), manna (John 6), abundant water (John 4), and life (John 11), and the people will be judged by their reaction to him (12:48). Those who look to him will be saved; for others, the rejection of Jesus through the use of a Roman cross *is* their judgment, showing that their deeds are evil. The theme of judgment culminates

---

70. The Wisdom of Solomon seems to have understood it in a similar fashion. In its interpretation of the events in the wilderness, the bronze serpent was given as a "symbol of salvation" (*symbolon sōtērias*) in order that the Israelites would remember the "command of your law, for the one who had turned/repented was not saved through the thing contemplated, but through you, the savior of all" (16:6–7, my translation). This suggests the bronze serpent was given in order to remind the Israelites of the Law and repent. Why would it do this? It could if, as suggested above, it was a symbol of their sin. It could cut through the fog of Israel's self-justification and reveal the shocking reality of who and what they were really following. Similar to the way that Moses grinds up the golden calf and makes Israel drink it (Exod. 32:20), here God is training Israel by making it contemplate its sin, represented by the serpent. How then, could this symbol of their sin also be a "symbol of salvation"? Wisdom 16 suggests that this particular revelation of their sin was also a sign of God's victory over the serpent, providing both an opportunity for their physical healing and their spiritual repentance. Some do turn and are saved from the poison that has taken hold of them.

in the trial and crucifixion sequence in 18:1–19:37. The dramatic irony builds and culminates in the lines: "Pilate asked them, 'Shall I crucify your King?' The chief priests answered, 'We have no king but the emperor'" (19:15). The rejection of the true king in the crucifixion reveals their true loyalties.

The bronze serpent was also a symbol of God's victory, for through it God healed the people of the serpents' poison. This physical healing of Israel suggests God's power to heal their sin. The cross is a similar symbol, in fact its fulfillment. The victory of God is accomplished through the healing of humanity's poisoned nature in the person of Jesus Christ, a healing involving his obedience to God's difficult yet life-giving ways. While Christ was tempted to follow the ways of Satan, he resisted those temptations throughout his life, culminating in his obedience to God's ways in spite of persecution, even to the point of death on a cross. Through Christ's obedience to God's ways, in himself he creates a new humanity purified from sin—a new humanity available to all who would follow him.

Requiring the people to look at the bronze serpent to be healed makes it a symbol of confession, repentance, and recommitment to follow God. The symbol of Christ on the cross is a reminder of Jesus's call to all who would follow him to take up their own crosses and follow in his way of costly discipleship.

These three meanings of Christ on the cross—judgment, victory, and call to discipleship—are packed into Jesus's cryptic statement about his impending death at a turning point in the Gospel of John: "Now is the judgment of this world; now the ruler of this world will be driven out. And I, when I am lifted up from the earth, will draw all people to myself." He said this to indicate the kind of death he was to die" (12:31–33).[71]

These thematic ties between the bronze serpent and the cross push one toward understandings of what Christ has done on the cross and how this brings us salvation—so-called atonement theories—that privilege notions of "recapitulation" or "headship." Drawing on Eph. 1:10, God's plan for "the fullness of time" is to "recapitulate [rehead] all things in him." Christ is the new head of the body of humanity. The larger story of salvation is told this way: Christ through his resisting temptation and his obedience fulfills the purposes for which humanity was created, namely, to be obedient to God, to have God's image shine in and through them, and to be in restored fellowship with God, with each other, and the rest of creation. He is the new Adam. Christ's suffering is both an internal struggle with sinful flesh (seen especially in Christ's temptations at the beginning of his ministry and in the garden of Gethsemane), but also a willingness

71. The Gospel of John also emphasizes that salvation flows out of this event of judgment. The ultimate goal is not punishment and judgment, but salvation and cleansing from sin. Blood and water, eucharist and baptism, flow from Christ's side. Those whom the Father draws "will look on the one whom they pierced," Christ crucified, and "they shall mourn for him" (John 19:37, quoting Zech. 12:10). But out of this piercing and mourning, salvation and cleansing will come: "On that day a fountain shall be opened for the house of David and the inhabitants of Jerusalem, to cleanse them from sin and impurity" (Zech. 13:1).

to suffer in the face of fallen "principalities and powers" (Christ's willingness to stand trial, be rejected, and crucified). We are saved by this new, cleansed, and righteous humanity created in Christ by having him dwell in us (John) through the power of the Spirit, by being united with Christ, being part of his spiritual body (Paul). Jesus Christ is our prototype, the "pioneer of [our] salvation [made] perfect through sufferings" (Heb. 2:10).[72]

In contemplating the cross, Christians—like Israel looking at the bronze serpent—can see in it God's judgment of and revelation of their sin, God's victory over sin, and a call to faith and discipleship. But unlike the bronze serpent, which suggested a way of discipleship, Christians can see hanging on the cross the one who fulfilled that way. Christians can see that their own way through the desert has been made straight and level by the one who successfully pioneered that path, and then pray they would be united with him through the power of the spirit. At least one central meaning of the Eucharist is precisely this, that we want to take into ourselves the manna from heaven, Jesus Christ, who is our life and our salvation, so that we will have the strength and faith to be obedient on the journey. The Israelites in the desert were shown the path and learned that they needed to trust in God for their spiritual healing. Christians in Christ's cross see the providence of God, the "plan for the fullness of time" made manifest. We pray to have that way imprinted in us yet more fully through the grace of God.

Reversal of Fortune: Journey to Moab and Holy Wars against King Sihon and King Og (21:10–35)

In the narratives following the seventh rebellion, Israel's fortunes have changed. In both the first and seventh rebellions, Israel complains generally about various misfortunes, and throughout the middle section of Numbers, Israel is defeated by problems and troubles from both within and without. But now, after the vow at Hormah (21:1–3) and the raising of the bronze serpent (21:4–9), Israel no longer suffers misfortune. Instead, it overcomes its enemies through the help of the Lord (21:14, 34).

The travel itinerary from Hormah to Moab (21:10–20) and the victorious battles against King Sihon (21:21–32) and King Og (21:33–35) all contain positive images that suggest that Israel's time in the wilderness is drawing to an end. The travel itinerary details the movement of Israel away from Mount Hor, a marker

---

72. While not precluding penal substitutionary themes, the resonances between the bronze serpent and the Gospels at least call into question their centrality. The themes of recapitulation surrounding the way Christ saves us through his work as foreshadowed in the bronze serpent are picked up by patristic interpreters and the Eastern Orthodox and have continued to be argued for by Christian theologians. For example, nineteenth-century theologian Thomas Erskine provides an exemplary analysis of the bronze serpent in *The Brazen Serpent; or, Life Coming through Death*, 2nd ed. (Edinburgh: Waugh & Innes, 1881), which was written in part as an argument against the penal substitutionary accounts of the atonement.

of the death place of Aaron, to the plains of Moab, the setting of the last third of the book on the edge of the promised land. (Mount Hor and the encounter with "the Canaanite" are noted in 33:40 and mark the beginning of the final part of the journey to Moab.)

The encounters with Sihon and Og are likewise positive. They have many structural and wording parallels with the negative encounter with Edom in 20:14–21. The wording of the messages Moses sends to the kings of Edom and Sihon are nearly identical (20:17; 21:22). These similarities make the contrast between the outcomes of these events all the more apparent. Edom successfully blocks Israel's progress (20:18), but when Sihon tries to do so, "Israel put him to the sword" (21:23–24). The obstacles in the path of Israel's journey have been removed.

Many historical questions arise (Ashley 1993: 406–31; Milgrom 1990: 175–84, 456–58) concerning the places mentioned, the Book of the Wars of the Lord (21:14), fragments of old songs (21:14–15, 17–18, 27–30), and Kings Sihon and Og. However, the most pressing theological question for contemporary Christians concerns the positive view of war in this section. The turning point of the fortunes of Israel in Numbers revolves around the utter destruction of entire peoples and God's blessing such a practice. While God does not directly command ḥerem, he does bless Israel's vow (21:3) and later says that "I have given him [Og] into your hand. . . . You shall do to him as you did to King Sihon" (21:34). How should such stories and images be received by contemporary Christians?

This is not an easily resolved question. Recent scholarship shows that the scriptures do not explicitly resolve the issue of how Christians or Jews should view war, but rather present a "bundle of biblical theologies which stand in tension with one another" (Wood 1998: 152). The Old Testament does not have a unified vision of holy war—rather various thoughts about holy war are present (Niditch 1993). Both Testaments also contain pacifistic visions for handling conflict in a nonviolent fashion, as well as just-war motifs.[73] Nor is there a simple progression from holy war to pacifism as one moves from ancient Israel to Christ (Wood 1998: 3). Nor has the church come to a final conclusion about participation in war, even given the strong message of peace in the New Testament.

In spite of the diversity of the biblical witness, we do see a clear direction and final goal. The witness centered in Jesus Christ proclaims that "the God of Abraham, Isaac, Jacob, Moses, David, and Jesus Christ is preeminently the God of shalom and not of war" (Wood 1998: 174). Wood concludes that—even though many interpreters throughout the Christian tradition derived direct moral sanction

---

73. Wood 1998: 149 provides an example of just-war motifs: "Deuteronomy 20:10–14 limits killing to the fighting population and calls for negotiation prior to attack. This is a far cry from the ḥerem, but reflects rather the traditional just war criteria, which, while recognizing the necessity of conflict, tries to impose severe restraints on warmaking." Elements of a pacifist vision of peace can be seen, for example, in the actions of the patriarchs (e.g., the actions of Judah and Joseph in Gen. 44:18–45:15), the vision of Isa. 9:1–7, and the teaching of Jesus to "love your enemies" (Matt. 5:44).

for holy wars from passages such as this[74]—we must make sense of these passages in light of the full revelation of the biblical witness. As such, one can read holy-war passages as "among those realms of ancient Hebrew morality which has been superseded by a better way." And the only biblically responsible descriptions of that "better way" are either pacifism or an "agonized participation" in certain wars as exemplified in certain understandings of just-war thinking (Wood 1998: 175).

Despite this clear direction, the portrayal of God's involvement in or approval of such wars pushes one to say that God is willing to be involved in activities and people that do not yet fully participate in the goal of shalom. Participation in war does not seem to be entirely alien to God's character—or else one must assume that the ancient Hebrews were totally mistaken in their understanding of God's leadership in such cases. While one could argue that pacifism makes the most sense in light of the full biblical witness, one must do so in a way that does not create an absolute antithesis between God as witnessed to in Numbers and God as revealed in Christ.

But Numbers should not be seen as simply pro–holy war. It is also pro-peace, and its literary construction suggests a certain reservation about the holy wars the Israelites engage in. Given the interpretation of the Aaronic blessing (→6:22–27) that sees shalom as the ultimate end of Israel's journey to the promised land, the activities of war that Israel enters into here can be seen only as penultimate means that stand in some tension with the ultimate end. The sense of the entire last part of the book (including the war against Midian in →31:1–54) is that Israel is only partially living into the vision seen in the first part of the book. Its practice of dedicatory holy war—while displaying renewed zeal, dedication, and courage— still pales in the light of this greater vision.

---

74. For Crusader and Puritan use of this passage, see Lisa Sowle Cahill, *Love Your Enemies: Discipleship, Pacifism, and Just War Theory* (Minneapolis: Fortress, 1994), 119–49.

6

GOD BLESSES ISRAEL THROUGH
BALAK AND BALAAM (22:1–24:25)

The story of Balaam is one of the best known portions of Numbers. Balaam's ass (22:22–35) and the prophecy about the "star" that "shall come out of Jacob" (24:17) are familiar to many readers of scripture. These two parts of the Balaam story are often depicted in Christian art[1] and, along with his association with Israel's worship of the Baal of Peor (Num. 25), referred to throughout the Bible (Num. 31:8, 16; Deut. 23:4–5; Josh. 13:22; 24:9–10; Neh. 13:2; Mic. 6:5; Matt. 2:2–3; 2 Pet. 1:19; 2:15; Jude 11; Rev. 2:14, 28; 22:16). Being well known, however, does not equate to being well understood. Traditions about Balaam have often been understood as conflicting, and interpretations vary. Yet, when viewed in light of its importance in Numbers and the theme of God's blessing of Israel, the story becomes clearer.

The central concern of this narrative is the blessing of Israel and how God accomplishes it through and in spite of Balak and Balaam. The narrative also raises many issues that resonate with larger concerns of Christian theology and practice, such as the relationship of God and his power to magic and religious practices, the temptations of religious leaders as they deal with spiritual matters, the dynamics of the providence of God in using even the enemies of his people for his purposes, and the content of God's blessing of Israel. While such an engaging and provocative

---

1. The scene of Balaam being encountered by the angel while on the ass has been paired in artworks with the scene of Paul on the road to Damascus or the appearance of the risen Christ to Thomas. The prophecy of the star is associated with the wise men of the east (often understood as the descendents of Balaam) following the star to Bethlehem.

story could stand on its own—and probably did at one point (Milgrom 1990: 467–68)—its current location forms a fitting climax to the story of Israel in the wilderness and contributes to the larger theme of blessing and cursing within the Pentateuch and the Bible.

The narrative can be divided into three sections for the sake of comment: the interactions between Balak and Balaam; in which the promptings of YHWH; the journey of Balaam to Balak on his donkey; and the oracles of Balaam.

Balak's Power, Balaam's Power, and God's Sovereign Power to Bless and Curse

The story begins as King Balak of Moab sees the great number of the Israelites on the doorstep of his kingdom. He and his people of Moab are "overcome with fear" (22:3). This detail highlights that now the nations fear Israel rather than vice versa (cf. 14:1, 9). Balak wants to drive the Israelites out, but does not trust that his power is enough to do so. Israel is "stronger than I," he confesses (22:6). So Balak calls on Balaam, a magico-religious specialist from a neighboring area, to curse them. Balak trusts in Balaam's effectiveness and says so to him: "Whomever you [Balaam] bless is blessed, and whomever you curse is cursed" (22:6).

The intention of Balak to curse Israel by using the power of Balaam sets up the dramatic tension that carries the narrative forward, for the reader knows that God intends blessing for Israel. "Who has the power to bless and curse?" is a central question that underlies the action. While most readers of the Bible will be able to guess the answer, the narrative details of the interactions between Balak, Balaam, and YHWH raise several issues and point to answers about the relationship between worldly power, magic or religious powers, and the power of God.

Balak's worldview has room for spiritual powers. But for Balak, spiritual forces are just one among many different kinds of power. His request to Balaam (22:5–6) and the detail about the messengers and elders carrying "the fees for divination in their hand" (22:7) make clear that Balak sees Balaam as a provider of spiritual services of blessing and cursing.[2] Balak is not seeking to submit himself in worship to Balaam's god, but rather he wants Balaam to deploy him/it as a weapon. His statement to Balaam, "I know that whomever you bless is blessed, and whomever you curse is cursed," echoes dissonantly with the promise of God to Abram and his descendents: "I will bless those who bless you, and the one who curses you I will curse" (Gen. 12:1–3). The terms "blessing" and "cursing" are reinterpreted

---

2. Origen 1996–2001: 2.271 assumes that such a practice would be exceptional: recognizing that Israel used the power of the word rather than physical arms, Balak seeks to combat "words with words and prayers with prayers." However, Moore 1990: 97 understands that such a practice would be unexceptional in such a culture, since kings often saw armies in combination with the supernatural forces that empowered them.

and domesticated as they are pressed into service within Balak's understanding of the world and gods/spirits. Blessing and cursing are stripped of the rich connotations of God's presence and intentions for shalom. They become instead means toward Balak's "greatest good" as he defines it, which here includes military victory over Israel.

As the narrative progresses, Balak's offer is at first turned down by Balaam, who tells him, "The Lord [YHWH] has refused to let me go with you" (Num. 22:13). Balak interprets this refusal as a ploy in order to get more honor or payment for his services. He does not take Balaam's initial refusal at face value, but rather treats Balaam as a shrewd negotiator (Moberly 1998: 9–10). And so he sends officials "more numerous and more distinguished" than those he sent at first (22:15–17). Balaam sees what Balak is doing and protests: "Although Balak were to give me his house full of silver and gold," he still would not be able to go (22:18).

When Balaam finally does come, Balak provides material resources for what could be typical sacrifices for exorcisms (22:41–23:3; Moore 1990: 104–9). Even as Balaam blesses Israel, first once, then twice, Balak persists in thinking that he can get the desired results from Balaam by somehow manipulating the ritual. Balaam in his first oracle speaks of God's election of Israel and the blessing apparent in their great numbers: "Who can . . . number the dust-cloud of Israel?" (23:10). In what may be satire, Balak seems to take this as a problem to be solved. He thinks Balaam is having difficulty seeing or numbering such a large amount of people, and so he moves Balaam to another place where Balaam "shall see only part of them" (23:13), perhaps making the cursing easier on Balaam (Levine 2000: 236).[3] In the end, Balak, after being frustrated a third time cuts his losses and fires Balaam from the job—"now be off with you! Go home!" (24:11)—holding back the silver and gold that he still thinks has motivated Balaam.

Throughout the narrative Balak is someone who thinks that spiritual blessing and cursing can be easily manipulated by Balaam and his magical rituals. He certainly recognizes the existence of spiritual powers, but his understanding of them, YHWH included, is that spirits and gods, like other forces in our world, are capable of being controlled by those with the proper know-how and influence. Magic/religion is a technology of control for Balak. "Blessing and cursing" are marketable spiritual commodities.

While Balak is a simple character who represents a rather straightforward desire for and understanding of worldly power, Balaam is much more complex. He moves between various roles, sometimes acting in ways typical of the seers and diviners, sorcerers and exorcists,[4] who practice their arts among the peoples

---

3. The reason for this change of venue is not given in the text; cf. Milgrom 1990: 198 and Ashley 1993: 475–76.

4. I follow the description and analysis in Moore 1990: 97–109, who differs from Milgrom 1990: 471–73. Milgrom understands the narrative to be driven by the tension between Balaam being a diviner and Balak wanting him to be a sorcerer.

surrounding Israel, and sometimes functioning as a true prophet of YHWH.[5] While Balaam's character changes (→22:22–35), the text makes clear that the different roles Balaam plays operate with quite different assumptions about God and his relationship to religious practices. He has one foot in the world of Balak, one foot in the world of Israel.

Balaam is understood to be a magical specialist of some repute and power. Given that Balak summons him from a place in another country, "Pethor, which is on the Euphrates" (22:5), and goes to the time, trouble, and expense of sending "the elders of Moab and the elders of Midian" (22:7) in order to secure his services, one can reasonably suppose that Balaam had a strong reputation for his magico-religious powers.[6]

The legendary power of Balaam is confirmed by the extrabiblical texts discovered in 1967 at Deir 'Alla. Plaster panels, probably attached to a column, with inked characters written on them were found in an Iron Age II temple (900–600 BC) near the intersection of the Jabbok and Jordan rivers. These panels confirm the existence of a legendary figure, Balaam son of Beor, and suggest that Balaam played both the role of a "seer" and an "exorcist" in the area.[7]

5. Viewing Balaam through the different roles he plays is central to the method Moore 1990: 11–16 uses. Moore cogently argues that this is a more fruitful approach than basing one's understanding of Balaam on the titles used of him or other magico-religious practitioners or trying to place Balaam definitively on the spectrum stretching from magic to religion, as is typical of cultural anthropologists and religionists. Moore points out the problems associated with typing and dichotomizing the two—such as the distinction of magic as primitive and religion as civilized—and he prefers a more fluid approach that carefully distinguishes between typical characteristics of shamans versus priests (17–18n60). For the text at hand, the question is less about magic versus religion, as if being religious in a general sense is what the text envisions as Balaam's proper response to YHWH, but more about the difference between a true prophet/priest of YHWH and the magico-religious specialists of the surrounding cultures. Moore writes: "Many of the ancient practices mentioned in the Hebrew Bible, for example, have been thoroughly edited and reedited by tradents quite hostile to magico-religious practices as a matter of religious principle" (46). This religious principle of Israel is what our text is interested in.

6. Milgrom 1990: 186 suggests Pethor should be identified with Pitru on a tributary of the Euphrates. If correct, the journey of four hundred miles would have taken twenty days.

7. Most scholars agree that the Deir 'Alla temple and texts are non-Israelite. The first of two main reconstructed panels highlights Balaam and his activity as a seer/diviner. In this text, Balaam is privy in a night vision to the future plans of the divine council (šdyn), which include "bolting up the heavens" so that light will not shine. Balaam then relates his troubling vision to his people. The much-debated second panel seems to suggest a connection between Balaam and either child sacrifice (Jo Ann Hackett, *The Balaam Text from Deir 'Alla* [Atlanta: Scholars Press, 1984], 75–89) or exorcism (Moore 1990: 87–96). If indeed the second panel refers to Balaam, he is a magical practitioner who plays more than one role—primarily a seer, but also a sacrificial priest or exorcist. His actions in the second panel are possibly intended to avert the disaster seen in the first (Hackett, *Balaam Text*, 80; Moore 1990: 93). Given this understanding of Balaam's roles in the Deir 'Alla texts, similar roles for him in or behind the biblical story might reasonably be imagined (Levine 2000: 241–75; Milgrom 1990: 473–76). For bibliography, see Moore 1990: 7–9. For more details, see Hackett, *Balaam Text*; and J. Hoftijzer and B. van der Kooij, *The Balaam Text from Deir 'Alla*

In the biblical text, the role of Balaam is primarily discussed in terms of his task to curse Israel. Balak summons Balaam: "Come now, curse this people for me" (22:6). But Balaam's words, actions, and titles reflect other roles, primarily that of "diviner" or "seer" (Moore 1990: 97–109; Milgrom 1990: 471–73). Terms used to describe Balaam's activity—*naḥaš* ("enchantment, looking for omens"; 23:23; 24:1) and *qesem* ("divination"; 22:7; 23:23)—his actions (e.g., night visions; 22:8, 20), and the consistent emphasis on seeing and not seeing (in the episode with the ass), all point to Balaam filling such a role. Joshua remembers Balaam practicing "divination" (*qesem*; Josh. 13:22), a picture that also coheres with the Deir ʿAlla texts.

In the cultures surrounding Israel, cursing was not the role of a diviner, but of a sorcerer or exorcist (Moore 1990: 33–41). For example, Mesopotamian magical texts show that when people were oppressed or threatened by evil spirits, which a *bārû* ("seer") would see or foresee, a specialist called an *āšipu* ("exorcist") would go through different rites to drive away the spirits and/or avert the impending danger. They would do this by performing purification rituals or cursing enemies (Moore 1990: 41). Some Mesopotamian sorcery practices were intended to "drive wedges between people and their protective deities" (Moore 1990: 40), and exorcism rites were the only known magical practices that involve sacrifices on seven altars (Moore 1990: 106). Given that Balak hired Balaam to curse Israel (22:6, 17), that Balak hoped he might be able to drive Israel out as a result of the curse (22:6), and that the rite included sacrifices on seven altars (23:1, 14, 29),[8] it seems that Balaam was being asked to function at least in part as an exorcist/sorcerer (contra Milgrom 1990: 473). Balak appears to be asking Balaam to perform an exorcist ritual that would drive a wedge between Israel and their god, YHWH, in this way cursing them so that he could in turn drive Israel out of the land (22:6).

Since practices of divination and sorcery/exorcism were outlawed in Israel, one would expect Balaam to be portrayed in a wholly negative light.[9] Yet, at many other points in the narrative, Balaam is portrayed not as a diviner or exorcist, but more like a prophet of YHWH.[10] The way that God and Balaam speak to each

---

Re-evaluated: Proceedings of the International Symposium Held at Leiden, 21–24 August 1989 (Leiden: Brill, 1991).

8. The sacrifice involved a bull and a ram on each of seven altars. Sacrificing a bull and ram together occurs in Ezek. 45:23; Job 42:7–9; and 1 Chr. 15:26. The first two texts refer to the sacrifices as *ʿōlâ*, but these burnt offerings probably had little to do with the regular offerings of the Israelites. Moore 1990: 107n44 thinks the word *ʿōlâ* was used simply because it was the closest word available to describe the rituals of Balaam.

9. Divination is condemned in scripture (Deut. 18:10–14; 1 Sam. 15:23; 2 Kgs. 17:17; Jer. 14:14), although something similar seems to have been sanctioned in the practice of the Urim and Thummim of the high priest (Exod. 28:30). Sorcery/exorcism (*kešep*) was also banned in Israel (Deut. 18:10; Exod. 22:18), and yet it was probably widely practiced because it and similar activities are so often condemned (2 Kgs. 9:22; 2 Chr. 33:6; Jer. 27:9; Mic. 5:12; Mal. 3:5). See Milgrom 1990: 471–73.

10. Based on descriptions of Moses in Exod. 7:1 and Deut. 5:22–23, R. W. L. Moberly, *Prophecy and Discernment* (Cambridge: Cambridge University Press, 2006), 4, lists the characteristics of an Old Testament prophet: (1) the prophet is "in essence *one who speaks for God*, a spokesman," (2) this

other implies intimacy and familiarity (e.g., 22:9). The commands by God (22:20) and the angel (22:35) to do and speak only what God commands show that the initiative of Balaam's activity lies with God, as it does with Israel's prophets. Balaam's refusal at first to go with the officials (22:13) is explained by his statement that "I could not go beyond the command of the LORD my God" (22:18), words that indicate his acceptance of God's authority. And Balaam's later description of having "the word" of God put in his mouth (22:38) and "the spirit of God [coming] upon him" before he utters his oracle (24:2) are what one would expect of an Israelite prophet, not an enemy of Israel.

What are we to make of these different roles? How is the action of God's spirit in inspiring the oracles of Balaam to be reconciled with Balaam not being an Israelite prophet and his engaging in practices contrary to the law of God?

Such tension in the story of Balaam is treated in different ways by interpreters. Many modern interpreters understand that Balaam was recognized as a prophet in earlier traditions still preserved in the text, but the pressure of priestly redactors and "the exclusive spirit of a later age could not tolerate the appearance of a true prophet of God among the heathen: it consequently took care to represent him in an unfavourable light" (Gray 1903: 320).[11] Thus the tensions felt in the text and the later largely negative biblical traditions about Balaam[12] are explained by the pressures of an intolerant traditioning process that presents him more like the diviners/sorcerers of the surrounding nations. Many modern interpreters accordingly seek to recover the theoretical earlier portrayals of Balaam that see him as a true prophet.

As the text stands, however, we have a portrait of a seer/exorcist/prophet pulled between different worlds. Propositioned by Balak to curse Israel, Balaam in his activity as a seer comes into contact with YHWH, the God of Israel. His interactions

---

is linked with "the natural correlative notion that the initiative for such speech lies with God," and (3) this initiative is "characteristically expressed in terms of the prophet being 'sent' by God, as a messenger by his/her master." Such a prophetic role, as in the case of Moses, is "based upon his proximity to God, his standing in the divine presence" (9).

11. Gray bases much of his work on M. M. Kalisch, who faults earlier interpreters for assuming that various references to Balaam's life (e.g., Num. 31:8) were faithful accounts.

12. In Num. 31:8, 16 Balaam is understood to have advised the Midianite women to invite the Israelites to sacrifice to their gods (cf. 25:1–2), thus tempting them to apostasy. Outside Numbers, Balaam is remembered as someone who was tempted by the gold offered by Balak (2 Pet. 2:15; Jude 11), was in some way behind the Baal of Peor episode (Rev. 2:14; cf. Ps. 106:28, 37), practiced divination (Josh. 13:22), and was actively trying to curse Israel (Deut. 23:4–5; Josh. 24:9–10). In Neh. 13:2 Balaam is clearly neutral, and only Mic. 6:5 portrays Balaam positively: "O my people, remember now what King Balak of Moab devised, what Balaam son of Beor answered him, and what happened from Shittim to Gilgal, that you may know the saving acts of the LORD." This passage puts Balaam in the company of Moses, Aaron, and Miriam, creating an analogy between him and these "saints of God" (Origen 1996–2001: 2.296). These tensions are taken as simply reflecting different Balaam traditions behind the text, most reflecting the received negative tradition, but a few still carrying on the "very old, favorable view" (Milgrom 1990: 470).

---

with YHWH challenge the assumptions of his typical magico-religious practices. The person of Balaam embodies the clash between two very different ways of envisioning and responding to God and gods.

The lesson of the text is clear: as opposed to the assumptions of typical magico-religious practices in the surrounding cultures, YHWH is not simply another god or spirit whose power can be used by magicians and kings to bring blessing and cursing as they see fit. The worldview represented by Balak is ultimately shown to be false. Balak's unsuccessful attempt to control Balaam, and Balaam's unsuccessful attempt to control his donkey, parody their lack of control over forces that are larger than they realize. Instead of Balak using God through Balaam to curse Israel, it is God who uses kings and prophets and magicians to bring forward God's purposes of blessing. Many of the confessions and statements that Balaam makes also reflect this understanding by upholding the transcendence and freedom of God in light of human activity. In contrast to Balak's statement in 22:6, Balaam says that he is subject to "the word of the LORD" (24:13) and only in accordance with the will of God can he speak blessings or curses upon Israel. He counters Balak's pretensions with statements that point to the ineffectiveness of these magical practices, turns his back on the rites of divination (24:1; cf. 23:23), and confesses that his will cannot bring forth blessing or cursing on its own (24:13).

While these chapters might be interpreted as merely pointing to YHWH being more powerful than the spiritual forces assumed in the world of Balak, we also see Balaam coming to deeper understanding. God's relationship to Israel is of a different quality altogether than the kind of relationship between gods and people that Balak and Balaam himself had presupposed. God cannot be controlled or manipulated. In fact, God transcends the battle of creaturely forces. In relationship to such a God, the only proper role someone like Balaam can play is that of *mediating* God's power, the proper role of the Israelite priest and prophet, as opposed to *manipulating* God's power, the role often assumed by the seer or sorcerer.

These realizations about YHWH are filled out in discussions in Christian theology of God's transcendence, impassibility (meaning God is not affected against his will), and sovereign freedom. In contrast to understandings of spiritual forces and gods that view them as simply powerful forces within our world that might be manipulated or controlled according to human will, the developed Christian view of God is one that sees God as transcendent, above the play of creaturely forces. That God is not simply one creature or spiritual power among others is *the* distinction that grounds a Christian understanding of God.[13] Recognizing God's transcendence means talking about God in a way that "avoids either simple identity or contrast with the qualities of creatures."[14] In other words,

13. Robert Sokolowski, *The God of Faith and Reason: Foundations of Christian Theology* (Notre Dame, IN: University of Notre Dame Press, 1982).

14. Kathryn Tanner, *Jesus, Humanity, and the Trinity: A Brief Systematic Theology* (Edinburgh: Clark, 2001), 4.

the way that creatures are and affect each other—exerting a kind of push on one another—is not the way that God relates to creatures. Instead, God creates the world and sustains active creatures; God does not act among creatures as yet another creature, even a quite powerful one. Therefore God is not subject to any power, coercion, or action by a creature that God does not want to be affected by; God is transcendent and impassible.

This last qualification is extremely important. The Bible clearly portrays that God chooses to be affected in some way or other by the creatures he has created—but not in precisely the same way that creatures are affected. While divine transcendence is a theological achievement, Christian thought about God is also determined by the incarnation of the Word in Christ and by Christ's involvement with human suffering. The paradox at the center of Christian orthodoxy is that the radical transcendence of God is precisely what allows God to be deeply involved with creation. The constant struggle to affirm and understand how God is transcendent and yet still deeply involved with creation and human suffering was a particular concern of twentieth-century Christian theology.[15] This concern was also at the forefront of the thinking that led to Nicene orthodoxy; patristic theologians sought to carve out a space in their thought and language that could make sense of the audacious claim that "the Impassible suffered."[16]

Such abstract statements about God may at first seem far removed from the Balaam story; yet such a view of God is reflected in these chapters and in the whole book. God is above manipulation—that is the main emphasis of this text—and yet God is also involved with humans, listens to their requests, and is passionately concerned to bless them toward a world of shalom.

Balaam, Donkey, and Angel: Religious Temptations and God's Providence (22:22–35)

In the middle of this larger story is the episode of Balaam, his donkey, the angel, and God. This story within a story satirizes Balaam's ability as a seer and traces the development of Balaam's character as well as his understanding of God. The

15. Barth 1936–77: 2/1.302; Jürgen Moltmann, *The Crucified God*, trans. R. A. Wilson and J. Bowden (London: SCM, 1974), esp. 27–235; William C. Placher, *Narratives of a Vulnerable God: Christ, Theology, and Scripture* (Louisville: Westminster John Knox, 1994).

16. Paul L. Gavrilyuk, *The Suffering of the Impassible God: The Dialectics of Patristic Thought* (Oxford: Oxford University Press, 2004), 172. Gavrilyuk writes further (173): "In contrast [to Docetists, Arians, and Nestorians], the orthodox theologians regarded qualified divine impassibility as being compatible with certain God-befitting emotions and with the incarnate Word's suffering in and through human nature. For the orthodox divine impassibility functioned as an apophatic qualifier of all divine emotions and as the marker of the unmistakably divine identity. Thus, the concern to protect the paradox of the impassible God suffering in the flesh became the driving theological force of the debates in question."

claim that Balaam's character develops, however, goes against most modern interpretations of the story. An interpretational challenge in the opening verse of this section leads to typical modern ways of interpreting the story.

"God's anger was kindled because he was going, and the angel of the LORD took his stand in the road as his adversary" (22:22). God's anger seems out of place, since two verses before "God came to Balaam and said to him, 'If the men have come to summon you, get up and go with them'" (22:20). This seemingly arbitrary change in God's mind, combined with the way the satirical and negative portrayal of Balaam in 22:22–35 seems to conflict with the more positive portrayal of Balaam elsewhere in the story, are two main reasons it is often assumed that a different Balaam story has been spliced into the middle of the main one.[17] If one removes 22:22–35 from the text and reads 22:36 as following 22:21, these interpretational challenges disappear. This leads most modern interpreters to read the text as holding in tension two conflicting accounts of Balaam, an earlier account that sees him as a true prophet outside the bounds of Israel, and a later tradition that sees him as a purported seer who cannot see spiritual realities when he meets them on the road. Since in this view the text does not present a coherent portrait of Balaam, the question of his development makes little sense. Like a not-quite-successful mosaic, it simply puts clashing pieces of tradition side by side. But such poor construction itself needs explaining.[18]

The principal problem with this understanding is that it ignores the text as it stands, which at least attempts to present a single, coherent narrative. There are good literary reasons to read the text as a coherent narrative. The episode of Balaam and the ass has clear connections to the surrounding text. For example, the three times that Balaam's intentions are hindered by the angel correspond to the three times that Balak's intentions are hindered by Balaam's blessings. Both the episode of the ass and the later episode where Balaam gives the blessings are permeated by the theme of "seeing" and "not seeing."[19] Whatever the history of the stories, they have been combined into a meaningful whole. The points of apparent tension in the narrative, instead of indicating sloppy editing or respect for two different traditions, might also indicate that a more complex,

17. Milgrom 1990: 468 notes the clash between 22:20 and 22:22, the change in scenery, the shift of protagonists, and other inconsistencies (similarly Levine 2000: 139). Noth 1968: 178 writes concerning God's apparent reversal: "It then appears as an act of irresponsible despotism on God's part if, according to v. 21aa, Yahweh's anger at this departure suddenly burst forth." This is one reason behind his understanding 22:22–35 as an interpolation.

18. Explanations typically involve the final redactors' respect for earlier traditions. The final textual result exhibits the ability of the scriptural redactors to hold differing traditions in tension without feeling the need to lift up one and denigrate the other. This is certainly a trait worth emulating in many circumstances, and a much needed one in our world of ethnic and religious conflict. But the question is still whether this is the most satisfying reading.

19. Olson 1996: 142 argues that the narrative is a coherent whole, drawing upon Robert Alter, *The Art of Biblical Narrative* (New York: Basic Books, 1981), 104–7.

multileveled interpretation is needed, such as the following one that highlights the development of Balaam's character.[20]

At the beginning of the story, Balaam starts off well. While his familiarity with YHWH is surprising, and his expectation that he can speak to YHWH seemingly at will is more typical of seers and diviners than of Israel's prophets (22:8), his response in 22:13, "Go to your own land, for the LORD has refused to let me go with you," seems entirely appropriate for a prophet or follower of YHWH.

In the next exchange, we see a turn for the worse. Balaam's response to Balak's second offer of increased honor seems above reproach, but it also suggests that Balaam is paying attention to the potential for gain: "Although Balak were to give me his house full of silver and gold, I could not go beyond the command of the LORD" (22:18). Balaam then attempts to try to have his cake and eat it too: "You remain here . . . so that I may learn what more the LORD may say to me" (22:19). What more could Balaam want to know? He apparently is unwilling to simply refuse the offer and is trying to find a way past YHWH's initial no. In this negotiating ploy, Balaam seeks a way "to evade the cost of discipleship" (Moberly 1998: 11).

YHWH's apparent reversal to Balaam's repeated request could be interpreted as a response to this change in Balaam. Perhaps YHWH is allowing Balaam to follow the desires of his heart (Origen 1996–2001: 2.295). In light of this, God's similar commands to "do only what I tell to you do" (22:20) and "speak only what I tell you to speak" (22:35) suggest that YHWH has a plan for using Balaam's wrong intentions for good—he will allow Balaam to go to Balak as he desires, but will guide his words and actions in a way that will bring about YHWH's desired results, not Balak's or Balaam's.

Origen interprets these interactions between Balaam, Balak, and God similarly, but like many premodern interpreters, he sees Balaam in a more negative light. Balaam approaches God a second time because he is lured by gain from the start. As a diviner, Balaam consorts with demons, and his apparently good responses to God are feigned. He is for Origen like the "scribes and Pharisees" who have a zeal for God, but only a simulated zeal. Balaam has the right words in his mouth, but not in his heart (1996–2001: 2.291).

According to Origen, God responds accordingly. God does not just hear his words, but sees his heart. So, instead of stopping him, he "abandons Balaam to

20. In the following I draw principally upon Origen (1996–2001: 2.266–309) and Moberly (1998; *Prophecy and Discernment*)—an ancient interpreter and a contemporary who attend to the tensions and complexities of the received form of the text about both Balaam and God. Origen begins his reflections on the text by noting the difficulties and praying that God would help him to explain the passage in a way fitting with the "reason and dignity" of the divine law, rather than treating it simply as a fable (1996–2001: 2.267). Origen devotes nearly seven full sermons to Balaam out of his twenty-eight on the book on Numbers.

the desires of his heart" as it says in Ps. 81:12.[21] God does not override Balaam's desires, but rather gives space for him to act freely (1996–2001: 2.290).[22]

Because Balaam is "obstinate in his passion for money" and because God allows him freedom, God rescinds his earlier decision and lets him go (Origen 1996–2001: 2.277). Thus, God's statement, "If the men have come to summon you, get up and go with them; but do only what I tell you to do" (22:20), is a concession on God's part to Balaam's evil intentions. Nevertheless, God is not pleased with Balaam's direction, even though he allows it, as is clear in the dialogue with the angel: "I have come out as an adversary, because your way is perverse before me" (22:32). Taking the story of the angel and ass at face value, such an interpretation makes sense; God is allowing Balaam to go but still wants to communicate his displeasure. Thus the angel's purpose is not to stop Balaam, but rather to inform Balaam and the reader that his path is not good. For Origen, the story of Balaam shows how, even though God allows evil to exist and have its play, God still watches over his people and will "keep" them (cf. 6:24). God acts in such a way that allows Balaam's evil will to exist and allows him to go to Balak and try to curse Israel. Nevertheless God eventually brings good by intervening and replacing his words of cursing with words of blessing.[23] God skillfully weaves together the good and ill wills of all people through his providence to bring forth blessing for his people.

Drawing on the terminology of 2 Tim. 2:20 and Acts 9:15, Origen reflects further on the way that God uses some people as "vessels of election" or "vessels of honor" and others, such as Balaam, as "vessels of shame." But it is precisely passages such as these that push us to look for a more charitable interpretation of Balaam's

21. Origen's use of the psalm is appropriate, for Ps. 81 is a meditation upon God's rescue of Israel from Egypt and their refusal to follow God's voice (important themes in Numbers): "Hear, O my people, while I admonish you; O Israel, if you would but listen to me! . . . I am the LORD your God, who brought you up out of the land of Egypt. Open your mouth and I will fill it. But my people did not listen to my voice; Israel would not submit to me. So I gave them over to their stubborn hearts, to follow their own counsels" (Ps. 81:8–12). Origen thus treats Balaam as a figure for Israel, especially its leaders, later on calling Balaam "a figure of the Jews," like "the Jews" in the Gospel of John who often have the words of scripture in their mouths but whose hearts are far from God.

22. The issue of why God gives space to evil, allowing evil intention and actions to continue to exist, is a question that continues to trouble many. This question interested Origen, and his main answer is that the existence of free evil beings and the freedom of human evil intentions and character create an environment in which humanity can grow and mature: "If the demons are deprived of free will, the athletes of Christ would not have adversaries." For an analysis of Origen's theme of divine pedagogy, see Jean Daniélou, *Origène: Le Génie du Christianisme* (Paris: Table Ronde, 1948).

23. This direct divine intervention against Balaam's will in the final oracles is the part of Origen's interpretation that seems to strain the most against a simple reading of the text. Moberly is also bothered by this commandeering of Balaam's mouth, but for a different reason: "But to suppose that God's grace in the oracles so overrules Balaam's understanding that he utters that which he himself not only does not believe but is opposed to, is to invoke a mechanistic or manipulative model of grace which has no foundation in Scripture or in Christian faith. . . . In essence, it replaces the Spirit with schizophrenia" (1998: 20).

character. "Vessels of shame" (NRSV has "ordinary utensils") is a metaphor for members of the congregation who are indeed "snared by the devil," but are still members of the household of God. In applying this picture of God's action to Balaam, seeing in it an example of the purification necessary to be used by God in a role of "honor," one might see Balaam himself as not evil and destined for destruction, but rather in need of purification and freedom from the influence of evil (2 Tim. 2:21, 26). Acts 9:15 is even more apropos to the Balaam story: here the "vessel of honor" is Paul, who was stopped by God on his way to kill God's people and was blinded and fell to the ground on the road to Damascus.[24] God revealed to Paul that his path was opposing God; his resulting blindness was a symbol of his lack of true understanding and sight. As a result, Paul went through a conversion/purification and became a true apostle or prophet of God, bringing God's "name before the Gentiles." Something very similar seems to happen to Balaam in our text.

After Balaam sets out for Balak on the back of the donkey, the road is blocked by "the angel of the LORD standing in the road, with a drawn sword in his hand" (22:23). YHWH could have stopped Balaam by any number of means, but instead sends a messenger that provides impediments to Balaam's course away from the way of God. In his response to these impediments, Balaam continues on his course, ignoring the signs of the unusual behavior of the ass, like an athlete who foolishly ignores subtle or not-so-subtle warnings of bodily pain (Moberly 1998: 17–18). The ass finally tells him in no uncertain terms: "Have I been in the habit of treating you this way?" (22:30). The angel then appears in a more direct revelation, and Balaam is told directly that his way is perverse in the sight of God. If he persists in it, he will likely be destroyed.

In response to this revelation of his sin, there is a second turn in Balaam. Balaam confesses, "I have sinned" (22:34). With this sincere confession of sin, Balaam is set back on the proper path and turns back from the world of Balak to the world of God (Moberly 1998: 16).[25] Rather than stopping Balaam outright, or informing the reader of the perverseness of Balaam's actions, this confession seems to be the reason God sent the angel.

Given the sincerity of his confession, the angel does not tell Balaam to return home, but, surprisingly, to continue on (22:35). At this point, Balaam becomes the willing tool of YHWH to be used to subvert Balak's plans. Balaam's purpose is now truly to say and do only what God says. In the following encounters with Balak, he seems to grow into his prophetic role, abandoning his divining (24:1) and receiving the spirit of God in a more direct fashion (24:2). Balaam now plays the role of the ass toward Balak: his unusual behavior puts roadblocks in the way of Balak's purposes, but Balak does not head the warnings. He too pushes on

24. I am unaware of any interpretation that fully draws out the parallels between Balaam and Paul, but Gerrit Claesz Blecker's 1634 painting in Museum Boymans (Rotterdam) places Paul's Damascus road experience side by side with Balaam's encounter with the angel.

25. Calvin 1852: 4.197 sees this statement as one more subterfuge on Balaam's part.

three times. He, however, does not repent, but instead brings on the blessing of his enemies and the oracle of his own destruction (24:17).

While the episode ends positively for Balaam, other biblical references suggest that he falls yet again. Several associate him with Israel's apostasy at Peor (Num. 31:8, 16; Rev. 2:14). Josephus suggests that after his encounter with Balak and giving his oracles, Balaam still feels the need to honor Balak, so he advises him and the Midianites how they might defeat Israel—this time not by turning YHWH against Israel, but by getting Israel to turn against YHWH. He reasons that because of God's care for the Israelites, there is little that could make a difference in God's continued blessing of them. But if Balak was to send attractive Moabite and Midianite women to the Israelites, they could seduce them and make the Israelite men desire them to stay. Then, "if they entreat them to stay, let them not give their consent till they have persuaded them to leave off their obedience to their own laws and the worship of that God who established them, and to worship the gods of the Midianites and Moabites; for by this means God will be angry at them" (*Antiquities* 4.130).

If this reconstruction is correct, the apostasy at Peor in Num. 25 is a terrible fall for both Israel and Balaam—a fall that for both occurs directly after their renewed dedication. If so, this is a terrible commentary on the way that God's people can so easily fall into sin. Familiarity and intimacy with God is no guarantee of holiness.

Regardless of Balaam's later history, he is a wonderful illustration of both "the miracle of grace" and the "depths of human sin" (Moberly 1998: 21). Rather than seeing Balaam as either all good or all bad, he is an example of how even those exposed to God's grace and gracious warnings can be seduced into turning away from the paths of God through subtle rationalizations or compromises and into trying to use and manipulate the power of God for one's own purposes, as Balaam seems to attempt (22:19). Given the history of both Israel and the church, such a warning is always needed.

Interpreted in this way, Balaam is a good symbol of the people of Israel in Numbers. Gifted by God with his presence, the people in the first chapters follow God obediently. However, when they enter into the wilderness, they are tempted by their various desires and fall into sin. Some of their temptations cause them to turn away from the good yet difficult path to the promised land, others revolve around the desire for or presumption of power in spiritual matters (→11:1–21:35). In response, the presence of God meets them, reveals to them their sin, and finally prompts their confession—"we have sinned" (21:7)—as well as their renewed dedication (21:2).

Later in Israel's priestly and cultic practice surrounding the temple, the line separating the mediation of God's presence and its manipulation was often crossed; consequently, the temple cult was often in need of reform by king and critique by prophet: "In the critique of the prophets, the cult has become a place of self-indulgence and satiation. Yahweh has become a function of religious enterprise that is manipulative and self-satisfying, but that has completely forfeited any reference to the sovereign God of the core testimony" (Brueggemann 1997: 678; cf. Isa. 1:11–15; 58:2–4; Jer. 7:4, 8–11; Hos. 6:6; Amos 4:4–5; Mic. 6:6–8).[26]

The domestication of God's transcendence in thought and in practices that grant God's blessing is a constant problem in the Christian tradition. In Christian theology, the blessing of God is mediated primarily through the sacraments, so one would expect the crossover from mediation to manipulation to occur there. And indeed, the central Reformation protests were critiques of the domestication of God and of the "captivity" of the blessings and grace of God mediated by Christian sacraments and penitential practice. Luther and other Reformers critiqued the practice of selling and buying indulgences because they manipulated God and domesticated his power—people were buying and selling forgiveness. In his treatise "On the Babylonian Captivity of the Church," Luther extended this critique to the entire sacramental system. Calvin's critiques of the sacraments tended to center around a misunderstanding of the sacrifice involved in the mass, but also included the practice of selling masses (1960: §4.18.14). Calvin saw in Balaam a warning against ministers who "usurp to themselves the prerogative of blessing without His commission" and included in his words of warning the abuses of indulgences: "Hence we gather, how vain it is for hypocrites, as they are wont to do, to purchase pardon from men in order to propitiate God" (1852: 4.187).

In response to such manipulations of God's grace, many Protestants reacted against any mediation of God by priest or sacrament and instead emphasized the unmediated grace of God to the individual received by faith. But this counteremphasis on faith in certain quarters may ironically have led to the same problems. Persons and traditions that emphasize faith—where faith is understood as an act of the will that leads either to salvation when one dies or to healing/health/wealth now—may also come perilously close to crossing the line between supplication and presuming to control the power of God for one's own blessing.

In modern times, religion in general and Christianity in particular have often been critiqued as involving the manipulation of God for one's own purposes. Barth's 1922 commentary on Romans critiqued religious practice as the functional equivalent of Paul's law in Rom. 7—a way to manipulate and control God. His more nuanced position in *Church Dogmatics* also saw that religion, considered as a human activity, is generally an expression of human unfaithfulness and unbelief, in that "it is the attempted replacement of the divine work by a human manufacture" (1936–77: 1/2.302). It is a technology for receiving blessing or self-justification and self-sanctification (280). However, Barth also holds out the possibility that religion can be "sublated" (*aufhebung*) by revelation—that

---

26. The royal reforms of Hezekiah and Josiah were also in response to the "exploitation and domestication of Yahweh" (Brueggemann 1997: 676).

God's grace and revelation can enter into humanity's attempts at religion and make it "become true" (325). The parallels to the Balaam story are striking. God commandeers the religious practices of Balak and Balaam, subverts (rather than sublates) them, and makes them true.

Balaam might then be seen not merely as a type of a pagan used by God for good, but also as a type of those who know the name of YHWH and are in the position of mediators of the spiritual realm—priests and prophets—and who are tempted to fall into the ways of spiritual manipulation for personal gain and power. Balaam might thus be an icon of the temptations that those who draw near to God and share the word and blessing of God must always face. As Paul writes to the Corinthian church: "Now these things occurred as examples for us, so that we might not desire evil as they did. . . . So if you think you are standing, watch out that you do not fall" (1 Cor. 10:6, 12).

Current scholarly wisdom concerning the history of this text is that priestly or theocratic writers took existing texts and traditions and brought them together to create the final (or at least relatively stable) canonical form of Numbers and the rest of the Pentateuch during and after the Babylonian exile. The older consensus also contained a certain suspicion about the priestly redactors, that their editorial work was primarily self-serving and in a sense domesticated earlier forms and understandings of God in order to bolster their status, authority, and theological views.[27] The Balaam story (along with 11:35–12:16 and 16:1–17:11) is a carefully constructed narrative that emphasizes that the blessing and power of God should not be understood to be in the power of priestly or prophetic mediators. These inspired priestly writers apparently maintained a healthy "hermeneutic of suspicion" about the possibilities of the corruption of their own roles and practices. One need not go behind the text for this; it is part of sacred scripture itself.

Balaam's Blessings

Once Balaam's journey is completed, Balak takes Balaam to several spots from which he could view Israel (22:41; 23:14, 28). Balak wants Balaam to now curse Israel, but instead, through the actions of God and Balaam, Balaam gives several oracles that function as blessings upon Israel.

These sayings of Balaam provide a climax to the theme of blessing in both Numbers and the Pentateuch. They are like the blessings of Jacob in Gen. 49, who

---

27. Of course, the possibility exists that later inspired redactors brought a more mature understanding of God and his will to their task. Brueggemann, suspicious of the suspicion, points out how Protestant wariness of the cult and hence the priestly tradition, as well as all forms of establishment and mediation, might still play a part in the way priestly writers are viewed and their work evaluated (1997: 651–54). Douglas's most recent works on Numbers (1993a) and Leviticus (1999) reevaluate the priestly writers. As opposed to her influential *Purity and Danger* (New York: Praeger, 1969), she no longer considers them to be using their position to impose purity laws that "exclude or subordinate people belonging to inferior classes or castes" (Klawans 2000: 18).

speaks suitable words about his sons' futures, in this way "blessing" them.[28] The oracles of Balaam give further insight into the content of the grace and blessing of God being passed on to Israel. The thematic progression in the four oracles shows that the blessing promised to Abraham is much more than the gift of many descendents.

Given the importance of blessing, it is noteworthy that this climactic series of blessings comes to Israel through Balaam, rather than through a priest of Israel. It underscores the freedom and power of God to bring forward his plans of blessing Israel and the world, both in spite of Israel's sin and outside regular channels. While it does not undercut the authority or efficacy of the priesthood in Israel in its role to bless and "place the name" of God on the people, it does undercut the *uniqueness* of the priesthood as a means of God's blessing and grace. God sets up and uses priests and the tabernacle/temple cult, but God's action and presence are not limited to them. As happens several times in Numbers, God uses people outside the regular hierarchy to guide, speak to, and bless his people (→10:29–32; →11:26–30). God is not bound by the failures of his people, the regular means of priesthood or tabernacle, or the evil intentions of earthly kings and powers. That God can and will use even the enemies of Israel to bless them highlights the freedom, power, and providential control of God as well as his great love for his sinful people and desire to bless them.

Each of Balaam's seven sayings is introduced by the phrase "and he/Balaam uttered his oracle" (23:7, 18; 24:3, 15, 20, 21, 23). A more literal translation is "and he took up his *māšāl*." While the NRSV translates *māšāl* as "oracle," the word is never used of the oracles or prophecies of Hebrew prophets, but rather is used of proverbs, riddles, poetry, lamentations, and sayings. It is elevated speech that is often metaphorical (Gray 1903: 344–45).[29] While seven in total, the sayings are clearly gathered into four groups. However, Balaam's third and fourth sayings use the word *nĕʾum* ("word, oracle") internally (24:3 [twice], 4, 15 [twice], 16), which the NRSV unfortunately translates with the same English word: "The oracle of Balaam son of Beor." There is a progression here, undoubtedly related to the introduction of the third saying: "Then the spirit of God came upon him" (24:2). This phrase is used of those inspired by the Spirit within Israel, as in David's oracle near the end of his life: "The oracle [*nĕʾum*] of David, son of Jesse, the oracle of the man whom God exalted. . . . The spirit of the LORD speaks through me, his word is upon my tongue" (2 Sam. 23:1–2). While God at first put a "word" (*dābār*) into Balaam's mouth (Num. 23:5, 16), Balaam's later words are oracles, words of Balaam yet inspired by God. The implication is that Balaam is *both* more inspired by God *and* speaking more fully from his own heart in the latter two groups of

---

28. Suggestive similarities between Gen. 49:1, 29 and Num. 24:14 and between Gen. 49:9 and Num. 23:24; 24:9 might indicate that Gen. 49 is being intentionally echoed.

29. Milgrom 1990: 181, 196 translates the word "theme" and also shows how it refers to the *mōšĕlîm* ("ballad singers") in Num. 21:27. The book of Proverbs is named for the *mišlê* it contains.

sayings, showing a greater intimacy in Balaam's relationship to God, as well as a deepening insight into the blessedness of Israel.

First Blessing: Election and Fertility (22:41–23:12)

In the first saying, Balaam is brought by Balak to Bamoth-baal, where he sees only part of the people (22:41). Balaam goes through his rites and then utters his *māšāl*, in which two central themes emerge: the chosenness or election of Israel that sets it apart from all other nations and the blessing of their great number—themes echoing the call of Abram in Gen. 12:2: "I will make of you a great nation." The center of Balaam's blessing is Num. 23:9–10: "Here is a people living alone, and not reckoning itself among the nations! Who can count the dust of Jacob, or number the dust-cloud of Israel?"—which echoes the passing on of Abraham's blessing to Jacob in Gen. 28:14: "Your offspring shall be like the dust of the earth." Balaam's blessing clarifies that Israel is unique ("alone") because it is different—it is an elect, "treasured possession" of YHWH (Exod. 19:5). He passes on the blessings of the patriarchs to the nation, even after its great disobedience and rebellions in the wilderness.

Israel's election is the basis of all its further blessings. It has been singled out by God to play a special role in the history of salvation. The theme of election was received in and transmitted through Christian theology (→1:1–54), but its connection to the role that God's people play in God's larger plans has often been lost or decentered, replaced by questions concerning God's eternal decisions about individual salvation. Here, however, we clearly see that the object of election is this people, a nation set apart from other nations.

The blessing of fruitfulness is appropriate as the first sign of this election. When God blessed humankind at the beginning, the first result was their fruitfulness: "God blessed them, and God said to them, 'Be fruitful and multiply, and fill the earth and subdue it'" (Gen. 1:28). In a similar way, when God makes a new beginning with Israel, a key sign of God's blessing is their fruitfulness. The great number of the people of Israel that Balaam sees—and that is reflected in the two censuses—shows that God is indeed with them and blessing them.

Balaam ends this *māšāl* with his own wish: "Let me die the death of the upright, and let my end be like his!" (Num. 23:10). Such a statement may simply reflect the hope that good will happen to Balaam at the end of his life. But it may also reflect the hope that Israel's blessing will spill over and include him. Such a hope fits with God's own plans for people like Balaam: "I will bless those who bless you, . . . and in you all the families of the earth will be blessed" (Gen. 12:3; cf. 22:18). The implications of Israel's blessing for others is spelled out: "And all the families of the earth will be blessed in you" (28:14). Balaam is blessing himself by referring to Israel, as suggested by an alternate translation of 12:3: "By you all the families of the earth shall bless themselves."

Unfortunately, Balaam will be disappointed in that hope. He did not die the death of the upright, but instead was cut down by the sword as part of Israel's revenge against the Midianites (Num. 31:8).

Second Blessing: Cleansing and Enlightening (23:13–26)

Balaam is now brought by Balak to the top of Pisgah, where he sees another part of the people (23:13–14). He goes through similar rites and gives his second *māšāl*, which centers on the recognition of the closeness of God to Israel and God's presence in their midst. God's presence both cleanses Israel of sin and enlightens them as to God's will, so that there is no need for divination or augury within Israel. This closeness also makes them like a lion—strong in battle.

This interpretation of the oracle depends upon several ambiguous phrases. The NRSV emphasizes God's protection of Israel from the outside, but the Hebrew supports an interpretation in which the blessed presence of God is recognized as transforming Israel from the inside.

The phrase "he has not beheld misfortune in Jacob; nor has he seen trouble in Israel" (23:21a) turns on the Hebrew words *'āven* and *'āmāl*. The King James Version and rabbinic tradition (e.g., Rashi) translate *'āven* ("misfortune" in the NRSV) as "iniquity" and "transgression" (Gray 1903: 353). *'Āmāl* ("trouble") means sickness or weakness and often has the connotation of moral evil, either because the people have "sick" hearts (Ezek. 16:30) or because the *'āmāl* of the land is a result of or tied to the people's iniquity (Jer. 14:2–3). Altering these translations changes the focus from evil outside Israel to evil within them. But the problem with translating the phrase as "he has not beheld iniquity . . . nor has he seen weakness" is that this is clearly not the case with Israel, as surrounding chapters show! Traditional commentators try to resolve this problem in several ways. Ibn Ezra says that the statement about God's friendship in 23:21b is dependent on there being no iniquity in Israel. Onqelos, another rabbinic source, argues instead that God *sees* no iniquity in Israel because of his love and friendship for it. I interpret Balaam's visions of Israel as in a sense eschatological, as descriptions of who Israel is called to be and will be, but is not yet. God's kingship among them is what brings this about: "The LORD their God is with them, acclaimed as a king among them" (23:21b). The fulfillment of God's reign among the Israelites is in part the cleansing of all iniquity, transgression, and moral weakness from among them.

The NRSV of 23:23 emphasizes God's protection of Israel. But Milgrom provides a better translation of the Hebrew: "Lo, there is no augury in Jacob, No divining in Israel: Jacob is told at once, Yea Israel, what God has planned" (1990: 200). The decision whether to translate the Hebrew preposition as "*in* Israel" or "*against* Israel" is driven by the wider sense. The most common translation is "in Israel," and the point is that because of God's prophets there is no need for the kind of divination and augury that Balaam and his ilk usually perform (Milgrom

1990: 200). This logic is reflected in Deut. 18:9–15, where those practices are forbidden in Israel.

Finally, the presence of God strengthens Israel "like a lioness" and "like a lion" (Num. 23:24). The image of Israel as a lion is found in the blessing of Judah (Gen. 49:9; cf. Ezek. 19:2–6), the tribe from which both David and Jesus emerge. It unambiguously points to the strength and prowess of Israel in battle, blessing and foreseeing the strength of Israel to stand up against its foes.

Altogether, this blessing pictures the presence of God within Israel as a divine force that blesses Israel into a pure, wise, and strong nation.

Third Blessing: Prosperity and Victory (23:27–24:9)

In the third blessing, Balaam is taken to the top of Peor by Balak (23:28). No longer looking for omens, seeing all Israel instead of part, and inspired by the Spirit (24:1–3), Balaam utters his third *māšāl*, which is now also called an oracle (*ně'um*).

Using rich poetic language, the first part of the oracle depicts Israel as a land of beauty, fruitfulness, and prosperity (24:5–7a)—language reminiscent of the Song of Songs. Israel is foreseen living in a land filled with palms, gardens, aloes, cedars, and water.

The blessings show a progression. Starting with a vision of the uniqueness of Israel, there is a movement to its sheer numbers as a sign of God's blessing. From there, the picture shifts to the moral and spiritual work that God must do within Israel to bring about his reign in it. God cleanses and enlightens his chosen people and makes them strong. The vision in the third oracle emphasizes the beauty, prosperity, and fruitfulness of the land. It is as if Israel has returned to the garden of Eden. Because of textual hints that Balaam is now seeing clearly and inspired by God, the emphasis on vision suggests that in this oracle we glimpse more clearly some of the final purposes of God for Israel.

The movement from the interior work of God in Israel in the second oracle to its material result in the third is significant. Often in Western Christianity there is a movement in thought and practice that privileges the spiritual over the material. As one becomes holier, one leaves off concerns with the material world and is instead occupied with the life of the spirit, which is understood often in opposition to the life of the body. Not so with ancient Israel. As the blessings of Deut. 28:1–14 also suggest, the promises and purposes of God for his people are quite earthy, quite substantial. Life in the Spirit for Israel is a life of renewed harmonies between humans and God, among humans, and between humans and the earth. It is a vision of shalom (→6:22–27). "Prosperity is a sign of God's blessing," and "asceticism and self-denial have little place in Jewish spirituality."[30] In light of the wilderness experience of Israel, in which self-dedication and some

---

30. Jonathan Sacks, *The Dignity of Difference: How to Avoid the Clash of Civilizations* (New York: Continuum, 2002), 97.

self-denial for a time are pictured as part of Israel's calling, this point needs to be slightly qualified. Especially in light of the cross of Christ, Christians will need to find some place for asceticism, self-denial, and suffering in our own spiritualities. However, the witness of this blessing will at least push us to consider whether we have overspiritualized or wrongly spiritualized our understandings of the purposes and blessings that God has in store for his people.

The second part of the blessing (24:7b–9) foresees that the king and kingdom of Israel will be exalted over the surrounding nations. It is an oracle of victory over the enemies of God's people. Victory over King Agag of Amalek was first accomplished by Saul (1 Sam. 15), with greater victories by David and Solomon over the Amalekites. On one level this oracle seems to have been fulfilled. But as with many messianic oracles, the oracle is taken up by later Israelite and Christian interpreters in an open-ended fashion, since the visions for Israel's blessings and defeat of its enemies have not been finally or fully fulfilled.

The introduction to the third oracle, "Balaam . . . set his face toward the wilderness" (Num. 24:1), uses the same Hebrew construction found in the final phrase of the Aaronic blessing: "The LORD lift up his countenance upon you and give you peace" (6:26). This third blessing has much of the same content as the Aaronic blessing and seems to function as the narrative conclusion to the picture of blessing given in the first part of the book. The surprise is that Balaam, rather than the high priest of Israel, pronounces this blessing. God here is bringing his intentions to pass in spite of the rebellions of Israel.

The final line of this third oracle brings to narrative conclusion the blessings that God is bringing on this generation of Israel. The words "blessed is everyone who blesses you, and cursed is everyone who curses you" point back to the blessings given to Abraham (Gen. 12:3; cf. 22:18) and Jacob (27:29). As Israel is about to cross into the promised land, Balaam's words recognize that the blessings and promises given to the patriarchs are being passed on to this people.

Fourth Group of Oracles: Rise of Israel's Future King and Defeat of Nations (24:10–25)

In the final interactions between Balak and Balaam, Balak's frustration at Balaam's threefold blessing of Israel comes to a head, and Balak fires his would-be sorcerer: "Now be off with you! Go home! I said, 'I will reward you richly,' but the LORD has denied you any reward" (24:11). This is followed by yet another ironic twist, for instead of cursing Israel, Balaam now utters four oracles that amount to curses of Israel's foes, starting with Balak's Moab. While Balak still believes he has the power to withhold rewards from Balaam, it is God who denies Balak any reward.

While there are many interpretational and translation challenges in this group of oracles (Wenham 1981: 178–84; Milgrom 1990: 201–11), including both the names and peoples referred to, the general sense is clear: the nations surrounding

Israel—namely, Moab, Edom, Amalek, the Kenites, Asshur, and Eber, both current and potential enemies—will be crushed by Israel or other nations. While Israel will be blessed, doom is pronounced on these nations.

The first oracle (24:15–19) is the longest and best known, mainly because of the star prophecy: "I see him, but not now; I behold him, but not near—a star shall come out of Jacob, and a scepter shall rise out of Israel" (24:17). This verse has been received by both Jewish and Christian interpreters as referring to a future ruler of Israel. The word "star" (*kôkāb*) is repeatedly used to describe rulers in Israel (Isa. 14:12; Ezek. 32:7; Rev. 22:16) and even more commonly elsewhere in the ancient Near East (Ashley 1993: 500). While the word for "scepter" can be translated differently, this is its most common meaning, referring to the king's insignia (Gen. 49:10; Isa. 14:5). Given this double royal reference, the vast majority of rabbinic and Christian interpreters have understood this to be a reference to a rising king of Israel.

This oracle is understood to refer first of all to David, whose victories over both Moab and Edom partially fulfill the prophecy (2 Sam. 8:2–14; 1 Kgs. 11:15–16). And yet, as both Edom (1 Kgs. 11:14, 17–22; 2 Kgs. 8:20; 14:7, 22; 2 Chr. 28:17; Ps. 137) and Moab (2 Kgs. 1:1; 3:4–5, 21–27; 13:20) rose again and were reconquered several times, those victories of David were short-lived (Ashley 1993: 503). Prophecies such as this need not refer to a single event, however, but often refer to a repeating or typological pattern. Jewish interpreters saw these verses as referring both to David and a later messianic figure near the time of Christ, Bar Kokhba (Milgrom 1990: 207).

Christians find this prophecy's fulfillment in Jesus Christ. The star mentioned in Matt. 2:2 is understood to refer to Num. 24:17, and the magi from the east coming and bowing down to Christ in the manger is understood as a partial fulfillment of this prophecy. Revelation 22:16 (cf. 2:28; 2 Pet. 1:19) also refers this prophecy to Jesus: "I am the root and the descendant of David, the bright morning star." The idea of Christ as both root and descendent of David refers to Christ's preexistence before his incarnation. Such an understanding is also seen in Jesus's own interpretation of Ps. 110, the great royal psalm associated with this oracle (Matt. 22:44; Mark 12:36; Luke 20:43; cf. Acts 2:35; Heb. 1:13; 10:13). Psalm 110 shares many words and themes with this oracle and is reasonably understood to be loosely based on it (de Vaulx 1972: 292; Wenham 1981: 183; Calvin 1852: 4.228).

How did Christ fulfill these prophecies, since during his incarnation he did not raise an army and defeat the surrounding nations? Calvin writes: "Hence it follows that the blessing, of which Balaam speaks, descends even to us; for, if the prosperity of the ancient people, their rest, their well-ordered government, their dignity, safety, and glory, proceeded from the sceptre as its unmixed source, there is no doubt but that Christ by His coming accomplished all these things more fully for us" (1852: 4.228). For Calvin, Christ fulfills this prophecy as he fulfills what he elsewhere calls the "royal office," shadows of which are seen throughout the kingship of the Old Testament. David is its prime exemplar; it is fulfilled in the rule and reign of Christ. For Calvin, this rule of Christ is begun in the ministry of Christ in Palestine, but will be fulfilled finally at the end of the age, when Christ returns in glory.[31] Thus this prophecy continues to look forward—as Rev. 22:16 does—to Christ's return, when indeed not only Moab and Edom, but all of the enemies of God and his people, including war, famine, pestilence, and death, will be finally conquered (6:1–8).

Balaam's oracles thus fill out the content of the blessing of Israel. Israel is blessed by God first in its election and fruitfulness. God also blesses through his presence, which cleanses, gives insight, and strengthens. This blessing leads to a life of harmony and prosperity in the promised land. Finally, God's blessing will include sending the Messiah, who will eventually bring victory over all the enemies of God's people. Understood in this way, the blessings of Balaam provide an overview of all salvation history.

31. William Kelly, *Lectures Introductory to the Study of the Pentateuch* (London: Broom, 1871), 398.

7

FINAL REBELLION
AND ATONEMENT (25:1–18)

While Balaam was blessing the Israelites from the top of the nearby mountain of Peor, all was not well in the valley below. While God was thwarting the plans of Balak and Balaam in order to bring blessing to Israel, the people of Israel, in the very last place they encamp before entering the promised land (33:49), Shittim, fall yet once more into sin.

This stark juxtaposition between the blessing brought by God and the sin of the people is familiar—there are many similarities between this pair of episodes and the giving of the law on Mount Sinai, which happens concurrently with the apostasy of Aaron and the people at Sinai (Exod. 32).[1] Both pairs include Israel's worship of other gods (Exod. 32:4–6; Num. 25:3); both pairs have similar settings: a mountain of revelation/blessing and the lowlands below where sin is committed (Exod. 32:1; Num. 23:28; 25:1); both apostasies result in a plague (Exod. 32:35;

---

1. The stark juxtaposition in these important events within the life of Israel also tells us something about God. It highlights the great mercy and patience of God while at the same time showing the great seriousness of sin. This picture of God's relationship to his people and their sin is admittedly complex, and yet clearly should call into question the stereotypical reduction of Israelite religion to "works righteousness." Many Protestant readers of Paul's Letters understand Israelite religion as Israel doing good works in order to make itself acceptable to God. At the very least, one can say that the Israelite understanding of God that shaped the composition of this text points in a different direction. While Israel is certainly called to purity and holiness, such purity is not the prerequisite of God's relationship with this people. The so-called new perspective on Paul (e.g., N. T. Wright, *Paul in Fresh Perspective* [Minneapolis: Fortress, 2005]) understands Israelite religion—and Paul's understanding of Israelite religion—in a way much more fitting of Numbers.

Num. 25:8–9); both have an immediate slaying of wrongdoers (Exod. 32:26–28; Num. 25:8), which respectively results in the priesthood of the Levites and the promise of perpetual priesthood of Phineas and his descendents (Exod. 32:29; Num. 25:13) (for more parallels, see Olson 1996: 153–54).

This episode thus provides a fitting bookend to the rebellions of the exodus generation. In the first apostasy at Sinai, God's words of judgment were open-ended as to the timing of punishment: "Whoever has sinned against me I will blot out of my book. But now go, lead the people. . . . Nevertheless, when the day comes for punishment, I will punish them for their sin" (Exod. 32:33–34). The punishment of that first generation began with the initial plague in Exod. 32, continued in the many plagues throughout Numbers, and culminates in this final one at Shittim. God's warning to Israel after the golden calf episode also points forward to this event with great precision: "You shall not make a covenant with the inhabitants of the land, for when they prostitute themselves to their gods and sacrifice to their gods, someone among them will invite you, and you will eat of the sacrifice. And you will take wives from among their daughters for your sons, and their daughters who prostitute themselves to their gods will make your sons also prostitute themselves to their gods" (Exod. 34:15–16).

As a result of their earlier apostasy at Sinai and their later rebellions in the wilderness (Num. 14:29–30), that entire generation died in the wilderness: "Among these there was not one of those enrolled by Moses and Aaron. . . . Not one was left, except Caleb . . . and Joshua" (26:64–65). That generation, in spite of God's repeated warnings and chastisements, ended up repeating the same errors Israel made nearly forty years earlier at Mount Sinai.

And yet not all is bleak. Phineas, a representative of the rising generation of Israel, acts decisively. He takes his place alongside Joshua and Caleb as signs of hope that the next generation will enter into the promises of God for Israel in the promised land. So while this episode in one respect closes the story of the rebellions and apostasies of the exodus generation, it is also naturally followed by the second census, which hopefully highlights the rise of the generation of the conquest.

The passage is easily broken down into three parts: the sin, its results, and the end of the plague (25:1–9); the epilogue concerning Phineas, Zimri, and Cozbi (25:10–15); and the final judgment on the Midianites (25:16–18) (Ashley 1993: 515; Wenham 1981: 185). While there are many intriguing linguistic and textual details in this passage (see Ashley 1993: 511–24 and Milgrom 1990: 211–18, 476–80), two aspects of this episode are of primary theological importance: the sin of the people and the response of Phineas.

The passage begins rather abruptly with the statement "the people began to have sexual relations with the women of Moab" (25:1). Other scriptural passages point to a story behind this story and suggest that Balaam instigated these relations and the following apostasy: "These women here, on Balaam's advice, made the Israelites act treacherously against the LORD in the affair of Peor" (31:16).

And John writes: "You have some there who hold to the teaching of Balaam, who taught Balak to put a stumbling block before the people of Israel, so that they would eat food sacrificed to idols and practice fornication" (Rev. 2:14). Origen reconstructs what he believes to have been Balaam's plan. After Balak's plan to curse Israel and defeat him with his armies does not work, Balaam suggests to Balak that he could still defeat them with different means. "Elegance disarms the warriors, beauty takes the sword captive," Balaam would advise. The undermining work of the Midianite and Moabite women would then include the enticement to sacrifice to Baal-Peor. To a certain extent the plan worked (Origen 1996–2001: 3.18–19). This reconstruction does not lessen the culpability of the Israelites, but it does make sense of the blame placed on the Midianites: "Harass the Midianites, . . . for they have harassed you by the trickery with which they deceived you in the affair of Peor" (Num. 25:17–18).

That Israel's apostasy came through the avenue of sexual relations and what may have seemed to be a slight religious accommodation to their attractive neighbors is of great contemporary interest. The people of Israel were not convinced to abandon YHWH through rational argument or at the point of a sword, but rather through an ancient equivalent of "missionary dating," generous invitation, and religious syncretism. The means of their downfall is a warning to the people of God today. Living in a society based on political liberalism and in a society greatly fearful of religious intolerance and fundamentalist violence, it is much easier for members of the academy and the church to condemn religious intolerance and fundamentalism than to speak of the need for religious purity and integrity. And yet the pressure of this passage—and indeed of the first and second commandments (Exod. 20:2–6; cf. 34:10–17)—is to push us toward the latter.

Living at the end or climax of the modern world, many movements and individuals within the church are calling for a renewed centering of Christian thought and practice on Christian tradition. They understand that Christianity has been accommodated to a reigning secular worldview. Theologian Stanley Hauerwas, for example, claims that much of modern Christianity in the West has already metaphorically "known" the Midianite women and sacrificed at the altars of nationalism, political liberalism, and secular rationality. In response, he calls Christians, especially Christian theologians, to "break back into Christianity."[2] There has been a related resurgence of interest in culture and Christianity's relationship to it.[3] This text relating the sin of Israel calls us to carefully consider the proper

2. Stanley Hauerwas, *Wilderness Wanderings: Probing Twentieth-Century Theology and Philosophy* (Boulder, CO: Westview, 1997), xii.

3. For example, D. Stephen Long's *Theology and Culture* (Eugene, OR: Wipf & Stock, 2008) examines contemporary movements in theology—such as postliberalism, communion Catholicism, Radical Orthodoxy, Anabaptists, philosophical communitarians, and postmodern feminists—who call for more coherent communities and traditions in the face of the breakup of the modern world. Both Long's book and T. M. Moore's *Culture Matters: A Call for Consensus on Christian Cultural Engagement* (Grand Rapids: Brazos, 2007) show the current interest in such discussions and take

relationship of the people of God to surrounding cultures and worldviews. It is a warning that God's people are easily tempted to abandon their loyalties to God for certain pleasures and relationships.[4]

The New Testament church also faced the issue of how to respond to the seductions of surrounding cultures that tempted the people of God to abandon their loyalty to God alone. These issues were especially difficult to discern given the breaking down of the cultural wall between Jews and Gentiles that Acts 10–11 records. Paul directly addressed the issue of eating food offered to idols in his letters to the Corinthian church and alluded to the apostasy at both Sinai (1 Cor. 10:7) and Shittim (10:8, 22). His directions to the Corinthians indicate he does not advocate total withdrawal from friendships with, relationships with, and hospitality toward others, but he does call for certain abstentions in certain cases: "If an unbeliever invites you to a meal and you are disposed to go, eat whatever is set before you without raising any question on the ground of conscience. But if someone says to you, 'This has been offered in sacrifice,' then do not eat it" (10:27–28). Given the great plurality of our own time, the lines between hospitality/openness and accommodation/apostasy are not always easy to draw. Yet Paul's reflections on Israel's sins should be taken seriously: "These things occurred as examples for us, so that we might not desire evil as they did" (10:6).

When Israel is seduced into worshiping Baal, the god of fertility and life, the climax of the event comes when Phineas pierces the Israelite man and Midianite woman with a spear. Their names, "Zimri son of Salu" and "Cozbi daughter of Zur" (25:14–15), are very suggestive of what is at stake. The Hebrew root *zmr* is related to an Arabic root meaning "thing to be protected, sacred, inviolable," while *sl'* has connotations of "weighty, consecrated" (BDB 275 #III, 698). Thus, the Israelite Zimri might be a symbol of Israel in general, a consecrated or holy people. The nominal roots *kzb* ("lie, liar") and *sr* ("adversary") mean "show hostility toward" and "vex" in their verbal forms (BDB 469, 865). The woman's name is also symbolic, since the Midianites vexed or harassed Israel through deceit or lies (25:17–18). These two figures thus beg to be read both literally and as symbols for their people; Israel, called to be a consecrated people, has been seduced by lies, deceit, and sin.

In the aftermath of Israel's apostasy, Phineas emerges as an exemplary character. Directly after Israel "yoked itself to the Baal of Peor," YHWH's "anger was kindled," and Moses is told to kill the chiefs of the people (25:3–4). Moses's response, however, is not in direct obedience to God; he instead tells the leaders that they should "kill any of your people who have yoked themselves to the Baal of Peor" (25:5). It could be that Moses is passing the buck, protecting leaders he knows personally, or perhaps even making the punishment more stringent

---

us much further in these discussions than H. Richard Niebuhr's famous typology in *Christ and Culture* (New York: Harper, 1951).

4. In his reflections on this passage, Origen 1996–2001: 3.19–33 ranges from the seductions of luxury and avarice to the results of various kinds of "spiritual adultery."

than what God intended; whatever the case may be, Moses does not seem to be carrying out God's judgment precisely (Olson 1996: 155).[5] Moses's plan is interrupted, however, by an Israelite and a Midianite princess who enter into a "tent"[6] near where Moses and others are praying to God to end the plague. Phineas son of Eleazar takes a spear and stops the plague by impaling them both. This action assuages the wrath of God, and the plague stops.

There is something disturbing about holding up this act of violence as exemplary. Some Jewish commentators even suggest that Moses would have excommunicated Phineas had not God declared that he had acted well (Milgrom 1990: 477). And yet God says that Phineas's action has "turned back my wrath from the Israelites by manifesting such zeal among them on my behalf that in my jealousy I did not consume the Israelites" (25:11). A more literal translation is, "in his becoming impassioned with my passion among them so I did not consume them in my passion." The focus of God's explanation is that Phineas mediated his own passion. It is his passion for God or impassioned action for God that was exemplary, that stemmed God's wrath and "made atonement for the Israelites" (25:13). A sacrifice is a representative intentional act that covers over, atones for, the sins of Israel and Israelites (→7:1–88), with the result that God might continue to dwell with the people. Phineas's action functions similarly. First, God accepts Phineas's act as representing the whole people, just as the deaths of the leaders (25:4) might have been accepted as representatives of the whole. And just as the intentional act of worshiper and priest is at the heart of the sacrifice, so too Phineas's zealous act—not the deaths of Zimri and Cozbi per se—is what God accepts as a sufficient atonement. Phineas is exemplary in his concern for the sanctity of God's people, that the relationship between God and his people be not damaged through sin.

Given this understanding, the early church was right to see Jesus Christ as "the true Phineas" in his own zeal for righteousness. Jesus's zeal was expressed not in the killing of sinners, but in his zeal for God's temple (John 2:17) and even more finally in his victory over sinful impulses through obedience even to the point of death on a cross (Phil. 2:8). His great act of zeal provides the final atonement for many.

Origen argues that Christians, instead of taking up a spear like Phineas, must take up the "sword of the Spirit," by which they can cut out the heart of sin in them and so approach with assurance the day of judgment (1996–2001: 3.55). The example of Phineas calls us to moral seriousness and the desire for spiritual growth and purity. And as a model for leadership, Phineas exemplifies the great passion a leader should have concerning the devotion to God of those he leads. One sees this passion also in Paul: "I feel a divine jealousy for you, for I prom-

5. Milgrom 1990: 476 states that the differences between the command of God, the command of Moses, and the action of Phineas are "the major critical problem in the text."
6. Some interpreters speculate that they entered the tabernacle, but the Hebrew word *qubbâ* perhaps suggests a marriage canopy (Milgrom 1990: 215).

ised you in marriage to one husband, to present you as a chaste virgin to Christ" (2 Cor. 11:2).

As a result of his action, God grants Phineas his "covenant of peace" (Num. 25:12). There is something a bit jarring about this, that peace is highlighted as a result of such a violent act. The phrase "covenant of peace" points to a state of shalom between God, his people, and the earth (Isa. 54:10; Ezek. 34:25). This promise to Phineas suggests that true peace, the end or goal of God's blessing, will come about only through the eradication of evil in Israel. Phineas plays a role similar to the star that will come out of Jacob in Balaam's fourth oracle (Num. 24:17), a Messiah who will crush the enemies of Israel and ultimately bring in the reign of God.

Phineas's great zeal for God and the purity of the people is fitting for his role as high priest, just as Joshua's courage is fitting for a leader who will take Moses's place. With leaders such as these, the rising generation of Israel can confidently approach the boundaries of the promised land.

PART 3

REORGANIZATION
OF ISRAEL (26:1–36:13)

God Prepares Israel for Life in the Promised Land

The third and final part of Numbers is a bittersweet portrait of the new generation. There is certainly much hope in these last eleven chapters of the book. The forty years in the wilderness is finally over, the new generation is emerging and is marked by a new obedience to God. The focus shifts from the rebellions in the wilderness to the particulars of life in the promised land. God has forgiven his people and will lead them forward. All this is good. And yet almost every chapter is marked with a sense that while everything is better, it is not quite as it should be. A strong sense of the penultimate, of the almost-but-not-there-yet, pervades.

This tone is heard especially clearly in considering the many parallels and subtle contrasts between Num. 1–10 and Num. 26–36. Just as in the opening chapters, Israel is given a new start, and an overall portrait of the new generation is painted. But while the ideal of Israel was set forth earlier, here the picture is a bit more gritty. The total from the new census is 601,730 (26:51), down just slightly from the initial 603,550 (1:46). The daughters of Zelophehad are given inheritance rights, a striking new development (Num. 27), but by the end of the book, some of their newfound rights are slightly curtailed (Num. 36). Moses is again told that he will see the promised land, but not enter it (27:12–13). The image of the Nazirite was originally presented as a vow undertaken by either man or woman (6:1–21), but

Num. 30 limits the vows of women, bringing women more in line with the status quo of Israel. In Num. 31 Israel, led in part by Phineas, triumphs over the Midianites and does so in obedience to God's commands, but not every command is realized immediately or as it should have been.[1] Perhaps even the holy-war idea that the Midianites and their idolatry must be cleansed by Israel pales in comparison with the self-dedication and self-purification of the Nazirite. As the Israelites near the promised land, two and a half tribes are not interested in entering it—although they are convinced to help the others do so (Num. 32). The rules concerning the cities of refuge, while showing that mercy is at the center of Israel's life, also bring a darker shade of realism to the vision of life in the promised land, for it implies there will be murder among the people (Num. 35). A hint is dropped that not all the inhabitants of the land will be totally driven out and that this will be a problem for Israel (33:55). The setting of these chapters, the plains of Moab rather than the slopes of Sinai (22:1; 36:13), is a fitting setting for the hopeful, but still-not-there-yet tone of these chapters. Perhaps the best example is at the center of these chapters, the detailed treatment of the Feast of Booths (29:12–40). In this central celebration of Israel, the people look forward to the final fulfillment of God's promises to Israel while living in booths, dramatically symbolizing that the physical and spiritual journey of the people is not yet complete.

"The theme of the Pentateuch is the partial fulfilment—which implies also the partial non-fulfilment—of the promise to or blessing of the patriarchs."[2] Numbers certainly reflects this theme—and adds its own particular emphasis to it. With its focus on the calling of Israel as a people, Numbers emphasizes that both the promise and the blessing have to do with the quality and shape of their life as a community. The calling of Israel to be a holy people in and through whom this blessing of God comes is set out in the first chapters. Israel fails miserably to live into this vision into the middle part of the book. In these final chapters, forgiven Israel begins to realize its calling but does not yet fully live as the people it is called to be.

The sense of hope mixed with awareness that God's promises and visions for the people are not yet fulfilled would certainly resonate with the people of Israel during and after the Babylonian captivity—the time when Numbers most likely came into its form as we know it. While the Christian church after the incarnation and coming of the Spirit at Pentecost is in a different place than Israel in the plains of Moab, the overall tone of these chapters is also apropos to us. A theme of the Eucharist, a feast with ties back to the Feast of Booths, is that it is a foretaste of the feast to come. We, like Moses, are able to catch a glimpse of the promised land and even taste a bit of its fruits, but we are still "living in booths." We are not yet home.

1. Olson 1996: 180 writes: "The portrait of the new generation emerges as a community devoted to God and God's commandments. But . . . the obedience is not over-idealized."

2. David Clines, *The Theme of the Pentateuch*, Journal for the Study of the Old Testament Supplement 10 (Sheffield: JSOT Press, 1978), 29.

8

A NEW START FOR ISRAEL (26:1–30:16)

Second Census: Preparation for Allotment of the Land (26:1–65)

The act of taking a second census of the people of Israel highlights that God's judgment on the first wilderness generation is over. The new generation in Israel is rising and ready to enter the promised land. As the first census exhibited God's ownership of and orientation of his rescued people, this second census marks a new start for Israel after forty years in the wilderness.

The unit can be divided into several parts: instructions for the census (26:1–4), results of the census (26:5–51), apportionment of the promised land as a primary reason for the census (26:52–56), enrollment of the Levites (26:57–62), and a coda emphasizing that all of the older generation, except Moses, Caleb, and Joshua, had died in the wilderness (26:63–65).

These different parts of the unit roughly parallel Num. 1–4. The results of the census are presented in the same tribal order (cf. 1:20–43). The directions for apportionment of the land in preparation for Israel's taking possession of the land, are analogous to the directions for ordering the camp in Num. 2 in preparation for their journey. A census of the Levites also followed the first census (3:14–37).

The parallels between the first and second censuses indicate several things. The census of the next generation shows the continuity of the covenantal promises and their partial fulfillment. The large numbers of both censuses point to the partial fulfillment of the promise to Abraham concerning numerous descendents (this is true whether 'elep means "one thousand" or "one unit"; →1:46; cf. Milgrom

1990: 219–20). That this new generation has arisen at all shows the steadfastness of God to those promises (Olson 1985: 68).

More specifically, that the second census is a repetition of the first underscores this as a new start for the people. It marks the end of the forty-year delay of Israel's journey and the beginning of the forgiveness by God of Israel. The final verses of the second census (26:63–65) directly refer back to 14:20–35, showing that the census marks the completion of God's promised judgment. As such, the census also marks the steadfastness, mercy, and forgiveness of God in giving them a new start. The overall ABA' structure of the book is quite apparent—the parallels between Num. 1, 14, and 26 are the crucial anchor points for the structure of the book.[1]

The way the census is reported combines this sense of forgiveness and new possibilities with reminders and warnings of judgment. On the one hand it is amazing that God provided for Israel so that even in spite of forty years in the wilderness Israel's population has not significantly dropped (the alternate reading of the census numbers shows a slight increase: from 5,550 to 5,730 men; cf. Milgrom 1990: 219–20), yet sprinkled in the narrative are reminders of the sin and rebellions of the people. For example, the census starts with the phrase "after the plague" (26:1), placing the entire census against the background of one of the rebellions. The census of the tribe of Reuben mentions Dathan and Abiram, who rebelled against Moses and Aaron and "became a warning" (26:10). These counterexamples are balanced by the daughters of Zelophehad (26:33), who become symbols of hope for the new generation of Israel (Num. 27, 36); the mysterious Serah daughter of Asher (26:46), of whom nothing more is known; and the sons of Korah (26:11), whose descendents became important in the temple service, both as singers (see the titles of Ps. 42, 44–49, 84, 85, 87) and as "guardians of the thresholds of the tent" (1 Chr. 9:19). Their special mention shows that their family, just like the people as a whole, was able to move toward a better future.

As the church reads Numbers, we should find ourselves identifying with the newer generation numbered in this census. Our situation as a church is similar to theirs—confident in the faithfulness of God and deeply grateful for God's forgiveness, yet knowing that God's promises and vocation for us have not yet been fulfilled. We are also challenged by the past failures of many believers and reminded that while God is merciful and faithful, God's grace should never be considered cheap—as Dietrich Bonhoeffer reminds us[2]—and never divorced from God's judgment of sin. In a sense, the day of the second census is quite similar to our own day and to the "today" of Ps. 95: "O that today you would listen to his voice! Do not harden your hearts, as at Meribah, as on the day at Massah in the wilderness, when your ancestors tested me. . . . For forty years I loathed that

---

1. The parallel between Num. 1 and Num. 26 is a "major structural edifice on which the organization of the book as a whole stands" (Olson 1985: 55). I agree, but also think this ABA' pattern is the best way to understand the design of the book.

2. Dietrich Bonhoeffer, *Discipleship*, trans. Barbara Green and Reinhard Krauss, ed. Geffrey B. Kelly and John D. Godsey, Dietrich Bonhoeffer Works 4 (Minneapolis: Fortress, 2001), 43–56.

generation. . . . Therefore in my anger I swore, 'They shall not enter my rest.'" The future of the new generation is open and poised between the wilderness and the promised land. The forgiveness and new start given to them open up new possibilities, new questions, and new choices.

Daughters of Zelophehad: Economic Justice and the Relationship between Men and Women (27:1–11)

Directly after the census, "the daughters of Zelophehad came forward" and "stood before Moses, Eleazar the priest, the leaders, and all the congregation, at the entrance of the tent of meeting" (27:1–2; cf. Num. 36; Josh. 17:3; 1 Chr. 7:15). The daughters—Mahlah, Noah, Hoglah, Milcah, and Tirzah—then make a request: "Give to us a possession among our father's brothers," backed by this rationale: "Why should the name of our father be taken away from his clan because he had no son?" (27:4).

This story of the bold action of these women naturally follows the account of the second census. One of the primary roles of the census was to apportion the land, and so this problematic case concerning land inheritance naturally fits here.

But this scene also plays another role in the narrative. It is the first action recorded in Israel after all the previous generation had died off in fulfillment of God's judgment on them (26:64–65). As such, it is a pregnant moment, in that these five daughters set the tone for the actions of this new generation. Their coming before Moses and Eleazar recalls similar actions by people in the larger story of Numbers. In 9:6–7 certain people "came before Moses and Aaron," asking why, even though they were unclean, they were not able to present "the LORD's offering at its appointed time" during Passover celebration. It also recalls the actions of Dathan, Abiram, and Korah, who "assembled against Moses and against Aaron" (16:3–5), seeking the right to offer incense before the Lord. Which story will this one be like? The action of these daughters raises questions not only about inheritance laws for women, but also about the character of this new generation.

In order to see more clearly what is at stake in the request of these daughters, we must consider the system of land distribution and inheritance in Israel. In 26:52–56 the basic laws for the initial distribution of land to the tribes were given, but they are ambiguous about how the two methods of casting lots and apportionment by size are supposed to work together. It appears that the general *location* of the tribal inheritances would be decided by lot, while the relative *size* of the inheritance would be apportioned according to the number of "names" within each tribe, so that a larger amount of land will be given to larger tribes, and a proportionally smaller amount of land given to smaller tribes.[3]

3. Milgrom 1990: 480–82 discusses the opinions of medieval rabbinic commentators on this issue and refers to the later biblical descriptions of the apportionment of the land in Num. 33:54; 34:13–29; Josh. 13:6; 14:1–2; 17:14–18; 18:6–11 to argue his case.

What kind of principles or motivating vision can be detected in this way of distributing the land? Determining the general location of each tribe's inheritance by lot shows both the great value attached to the tribal system and the understanding that the land is God's to give as a gift to each tribe. Determining an issue by lot is understood to put the decision in the hands of God, not in the hands of chance. This shows a basic trust in God's providence.[4]

But the second part of the method, apportioning land according to the number of people—as opposed to other possibilities such as determining it by birth order, strength, favor, or merit—shows a concern for relative economic equality and opportunity; it is justice based more on need and equality than deserts. The land is distributed according to the equal need of every person to have land, to have the means of economic sustenance.[5]

Israelite land inheritance was patrilineal—a father's land was handed down only to his sons. In other neighboring cultures (e.g., Mesopotamia and Egypt), women both owned and inherited land in different ways and to different extents (Milgrom 1990: 482). Why did Israel remain so patriarchal in this respect? It is reasonable to understand that the patrilineal system of inheritance was motivated in part by the desire to preserve the tribal structure. "The Bible, in its earliest stages, presumes a tightly knit clan structure; the foremost goal of its legal system was the preservation of the clan" (Milgrom 1990: 482). If the land were equally distributed to both sons and daughters upon their parents' death, marriages between tribes would quickly dissolve the tribal land system.

The request of the daughters of Zelophehad thus takes on deeper meaning. Since the land was distributed according to the number of "names," they are asking that their family unit, represented by their father's "name," be counted in determining the size of the proportion given to the clan of Manasseh, and furthermore that they become caretakers of this portion. This was not an inconsequential request: counting them meant that ten rather than nine portions were given to the tribe of Manasseh on the west side of the Jordan (Josh. 17:3–6). Their request to Moses thus raised the issue of what principle was more basic—that of patrilineal inheritance or that of equitable distribution according to economic need.

This request puts Moses in a difficult situation, for it is a genuine conflict of principles. Members of other tribes who would lose land could rightly point to

4. More practically, it also avoids squabbling and difficult decisions about which land is better and which tribe would get the land perceived as better. In this way it helps to sustain the tribal system by avoiding such contentious issues.

5. That the land can be bought and sold (i.e., Lev. 25:14) shows that individuals and families could expand their holdings, but such increases were not without their limits. Both concerns—for the maintenance of the tribal structure and for a relative economic equality—are evidenced in the Levitical laws concerning the year of Jubilee (Lev. 25) in which every fifty years the land is redistributed according to those initial allotments to the tribes. Harvard economist Hermann Daly derives the following minimal principle from Israelite land laws concerning distribution, inheritance, and ownership: "Thou shalt not allow unlimited inequality in the distribution of private property" (Herman Daly, *Beyond Growth* [Boston: Beacon, 1996], chap. 14).

the patrilineal system as a reason to deny the request. But the answer God gave to Moses was this: "The daughters of Zelophehad are right in what they are saying; you shall indeed let them possess an inheritance among their father's brothers and pass the inheritance of their father on to them" (27:7). This answer upheld the equitable distribution to the clan of Manasseh—it was a matter of fairness first of all to their clan.

But given that the law concerning daughters in their situation was perpetual, and thus not simply a matter of the initial division of the promised land, more is at stake—namely the economic independence and livelihood of the daughters and other women in similar positions. God's ruling allowed the daughters to possess the portion of the tribal lands owned by their father until their own deaths, thus taking care of their own economic needs. At the same time, it upheld the tribal land system in that, after their deaths, the land would be passed on through their father's brothers.

God's resolution made clear that the most basic principle of the distribution and inheritance system is not that women cannot possess or inherit land. The ruling showed that the patrilineal system was in service to the more basic concerns that the tribal land structure should remain intact and that there should be an equitable distribution of land to the tribes and the members of the tribes according to their need.

This ruling has implications for women's rights within the people of God. One can reason that, given the demise of the tribal land system in Israel's later history, there is no reason for women not to own and inherit land. A later group in Judaism allowed daughters to own and inherit land equally with sons and based this on the belief that the laws concerning inheritance and the daughters of Zelophehad applied only to land holdings in the promised land.[6] Thus while later rabbinic interpreters held that God had intended only males to inherit land, some groups rightly understood that this aspect of the patriarchal system of Israel was only in service to the tribal land structure of the promised land.

This ruling also informs Christian understandings of the relationships between men and women. Here God seems to be guiding Moses and Israel in such a way that suggests one aspect of the patriarchal system of Israel—the typical passing on of land from fathers to sons, rather than from parents to sons and daughters— should *not* be interpreted as a signpost toward some kind of natural law set up by God concerning the relationship between men and women. Instead, it is best interpreted as a contextual system set up in part to preserve the tribal structure of Israel, not as a universal system based on the natural authority and rights of men. At the very least, the recorded divine guidance concerning male inheritance rights is secondary to divine concerns for the equality and economic viability of

6. Milgrom 1990: 484 cites the Karaites, a ninth-century group distinguished from rabbinic Judaism by rejecting the authority of the Talmud, holding only to the authority of the Tanak, the Old Testament.

women, should the two come into conflict. In places and parts of the Christian church where the relationship between men and women is still being negotiated, Num. 27 provides one example of how God is at work within the people of God, showing at the very least that concern for the economic viability of women is more important than upholding systems of male privilege.

The daughters of Zelophehad seem to have understood this. Their boldness in approaching Moses, Eleazar, and the tent of meeting suggests that they thought that God and Moses would recognize that the good of the clan, including themselves, should come before upholding customs of male-only inheritance. These women shared or understood the larger vision that God had for his chosen and holy people, and they were rewarded by God's statement: "The daughters of Zelophehad are right in what they are saying" (27:7).

In this first significant narrative event of the new generation, the new generation, represented here in these daughters, has taken a good first step in their journey. Dathan and Abiram and Korah—the other main group of individuals specially mentioned in the census account in Num. 26—also complained about their lack of inheritance: "It is clear you have not brought us into a land flowing with milk and honey, or given us an inheritance of fields and vineyards" (16:14). But rather than appealing to Moses, they sought to overturn Moses's leadership. In contrast to this, the boldness of Zelophehad's daughters is based on their trust in the goodness and justice of Moses and God and in their right understanding of what that goodness and justice entailed.

Joshua Commissioned by Moses: Succession and Leadership Qualities within the People of God (27:12–23)

God commands Moses to go up a certain mountain (identified as Mount Nebo in Deut. 32:48–52) in the Abarim range in order to see the promised land and then to die (Num. 27:12–13). However, the thematic center of the passage is arguably not the death of Moses, but the commissioning of Joshua (so Sakenfeld 1995: 153).[7] This scene in which the mantle of leadership is transferred from Moses to Joshua is filled with images that help form the ideals of Israelite understandings of leadership and that can helpfully inform the church's imagination as well.

Just as the first third of the book highlights the leadership of Moses and Aaron after the people are counted, organized, and prepared for their journey, so now Joshua is commissioned as leader (27:12–23) in preparation for the occupation of the promised land after the new generation is counted and reorganized (Num. 26). The transfer of the high priesthood from Aaron to Eleazar has already taken place in a narrative similar to the one here (20:22–29). The command about

---

7. Interpretations that see the thematic center as the death of Moses struggle to answer why the command to Moses to go to the mountain is given here but only fulfilled in Deut. 34. See Milgrom 1990: 233 and Olson 1996: 168–69.

Moses's death thus serves to introduce the need for his own successor. The passage mainly focuses on the acts that complete the transfer of leadership from the old generation to the new.

Moses is told by God to "lay your hand" on Joshua in front of the people (27:18). This ritual stresses the passing on of something—whether a blessing, guilt, "spirit," and/or a role—from one person to another (Ashley 1993: 551–54). It shows that Joshua follows in the same tradition as Moses and does so with the blessing of both Moses and God. An orderly and nondisruptive way to transfer leadership from Moses to Joshua, it emphasizes both continuity from one human to the next as well as God's blessing and empowerment.

The orderly transition from one leader to the next by the laying on of hands continued to be the norm for Israel and, later, the church. It shows that the gift of God's authority to lead Israel is usually mediated through the regularized human channels of his people. However, there are several examples in both Israel and the church where such succession of leadership was not "orderly," that is, not mediated through regular channels. The rise of David was authorized by God through Samuel the priest, but not through Saul the king (1 Sam. 16:1–2), leading to great bloodshed. The mysterious figure of Melchizedek (Gen. 14:18; Ps. 110:4) is another important example of someone recognized as a priest of God and a king but not commissioned through the ordinary channels of the people of God.

The succession of God-given authority within the people of God has been a matter of great debate between different Christian traditions, a debate often concerning the term "apostolic" in the Nicene Creed: "I believe in one, holy, catholic, and apostolic church." Certainly the crucial matter in carrying on the mission of the apostles is God's authorizing of and gifting for such a task. A concern for this is seen in the linking of God's election of Joshua to the "spirit" in him (27:18) and his faith in God, both evidenced by his good report about the promised land. Protestants stress similar themes in debates about apostolicity. But the orderly transition from Moses to Joshua also supports Catholic, Eastern Orthodox, and Episcopalian emphases on the historic succession from one bishop to the next. The important ecumenical document *Baptism, Eucharist, and Ministry* reflects the balance seen in Num. 27:

> The orderly transmission of the ordained ministry is therefore a powerful expression of the continuity of the Church throughout history; it also underlines the calling of the ordained minister as guardian of the faith. Where churches see little importance in orderly transmission, they should ask themselves whether they have not to change their conception of continuity in the apostolic tradition. On the other hand, where the ordained ministry does not adequately serve the proclamation of the apostolic faith, churches must ask themselves whether their ministerial structures are not in need of reform.[8]

8. *Baptism, Eucharist, and Ministry*, Faith and Order Paper 111 (Geneva: World Council of Churches, 1982), "Ministry," §35.

Besides highlighting the means of commissioning, the passage also tells us that Joshua's authority is less than and different from Moses's. Moses asks that Joshua be given the same authority that he had, but God says "you shall give him some of your authority" (27:20), not all of it, and commands that Joshua must inquire of Eleazar the priest for the will of the Lord. Furthermore, Eleazar must "inquire for him by the decision of the Urim before the LORD" (27:21). Dice or small chips with letters of the alphabet on them, the Urim and Thummim were carried by the high priest and used to "inquire of God" about his will concerning some specific question (Milgrom 1990: 484–86). While Moses's relationship with God was quite direct, leaders after Moses did not have the same intimacy with God—even the priest inquired of God through the Urim. As a result, their authority to speak for God and lead in his name was less. God also instituted certain checks and balances in the authority structure to distribute this lesser authority. Later in Israel's history, the lessened authority of its leaders is made apparent in the strong contrast between them and the authority of Jesus in the Gospels: "They were astounded at his teaching, for he taught them as one having authority" (Mark 1:22; cf. Matt. 7:29; Luke 4:36). Jesus's great authority was a sign that one like or greater than Moses was in their midst.

Perhaps the most important issue raised by this passage is what kind of qualities and character leaders of the people of God should possess. Several details highlight the character of Moses, creating a picture of his exemplary leadership. First, Moses, unlike Aaron, is not given a command concerning his successor. Instead Moses requests one for Israel. When told of his approaching death, his concern is not for himself, but rather for his people (cf. Jesus's prayer for his disciples at the hour of his death; John 17:6–24). Moses also suggests that his successor have the authority to "lead them out and bring them in" (Num. 27:17)—that is, that the successor have equal authority to Moses, to be able to speak and lead in the name of God just as Moses had. Both requests highlight Moses's selflessness and compassion for the people he leads. Not many leaders desire their successor to be as powerful as they are!

The phrase "lead them out and bring them in" is arguably tied to the main image that Moses uses to portray his leadership of the people: a shepherd with their sheep.[9] Moses asks God for a successor to himself "so that the congregation of the LORD may not be like sheep without a shepherd" (27:17). The shepherd image tells of Moses's understanding of the purpose of leadership—guiding and protecting the people—as well as the manner of his leadership. The shepherd is an image of guidance and protection, similar to "king," "lord," or military "captain."

9. The idiom "lead them out and bring them in" is taken by most to refer to military leadership. But the only other attestation of this form of the phrase is 2 Sam. 5:2, where the tribes of Israel come to David and say: "For some time, while Saul was king over us, it was you who led out Israel and brought it in. The LORD said to you: It is you who shall be shepherd of my people Israel, you who shall be ruler over Israel." It seems rather that the basic image is of a shepherd who takes out the flock and then brings it back to the fold—an image then applied to the military career of David rather than vice versa. The leader of Israel is also called a shepherd in 1 Kgs. 22:17 and 2 Chr. 18:16.

But unlike them, the shepherd image disassociates leadership from worldly glory, prestige, or coercive power.

This positive portrait of exemplary leadership is made even clearer through the contrast with Moses's sin. God tells Moses: "You did not show my holiness before their eyes at the waters" (27:14). Moses's sin was a lapse in both Moses's faith in God and in his care for the people (→20:2–13). That this sin was so grave in God's eyes that it cost him the privilege of leading the people into the promised land underlines the importance of these shepherdlike qualities in a leader of God's people.

The image of a shepherd with sheep is used for *God's* leadership of Israel (Ps. 23:1; 28:9; 37:3; 80:1; Eccl. 12:11; Isa. 40:11; Jer. 31:10; 50:19) and also of human leaders (Jer. 3:15; 23:4). This double use suggests that Israel's leaders should mediate God's leadership of the people, and do so in a way similar to how God leads his people. David, the shepherd who becomes king, and Moses are specifically mentioned as leaders who led Israel like shepherds (Ps. 78:71; Isa. 63:11; Ezek. 34). When the leaders of Israel fall short of these role models, the prophets, especially Jeremiah and Ezekiel, indict them. They critique them for being bad shepherds, for taking advantage of their power over the sheep and for not guiding them well in God's ways (Jer. 10:21; 12:10; 23:2; 25:34–36; 50:6; Ezek. 34:2–23).

This image is regularly applied to Jesus. Christ is called the "good shepherd" or the "shepherd of his people" throughout the New Testament (Matt. 9:36; 26:31 [alluding to Zech. 13:7]; Mark 6:34; 14:27; John 10:11–16; Heb. 13:20; 1 Pet. 2:25). In a direct allusion to Num. 27:17, Jesus sees the crowds, "and he had compassion for them, because they were like sheep without a shepherd" (Mark 6:34 par. Matt. 9:36; the phrase "sheep without a shepherd" occurs only in these Gospel accounts and Num. 27:17; 1 Kgs. 22:17; 2 Chr. 18:16).

It is no surprise that this image has deeply shaped Christian understandings of leadership. Jesus's commissioning of Simon Peter to lead his "lambs" is carefully structured around this image (John 21:15–19). Three times Jesus asks Peter, "Do you love me?" And Peter is told to feed and tend Jesus's people. Love for Jesus and compassion for God's people are shown to be at the center of Christian leadership. The term "pastor" extends this image, as does the shepherd's crook carried by many ecclesiastical leaders as a symbol of their role. The images of Jesus as good shepherd, washer of the disciple's feet, and crucified Messiah all combine to give an image of leadership of God's people in which love, service, and guidance are emphasized, while prestige and use of coercive power are severely critiqued. This has and should continue to shape how Christians understand leadership within the church.

In the early church, the image of Jesus as good shepherd was by far the most frequent iconic image of Jesus, but that eventually changed and was replaced by images of Christ as teacher and king.[10] It is not difficult to imagine why. Given

10. Boniface Ramsey, "A Note on the Disappearance of the Good Shepherd from Early Christian Art," *Harvard Theological Review* 76 (1983): 375–78.

the rise of the Christian rulers Constantine and Theodosius, images of leadership in the surrounding culture influenced the preferred images of leadership within the church, rather than the other way around.

Throughout church history, it has been extremely difficult for Christian leaders to consistently articulate and live into such biblical images of compassionate and servantlike leadership rather than falling into images and practices that lack faith in God and compassion for the people. There is much contemporary concern about leadership issues in both North American Protestantism and Catholicism, especially given the lack of confidence in leadership due to decreasing numbers in the mainline Protestant churches and scandals in the Roman Catholic Church. Many models of leadership draw more from modern business models than from biblical models. One book that helpfully enters into this discussion is *Treasure in Clay Jars*.[11] The authors spent time with churches—from Roman Catholic to Mennonite—that were identified as "missional."[12] Part of their reflection concerned the leadership patterns of these churches, which they found to be countercultural: "The chasm between the church's understanding of authority and that of the dominant culture is much wider than we realized. A church conditioned by Christendom is often tempted to begin with the concept of authority as defined by culture and then seeks to find whether the church has that kind of authority. . . . We needed a more biblically based understanding of authority in order to sense the pattern of missional authority in these churches."[13] Quality and style of leadership is arguably tied to the overarching vision of these missional churches, namely that their life together is "a foretaste of where God is inviting all creation to go."[14] As Moses also discovered, the ends of his leadership (leading Israel into a certain way of life, a life in which the reign of God was actualized in a certain place so that God's holiness and glory might be seen) could not be divorced from the means (the quality and character of his leadership).

Liturgical Calendar: The Structure of Israel's Year in the Promised Land (28:1–29:40)

The sacrifices appropriate to the different feasts that were part of Israel's worship life throughout the year are described next. This movement of the narrative

---

11. Lois Y. Barrett et al., *Treasure in Clay Jars: Patterns in Missional Faithfulness* (Grand Rapids: Eerdmans, 2004).

12. The phrase "missional church" is defined by Eddie Gibbs this way: "A community of God's people who live in the imagination that they are, by their very nature, God's missionary people living as a demonstration of what God plans to do in and for all of creation in Jesus Christ" (in Alan J. Roxburgh and Fred Romanuk, *The Missional Leader: Equipping Your Church to Reach a Changing World* [San Francisco: Jossey-Bass, 2006], xv). This vision of God's people is quite similar to the vision for Israel described in Numbers.

13. Barrett, *Treasure in Clay Jars*, 140.

14. Roxburgh and Romanuk, *Missional Leader*, xv.

has a similar shape to the opening chapters of Numbers. After the people are organized and their leadership described (Num. 1–4), their worship life is outlined (Num. 7–10). So now, after the new generation is reorganized and the old leadership passes on (Num. 26–27), the worship life of the people is once again outlined (Num. 28–29). While the three main festivals of Israel were alluded to in 9:1–10:10, here the entire liturgical calendar is described. The sacrifices for every important feast are detailed, sacrifices that would be possible only given their upcoming settled life in the promised land.[15] Worship was central to Israel's life, and its year was structured according to these celebrations.

This unit has six parts: general introduction (28:1–2); daily, Sabbath, and new moon sacrifices (28:3–15); Pesach sacrifices (28:16–25); Shavuot offerings (28:26–31); Sukkot offerings (29:1–38); and a small coda (29:39–40). In comparing this treatment of Israel's liturgical year with that of Lev. 23, two items stand out: greater emphasis on the daily and new moon offerings and greater emphasis on Sukkot.

This unit focuses on the details of the sacrifices. Because of this, it is easy to overlook the importance of the liturgical calendar and the meanings of the sacrifices and feasts for Israel. Yet its placement within the larger narrative of Numbers draws attention to the overall shape of the worship life of Israel and the way that these feasts and celebrations formed it to be a holy people in theology and practice (Ashley 1993: 555–72; Milgrom 1990: 237–50).

The first celebrations are the daily, Sabbath, and monthly offerings. The cycles of day and night and the weekly and monthly rhythms of the year are marked by Israel's worship.

Besides these regular occasions, three main pilgrimage feasts punctuate the Jewish calendar: Pesach, Shavuot, and Sukkot. These celebrate or came to be linked with important events in Israel's history.[16] Israel is told by God that "three times in a year you shall hold a festival [*ḥag*] for me" and that "three times in the year all your males shall appear before the Lord GOD" (Exod. 23:14–17). The word *ḥag* ("pilgrimage") and its related verb ("to celebrate a pilgrimage feast") are better known to modern readers through the Islamic Hajj (pilgrimage) to Mecca.

In Numbers the term "holy convocation" (*miqrā' qōdeš*) is used as a general term for gatherings of the people at the sanctuary (Levine 2000: 381–83). Seven holy convocations took place at the three annual feasts. The word *ḥag* is used in

---

15. Three other glimpses of the full liturgical calendar in Exod. 23:14–17; Deut. 16:1–17; and Lev. 23 also give similar, yet slightly different, accounts of the regular celebrations of Israel. Cf. Ezek. 45:13–46:15.

16. While the older scholarly consensus is that all these celebrations were originally celebrated as nomadic (Passover) or agricultural (Unleavened Bread, Weeks, Booths) festivals by Israel and then over time were linked with the events of salvation history as recorded in the text, there is no direct evidence of this (J. G. McConville, *Deuteronomy*, Apollos Old Testament Commentary 5 [Downers Grove, IL: InterVarsity, 2002], 270–71). In regard to Passover and Unleavened Bread in particular, more convincing arguments link these celebrations directly to the exodus (John Hartley in *NIDOTTE* 2.1065–68).

Numbers only with the Feast of Unleavened Bread (28:17) and Feast of Booths (29:12), both of which were celebrations lasting at least a week (Shavuot is called a *hag* in Deut. 16:10; Levine 2000: 394–95, 407–18). This is the annual feast calendar as detailed in Numbers and elsewhere:[17]

Date	Holy Convocation
Nisan 14	Pesach (Passover)
Nisan 15–21	Chol Hamoed (Unleavened Bread)
Nisan 21	Final Holiday (Firstfruits)
[Sivan 6]	Shavuot (Pentecost or Weeks)
Tishri 1	Trumpets (later called Rosh Hashanah, New Year)
Tishri 10	Yom Kippur (Day of Atonement)
Tishri 15–21, 22	Sukkot (Booths)

The seven convocations form three basic groups, and these larger festivals are commonly referred to as Pesach, Shavuot, and Sukkot.

These festivals were the highest expression of Israel's life together as a people. In these feasts, Israel comes together before the Lord at the sanctuary, celebrates before YHWH as a people, offers sacrifices of thanksgiving and atonement, remembers the formative events and providence of God, and recommits themselves to be and live as God's holy people. They are rich and full of meaning, and their history and development are complex, fascinating, and multifaceted.

These worship times formed Israel's understanding of God and its own identity and vocation in part by helping it remember the history of its relationship with the Lord. While the daily, weekly, and monthly offerings marked basic and ongoing aspects of Israel's life with God as creator, the pilgrimage feasts can be related more clearly to the specific history of God with Israel as a chosen people. Passover remembers the redemption of Israel from Egypt; Shavuot became linked with God's guidance of his people, especially through the giving of the law and covenants; and Sukkot looks forward to God's future judgment, mercy, and final victory as king. Together they create a sweeping portrait of God's history and plan for Israel. These festal celebrations of Israel became a primary way the people gained their vision of who they were and who God is—it was their catechism.

The powerful events at the heart of these celebrations contain images and meanings that Jesus Christ took and wrapped around himself in his teaching and activity. His disciples and the New Testament writers in turn used them to better understand and proclaim who Jesus was and the larger story of God's plan

17. The months are simply numbered in the text, except for the dating of Passover in Exod. 13:4, which uses the preexilic name "Abib" rather than "Nisan" for the first month. The names of the months are a later development taken from the Babylonian calendar. The specific date for the Feast of Weeks is not given, but is seven weeks plus one day after the firstfruits offering. Sivan 6 is the date commonly used by contemporary Jews.

of salvation for the world. They consequently provide an important background for understanding Christ, the Lord's Supper, and the Christian liturgical year.

Daily, Weekly, and Monthly Offerings: Creation and Providence (28:1–15)

In the daily, weekly, and monthly offerings, Israel recognizes and gives thanks for God's providence. While the three great pilgrimage festivals also recognize the goodness of God in the yearly cycles of harvest, they came to be tied most closely to the remembrance of and hope in God's redemptive activity in the history of Israel. Without making too strict a dichotomy, the pilgrimage feasts focus more specifically on God's plans to move his people forward to his future purposes for them (the economy of redemption), while the daily, weekly, and monthly offerings—structured by the regular cycles of sun and moon—are tied more closely to the regular providential activity of God in sustaining and guiding the creation, thus providing food and basic sustenance for his people (the economy of creation).

The opening lines of this unit show that the sacrifices were in part understood as food, drink, and scent offered to God: "My offering, the food for my offerings by fire, my pleasing odor, you shall take care to offer to me at its appointed time" (28:2). The different kinds of sacrifices represent different kinds of transactions between the individual or group that offers them and God (→7:1–88). The sacrifices in this passage are clearly meant to be edible (Lev. 21:6; Num. 28:2) or burned to create an odor (Gen. 8:21; Exod. 29:18; Lev. 1:9; Num. 15:3; 28:2–6). In Lev. 21:6 the sacrifices are directly called "the food of . . . God."[18] The idea of gods needing food and drink was common in the cultures surrounding Israel (Milgrom 1990: 486–88). However, the Israelites were clear that this idea of God desiring food should not be taken in a crass way: "Do I eat the flesh of bulls, or drink the blood of goats? Offer to God a sacrifice of thanksgiving, and pay your vows to the Most High" (Ps. 50:13–14).

So why would God want human food? The offering of food to God in the šĕlāmîm sacrifice symbolizes that the offerers are enjoying a feast together with God; it is a celebration of the anticipated shalom involving humans, God, and the earth, which is in part experienced by God's people. But Ps. 50 suggests that these burnt offerings are an act of thankfulness for the abundance of the land and the providence of God that causes that abundance. Psalm 104:14–15 also suggests these meanings: "You cause the grass to grow for the cattle, and plants for people to use, to bring forth food from the earth, and wine to gladden the human heart, oil to make the face shine, and bread to strengthen the human heart." The providence of God in sustaining all the natural forces and seasonal rhythms of the world is being celebrated. The grain, oil, and wine mentioned are the elements of the sacrifices (→15:1–21) and correspond to the three main harvests of the year—grain

18. Corrine Carvalho, "Finding a Treasure Map: Sacred Space in the Old Testament," in *Touching the Altar: The Old Testament for Christian Worship*, ed. C. Bechtel (Grand Rapids: Eerdmans, 2008), 128.

in May–June, grapes in August–September, and olives in October. The link to the creational cycles of days, Sabbaths (a celebration linked to God's creation), and new moons suggests that in large part these sacrifices are a thanksgiving gift to God. The worshipers give back to God a portion of what they have received, showing their dependence on and thankfulness for his providence and gift of life.

Sabbath was tied not only to God as creator (as the Exod. 20 Sabbath command suggests), but also to God liberating those enslaved to work (as the Deut. 5 command emphasizes).[19] The creational patterns remembered and enacted in the celebration of the Sabbath are related not only to what moderns understand as the environment, but also to just patterns of human society. Put otherwise, justice in human relationships is also part of the creational, providential patterns of God recognized in these celebrations. That is in part why the prophets saw it as an act of hypocrisy on Israel's part when they celebrated these festivals but did not live into their implications: "Your new moons and your appointed festivals my soul hates; they have become a burden to me, I am weary of bearing them" (Isa. 1:14; cf. 1 Sam. 15:22; Ps. 50:7–15; Hos. 6:6). The reasons given in Isaiah and the other prophets for these critiques is not that God hates the practice per se, but rather that the practice is done hypocritically, as evidenced by the injustice allowed in Israelite society by its leaders. In contrast, in the grand vision of the renewed Israel seen in Ezek. 40–48, the new moon and other regular offerings are mentioned as part of its renewed life. The prince who will come to present the regular offerings (45:13–17) will have put away the "violence and oppression" (45:9) and dishonesty (45:10–12) that came to characterize the politics and economics of Israel.

Christians should see that at least part of Israel's worship was a celebration of God's providence in the rhythm of natural forces. Many Christian theologians and biblical scholars make too great a distinction between Israel and the surrounding cultures of the ancient Near East, suggesting that the pagan cultures focused on nature while Israel focused exclusively on God's acts in history: "The Old Testament can never be regarded as a typical mythology in part or in whole, because it proclaimed God as the Lord of history in contradistinction to the polytheistic patterns that made life and History in general dependent upon the rhythm of natural forces."[20] While there is a distinction to be made, the distinction is not a dualism. Part of the daily Israelite piety imaged here is a continual sacrifice that recognizes Israel's dependence upon and thanksgiving for the daily meat and bread God provides.

19. Dennis Olson, "Sacred Time: The Sabbath and Christian Worship," in *Touching the Altar*; and Abraham Joshua Heschel, *The Sabbath: Its Meaning for Modern Man* (New York: Farrer, Straus & Giroux, 1951).

20. R. K. Harrison, *Introduction to the Old Testament* (Grand Rapids: Eerdmans, 1969), 457. On the other hand, many scholars seek to explain Israel's worship in light of the pagan practices of the surrounding cultures, often reducing the meaning of its worship to them. They often see the connections of the pilgrim feasts to God's redemptive acts in history as the impositions of later writers.

These patterns of regular thanksgiving and sacrifice celebrating the providential activity of God have much to say to Christians. Regular thanksgiving and recognition of the gift that food, drink, and daily sustenance is for us are the soil out of which grow the simple, yet profound Jewish and Christian practices of prayers before and after meals, regular times of prayer and worship throughout the day, and the weekly practices of Sabbath rest and worship. These practices in turn have the potential to form our vision concerning just and proper ways of being in relationship with all of creation.[21]

Israel's practices of regular food and animal sacrifice may seem quite foreign to us. This is in part due to agriculture and the raising and killing of animals for our food being hidden from most people in the modern West. "Factory" production of food can hide the reality that other beings—plants and animals—have given their life so that we might live. While reinstituting the sacrifice of animals in public is not an option for us, the prayerfulness by which animal life was taken in Israel can inform at least our prayers before eating and can critique many modern practices of agriculture and animal husbandry.

A well-known modern prophet speaking for a relationship of care and thankfulness toward creation in agriculture, forestry, and animal husbandry is Wendell Berry. In many essays he contrasts the destructiveness of the modern economy that sees the world as raw material with the thankfulness toward God and care that comes from seeing the world as filled with fellow creatures: "Care, on the contrary, rests upon genuine religion. Care allows creatures to escape our explanations into their actual presence and their essential mystery. In taking care of our fellow creatures, we acknowledge that they are not ours; we acknowledge that they belong to an order and a harmony of which we ourselves are parts."[22] Such genuine religion is embodied in the daily, weekly, and monthly sacrifices of Israel.

Festival of Passover: Pesach (28:16–25)

The sacrifices for the public parts of the larger Passover and Unleavened Bread festivals are now detailed. Many of the meanings of the larger festival are tied to its three main symbols: the blood of a lamb, unleavened bread, and bitter herbs (Num. 9:11; Exod. 12:8). All of these symbols point back to the exodus event, and all three add to the meaning at the heart of the celebrations—redemption by God.

During the Passover celebration, bitter herbs are eaten. The symbolism of these herbs is fairly straightforward—they point to the bitterness of the slavery and oppressions that Israel experienced in Egypt. Remembering the bitterness of their situation is not without significance. Israel often looks back with a wistful eye to their situation in Egypt, perhaps remembering it as better than it was. Several times they long for the food and comforts of their time there (Num. 11:5, 18, 20;

21. Olson, "Sacred Time," 26–30.
22. Wendell Berry, *Another Turn of the Crank* (Washington, DC: Counterpoint, 1995), 77.

14:3; 21:5). Taking time to remember the difficulties of life before God redeemed them helps one to be thankful for the new start God gave them.

The Passover lamb with its blood is a much more complicated sacrifice and symbol. No other sacrifice is quite like this one. The earliest Passover tradition is that lambs are slaughtered in each family's home, rather than in the tabernacle, and that the blood is placed on the doorposts and lintel of their dwelling, just as was done during Passover in Egypt. In one way this resembles a sin offering. An animal is given and killed so that one's sin is covered and the wrath of God will pass over. The animal is then eaten by all—which is more like a fellowship offering.

The Pentateuch gives two main emphases to unleavened bread. Unleavened bread is a symbol of the haste of the Israelites as they left Egypt; they did not even have time to let their bread rise. This meaning of the bread simply points back to the circumstances of their escape from Egypt, highlighting the narrowness of their escape and precariousness of their redemption. On the other hand, in several places the stress is laid on not eating leavened bread—it is the leaven that must be avoided: "For seven days no leaven shall be found in your houses" (Exod. 12:19; cf. 12:15, 20; 13:7). Leaven is a powerful symbol of something unseen that has great effects. Furthermore, given the practice of saving leaven from one batch of dough to the next, it is also a wonderful symbol for a long-term tradition or habit. Cleaning out the leaven from a house represents a new start in the household's habits and practices and is explicitly linked to Israel's fresh start when leaving Egypt: "For on this very day I brought your companies out of the land of Egypt" (12:17). And the punishment for eating leaven is being "cut off from the congregation of Israel." This keeps the "leavened" person away from the new dough of Israel. This latter meaning of the feast and of cleaning out the leaven is emphasized by later Jewish traditions and by Jesus and Paul. Evil intentions and evil persons (like "bad apples") and, conversely, the holy intentions and patterns of the kingdom of God are all likened to leaven (Matt. 13:33; 16:6, 11–12; Mark 8:15; Luke 12:1; 13:21; 1 Cor. 5:6–8; Gal. 5:9).

In all these ways, the festival focuses specifically on the redemption of Israel from Egypt, God's bringing Israel out of the bitterness of slavery and giving them a fresh start as a people. In this celebration, Israel looks to the past, remembering the bitterness of this slavery and the graciousness of God in freeing his people to begin again. But Pesach also becomes a time for Israel to start ever afresh, to look inward for the different kinds of "leaven" that have become part of it, and to purge these habits and evil patterns as it moves into the future.

Aspects and themes of Pesach have shaped Christian practices of Lent and Holy Week and understandings of Christ's death and resurrection. The Gospel of John especially draws explicit connections between Jesus's death on the cross and the Passover sacrifice.[23] Christians prepare for the celebration of Christ's paschal

---

23. Raymond Brown, *The Gospel according to John xiii–xxi*, Anchor Bible 29a (Garden City, NY: Doubleday, 1970), 930. John 13:1 stresses that the passion was set during Passover. Details of

sacrifice on Good Friday and the new beginning of his resurrection life on Easter throughout the penitential season of Lent, a season with connections to the fast from leaven of the Israelite celebration of Unleavened Bread. And themes of the pilgrim feast, together with those of Shavuot and Sukkot, provide the background for fully understanding Jesus's actions during the Last Supper.

Festival of Weeks: Shavuot (28:26–31)

The Feast of Weeks has various names. It is most commonly called Feast of Weeks (*ḥag haššābu'ōt*), from which is derived the common Jewish name for the feast, Shavuot (Exod. 34:22; Num. 28:26; Deut. 16:10, 16; 2 Chr. 8:13; cf. Lev. 23:16–21). It is also called "the festival of the harvest" (Exod. 23:16) and "the day of the first fruits" (Num. 28:26). The term "weeks" refers to the day of the celebration occurring seven weeks plus one day after the firstfruits offering concluding the barley harvest. As the alternate names suggest, Weeks is associated with harvest as well, this time the wheat harvest. Its festival and offerings recall God's providential care and sustenance through the period of harvest; the occasion is marked by the presentation of two loaves of bread (as opposed to simply sheaves of grain fifty days before) to God (Lev. 23:17) in addition to the sacrifices. The lack of difference between the description here and in Leviticus (besides reversing the number of bulls and rams in Num. 28:27 and Lev. 23:18) makes it likely that this section was included primarily to fill out the entire festival structure of Israel's yearly calendar.

While the celebration is an agricultural festival, this festival is also tied to the history of God with Israel in several ways. The liturgy in Deut. 26:1–11 was probably used at this harvest festival.[24] In it, the harvest is associated with God's bringing of Israel into the promised land: "The LORD brought us out of Egypt with a mighty hand and an outstretched arm, with a terrifying display of power, and with signs and wonders; and he brought us into this place and gave us this land, a land flowing with milk and honey" (26:8–9). Thus while Passover is associated with delivery from Egypt, the harvest itself is associated with God's power and guidance in bringing them into their present state of settled existence and plenty. The pillar of cloud and fire serves as a fitting signpost to this feast, serving as a symbol of God's leadership and guidance of his people to the promised land (→9:15–23).

In Israel's later history, the feast also becomes associated with God's making covenants with Israel. According to Jubilees, written probably in the second century BC, God's covenants with Noah (*Jub.* 6.17), Abraham (15.2), and Moses (1.1–2) were all completed on the same day of the Jewish calendar—the Feast of Weeks. Dating the giving of the law on Sinai fifty days after the departure from Egypt roughly fits with the timeline in Exod. 19:1. The title of the book, "Jubilees," is

---

the crucifixion (hyssop and wine in 19:29; no broken bones in 19:33; the time of the slaughter of Passover lambs in 19:14) connect Christ's death with the Passover sacrifice.

24. H. H. Rowley, *Worship in Ancient Israel: Its Forms and Meanings* (London: SPCK, 1967), 89; McConville, *Deuteronomy*, 377–80.

itself a reference to the number fifty (seven times seven plus one), and it contains fifty chapters. Thus, the celebration recalls the covenant with Noah in which God vowed that "as long as the earth endures, seedtime and harvest . . . shall not cease" (Gen. 8:22). It also recalls the promise to Abraham that God will give them the land of Canaan (12:1), a promise whose partial fulfillment is celebrated in Deut. 26:8–9. And finally, it celebrates the giving of the law to Moses on Sinai, an event also associated with the cloud and fire of God's presence.

Thus, Shavuot can be understood as most centrally a celebration of God's guidance of Israel, both directly and through the law, toward the fulfillment of God's purposes for it.[25] The harvest of Deut. 26, the pillar of cloud and fire, and the covenants are all symbols of the guiding care of God for his people.

The New Testament Feast of Pentecost begins the fulfillment of the "new covenant" prophesied by Jeremiah (31:33). The tongues of fire and loud sound recall the events of Sinai,[26] but rather than the law being given the Spirit is instead poured out on all. Rather than guiding his people by a pillar of cloud and fire or by tablets of stone, God is now guiding his people by giving them his Spirit—in a way similar to how God led the prophets (Acts 2:17; cf. Joel 2:28–32). As a result of this outpouring of the Spirit, "wonders and signs" now accompany the apostles (Acts 2:43; cf. Deut. 26:8–9). Due to the work of Jesus the Messiah and his sending of the Spirit (Acts 2:29–33), the blessings promised to Abraham (3:25–26; cf. Gen. 12:1–3) and Israel are now being realized in the new community of the church. People are healed, and "there was not a needy person among them" (Acts 4:34)—both signs that the promises of the covenant were being fulfilled (Deut. 15:4).

This second pilgrim feast of the Jewish calendar in this way informs the biblical narrative in Acts about Pentecost and the work of the Spirit, providing the background for the second most important Christian celebration of the church year, Pentecost.

Festival of Booths: Sukkot (29:1–40)

Three "holy convocations" (29:1, 7, 12) are associated with Sukkot (*sukkôt*), the Feast of Booths. Occurring in the seventh month of the year, this festival highlights themes of divine judgment, mercy, and God's final victory. The different moments of the feast dramatically enact striking biblical images associated with the coming of God to judge. It is an apocalyptic or eschatological feast, in that many of its themes and images are concerned with God's judgment at the close of the year or even the end of the age. However, like all the feasts, many other meanings are bound up in its celebrations.

25. Michael Strassfeld, *The Jewish Holidays: A Guide and Commentary* (New York: Harper & Row, 1985), 80, notes that King David—another symbol of God's guidance of Israel—also becomes associated with this festival in later times.

26. Luke Timothy Johnson, *The Acts of the Apostles* (Collegeville, MN: Liturgical Press, 1992), 41–47.

The first holy convocation is the Festival of Trumpets (29:1–6; cf. Lev. 23:23–25). It is "a day for you to blow the trumpets," and a burnt offering, grain offerings associated with the burnt offerings, and a sin offering are made. In many biblical passages, trumpets (*ḥṣr*) are a symbol associated with the call to holy battle and the enactment of divine judgment: before the battle with Midian (Num. 31:6), as the ark of the covenant is processed into the temple (2 Chr. 5:11–14), at the start of a battle in which "God is . . . at our head" (13:12). Victory is seen as God's judgment on those who had done wrong.[27] Trumpets are blown in Ezek. 7:14–19 and Hos. 5:8–10, but because of the apostasy and sin of Israel, the battles that follow turn out to be judgments against Israel. God's "wrath" is "poured out" on Israel. The Feast of Booths is also known as the Feast of Ingathering because it concludes the final harvest season when summer fruit, most importantly grapes and olives, was gathered.[28] Trumpets, judgment, grapes, and the pouring out of wrath are often tied together in biblical imagery (Joel 3:13), and all these images are closely tied together in the Festival of Booths.[29] A tractate in the Mishnah, *Rosh Hashanah* ("New Year"), is entirely devoted to this first part of the celebration, showing that later Jews understood this as a day of judgment and penitence, when every person had to give an account of their actions in the past year (Hendrik Bosman in *NIDOTTE* 3.1023). The trumpets sound, and God comes to judge.

The second holy convocation is the Day of Atonement, or Yom Kippur (*yôm hakkippurîm*). This important celebration gets little attention in Num. 29:7–11. Compared to the complex of ritual actions given in Lev. 16 (cf. 23:26–32), very little detail is given to this day. It does mention the "sin offering of atonement," but little else—likely because the themes of the first and final convocations rather than the Day of Atonement are much more closely connected with the central themes of Numbers. This is a day in which Israel is told to "deny yourselves" (29:7; Lev. 16:31; 23:27). The Hebrew literally means "to torment or afflict your bodies," but in biblical usage this usually means to fast from food (similar phrases in Ps. 35:13 and Isa. 58:3–5 refer to comparable penitential practices). The proper corresponding actions of Israel to God's mercy in allowing Israel's sins to be covered (→7:1–88) are humble repentance and fasting. The drama of the larger festival is heightened during this day. After the trumpet call, alerting one to the coming of God in judgment, God is merciful in covering over and forgiving the sins of the people.

The final festival is the Feast of Booths (*hag hassukkôt*), or the Feast of Ingathering (Exod. 23:16; 34:22), or even simply "the Feast" (1 Kgs. 8:2; 12:32). It is

27. Ps. 98:6 speaks of the blowing of trumpets and the horn, which signal "the presence of the LORD, for he is coming to judge the earth" (98:9).

28. See Oded Borowski, *Daily Life in Biblical Times* (Atlanta: Society of Biblical Literature, 2003), 27–28.

29. A postscript (commonly read as a superscript to the subsequent psalm; see Robert O'Connell in *NIDOTTE* 1.904–5) to three psalms may be read as "to the melody of the female winepressers," thus associating Ps. 7, 80, 83 with this festival. All three psalms call for God's judgment on Israel's foes.

the largest feast of the year. The great number of sacrifices detailed here, greater than all the other festivals put together, stresses the major character of the feast. The number of bulls starts at thirteen on the first day, decreasing to seven on the seventh day, for a total of seventy bulls during the week, leading to the final celebration on the eighth day. The booths refer to the temporary houses used by the Israelites during the forty years in the wilderness (Lev. 23:42–43; cf. Neh. 8:13–18); for this reason this feast is particularly relevant for Numbers.

This feast is linked to the ingathering of all the final produce from the fields, especially the grape harvest. But the celebration is also tied to the remembrance of the wilderness period, which is why Israel must live in booths (Lev. 23:42–43). The building of booths became standard practice at the time of Ezra: "From the days of Jeshua son of Nun to that day the people of Israel had not done so" (Neh. 8:17). Both Philo and Maimonides (*Guide of the Perplexed* 3.43) understand that part of the meaning of this practice is to point out the shortness and fragileness of our lives. The theme of leaving the security of home and entering into the more fragile dwelling is certainly in keeping with the lessons of wilderness. The wilderness time of Israel becomes a figure for all of our lives on this side of judgment.

The seventh day of the festival in later traditions (*Leviticus Rabbah* 37.2) is given the name Hoshanah Rabbah ("Great Hoshanah"). During the whole week, palm bundles (Lev. 23:40) are waved as people process around the altar; on the seventh day, they process around the altar seven times (Mishnah, tractate *Sukkah* 4.5). During these processions, psalms and prayers containing the words *hôšî'â nâ'* ("save us") are said.[30]

The eighth day of the festival celebrates the possibility of new beginnings after judgment: all of God's promises will be consummated and all creation will enter into the rest that God promises.

In later biblical and rabbinic traditions the feast is also associated with God's plans for nations outside Israel. Zechariah 14 gives a vision of the great day of the Lord, when nations will battle against Jerusalem. As a result of this final battle, "the LORD will become king over all the earth" (14:9). The people who are left in the nations "shall go up year after year to worship the King, the LORD of hosts, and to keep the festival of booths" (14:16). The image of the sanctuary's holiness extending outward has every cooking pot as "holy as the bowls in front of the altar" (14:20). God's final victory envisioned in the festival will result in his holiness and blessing extending to all the nations and all the nations coming to worship God.[31]

---

30. Willow branches are beaten on the ground, and the falling of their leaves may be a symbol of mortality. The themes of death and judgment are part of the celebration even at this point, since God's judgment is sealed not on Yom Kippur but on Hoshanah Rabbah, according to some rabbis. Other traditional aspects of the celebration (e.g., water libations, lighting large lamps) deepen the meanings of the feast: God will come to quench the thirst of God's people and give them light.

31. The Babylonian Talmud teaches that the seventy bulls offered in the temple during the feast serve as atonement for the seventy nations of the world (tractate *Sukkah* 55b).

The future orientation of this feast is apparent. Booths completes the cycle begun with Passover and Pentecost by looking forward to the consummation of all of God's promises for Israel, when God will judge the nations, fully atone for sin, and begin the great feast.

The themes of this feast resonate well with the whole book. In Num. 10:1–10 the silver trumpets of judgment were made. The blowing of these trumpets will mean God's judgment on Israel's foes as it moves forward in its journey. But as the narrative unfolds, it is primarily Israel who is judged. In the middle of the book, after the seventh rebellion of Israel, a symbol of atonement for Israel is commanded by God (21:5–9), and atonement is also later made by Phineas on behalf of the people (25:10–13). Now, as the people of Israel wait in the plains of Moab, they look forward to the consummation of God's promises for them in the promised land, but they are still dwelling in booths and have not yet reached home or entered God's rest. Numbers could be seen as a narrative enactment of this great festival of Israel.

As Passover resonates with the church liturgical season of Lent and Holy Week, and Pentecost with Pentecost, the Festival of Booths has its Christian counterpart in Advent. The great themes of Sukkot are judgment, mercy, and the final coming of God as king. Just as the wilderness was a place of testing and judgment on Israel, so too these themes are developed in the lectionary readings of the modern Advent season.

Advent has a double focus. It both remembers the coming of Jesus Christ to Israel and anticipates his coming again to judge the world and bring to consummation the reign of God in all of creation. John the Baptist's cries—"Repent, for the kingdom of heaven has come near. . . . Prepare the way of the Lord. . . . Who warned you to flee from the wrath to come? . . . Even now the ax is lying at the root of the trees" (Matt. 3:2–10)—all seem out of place given our typical practices of Advent in contemporary culture, but in light of the Festival of Sukkot they are quite fitting. The angels bearing trumpets, both on our Christmas cards and in Rev. 8:2, announce the coming of judgment. But thankfully the one who judges is none other than the Lamb, who through his atoning sacrifice of obedience and zealous self-offering takes away the sin of the world: "Then I looked, and there was the Lamb, standing on Mount Zion!" (14:1). While Jesus was revealed to Israel in a veiled way during his first coming,[32] he will be revealed in glory at his second. In that great harvest and ingathering at the end of the age (14:17–18), "all nations will come and worship before you, for your judgments have been revealed" (15:4). After judgment and atonement comes the great feast, the eighth day, the

32. Connections between Jesus and the meanings of this feast are clearly made in the Gospel of John, which places Jesus in the temple during this festival (John 7:2, 37). Jesus's statements—"let anyone who is thirsty come to me" (7:38) and "I am the light of the world" (8:12)—clearly associate him with the symbolic actions of pouring libations of water and lighting lights during this great feast. See Raymond Brown, *The Gospel according to John i–xii*, Anchor Bible 29 (Garden City, NY: Doubleday, 1966), 320–31.

day of resurrection, the marriage feast of the Lamb (19:7). The wife suspected of unfaithfulness (Num. 5) is finally made faithful, and she will dwell with God in the promised land: "Come, I will show you the bride, the wife of the Lamb ... the holy city Jerusalem. ... It has the glory of God. ... And the wall of the city has twelve foundations" (Rev. 21:9–14).

Vows Made by Women (30:1–16)

Vows and oaths are the next topic of discussion.[33] A general principle about vows and oaths is given first: "When a man makes a vow to the LORD, or swears an oath to bind himself by a pledge, he shall not break his word; he shall do according to all that proceeds out of his mouth" (30:2). Four cases of women's vows and oaths are presented next: those taken by a woman in her father's house (30:3–5), those taken before a woman is married (30:6–8), those taken by widows and divorced women (30:9), and those taken while a woman is married (30:10–15). In all these cases, the general rule is that vows and oaths made by a woman are valid unless a man who is in charge of her—father or husband—upon hearing of the vow, or relatively soon after that, repudiates them. These laws reflect a culture where men had authority over women as fathers and husbands.

While the laws themselves are fairly straightforward, the validation of vows and oaths might at first seem contrary to later biblical texts that critique vows. In addition, the ability of husbands and fathers to limit their wives' or daughters' religious commitments—and the portrayal of women as apt to make rash vows—does not seem to match well with the New Testament's trajectory toward the full equality of women. These features are especially disturbing given that "the LORD has commanded" (30:1) them. Given that Numbers gives prominent attention to both vows (6:1–21; 15:3, 8; 21:2; 30:1–16) and laws concerning women (5:11–31; 27:1–11; 30:1–16; 36:1–13), one wonders if there is a deeper significance to the placement of this passage or the larger themes connected with these laws. These issues raise questions about how this text might be best read as Christian scripture.

Vows and oaths are commitments or statements that use the name of God. While there is not much difference between "oath" (*'issār*) and "vow" (*neder*), there is an important difference between oaths and vows that promise something *to* God and those that are sworn *by* the name of God (Milgrom 1990: 488–90). Numbers 30 focuses on the first type, which can involve an action, an offering, or an abstention. Israelites took vows and oaths quite seriously: people who break a vow or oath must "bear guilt [*ăwôn*]," an important phrase in Num. 5:15, 31; 14:18, 19, 34; 15:31. If this happens, one's sin or guilt is without a protective covering before God (→7:1–88), and God's wrath will break freely upon the individual: "Because of having despised the word of the LORD and broken his

33. Num. 30:1–16 in English Bibles is numbered 30:2–17 in the Masoretic Text.

commandment, such a person shall be utterly cut off and bear the guilt" (15:31). Vows are like the covenant in miniature, and the consequence of breaking a vow is similar to Israel's breaking covenant with God. The tragic story of Jephthah's vow shows that he took his vow to God so seriously that he would rather kill his own daughter than break his vow (Judg. 11). This story also implicitly questions the wisdom of making *any* vows to God. In fact, the history of vows in Christianity shows ambivalence toward them and raises the deeper question: Why make a vow at all when the consequences can be so extreme?

One might make a vow to God as a means of trying to gain God's help—as in the case of Jephthah, Hannah, and other biblical figures. In such cases, one vows to God in order to gain a benefit; that is, a vowed action is traded for a benefit from God. Swearing an oath *by* God's name can be a means to make other people trust our word. Our own cultural practice of having people swear something with one hand on the Bible is similar. This sort of vow secures a kind of religious collateral offered to another person or calls upon God to act as a witness. In both cases, one is using a religious practice as a means for securing one's own benefit. But a vow can also be a means of religious devotion and self-offering, as in the Nazirite vow (6:1–21). This vow is a means of declaring one's intention and binding one's future will; taking the vow deepens one's covenantal obligations by committing oneself to further abstentions or duties. It is in this sense a gift of devotion to God that embodies one's zealous love for God. This kind of vow has great similarities to marriage vows. So, while different vows may share common features, they place different expectations on divine action and are driven by very different motivations.

These different expectations and motives for making vows make sense of the ambivalence that later biblical and Christian traditions had to vows; they also make better sense of how the commands of Num. 30 can still guide Christian thinking and practice.

Jesus responds to the practice of making vows by saying: "Do not swear at all. . . . Let your word be 'Yes, Yes' or 'No, No'; anything more than this comes from the evil one" (Matt. 5:33–37; cf. Num. 30:2; Lev. 19:12; Deut. 23:21). He is addressing a proliferation of vows of the "religious collateral" type. His words point to one principle that guides the Numbers passage: followers of God must be people of integrity, people whose word is truthful and trustworthy. But Jesus also seems to call into question the propriety of making any vows, at least of this kind.

Jesus critiques a different use of a formal religious commitment similar to a vow in Mark 7:6–13. He states that while on the outside certain people seem to honor God, yet "their hearts are far from me; in vain do they worship me." Jesus then critiques those who declare something "Corban (that is, an offering to God)," a vow that dedicates possessions to God, seemingly in order to get out of family obligations. Under the guise of religious dedication, they secure their own purposes and undercut their duty to their parents. The act might seem holy, but the practice is not truly motivated by zeal for God.

In other instances, both Jesus and Paul support vows. Jesus himself might have made a Nazirite commitment (Matt. 26:29), and Paul financially supported what appear to be Nazirite vows by others (Acts 21:23–24). Considering the motivation behind the vow and its implicit divine expectations help make sense of Jesus's and Paul's practice—they supported vows of dedication while critiquing vows made for self-serving reasons. These distinctions also make sense of the ambiguous response to vows in later Christian traditions.

Within the Protestant tradition, vows were challenged by Calvin and Luther. They viewed them negatively as part of the superstition prevalent in their day, or as yet one more "work" that Christians took on themselves in order to please God. They opposed this kind of "works righteousness" by the principle of justification by grace through faith.[34] In addition, they challenged the vow of chastity by those joining religious orders, seeing it as against the "universal condition of men," and thus rash, and the cause of much hypocrisy.[35] Nevertheless, Calvin does see that certain vows are part of the normal Christian life: the baptismal vow, confirmation, and even the Lord's Supper are all seen as healthy vows toward God.[36] The response of the Roman Catholic Church to questions about the vow of celibacy has been to stress the link between the vocation of priesthood and celibacy. The vow to be a priest involves a spiritual marriage to the church, who in turn is the bride of Christ.[37] The Roman Catholic Church has not had the same kind of reservations that Protestants have had toward religious vows; they affirm that vows can embody a person's dedication to God instead of simply being a superstitious manipulation of God.

There is no discussion of motivations in Num. 30:2. Instead, the principle held up is that, regardless of motivation, one should keep one's word, especially in religious vows.

But then why the limitations on vows and oaths by women? These limitations may simply reflect the patriarchal context in which the obligations and decisions of a woman were subject to the man (father or husband) in charge of her. Or perhaps this evidences the belief that women are particularly apt at making rash vows, as suggested by 30:6: "If she marries, while obligated by her vows or any thoughtless utterance of her lips." The Hebrew behind the translation does not necessarily mean "thoughtless" (Milgrom 1990: 252). Another possible translation is, "If she should marry while her vow or the commitment to which she bound

34. "At this point [concerning vows] superstition has been strangely prevalent in all ages. . . . But we see that for some centuries nothing has been more usual than this wickedness: whole people everywhere, despising God's law, burned with a mad zeal to vow anything that had tickled them in dreams" (Calvin 1960: §4.13.1).

35. "In this class [rash vows], celibacy holds the first place for insane boldness. For priests, monks, and nuns, forgetful of their own infirmity, think themselves surely capable of celibacy" (Calvin 1960: §4.13.3).

36. Other than these, Calvin's advice is to "undertake only sober and temporary vows" (1960: §4.13.6).

37. See for example, *Sacerdoltalis caelibatus: Encyclical of Pope Paul VI on the Celibacy of the Priest* (June 24, 1967).

herself is still in force." A third possibility is suggested by 30:13: "Any vow or any binding oath to deny herself, her husband may allow to stand, or her husband may nullify." Here, the oath in question appears to be some kind of commitment to denial, such as the Nazirite vow, which is open to both men and women. This scenario may imagine the use of a religious vow by a woman to secure her own space—not so much with the intention of dedicating herself to God, but rather of using religion as a way of avoiding obligations to her family or spouse. She might "dedicate herself" to God with the real motivation of securing her autonomy. The text seems to be safeguarding obligations to family and clan against this.

This last possibility makes sense in light of the larger context of legislation dealing with vows and women. The underlying principle, as in Jesus's critique of the practice of Corban, is that one should not use religious freedoms, rites of dedication, or inheritance legislation in order to subvert one's obligations to the tribe or community. Understood in this way, Num. 30 and Num. 36 do not harbor a distrust of women per se, but rather recognize how easy it is to surreptitiously use religious practices for one's own benefit, rather than as opportunities for service to others or dedication to God.

Given this, one should not critique these laws on the grounds of female autonomy, but rather because the text does not similarly charge the men. They too should not use vows or oaths as a way of avoiding obligations to their families and tribes. Men too should offer themselves readily to God and to their families, including their wives. Such are the directions Paul often takes in his letters to the churches (1 Cor. 7:3–5).

Finally, is it possible to see the women in this passage as veiled figures of Israel in relationship to God? The placement and details of Num. 5:11–31 invite the reader to see Israel as the woman suspected of unfaithfulness; is Num. 30 inviting a similar reading? If so, this hints at something quite profound—that the husband (i.e., God) might in certain cases take on the negative repercussions of his wife's failed vows (i.e., Israel): if the husband "nullifies them [his wife's vows] some time after he has heard of them, then he shall bear her guilt" (30:15). The exodus generation for forty years had borne the guilt of its own sin as a result of unfaithfulness (14:35). For this new generation, these laws here might hint that God as the husband of Israel will himself bear the guilt and not enforce the entire fulfillment of all the punishments for unfaithfulness required by the covenantal vows of Israel.

This figural reading of the text also suggests something about Israel. Israel, as the woman in this passage, will not be allowed to use "the name of God" for the wrong intentions. So often the history of God's people has been precisely that—rather than vows being a way to further dedicate oneself to God, vows have become means by which the people of God seek to manipulate God to serve their own purposes or undermine their obligations to others. This chapter is one more warning and prohibition against this use of religion.

9

FINAL STAGES AND SUMMARY OF THE FORTY-YEAR JOURNEY (31:1–33:49)

Israel's Holy War against Midian (31:1–54)

Like the battle scenes detailed in 21:1–3, 10–35, aspects of the battle against the Midianites and its aftermath—especially its underlying idea of holy war—raise difficult questions about how to read this passage as scripture. There are apparent tensions between the image of God and the attitudes toward killing seen in this chapter and elsewhere in scripture, both Old Testament and New. Several of its details highlight how this text functions within Numbers and the journey of Israel, raise the issues of the propriety of such a holy war, and show how the text itself seems to call for being read in a more spiritual manner, as it has throughout the Christian tradition.

The opening command of the Lord to Moses—"avenge the Israelites on the Midianites" (31:2)—recalls the story about Midianite women being partially to blame for the apostasy at Peor. Placing the census of the new generation (Num. 26) between the command (25:17) and its execution highlights that the old generation did not accomplish it. The final act of the old generation was its final apostasy, apparently incited by the Midianites. The newer generation is able to overcome and seek the vindication of the wrongs done to Israel and to God by them. The victory of the Israelites over the Midianites in this passage foreshadows the success of this newer generation of Israel in the conquest of Canaan. While Moses is involved in the battle as one of his final actions—"afterward you shall be gathered to your people" (31:2)—the battle is waged by selected troops led or supported by Phineas, who because of his zeal is the key priestly figure of the younger generation.

This war was regarded as a religious enterprise. God's explicit command to avenge the Israelites, Phineas's going into battle with both "the vessels of the sanctuary and the trumpets for sounding the alarm" (31:6), the burning of Midianite towns and encampments (31:10), the dedication of at least part of the booty to God (31:28–29), and the final offering to God (31:50–54)—all these elements are part of what is often referred to as "holy war" or "YHWH war" (→21:1–3 and →21:10–35) (Wood 1998: 19; Niditch 1993).[1]

In certain forms of holy war, all enemies are supposed to be "dedicated" to God as a kind of sacrifice (→21:1–3).[2] Moses's anger at the commanders who return (31:14) might be based on this understanding, because Israel had *not* killed every person. But his response, "have you allowed all the women to live?" (31:15), and the further explanation that these women had "act[ed] treacherously against the LORD . . . so that the plague came among the congregation" (31:16) make clear that the Israelites were to have exacted retribution for these particular sins. This was not simply a holy war of dedication. The motive for the war instead appears to be retribution or vengeance, especially against the women of Midian.[3]

Calvin reads the text in this way. For him the war served to execute God's justice. He further understood that even in his day God might act similarly, placing at times the prerogative on his church "to execute vengeance upon the heathen." The church, like Israel, should not simply avenge their own injuries, but "they are the just and legitimate executioners of God's vengeance, when the sword is put into their hands" (1852: 4.263–64). For Calvin, the key is whether God commands vengeance or not, and so the church, just as Israel, must be ready "to pardon the Midianites" as well as punish them as God desires (264). Of course, the trick for the church is discerning God's command correctly, as Protestants, Catholics, and Puritans found out during the centuries of slaughter that followed the Reformation.[4]

Moses's commands complicate matters further. He tells the commanders that all the virgin women should be spared, but to kill the young men and "every woman who has known a man" (31:17). Rather than justice, the purity of the people now appears to be at stake. Susan Niditch argues that the "priestly ideology" informing the report of this war sees the Midianites as unclean and needing

---

1. Contra Gerhard von Rad, *Holy War in Ancient Israel*, trans. Marva J. Dawn (Grand Rapids: Eerdmans, 1991), 41–51, there is not one common understanding of holy war in Israel, but rather different understandings and traditions that often, but not always, share certain features.

2. In Niditch's taxonomy of seven different ideologies of war in ancient Israel, this fits the category "The Ban as God's Portion" (1993: 28–55).

3. In Niditch's taxonomy, this is "The Ban as God's Justice" (1993: 56–77).

4. Lisa Sowle Cahill, *Love Your Enemies: Discipleship, Pacifism, and Just War Theory* (Minneapolis: Fortress, 1994), 119–49.

to be eradicated (1993: 83–86). The virgin women alone are spared, because they have not yet been marked as impure through sexual relations with enemies. Even inanimate booty needed to be purified through fire and/or water before it could be brought into the camp (31:21–24) since it had come into contact with the impure Midianites.

The view of war underlying this text—that holy war needs to be waged out of concern for purity—is perhaps even more frightening in its potential for abuse than a holy war waged out of concern for justice. This view seems to be similar to policies of ethnic cleansing that continue to scar the world. The enemy is seen as a disease that needs to be eradicated or a tumor that must be cut out. Such a view fits quite well with the major themes of the book—that Israel is called to be a holy and pure people. But the war against Midian shows potentially serious problems with concerns for holiness and purity. Can zeal for holiness and purity be embodied in such a way as to not dehumanize the unclean? In our own day, similar attitudes often dehumanize groups considered unclean and foster attitudes of fear and hatred of them.

In small ways, this text begins to raise such questions. Perhaps the authors and redactors of Numbers sensed some of these difficulties with holy war and with Israel's call to holiness and purity. A least four aspects of the text suggest that the killing of the Midianites, while serving some good, is not the "final solution" for the holiness problem of the people of Israel.

The first aspect is attention to the uncleanness that results from contact with corpses. Corpses are unclean because they represent death and the breakdown of God's life-giving order within creation (→5:1–4). The logic underlying the purity system emphasizes that God seeks to give life and resist death. In the practice of holy war, as the participants kill others they become unclean themselves, which sets up a conflict between means and ends at the very center of the practice. Those who participated, rather than immediately entering the camp as heroes, may not reenter the camp until going through a purification process: "Camp outside the camp seven days; whoever of you has killed any person or touched a corpse, purify yourselves and your captives on the third and on the seventh day" (31:19). Here, at least a temporary conflict between killing another person and proper worship of God is recognized. Such a conflict was also recognized by the writer of Chronicles when David was not allowed to build the temple because he "waged great wars" and "shed so much blood" (1 Chr. 22:7–8; 28:3).

Second, the gift of atonement (Num. 31:50–54) may also indicate that the war with the Midianites was sensed to conflict with the ultimate purposes of God. The officers bring crafted jewelry and articles of gold to Moses and Eleazar "to make atonement" for themselves; Moses and Eleazar bring them into the tent of meeting "as a memorial for the Israelites before the LORD." The atonement and memorial could be an extraordinarily rich payment of the silver tax required for taking a census (Exod. 30:11–15), if the counting of the troops in Num. 31:5, 49 is understood as a census (Milgrom 1990: 264–65; →1:1–54). Or it could be a kind of sin offering to atone for Israel's apostasy at Peor or even the earlier one at Sinai, an offering that fittingly concludes the matter.[5] Or it could be an atonement offering for the shedding of the blood of the Midianites and its resultant defilement (Sakenfeld 1995: 169; Olson 1996: 179; Niditch 1993: 88; Wenham 1981: 212; de Vaulx 1972: 359). If the latter, the Israelites themselves sensed that battling, even under the direction of God, involved them in a practice for which they needed atonement.

Third, the structure of Numbers might suggest that the highest form of zeal and dedication to God is a *self*-dedication rather than a dedication of the enemy (→21:1–3), and the highest form of concern for purity and holiness is that of faithfulness and obedience to God, rather than "cleansing" the infidel and killing off tempting influences such as the Midianite women. The first third of the book's high view of the people of God features the self-dedication of the Nazirite (Num. 6) and the ideally faithful bride (Num. 5). While the second generation featured in the last third of the book is given a new start and is much more faithful than the wilderness generation, this generation is not idealized or pictured as having fully entered into the vision set forth in the first part. They are still Israel "on the journey," not yet entering into the fullness of what God has planned. Certainly in the light of Christ's teaching—for example the way Christ stresses the interior heart of the law in the Sermon on the Mount (Matt. 6–8)—Israel's concern for zealous defeat of outward enemies and outside temptations is a good, but not the highest good.

Fourth, the battle with the Midianites seems to call for an allegorical or spiritual reading. While this does not negate the historical reading, it suggests physical battles are not the ultimate or even most important battles that Israel must face. In this allegorical reading, this is a battle for Israel's soul, a battle not against flesh and blood per se, but rather against the spiritual forces or temptations that confront Israel and keep it from fulfilling its role to be a holy nation.

The list of defeated kings of Midian (31:8) could be simply names, but they also have suggestive meanings, which without much difficulty can be related to many of the temptations Israel faced in the wilderness:

name	root
Evi	*'wn* ("trouble, sorrow, wickedness") (BDB 19)
Rekem	*rqm* ("variegated" and hence, "impure") (BDB 955)
Zur	*ṣr* ("adversary, foe") (BDB 865)
Hur	*ḥrr* ("to bore or pierce, to be parched" or "a parched place") (BDB 359)
Reba	*rb'* ("to lie down, copulate") (BDB 918)

5. Given the parallels between turning gold jewelry into a memorial in this passage and into the golden calf in Exod. 32:24 and 33:4–6 and the parallels between Exod. 32 and the apostasy in Num. 25, this is a plausible option.

The number of Israelites battling the Midianites—one thousand from each tribe—also seems stylized (→1:46), with the symmetry suggesting that the portions from each tribe represent Israel as a whole. That Phineas the priest leads them into battle, blowing the trumpets of judgment (mentioned only here and in 10:1–10) and carrying "the vessels of the sanctuary" (31:6) or "holy things," also gives this battle a particularly priestly tone. Finally, the concern to carefully detail the purification of people and booty after the battle sets this story apart from most others.

Given these details, a more spiritual or allegorical reading seems called for (as Origen suggests). Historically, the text relates how Israel encountered people who tempted them, through their women and religious practices, to turn away from God and forsake the journey to the promised land. God commands Israel to harass their enemies and defeat them. But the spiritual reading emphasizes that Israel's adversaries were not only outside them, but also inside them, as the sevenfold temptation and rebellion of Israel in the wilderness showed. Unlike the kings of Midian, who were entirely defeated without cost to Israel, the sins of Israel continued to be thorns in the flesh that continued to harass it throughout history (cf. 33:55).

The battle witnessed to in this passage is both perennial and penultimate. Yes, God was faithful to lead Israel to victory over adversaries who harassed it on the way to the promised land. But Israel also needed to fight a constant spiritual battle against sins inside and among it—an inability to deal with misfortunes; to rise above basic hungers, thirsts, and sexual appetites; to follow God wholeheartedly; and to see through lies and deceptions. This battle was not won once for all in Israel. As the yearly trumpets of the Feast of Sukkot suggest, it must be fought repeatedly with "holy things," the weapons of its worship life, as the people of God continue on in their journey of purification toward the ultimate victory and rest of the promised land.

Allotment of Land in the Transjordan: Fully Following or Compromise (32:1–42)

Israel has almost made it to the promised land. Having battled the last enemy blocking the way, it encounters yet another problem: some of the tribes decide that they would be better off not crossing the Jordan into the promised land. Like the ten leaders in the central rebellion of the exodus generation, these tribes decide that their life would be better outside the land flowing with milk and honey. Because they "owned a very great number of cattle" (32:1) and the Transjordan appeared to be a good place for their cattle or livestock, they requested, "Let this land be given to your servants for a possession; do not make us cross the Jordan" (32:5).

Like several passages in the final third of the book, the new generation of Israel is seen to be following God and doing much better than their forebears in the wilderness, and yet it is still not quite reaching the ideals expected of the people of God. While this potential crisis has a good ending, the tribes at issue do not behave ideally. Instead, a compromise solution allows all the Israelites to move forward.

The compromise suggested by Gad and Reuben, who were later joined by half the tribe of Manasseh, is that men from their tribes would act as a "vanguard" for the other tribes, and these men would not return to their little ones, wives, and livestock until all the promised land was subdued (32:16–19, 31–32). Their inheritance would be in the Transjordan, however, not with the other tribes in the land God promised.

The ambivalent portrait of these tribes is highlighted by the episode being structured around the sevenfold repetition of five key Hebrew phrases: "Gad and Reuben," "cross [the Jordan]," "be picked/shock troops," "holding/share," and "before the LORD" (Milgrom 1990: 492–94). These terms are part of a larger chiastic structure that centers on 32:25–27, where Gad and Reuben accept Moses's compromise (the list of nine cities and the request of Gad and Reuben in 32:1–6 parallels the gift of the land by Moses and the list of fourteen towns in 32:34–38; similarly 32:16–24 parallels 32:28–32). The center of this tightly constructed story emphasizes the *obedience* of the two and a half tribes to the compromise solution of Moses; this appears to have been the original story. The actions of the two tribes are viewed as "half full."[6] However, 32:7–15 does not fit well into this structure and was perhaps added later. Moses's speech in those verses reminding the people of the rebellion of Num. 13–14 suggests that this generation, represented by the Gadites and Reubenites, is falling into the same problem of not "unreservedly following" God. Thus, later editors/authors perhaps presented Moses's speech here to emphasize the incongruence of obedience and not fully following God, thus lending a "half empty" emphasis to this ambiguous episode.

In the end it is Moses, and not YHWH, who gives the Transjordan tribes their inheritance. The promised land was to be "apportioned by lot" (26:55), emphasizing God's apportioning of it. Yet here, "Moses gave to them" (32:33). The inheritance of the two and a half tribes is thus not of the same status (as reflected in Josh. 22).

An important phrase describing the virtues of Joshua and Caleb—"unreservedly followed me" (32:12; cf. 32:11)—is a direct quotation of 14:24: "But my servant Caleb, because he has a different spirit and has followed me wholeheartedly, I will bring into the land." The ideal of "fully following" (*milĕ'û 'aḥărê*) after God is a strong theme in Numbers and resonates with the ideal of zeal for God. Nazirites unreservedly give themselves to God (Num. 6); Caleb and Joshua's actions contrast

---

6. Olson's relatively positive evaluation of them fits this emphasis: "The new generation continues to be characterized as faithful but also creative adherents to God and the traditions of the past" (1996: 183).

with that of the rest of the leaders (Num. 13–14); and Phineas is similarly zealous in defending the honor of God (25:11).[7] It is these kind of people who inherit the land and fulfill what God desires for his people, and it is their self-offering and self-dedication to God that often brings atonement (25:13), in contrast to the sloth, unfaithfulness, and selfish ambition of Israel manifested in Num. 11–21. The phrase is highlighted later when Caleb receives his inheritance (Josh. 14:8, 9, 14). In contrast, Solomon did not "fully follow" God (1 Kgs. 11:4, 6); he was drawn by his wives into following other gods, with the result that the land and the kingdom were torn in two. Finally, echoes of this Old Testament phrase can be heard in Jesus's call for his disciples to "follow me."

Thus, a contrast is set up between the ideal that Israel should "fully follow" after God and the responsible, yet not ideal, actions of these tribes. They work to help others enter the land and take possession, yet they themselves do not fully enter in. Their hearts and their treasures are not fully invested in the promised land. Instead of fully following after God, they simply seek to obey the commandments of God and the words of Moses to ensure their continuance as part of God's people and avert God's anger—a subtle but profound difference. Dietrich Bonhoeffer makes a similar contrast in his book *Discipleship*: following after God, following after Jesus, is not following "a general law; it is rather, the exact opposite of legalism." "Follow me, walk behind me! That is all."[8]

Reading this journey of Israel as a spiritual journey of the people of God shows many parallels to Jesus's teachings about discipleship and life in the kingdom of God. For example, the Gadites and Reubenites might be seen as similar to the soil with weeds in Jesus's parable of the sower. They accept the word, yet are choked by the cares of the world and do not—either individually or as a group—bear kingdom fruit as they should. Bishop Paterius read this chapter similarly: "By analogy [to the Gadites and Reubenites] many people, although they are believers, are occupied with present cares, as if they were feeding flocks across the Jordan. Contrary to the faith they professed in baptism, they serve perishable things with their whole minds and all their desires. But, as we said, when a temptation against faith arises, they gird on arms to defend it" (cited in Lienhard 2001: 261). Origen compares settling on the other side of the Jordan to that place in the spiritual journey of Christians whose lives are like the "arid" land they settle for, a life without charity, justice, chastity, and piety, a life that will not bear the fruitful harvest of the word of God (Origen 1996–2001: 3.255). Like the Reubenites and Gadites, the people of God can live in a way that is not open rebellion, but is still a second-rate faithfulness not fully in accordance with the vision of who the people of God are called to be. Numbers calls us to something better.

7. While the zeal of the Levites is not explicitly mentioned, the phrase "unreservedly given" (Num. 3:9; 8:16) seems to be an echo of their zeal in Exod. 32:25–29.
8. Dietrich Bonhoeffer, *Discipleship*, trans. Barbara Green and Reinhard Krauss, ed. Geffrey B. Kelly and John D. Godsey, Dietrich Bonhoeffer Works 4 (Minneapolis: Fortress, 2001), 58.

Israel's Wilderness Itinerary (33:1–49)

With the battle against the Midianites and the episode with the Gadites and Reubenites, the new generation of Israel has overcome the final external and internal threats to the completion of its journey to the promised land. So it is now appropriate that the entire itinerary of the long journey from Egypt to the edge of Canaan is rehearsed. Following this travel itinerary will be the final "commands and ordinances" (36:13) that the Lord commanded Israel through Moses concerning life in the promised land. After the long journey is remembered, the new generation will turn their imagination toward crossing the Jordan River and hear final instructions about the shape of life in the promised land.

The travel itinerary functions as a summary of the journey through the wilderness. In form, it is similar to other ancient Near Eastern itineraries that record, for example, the movements of armies in military campaigns (Milgrom 1990: 497–99). Israel's journey was a campaign of sorts, but while it did encounter outside enemies, its chief adversaries were its internal sins and temptations.

While the itinerary records Israel's physical journey, its structure and presentation also suggest something about Israel's spiritual journey, Israel's journey in its relationship to God and toward the calling they are to embody in the promised land.

The journey has forty-two stages, a number that may have deeper significance.[9] Three small explanations and interpolations break the rhythm of the itinerary (33:8, 9, 14) with suggestive details—"three days," "twelve springs," "seventy palm trees"—that might be symbolic. But by and large the journey's itinerary has three main markers: Passover at Rameses at the beginning of the journey, the death of Aaron at Mount Hor, and the end point at the plains of Moab next to the Jordan River. The first two have explicit dates: "the fifteenth day of the first month" (33:3) and "the fortieth year after the Israelites had come out of the land of Egypt, on the first day of the fifth month" (33:38). Using the exact words found in 21:1, the reference to "the Canaanite, the king of Arad, who lived in the Negeb in the land of Canaan" who "heard of the coming of the Israelites" (33:40) also breaks the itinerary at Mount Hor and recalls the events directly after Aaron's death at Mount Hor: the battle at Hormah, which is a positive turning point in the fortunes of Israel (21:1–3), and the seventh and final rebellion of Israel in the wilderness

---

9. While speculative, if one divides the forty-two stages into seven parts, each with six stages, there are interesting results. At the end of the first part Israel is camped at Elim, with its suggestive mention of twelve springs and seventy palm trees. They cross the Red Sea and arrive at Mount Sinai in the twelfth stage. Immediately after this comes the places associated with the first rebellion (11:1–2). The seventh group starts with Oboth, the first place mentioned (21:10) after the turning point of the narrative in 21:1–9. Given the association of rest with the seventh day, the Sabbath, and God's statement in Deut. 12:9 and Ps. 95:11 that "they [the exodus generation] shall not enter my rest," perhaps the seven divisions can be associated with the seven days of the week, ending with the Sabbath. Then, the final group of stages—associated with the final third of the book—is fittingly concerned with the preparation to enter into the rest of the promised land.

(21:4–9). While the wilderness of Sinai is mentioned (33:15–16), there is no mention of the many important events that took place at Mount Sinai.

While the details may suggest that the itinerary has greater allegorical significance, the main theme is that Israel was in the wilderness for forty years—the forty years mentioned in 14:34 as the time that Israel would "bear [its] iniquity" and "know [YHWH's] displeasure." The writer(s) of Numbers is most interested in telling the wilderness journey of Israel from Egypt to the borders of the promised land as a story of the uncovering of Israel's sin—and of the atonement or covering of sin that would allow it to move ahead as the people of God. The details of the itinerary at least point to this spiritual aspect of Israel's journey.

The itinerary also makes the point that Israel was on a real, historical, flesh-and-blood journey. Moses wrote the itinerary (33:2)—the only direct claim of Mosaic authorship in Numbers. Given the mythic proportions of the encounters between God and Israel narrated throughout the book, the itinerary helpfully anchors the journey of Israel squarely on the plane of history. It is similar to the phrase in the Apostles' Creed, "crucified under Pontius Pilate," and Luke's famous sentence, "this was the first registration and was taken while Quirinius was governor of Syria" (Luke 2:2), which put the story of Jesus squarely in the context of the politics of his day. There is little reason to doubt the itinerary's ancient character (Ashley 1993: 622–26).

A long history of Christian commentary reads the itinerary as pointing not only to the physical and spiritual journey of Israel through the wilderness, but as a description of the journey of the Christian believer's soul progressing toward virtue and union with God, the soul's true promised land. While Origen's famous twenty-seventh homily on Numbers is perhaps the best known (1996–2001: 3.266–347), Isidore of Seville and Ambrose of Milan also wrote on the stages. The Hebrew names of the forty-two stations become pointers to the stages in the soul's journey. For example, Origen writes concerning the journey from the second to the third camp: "Then when the soul thinks it is ready, it sets out from Succoth and camps at Buthan [Etham]. Buthan means 'valley.' Now we have said that the stages refer to progress in the virtues. And a virtue is not acquired without training and hard work. . . . So the soul comes to a valley. For in valleys and in low places the struggle against the devil and the opposing powers takes place" (cited in Lienhard 2001: 264–65).

Using Augustine's rule that any reading of scripture that promotes love is a good reading, we can appreciate these beneficial figural readings of Origen. But Numbers pushes back against at least a sole emphasis on individual growth: the main spiritual struggles of Israel concern its corporate life as a people. These are the struggles of the people of God and its leaders to live into its calling to be a holy people and public light to the nations. Especially in a context where the gospel is often overspiritualized and overindividualized, we should hesitate to move too quickly to readings that highlight the inner journey of the soul without also considering the public life of the people of God.

The spiritual journey of Israel recorded throughout Numbers can be a convincing and helpful picture of the journey of the Christian church, both corporately and individually. One need not turn only to allegorical readings of the forty-two stages for contemplation of the Christian life. Stories about and reflections on the main problems that Israel faced in its journey—bodily needs and desires, pride, religious/political leadership, sloth and despair, and the constant pull of idolatry and apostasy—provide an apropos and timely catalog of temptations that confront the church on its journey as God's people in the world. The itinerary does its best work by reminding us of the historical *and* spiritual journey of Israel during its forty years in the wilderness.

10

FINAL COMMANDS
AND ORDINANCES CONCERNING
LIFE IN THE PROMISED LAND
(33:50–36:13)

In the last part of Numbers, Israel is given final instructions concerning its life in the promised land before it crosses over the Jordan. The journey to the edge of the promised land is now complete, as marked by the itinerary in 33:1–49. The forty years are over, and God now gives Israel one final vision of what life is to be in this new land through the commandments and ordinances recorded here. Like the opening of the book, this closing part paints a bird's-eye view of the organization of Israel, but now in the promised land rather than in the camp.

The promises originally given to Abraham and passed on to his seed involved offspring and land. The double numbering of the people of Israel emphasized fulfillment of the promise of offspring; these final chapters look to the fulfillment of the promise of land. But the promise is much more than *merely* land and offspring. The goal of the promise is an embodied social reality, the life of the fruitful and priestly people of God in that promised land. The laws and narratives in both the opening and closing sections of Numbers paint a detailed picture of this social reality, this land and people of salvation.

These commands and ordinances are clearly sectioned off by introductory statements—"in the plains of Moab by the Jordan at Jericho, the LORD spoke to Moses" (33:50; 35:1) and "the LORD spoke to Moses" (34:1, 16; 35:9)—and concluded by "these are the commandments and the ordinances that the LORD commanded through Moses to the Israelites in the plains of Moab by the Jordan at Jericho" (36:13). In addition, each command begins with a statement—for example, "when you cross over the Jordan to the land of Canaan"—that makes clear that these ordinances concern life in the promised land. Only the final episode, the revisiting of the legislation about Zelophehad's daughters, begins differently, yet its ending marks it off as also part of this last group of commands and ordinances.

These clear literary markers easily divide the section into six parts: driving out all the inhabitants of the land (33:50–56), boundaries of the land (34:1–15), leaders of each tribe responsible for apportioning the land (34:16–29), forty-eight towns designated for the Levites (35:1–8), cities of refuge (35:9–34), and inheritance rights for Zelophehad's daughters (36:1–13).

These sections have many parallels to the opening chapters of Numbers, where the camp was organized according to tribes, the Levites and priests were set apart from the people and put in charge of the tabernacle, and legislation was given that highlighted the calling of Israel to be holy, so that the "name" of God might be "on the Israelites" (6:27). Now, Israel is organized in the land according to tribes, the designated towns of the Levites are set apart, and legislation concerning murder and cities of refuge is given. This latter legislation is given so that "you shall not defile the land in which you live, in which I also dwell; for I the LORD dwell among the Israelites" (35:34). Discussion of the inheritance rights of Zelophehad's daughters does not fit this parallel structure, but seems instead to carry its own particular purpose.

Reflecting on these parallels shows that the central concern is quite similar: Israel is to be a people among whom God will dwell. Therefore, the way that it is organized and lives matters greatly. The concern with murder in 35:34 expresses the same truth and concern as the earlier legislation concerning corpses: "They must not defile the camp, where I dwell among them" (5:3). God is a God of life and a God of holiness—God's people must be clean and holy.

And yet the vision in these chapters of Israel as a holy people seems a bit less glorious than that given in the opening chapters. Rather than presenting a vision of a whole twelve-tribed Israel symmetrically centered around the tabernacle, or implicitly likened to the zealous Nazirite, the ragtag nine and a half tribes are now presented with laws that presume some of them will murder each other. Has God simply lowered the bar in light of the all-too-apparent sinfulness of Israel? Perhaps. But maybe these new laws also deepen Israel's understanding of the holiness it is called to. The stress in these chapters is on a different, but nonetheless just as important, aspect of Israel's holiness. Rather than the purity of the tabernacle, the symbolic centers of holiness in this portrait are the cities of refuge; the stress on purity is supplemented with a stress on mercy and openness to those in trouble. The cities of refuge may in fact reflect something quite deep about the heart of God and the content of Israel's holiness.

Driving Out the Old Inhabitants of the Land: The People of God and Other Cultures (33:50–56)

"Out with the old, and in with the new." These chapters about what Israel should do when it crosses the Jordan begin with a message about cleansing the land of the old inhabitants and their idols. Canaan, the promised land, is to be cleansed and purified of old inhabitants and old religious places and items—like old leaven during Passover—so that Israel can settle in with a clean start. This practice raises many questions about proper Jewish and Christian attitudes toward surrounding cultures and religious practices.

The proper thing that Israel should have done upon entering the land is fairly clear: "Drive out all the inhabitants of the land from before you" (33:52). Other scripture passages envision God driving out the inhabitants through God's "angel" or "pestilence" (Exod. 23:23, 28) or through the agency of Israel in holy war (Deut. 7:2–6, 16; 20:16; Josh. 10:40–43).

The motivation for this is so Israel would not fall into idolatry, but instead follow God alone and maintain its covenant with God. Israel is to be a treasured possession and a holy people, and this entails not entangling itself with other gods. Israel is commanded to destroy all the idols and high places in the land (Num. 33:52), and elsewhere it is told not to intermarry (Deut. 7:3; Josh. 23:12) or even make covenants with the people in the land (Exod. 23:32; 34:12). All these commandments come with warnings that Israel will be snared, trapped, or hurt if it fails to do so. If they worship other gods, apostatize, and break their covenant relationship with God, God says that "I will do to you as I thought to do to them" (Num. 33:56).

Israel in fact did not drive out all the inhabitants. It intermarried, made covenants, and worshiped the Canaanite gods (Judg. 2:1–5, 11–15; 3:1–6) and, as a result, was eventually thrown out of the land and fell back into captivity.

How should the command to "drive out the Canaanites" inform the continuing life of the people of God? Positively, the command calls the people of God to live a corporate life of single-hearted devotion to God—in thought, worship, and practice. But it also calls the people of God to drive out evil influences from their midst. While easy to understand in the abstract, putting these directives into practice well and wisely is extremely difficult. The ongoing significance of God's command to "drive out the Canaanites" is a deep and abiding question for both Jews and Christians. It can be understood at different levels—land, community, individual—and in different ways: are "the Canaanites" people without or temptations and demons within? It historically becomes the question about Jewish racial purity, the question about whether to free the holy land from infidels, the question of "Christ and culture," the question of excommunication and church discipline, the question of the grounds of eucharistic fellowship, and the question asked of Christian baptismal candidates: "Do you reject Satan and all his ways?" Different answers to these analogous questions were *the* dividing lines between many Jewish sects at the time of Christ: Zealots, Pharisees, and Essenes. Different practical answers to these questions continue to be fault lines dividing many Christian communities and traditions today.

While such questions are not easily resolved in the abstract, several parts of the New Testament witness are helpful for carving out a path between reading this and similar texts in extreme ways or simply ignoring them. That Jesus rejected the Zealot option of violent expulsion of the Romans from the land closes off violent options of religious war and ethnic cleansing as responsible Christian options for engaging with cultures and religions opposed to Christianity (→21:1–3; →31:1–54). And Jesus's teachings (e.g., the parable of the wheat and tares) and his practice of "eating with tax collectors and sinners" point us away from facile forms of cultural separation leading often to hypocrisy and judgmentalism. And yet, Christ's call to repentance, baptism, discipleship, and holiness within the Christian community does not create a culture of mere openness, but rather a culture of hospitality mixed with discernment and discipline. Christ's Sermon on the Mount includes the statement "if your right eye causes you to sin, tear it out and throw it away" (Matt. 5:29; cf. 18:15–20), and Paul's disciplinary advice to the Corinthians includes the statements "clean out the old yeast so that you may be a new batch" (1 Cor. 5:7) and "drive out the wicked person from among you" (5:13).

In the past fifty years, there has been heightened interest in the relationship of the Christian church to culture,[1] in recovering a robust ecclesiology, and, given renewed appreciation of the sacraments among mainline and evangelical Protestants, in the grounds of eucharistic fellowship.[2] Such careful discussions model the contextual sensitivity needed to negotiate these difficult questions well.

Boundaries of the Land and Leaders for Apportioning It: The Land and Occupying Salvation (34:1–29)

God details the boundaries of the promised land (34:1–15) and tells Moses which leader from each tribe he should appoint to apportion the land (34:16–29). After describing the geographic boundaries of the land, Moses is then reminded that the land will be divided among only nine and a half tribes since Gad, Reuben, and half of Manasseh have already received their land in the Transjordan (34:13–15). This naturally leads into the narrative in which leaders from the nine and a half

---

1. D. Stephen Long, *Theology and Culture* (Eugene, OR: Wipf & Stock, 2008); T. M. Moore, *Culture Matters: A Call for Consensus on Christian Cultural Engagement* (Grand Rapids: Brazos, 2007); Kathryn Tanner, *Theories of Culture: A New Agenda for Theology* (Minneapolis: Fortress, 1997).

2. One example of the renewed discussion about "open table" practice among mainline Protestants is *Invitation to Christ: A Guide to Sacramental Practices*, a document published by the PC(USA) Office of Theology and Worship in 2006.

tribes are named to "apportion the land to you for inheritance" (34:17) under the direction of Eleazar and Joshua.

This unit has parallels to earlier lists of tribal leaders (1:4–16; 13:3–16) and the description of the land in 13:21–29. These parallels once again highlight the threefold ABA' structure of Numbers.

This description of the physical boundaries of the land provides some sense of completion to the story of the journey of Israel. At the beginning of the book, Israel is prepared as a people for its vocation in the land, but throughout the middle third of the book rejects or fails in its vocation. Now, after being given a new start, it is once again prepared to enter into the land at the end of the forty-year journey.

The boundaries named here are an idealized or promised set of boundaries that apparently never described the actual boundaries of Israel once it entered the land.[3] Even during the reigns of David and Solomon, when the extent of Israel's control to the north and south was at least as great as those described here, the Philistines occupied territories in the southwest along the Mediterranean Sea, keeping Israel even at its height from fulfilling this vision. A more typical description of Israel's lived boundaries was the area "from Dan to Beer-sheba" (Judg. 20:1; 1 Sam. 3:20; 1 Kgs. 4:25), a much smaller area.

At least three points of interest concern these boundaries. First, the promised boundaries correspond to descriptions of the Egyptian province of Canaan dated to the New Kingdom, during the time of the exodus (Milgrom 1990: 501, drawing on work by Benjamin Mazar). It follows that the Israelites may have taken this understanding of the bounds of Canaan from the Egyptians. While of historical interest as a piece of data supporting the antiquity of these boundaries, this connection to Egypt also shows that the gift of the land to Israel was another kind of triumph of Israel and YHWH over the Egyptians. The reality of life under the Egyptians is being replaced by the promised life under God.

Second, that Israel never came to fully occupy those boundaries is another indication that the hopes of and promises to Israel were not fully fulfilled. While Israel's new generation did cross the Jordan and enter the land, it did not fully follow God's commands (Num. 33:55–56); as a result, it did not fully receive the inheritance and promised life in the land. It neither fully occupied the land nor achieved the rest and peace envisioned for life in it.

3. The boundaries here are similar to those given in Ezek. 47:15–20 as part of Ezekiel's magnificent vision of the restored Israel. The north and south points are mentioned in the brief summary statement of the extent of Israel during Solomon's reign (1 Kgs. 8:65). While the southern boundaries described here were those actually occupied by Judah after the conquest (Josh. 15:1–12), the northern and eastern extents of the idealized territory were not fully occupied by the tribes. Another set of ideal boundaries in Gen. 15:18–21; Exod. 23:31; Deut. 1:7–8; 11:24; Josh. 1:4 has the promised land extending from the Nile to the Euphrates and bounded by the desert on the east—but Numbers does not mention these.

Finally, it is significant that the inheritance of Israel was a land with real borders. While much Christian thought moved quickly to a spiritualization of salvation, the salvation Israel was looking forward to in Numbers was quite earthy, quite substantial. The covenant of God with Israel is intended to lead Israel toward the renewal of human life in the land. God and his people are to dwell again together in peace and harmony, in shalom (6:22–27). On the other hand, we must not reduce the vision of the promised land to simply a promise that Israel would acquire a certain parcel of ground. That vision is of a substantial life in the land lived according to the covenant: "The land as a social reality, that is, not simply as a one-dimensional piece of real estate, takes on a different quality, depending on the attitude, conduct, and policies of its inhabitants."[4] Salvation is a vital social reality, the life of the renewed people of God living in a way that reflects and corresponds to the holy God in their midst. As this vision is taken up in the New Testament, salvation is not dematerialized, but rather "spiritualized" in another sense in Acts 2. With the coming of the Holy Spirit at Pentecost, the embodied life of the believers was described as salvation and as a foretaste of the full realization of the promises given in the Torah concerning life in the land. The summary description of the post-Pentecost church in Acts 4:32–35 (cf. 2:42–47) contains a direct allusion back to the promised blessing of Deut. 15:4: "There will, however, be no one in need among you, because the LORD is sure to bless you in the land that the LORD your God is giving you as a possession to occupy."

Levitical Towns, Cities of Refuge, and Manslaughter: The Holiness of Justice and Mercy (35:1–34)

God now tells Moses which cities the Levites should live in and specifies what pasturelands they will possess. He also gives details about the special cities of refuge for those who commit involuntary manslaughter. Like in the opening bird's-eye view of the tribes and the Levitical and priestly precincts, the closing description and allotment of land to the tribes is followed by the description of the cities of the Levites. The Levites, since their work is work associated with the worship life of Israel and their income comes through the tithing of the other tribes (18:20–24), do not receive an allotment of the land. Instead they receive forty-eight cities with the associated pastureland for their animals. The dimensions of the border of pastureland surrounding the cities is a realistic portrayal of the needs of the Levites for their livestock, as the amount of pastureland would grow as their cities grew (Milgrom 1990: 502–4).

4. Walter Brueggemann, "'Placed' between Promise and Command," in *Rooted in the Land: Essays on Community and Place*, ed. W. Vitek and W. Jackson (New Haven: Yale University Press, 1996), 125; see also idem, *The Land: Place as Gift, Promise, and Challenge in Biblical Faith*, 2nd ed., Overtures to Biblical Theology (Minneapolis: Augsburg Fortress, 2002).

The instructions about cities of refuge and their relationship to manslaughter add to the portrait of the people of God. The initial Levitical concern to protect the tabernacle against pollution—"but the Levites shall camp around the tabernacle of the covenant, that there may be no wrath on the congregation of the Israelites" (1:53)—is matched here with a concern to protect the land against pollution: "You shall not pollute the land in which you live; for blood pollutes the land. . . . You shall not defile the land in which you live, in which I also dwell" (35:33–34). The Levites and the cities of refuge are part of the system that keeps manslaughter from defiling the land.

The Levites are given forty-eight cities, but it is unclear what, if any, significance the number has (a multiple of twelve?). Of those cities, six are designated as cities of refuge: three in the promised land and three in the Transjordan. If a person kills someone, the loss of the blood or life creates a debt that must be reckoned with. God owns all life, and so one incurs a debt to God by taking a life either intentionally or unintentionally—and this debt must be repaid. It is the responsibility of the *gōʾēl* ("avenger, kinsman redeemer") to make sure that this debt is repaid by killing the one who has killed. The term *gōʾēl* refers to a next-of-kin male who is responsible to uphold the rights of a family or restore its losses (→5:8).[5] The avenger both collects a debt to the family and atones (*kippur*) or covers over the sin so that God will be able to dwell in the land (35:33). However, if this killing takes place unintentionally—intention is largely determined by the mode of death (35:16–23)—then the slayer may flee to a city of refuge, to eventually stand trial by the council. If found not guilty of murder, but rather of manslaughter, then the slayer can live in the city of refuge until the high priest dies. The death of the high priest in this case covers or substitutes for the life taken. The high priest redeems the debt to God both by assuring that it is paid and by being the payment itself.

The concerns treated here—the *gōʾēl* and the sacrifice that makes *kippur* for a debt—are also found in 5:5–10, where the *ʾāšām* (or restitution) is given to the *gōʾēl*. In both cases, wronging one another (5:6) or killing a person (35:11) not only creates a disruption of the relationship within the community, but also with "the land" and/or God. In both cases the ethical principles at stake move beyond a concern for wrongs done to the family to include the debt to God.

These laws and provisions give two important insights into who Israel and its God are. First, they show that Israel is being trained by God to have a great respect for human life. Israel is being restrained from any presumption that lives are cheap or that people can dispose of life—their own or anyone else's—as they see fit. The practice of holy war and the many deaths caused by God throughout the book,

---

5. The kinsman—a brother, uncle, cousin, or other male relative—has an obligation or opportunity to redeem a person sold into slavery (Lev. 25:39–55) or a piece of family property (25:25–34), to buy a piece of land to keep it from passing out of the family (Jer. 32:7–15), or to do a kinsman's part with a kinsman's widow (Ruth 3:6–13) in order to keep the name from passing out of the family, in a sense "redeeming" the name or lineage of the kinsman from death (4:10). In both Num. 5 and here, the kinsman collects a debt to the family—and to God. See Ashley 1993: 115–16, 650–51.

however, show that the principle that informs this particular understanding of the sacredness of life is not equivalent to modern notions of the right of a person over their own life. Life is God's, not ours.

Second, the provision of the cities of refuge and the related substitution of the high priest's life for the life of an unintentional slayer show something about the content of God's justice. Just as the episode of the bronze serpent in the wilderness (21:4–9) revealed both the sin of the people and the mercy of God, the provision of the cities of refuge makes sure that the debt of the life is dealt with, while at the same time providing a means of mercy for the one who has killed. Justice and mercy are intertwined in this picture of the land.

This combination of justice and mercy in the structure of Israel's life in the land reveals something of the heart of God. The way the righteousness of God is combined with his mercy is most fully revealed in Jesus Christ, the great high priest. Early Christian commentators often understood these particular provisions to provide "shadows" of Jesus, the great high priest. Paterius puts it this way: "What does it mean that a homicide returns for absolution after the death of the high priest, except that the human race, which brought death upon itself by sinning, receives absolution for its guilt after the death of the true priest, namely our Redeemer?" (cited in Lienhard 2001: 273). In Jesus Christ, God is acting as kinsman redeemer and high priest on our behalf. The same zeal for justice intertwined with mercy should also characterize the life of the people of God.

Inheritance of Heiresses: The Goal and Means of Inheritance (36:1–13)

The final chapter of the book revisits the issue of the inheritance of Zelophehad's daughters. "The heads of the ancestral houses" of some Manasseh clans come to Moses with a concern that the earlier ruling (Num. 27) about the daughters of Zelophehad might jeopardize the integrity of the tribal inheritance (36:2–4). The episode, and the whole book, ends with the obedience of the daughters of Zelophehad to the new legislation, which solves the problem. It provides a fitting ending to the book: the inheritance of the tribes—the goal of the journey of Israel—is safeguarded by the proper boldness of the daughters of Zelophehad tempered with their humble obedience—the necessary means for their spiritual journey into the life of the promised land.

Several key principles were at play in the daughters' inheritance (27:1–11): the system of patrilineal inheritance, the rights and good of the larger tribe, the relative economic equality served by the land distribution system, and the economic well-being of the daughters of Zelophehad and women in similar positions. The solution clarified the hierarchy of these goods: the patrilineal system was not the highest good, but rather was intended to serve the integrity of the land holdings of the tribe from generation to generation (27:8–11). The economic well-being of the daughters was also of concern.

The problem now is that if the daughters gain control of the land and then remarry someone of another tribe, their land will be added to the holdings of that other tribe. Not even the year of Jubilee would make it possible to recover that land, for only land that is sold, not inherited, returns to the original tribe (Lev. 25:10–34, esp. 25:28).

The proposed solution is that widowed women may choose whom they like to remarry, so long as they remarry within their tribe (Num. 36:6). This limits their personal freedom of choice (actually, the choice made for them by the larger family). But this limitation serves the good of the tribe and also the larger good of relative economic equality that the tribal land system itself serves.

The two episodes featuring the daughters of Zelophehad bookend the final third of Numbers, which details both the laws concerning the land and the actions of the new generation. The new generation is counted in Num. 26, and the first encounter with the daughters of Zelophehad occurs immediately afterward. That Numbers ends with the second encounter makes it probable that some importance is attached to these episodes by those who wrote and edited the book. Certainly the two main presenting issues—assuring the continued proper inheritance of the land and the character of the daughters as representatives of the new generation— are both central to this final third of the book.

The tribal structure of land inheritance is important for several reasons. Closing loopholes that would potentially undo the system of land inheritance shows the providential working of God to preserve his promises to the tribes. The land is both symbol and partial content of God's promises to Israel. But the land is not simply real estate (→34:1–29); it also represents a larger social reality, one that includes relative economic equality.[6] Throughout the Pentateuch, laws about Israel's life in the land envision a way of life counter to the life of the surrounding nations.

In addition, the character of the daughters is highlighted. They are properly bold, in contrast to the cowardice of the ten spies (Num. 13–14). But they are also properly obedient, willing to limit their choices and options in service to the larger tribe, in contrast to both Miriam and Aaron (12:1–16) and Korah, Dathan, and Abiram (Num. 16). The final words of the episode highlight both the obedience of the daughters and the integrity of the tribal inheritance: "The daughters of Zelophehad did as the LORD had commanded Moses. Mahlah, Tirzah, Hoglah, Milcah, and Noah, the daughters of Zelophehad, married sons of their father's brothers. They were married into the clans of the descendents

6. Richard Bauckham, *God and the Crisis of Freedom: Biblical and Contemporary Perspectives* (Louisville: Westminster John Knox, 2002), 119, writes: "In premonarchical Israel the egalitarian ideal seems to have achieved a reasonable—in its historical context, remarkable—degree of practical realization. The *form* that egalitarianism took was the basic economic equality of family households." The inheritance rights of the tribes served that end.

of Manasseh son of Joseph, and their inheritance remained in the tribe of their father's clan" (36:10–12).

This boldness mixed with obedience safeguards the inheritance of the social reality that the land represents. The ultimate goal of life in the land is salvation, a new life for Israel in which God will dwell among them and bless them (cf. 6:22–27; 24:2–9) so that all nations will see their life, glorify God, and receive the blessing of God as well (cf. Gen. 12:1–3).

The New Testament equivalent of "life in the land" is "life in the church." The qualities expressed by the daughters are similarly stressed throughout the New Testament: "Like obedient children, do not be conformed to the desires that you formerly had in ignorance. Instead, as he who called you is holy, be holy yourselves in all your conduct. . . . Now that you have purified your souls by your obedience to the truth so that you have genuine mutual love, love one another deeply from the heart" (1 Pet. 1:14–15, 22). Such a life in the church will cause the Gentiles to "glorify God when he comes to judge" (2:12).

In our modern culture, any curtailment of personal freedom is difficult to swallow, especially when it is the rights of women and other people who have all too often been wrongfully oppressed. Yet this passage need not be read exclusively in this light. It might instead be recognized for the remarkable visibility of women in it and for the way it helps preserve a system of land distribution that was remarkably egalitarian, in stark contrast to the monarchical systems of Israel's neighbors, including that of Egypt from which it was rescued.[7] The daughters of Zelophehad—equal heroes in Numbers alongside Joshua, Caleb, and Phineas—mix boldness to confront systems that do not serve their proper ends with the obedience that is willing to curtail certain freedoms for the good of the community. They are an icon of character we desperately need to contemplate.

Numbers fittingly ends in this way—concerned with the holy social reality of Israel in the promised land and presenting a model of the obedience and faithfulness required of the people in order to overcome the temptations and obstacles that plague its journey toward living in that promise. This daring and God-given vision of the calling of the people of God and the bold and zealous obedience to God needed to fulfill it are the main equipment Israel needed for the spiritual journey it undertook in Numbers. That vision and the faithful obedience needed to pursue it are of continuing importance for the people of God. They are certainly needed in the worldwide church today.

---

7. Bauckham, *God and the Crisis of Freedom*, 116–27.

BIBLIOGRAPHY

Works cited frequently are listed here. Other works are documented in the footnotes.

Ashley, Timothy R. 1993. *The Book of Numbers*. New International Commentary on the Old Testament. Grand Rapids: Eerdmans.

Balentine, Samuel E. 1999. *The Torah's Vision of Worship*. Overtures to Biblical Theology. Minneapolis: Fortress.

Barth, Karl. 1936–77. *Church Dogmatics*. Edited by Geoffrey W. Bromiley and Thomas F. Torrance. Edinburgh: Clark.

Brueggemann, Walter. 1997. *Theology of the Old Testament: Testimony, Dispute, Advocacy*. Minneapolis: Fortress.

Budd, Phillip J. 1984. *Numbers*. Word Biblical Commentary 5. Waco: Word.

Calvin, John. 1852. *Commentaries on the Four Last Books of Moses*. Translated by Charles William Bingham. 4 vols. Edinburgh: Calvin Translation Society.

———. 1960. *Institutes of the Christian Religion*. Edited by J. T. McNeill. Translated by F. L. Battles. 2 vols. Library of Christian Classics 20–21. Philadelphia: Westminster.

Douglas, Mary. 1993a. *In the Wilderness: The Doctrine of Defilement in the Book of Numbers*. Journal for the Study of the Old Testament Supplement 158. Sheffield: JSOT Press.

———. 1993b. "The Forbidden Animals in Leviticus." *Journal for the Study of the Old Testament* 59:3–23.

———. 1999. *Leviticus as Literature*. Oxford: Oxford University Press.

Gottwald, Norman K. 1979. *The Tribes of Yahweh: A Sociology of the Religion of Liberated Israel, 1250–1050 BC*. Maryknoll, NY: Orbis.

Gray, George Buchanan. 1903. *A Critical and Exegetical Commentary on Numbers*. International Critical Commentary. Edinburgh: Clark.

Hoffmeier, James K. 2005. *Ancient Israel in Sinai: The Evidence for the Authenticity of the Wilderness Tradition*. Oxford: Oxford University Press.

Hutton, Rodney R. 1994. *Charisma and Authority in Israelite Society*. Minneapolis: Fortress.

Kiuchi, Nobuyoshi. 2007. *Leviticus*. Downers Grove, IL: InterVarsity.

Klawans, Jonathan. 2000. *Impurity and Sin in Ancient Judaism.* New York: Oxford University Press.

Levine, Baruch A. 1993. *Numbers 1–20.* Anchor Bible 4a. New York: Doubleday.

———. 2000. *Numbers 21–36.* Anchor Bible 4a. New York: Doubleday.

Lienhard, Joseph T. 2001. *Exodus, Leviticus, Numbers, Deuteronomy.* Ancient Christian Commentary on Scripture: Old Testament 3. Downers Grove, IL: InterVarsity.

Milgrom, Jacob. 1990. *Numbers.* JPS Torah Commentary. Philadelphia: Jewish Publication Society.

———. 1991. *Leviticus 1–16.* Anchor Bible 3. New York: Doubleday.

———. 2000. *Leviticus 17–22.* Anchor Bible 3a. New York: Doubleday.

Moberly, Walter. 1998. *Can Balaam's Ass Speak Today? A Case Study in Reading the Old Testament as Scripture.* Cambridge, MA: Grove.

Moore, Michael S. 1990. *The Balaam Traditions: Their Character and Development.* Society of Biblical Literature Dissertation 113. Atlanta: Scholars Press.

Niditch, Susan. 1993. *War in the Hebrew Bible: A Study in the Ethics of Violence.* New York: Oxford University Press.

Noth, Martin. 1968. *Numbers.* Translated by James D. Martin. Old Testament Library. Philadelphia: Westminster.

Olson, Dennis T. 1985. *The Death of the Old and the Birth of the New: The Framework of the Book of Numbers and the Pentateuch.* Brown Judaic Studies 71. Chico, CA: Scholars Press.

———. 1996. *Numbers.* Interpretation. Louisville: Westminster John Knox.

Origen. 1996–2001. *Homélies sur les Nombres.* Edited by Louis Doutreleau. 3 vols. Sources Chrétiennes 415, 442, 461. Paris: Cerf.

Sakenfeld, Katharine Doob. 1995. *Journeying with God: A Commentary on the Book of Numbers.* Grand Rapids: Eerdmans.

Vaulx, J. de. 1972. *Les Nombres.* Sources bibliques. Paris: Gabalda.

Wenham, Gordon J. 1979. *The Book of Leviticus.* New International Commentary on the Old Testament. Grand Rapids: Eerdmans.

———. 1981. *Numbers.* Tyndale Old Testament Commentaries. Downers Grove, IL: InterVarsity.

Wood, John A. 1998. *Perspectives on War in the Bible.* Macon, GA: Mercer University Press.

SUBJECT INDEX

SCRIPTURE INDEX